Essays on American Literature
in Honor of Jay B. Hubbell

ESSAYS ON
AMERICAN LITERATURE

IN HONOR OF

JAY B. HUBBELL

Edited by

Clarence Gohdes

DUKE UNIVERSITY PRESS

DURHAM, N. C. 1967

L.C.C. number 67-25597

I.S.B.N. 0-8223-0070-2

Second printing, 1971

Printed in the United States of America

Preface

This book contains more than a score of essays which deal with various topics of interest especially to serious students of the literature and social history of the United States. No theme or method or organic principle is either sustained or illustrated throughout. The essays, all printed for the first time, have been gathered as a token of esteem, to honor a man who has contributed so notably to the development of the academic study of the national letters that the chief body of experts in the field, the American Literature Section of the Modern Language Association, has given his name to its medal of honor periodically awarded to especially distinguished members of the society.

Jay Broadus Hubbell is known in all quarters where the literature of the United States is the subject of advanced study and research. He was the founding editor of the first, and still the foremost, scholarly journal devoted solely to research in American belles-lettres. And, on the basis of his own publications, he ranks as the most eminent authority on the authors of the Southern states. He was not only a pioneer in initiating programs of instruction and research in his province at Southern Methodist University, Duke University, and the University of Vienna, but has endeared himself to hundreds of younger scholars in other schools whom he has taught in the classroom or otherwise encouraged. Though he has not always approved or really believed in the validity of all the varied critical "isms" that have accompanied the flood of literary comment emanating from academic purlieus, he has never inveighed against the Young Turks who have followed paths untrod in the graduate schools of his own generation. He has always readily accepted the fact that the present lives continually on the verge of the future, as well as the past, and he vividly remembers the oppressive nature of the doctrines of his own academic elders who viewed the study of English literature later than the era of John Dryden as too easy to warrant serious effort, or considered research in American literature as no more than a species of intellectual slumming.

It was altogether fitting that five of his younger friends should have proposed a book to honor Mr. Hubbell—in their words, "not only as the responsibility of the university which he served so long and to which he brought such distinction and reputation, but also as a responsibility of the scholars all over the world who have built upon the foundation which he laid." These five men are all represented in this volume: Charles R. Anderson, Ray M. Atchison, Lewis Leary, Henry Nash Smith, and James L. Woodress, Jr.

In planning the resultant book, the first decision made—and it was made reluctantly—was to limit the contributors to Mr. Hubbell's own countrymen; the next was to assemble contributions from veterans representing institutions scattered from coast to coast. There was no thought of confining the list to his former students, though several of them appear in these pages. Indeed, it would be impossible to garner a sheaf of essays written by prominent scholars in the field—whatever the basis of selection—without including the work of Mr. Hubbell's former pupils. The first letters sent out to prospective contributors elicited such a prompt and cordial response that, in order to keep the *Festschrift* within allowable size, a number of scholars whose collaboration would have been warmly welcomed had to be passed by. The purpose of covering the country, so to speak, has, however, been accomplished, for all sections of the United States are represented by the writers of these essays, from Maine to California, from Georgia to Wyoming. While several of the essayists have won Pulitzer prizes for biography, quite a few have been Guggenheim Fellows or Fulbright lecturers abroad, and a substantial group have served on the editorial board of *American Literature*, the authors of this book are to be considered as men and women who represent the large company of professional students of the literature of the United States—"representative men," in the Emersonian sense.

At the outset a suggestion was made that scholarship might perhaps be advantageously broadened if the literary figures chosen as subjects for the essays were to be selected from authors not presently fashionable in academic circles. Most readers who may be expected to turn the pages of a book like this one are aware of the fact that regnant fashions in scholarship and criticism tend to produce vogues for certain authors, to the neglect of others. The domain of American literature has of late assuredly illustrated the phenomenon. And editors of learned journals as well as of critical quarterlies have bemoaned the proliferation of articles concerned with a mere handful of authors. A Frenchman has actually characterized the vast glut of treatises on Herman Melville as "indecent." It cannot be said, however, that the contributors to this book have all followed this original suggestion.

The initial essay, for example, stands apart from the others and has to do with "American Studies," a term which has come into special use largely since the Second World War. As defined by Walter Johnson in a report from the U. S. Advisory Commission on International Educational and Cultural Affairs dated July, 1963, "American Studies" means "the study of the past and present civilization of the United States through specific courses in academic departments . . . of universities and colleges and in secondary schools." And Mr. Johnson further explains that the term as he defines it does not correspond exactly to the meaning attached by the American Studies Association in the United States: "to designate a collectivity of courses, organized as an 'area study'; that is the study of the United States as an entity by itself outside of the traditional academic departments." The earliest known proposal for such an area study was made, without result, in the 1860's to the Senate of Cambridge University in England, and the central connection with literature was obvious, for the proponents wished to invite James Russell Lowell as the first professor of "American civilization." Only in recent years have such programs come into being. But in almost all of them literature has provided the core.

While there are of course diverse reasons, varying from university to university, for the introduction of "American Studies," and Henry Nash Smith and others have raised the question whether such interdepartmental enterprises can develop a "method" peculiar to their especial requirements, their fundamental purpose has been largely taken for granted. In the first essay contained in this book Howard Mumford Jones addresses himself to this important problem, especially as it concerns institutions of learning in the United States. His views on the subject, one may venture to prophesy, are not likely to lapse into innocuous desuetude.

The three essays which follow that of Professor Jones deal with authors of the Colonial period, surely an epoch sadly neglected by recent students. And among the other disquisitions appear two treatments of Harriet Beecher Stowe and appraisals of the work of

Jack London and Thornton Wilder—all authors of world-wide renown who are seldom discussed by critics in the American academic fold. Fittingly enough, four writers from the South are also treated in this book, two poets, Poe and Lanier, and two writers of fiction, Kate Chopin and O. Henry. And Lafcadio Hearn may also belong to this category, for his most signal productions prior to his departure for Japan all came during the period of his residence in New Orleans. Further delineation of patterns in the contents of this volume would be perhaps as factitious as it would be supererogatory. Let it suffice to say that the range is considerable—from an analysis of one of the major novels of Henry James to a careful survey of the total output of Dashiell Hammett. One may safely assert that this memorial to a distinguished authority and a friend with a warm heart can stand in its own right as a solid contribution to scholarship in his field. This is as it ought to be, for in the long run scholarship alone honors scholars.

CLARENCE GOHDES

Contents

*Essays on American Literature
in Honor of Jay B. Hubbell*

AMERICAN STUDIES
IN HIGHER EDUCATION*
Howard Mumford Jones

Harvard University

Among the subjects in which graduate schools offer instruction, courses in science and mathematics aside, I think none makes severer demands upon the disciplined intelligence or requires a richer and wider consideration than what we call American Studies, a term we leave persistently undefined. I also note with regret that in few other areas is the gap between lofty aim and actual performance, between the intent of the programs and preparation for carrying out programs, more evident than in this field. I think it important that the gap be lessened, that our philosophy of the subject be re-examined and our notion of the place of American Studies in higher education be more carefully thought through. To this topic—the demands of the field, the inadequacy of our present preparation for it, and some principle by which these inadequacies can be lessened—I address my remarks.

I find the notion that American Studies are difficult is one many persons refuse to accept. All sorts of considerations seem to move in an opposite direction. In the matter of the time span covered in American Studies they argue that the historical period is recent and the lapse of years not great. The total life of the United States as an independent nation is, for example, shorter than the number of years separating Julius Caesar from Marcus Aurelius Antoninus. Even when we reckon all the years that have elapsed from the discovery of the New World by Columbus to the age of President Johnson, a stretch that seems immensely long to the American imagination, we have used less than half the years that separate the fall of Rome in 476 from the capture of Byzantium in 1453. Surely then, it is argued, to say that the study of the develop-

---

*The substance of this article was delivered as a lecture at Marquette University in May, 1966.

ment of American culture is more difficult than the study of the classical past or the Middle Ages is to make a rash assertion.

Moreover, American Studies are carried on in a familiar language. Most of the relevant documents are in English, and virtually none of them goes back even to Middle English. Students therefore do not need the linguistic preparation necessary for classical studies, or for the medieval world, or for the Orient, or for Africa, or for Polynesian anthropology. American life lies all around us. We are born in it, we are schooled by it, we participate of it. Where, then, is the difficulty? Few elements of American Studies are remote as the concept of chivalry, or of Buddhism, or of the perplexing tangle of values in Vietnam is remote.

But here, precisely, is one difficulty. An experience of some twenty-five centuries has gone to the making of classical scholarship. The student who wants to be a classical scholar knows at once that he must master not only Latin and Greek but also something quite alien from his own time, something called the classical world. The outlines of that world are fairly fixed, whatever the archeologists may do; and though the modern historian may have his fresh interpretation of Caesar or of Constantine, though he may endlessly debate whether the so-called fall of the Roman Empire was due to climatological change, or too much bureaucracy, or malaria, or too much slaughter and a falling birth-rate, or to a general failure of nerve, or to slavery, or to the clogging of old trade routes, he plays a game the rules of which were established long ago.

So likewise the scholar who goes in for Oriental studies or the study of Saracenic culture or for an examination of Slavic traditions enters a game, the rules of which are stabilized. There is the necessity of getting up the appropriate languages, there is the acceptance of the fact that the subject he pursues is different from, other than, the pattern of culture around him, there is the truth that as a matter of course he must make an imaginative leap from one sort of human existence to another. If these examples are extreme, it is also true, though in lesser degree, that the scholar in Romance languages or Latin-American studies or almost any other branch of more recent Western historical inquiry is guided by intellectual and imaginative patterns that have long worked reasonably well.

Fixity of pattern in this loose sense has also generally character-ized our departments of history wherein the study of American history has followed much the same trends as the study of British history or any other branch of inquiry. We have on the whole gone along with historiography as Europe has developed historiography. When a providential theory of history reigned in Europe, a providential theory of history was regnant here—quite baldly in the case of Cotton Mather, somewhat genteelly concealed in the case of George Bancroft. When the doctrine of the Germanic origins of free institutions swept European universities, American historians— Henry Adams is an example—obediently followed, and traced the origins of the New England town meeting back to the folkmoot held under the mighty trees of the Teutoburg forest. After the opening of this century much was made for a time of something called the "New History," but the "New History," however novel in American colleges, was a version of social and cultural history already practiced abroad. The one novel element was perhaps Turner's celebrated thesis about the frontier; but since social historians took in already vast sweeps of time and actions, there seemed to be no good reason why in conventional history departments courses in American cultural history and in the history of ideas in America could not be competently taught.

But enthusiasts for American Studies were not satisfied to leave American Studies, whatever they might be, to the department of history or, for that matter, to the department of English. They wanted a program of their own devising. They felt with some justice that English departments suffered from a kind of intellectual arthritis that made free movement painful. However excellent instruction in American history had been—and no department of humane scholarship in this country has produced more first-rate names— proponents of American Studies felt that some fusion of American history and American literature would not merely produce a goodly harvest but would also allow for a degree of scholarly experimentation not possible in tradition-bound departments. Nor could they see any reason why American painting, American architecture, American philosophy, or any other major American activity should not be added to this attractive enterprise. In 1949 they founded a magazine, *The American Quarterly*, for their very own; and in 1950 they created the American Studies Association, an organization at once national and regional, both scholarly and pedagogical. In addition, *American Studies News* is regularly published by a committee with one of the longest names in history—the Committee on International Exchange of Persons of the Conference Board of Associated Research Councils. The periodical is global in scope; in the December, 1965, issue, for example, I read about American Studies in countries as diverse as Thailand, Germany, Ceylon, South Africa, and Yugoslavia. I note also that foreign scholars of the status of Sigmund Skard of Oslo have written extensively on the theory and practice of American Studies programs. In some sense one has to go back to the Italian Renaissance to find a like instance of a branch of the humanities pursued with this same exhilaration.

Why, then, am I troubled? Scholarly enthusiasms are not so common we can afford to deride them. Perhaps a young subject like American Studies is only following the pattern of other young subjects—for example, sociology, which was young only a hundred years ago. Let us be patient with the infant.

Alas, however, for parallels! The characteristic fallacy of sociology in its younger years was the facility with which its practitioners constructed easy generalizations supposed to be "scientific." But the difficulty in American Studies is precisely an opposite one. I find it almost impossible to discover the generalizations on which or towards which American Studies are supposed to build. It is probably true, as John Stuart Mill somewhere observes, that the first principles of any branch of learning are really the last results of metaphysical analysis. But Mill insists that all action is for the sake of *some* end and that the rules of action, one supposes, must take their whole character from the end to which they are subservient. What is the end of American Studies? What is the philosophical purpose of these actions?

The aim of American Studies cannot be quite the same as the aim of the department of history, since enthusiasts for American Studies have removed, or tried to remove, their actions from that department. Nor can the aim be that of the department of English, for the same reason. Nor can it be precisely that of the department of art or of music of any other previously existing department; so that we face the logical absurdity that a thorough knowledge of art or of philosophy or of music is improper to American Studies, or at least not useful to them, whereas an imperfect control of some of these subjects is somehow good.

It is sometimes said that the great virtue of American Studies is that they are interdisciplinary. But interdisciplinary training can be no more than the sum of its parts unless some governing idea fuses these parts into a new unity; and though the concept of interdisciplinary studies may have the negative value of a practical protest against too much specialism, its positive contribution is nil unless interdisciplinary training is directed towards some particular philosophic end. Otherwise we are back in the absurdity of supposing that having an imperfect understanding of three, four, or five subjects is somehow preferable to having a thorough understanding of some one of them. "Interdisciplinary" is not an aim but a mode, and as a mode it merely postpones the issue.

Nor does it help very much to talk vaguely about the American way of life, or the American rhythm, or American innocence or guilt, or, for that matter, Americanism. To say that American Studies exist for the sake of studying Americanism is an obvious tautology.

It has been urged, usually as a reproof, that American Studies are in fact a branch of propaganda. I think this is not wholly bad, and I think the allegation perhaps puts us on the right trail. American Studies are propaganda because they are an attempt to explicate and make persuasive a set of values satisfactory to the American people; and because the American people believe these values, or some of them, may benefit other nations, they are engaged in a mighty effort to make these values comprehensible both at home and abroad. Why else do we have these required courses in American history? Why were we so insulted as a nation a century or more ago when the Reverend Sydney Smith asked his hateful question: "In the four quarters of the globe who reads an American book?" Why is public money spent on American Information Libraries abroad, too frequently the object of mob action? Why do we spend counterpart funds under the Fulbright Act to send scores of scholars and teachers to Dijon and Cairo, Allahabad and Athens, Bogotá and Tel-Aviv except to explain the American value system, persuade others of its excellence, and lure them to try parts of it themselves? This is an ancient formula. If the Romans conquered the world by force of arms, the Greeks conquered the Romans by force of culture. Again: the missionary movement, from the crude days of converting whole peoples by the sword through the prolonged effort of the Jesuit fathers to compel Chinese respect for Western learning and so make room for the faith, down to our time, is a parallel. I respect intelligent propaganda; and in a world where radio and television, newspaper and magazine, public statement and what we quaintly call trial balloons contend for the opinions of mankind, there is in one sense no good reason why America should hide its light under a bushel. Of course we do not have Russian Studies in this sense, though the Russians are great propagandists, and even General de Gaulle has not yet launched a worldwide series of French Studies paralleling American Studies, but perhaps this merely indicates Yankee forehandedness. We have been propagandizing the American value system at least since the days of Benjamin Franklin.

But scholarship does not find propaganda an altogether satisfactory term. Scholars do not want to become an arm of the government. The end of scholarship is, they think, truth, not propaganda; and though there is a sense in which the most elementary instruction in any set of ideas—for example, Plato—is propaganda for that set of ideas, we do not feel that the primary aim of the scholar in charge of the course in Plato is to turn out little Platonists but rather to examine Plato's ideas and their influence as dispassionately as he can. This implied ideal is, of course, shadowed by another and contradictory idea; namely, that the bright student goes to sit at the feet of some powerful personality or to enroll in some notable department because he wants the coloring of the department or the stamp of the personality. But this idea, though human, suffers from the same weakness that propaganda exhibits. We do not want to multiply little replicas of great men; we want independent minds, even though discipleship has great value. Mill says that all action is for the sake of some end and that the rules of action take their character and color from the end to which they are subservient. Most of us cannot be satisfied with the doctrine that what differentiates American Studies from other studies of like kind is either their importance as propaganda or their potentiality as discipleship. We shall have to dig a little deeper.

I turn therefore to a more complex topic that at first sight seems to answer our question simply; namely, the theory that the primary aim of American Studies is to examine the Americanization of culture. This theory emphasizes two obvious truths. The first is that we have had even before the founding of the republic a demand for the nationalization, so to speak, of our cultural expressiveness. The second is the theory that there is something called Americanization going on elsewhere as a result of American influence—for example, in Mexico or Japan—which seems to acknowledge the truth that the Americans have created a recognizable culture and that this culture is both desired and feared by old foreign nations. This idea is somewhat different from the proposition that there is a recognizable American way or a recognizable American rhythm, because it inquires: how did this American way or this American rhythm come into being?

I think the principal elements of the problem are two. The first is the patent fact that the foundations of civilized life in the United States have all been imported from Europe. We swept away aboriginal culture, however a few sentimental spirits may nostalgically want to return to it. As early as the coming of the Puritans, and more firmly after the creation of the republic, we insisted that we could not be, we would not be, a mere province of Europe; that, however much we might borrow, whatever these borrowings might be, it was our national duty to turn them into something worthy of the New World, or, by and by, the new nation, or, if some Americans—the kind who went to boarding schools, who lamented with Hawthorne there was no proper romantic light and shade in New England or who married their daughters to French counts and English dukes—insisted upon regarding European culture as a norm, it was our national duty to create a special and unique culture that would parallel, overwhelm, and deny this assumption. Hence it is that the young Emerson, speaking for a whole generation, implored us to forget the courtly muses of Europe, and Walt Whitman adjured us to divest American culture of the last vestiges of feudal society.

This conflict of values was first clearly defined in the political sphere. The colonists came by and by to insist that in crossing the ocean they had not given up any of the rights of freeborn Englishmen and then to insist that these rights should be directly expressed in colonial legislatures and not indirectly and imperfectly by the king in council or the imperial parliament. By and by this problem of rights underwent an enormous transmogrification—and to this I shall return—when the colonies left a monarchical empire and set up an establishment of their own, from which not only the crown but all such elements as a hereditary aristocracy and an established church were excluded. We were not going to parallel the crowned republic of Victorian England, we were going to be an American republic without a crown; and though words like "president," "senate," and "capitol" indicate that important parts of our governmental procedures were modeled upon classical practice, we were to become a unique experiment in the world—a single enormous republic in a universe of monarchies.

To this, as I say, I shall return. But as all practitioners of American Studies know, the question of nationalism in American letters occasioned a debate that has lasted from 1789 to the present day and has been the theme of innumerable scholarly studies. The issue, in one sense, is simple; the solutions have been complex and thoroughly unsatisfactory. It was argued on the one hand that by the very law of its being, a republic ought immediately to produce a mature literature of the people and, moreover, since the republic lay in the New World, that this literature would express new world scenery, new world manners, and new world values. On the other hand, equally ardent patriots argued that the United States could best evidence its maturity, not by repudiating a Europe rich with the spoils of time, but by profiting from the ageless culture of Europe, by emulating it, by making a contribution comparable in richness to that of Britain, France, or Germany. Despite early proposals to scrap British common law and the English language, you could not get along without using English. Let us therefore insist that Chaucer and Shakespeare and Milton are part of our inheritance, and, for that matter, Homer and Dante and Cervantes. To this the reply was sometimes made that we might, indeed, have to use the English language but that we should use it in our own way, neither talking nor writing an imported British idiom; and that even though, or perhaps because, the great European writers were part of the heritage of civilized man, our duty was to produce a genius comparable to them, or an American epic, or the great American novel, or something of that kind.

But difficulties appeared. Were, for example, the humorists of the Southwest frontier with their grotesque spelling, their burlesque of rude, uncultivated humanity, their lack of subtlety and their slapstick humor somehow "American," whereas Henry James, who spent most of his life abroad, who deplored the crudity of American culture, and who knew Flaubert, George Eliot, and Turgeniev, was somehow less "American" or even not American at all? Was Melville an American writer when he wrote *Pierre*, most of which is laid in the United States, and non-American when he wrote *Typee* and *Omoo,* which are laid in the Pacific? Everybody agrees that Mark Twain in a book like *Huckleberry Finn* was quintessentially national, but did he somehow fall short of the demand of nationalism when—I waive all aesthetic considerations—he took on Edward VI in *The Prince and the Pauper,* Malory's *Morte d'Arthur* in *A Connecticut Yankee,* and Joan of Arc as seen through the eyes of Sieur Louis de Conti? Walt Whitman is an American bard, who lived in Camden, New Jersey; is Wallace Stevens, an American poet who lived in Hartford, Connecticut, less so? Nobody denies that among the *Tales of a Wayside Inn* "Paul Revere's Ride" is as American as the Declaration of Independence; what, then, does one do with the magnificent "Saga of King Olaf" in the same collection, or with the even more magnificent sonnets on Dante's *Divine Comedy?* If there be an identifiable something called an American rhythm, is this found in Gertrude Stein, whom most Americans do not read, or is it only to be discovered in, say, Raymond Chandler's *Farewell, My Lovely,* which they read in thousands of copies? Does an American idiom show up in Carl Sandburg, son of Swedish immigrants, and disappear from *The Education of Henry Adams,* the author of which was in the sixth generation of probably the most famous American family? Finally, in this list of embarrassing rhetorical questions, is Mrs. Anna Cora Mowatt's *Fashion; or, Life in New York,* with its obvious indebtedness to the European theater, somehow more American than Archibald MacLeish's *J.B.,* with its obvious indebtedness to the Book of Job in a setting vaguely somewhere along the Eastern seaboard when it is not in heaven or no man's land? The matter, even in so relatively simple an area as American writing, is more than a little troubling.

If the struggle toward national expression in literature is the best-known phase of this problem in cultural interpretation, as soon as one turns to some of the other arts, the question becomes even more baffling. In painting, for example, it is argued that when we arrived at the Hudson River School we arrived at a true and mature American art, at painting that expresses the vastness, the elemental grandeur, the coloring, and the melancholy of the American scene. In some degree this is true. But these propositions are no sooner advanced than somebody comes along to point out that these painters are derivative in design, coloring, aesthetics, and moral principles.

They are influenced by baroque landscape painters in Europe, by Claude and Poussin, by Constable and Turner, and by others. If one asks, for instance, wherein the theatricality of an allegorical canvas by Thomas Cole—say, "The Voyage of Life" series—differs from the theatricality of a canvas by the painter John Martin—for example, "The Fall of Babylon"—it is difficult to say what in these two artists, contemporaries as they were, makes the one American and the other British. At the Centennial Exposition at Philadelphia in 1876 Thomas Moran was awarded a medal for painting the "Mountain of the Holy Cross" in Colorado, a vast panorama of the wilderness. But in the fifties the American painter Frederick E. Church went to Ecuador where he painted "Cotopaxi," a vast panorama of the wilderness that won the admiration of John Ruskin. Was the one painter American because he painted the Rocky Mountains in Colorado and the other somehow less American because he painted a volcano in the Andes? Or, to turn to something more modern, much is made of the proposition that abstract art is to be valued because it expresses the mechanical perfection of American culture. Perhaps it does. The only difficulty is that abstract painting had its roots abroad. So far as I know, the first statement of abstract theory was Kandinsky's little book *Concerning the Spiritual in Art*, published in 1910, and abstract painting did not really get under way in this country until Katherine Dreier put on an exhibit of the leading European abstractionists at the Brooklyn Museum in 1926. I add that the Association of American Abstract Artists was not founded until 1936. As American painters have commonly gone to school abroad—to London or Paris, to Italy or Germany—there is nothing surprising in these facts, but we are back at our original difficulty: the American spirit seems to be nourished on imported foods. I for one find it difficult to go through the Museum of Modern Art in New York and determine by inspection any specific difference between an abstract painting by an American and an abstract painting by a European. But I do not pretend to be an art critic.

If, on the other hand, one picks up almost any book about American music—that by Gilbert Chase[1] is a good one—one confronts a similar difficulty. Until well into the twentieth century what I shall rudely call highbrow musicians—examples are Edward MacDowell

---

1. Gilbert Chase, *America's Music, from the Pilgrims to the Present* (2nd ed.; New York: McGraw Hill, 1966).

and the Boston classicists like Horatio Parker—were educated in Europe or in Europeanized conservatories here and had no great vogue in this country until they had acquired a European reputation. An amusing instance is that of the tenor, Eduoardo di Giovanni, a star of the Chicago Opera, who was born in the New World as Edward Johnson, but who had to go abroad and Italianize his name in order to succeed in the United States. Composers, when they wrote on a supposedly American theme—for example, MacDowell's "Indian Suite"—also Europeanized; MacDowell, indeed, said in good set terms: "I do not believe in 'lifting' a Navajo theme and furbishing it into some kind of musical composition and calling it American music." Possibly our difficulty is that we do not distinguish between music in America and American music.

What, then, is American music? Jazz is supposed to express the national temperament in succession to ragtime and the blues, and we are rightly proud of Gershwin's *Porgy and Bess* and of various trumpeters, combos, and jazzmen of one sort or another. But jazz, however it may express the American temperament, is scarcely an American invention in the usual meaning of that phrase. Jazz, the blues, Negro spirituals, walk-arounds, and ballads are not uniquely American in the sense that they are original with us; on the contrary, their origins are traceable to imported Methodist hymn tunes, African chants, and rhythms and harmonies reaching us by way of the West Indies from Moorish Spain, not to speak of the blending-in of elements from the Indian population of the Caribbean and the Southwest. This last element of course shifts the meaning of the word "American," which now means "American aboriginal," a quite different notion. As for jazz as a characteristic American musical expression, Neil Leonard's admirable study *Jazz and the White Americans*[2] shows how middle-class white Americans fought it off as long as they could.

These speculations are not necessarily decisive. Cultural history again and again demonstrates how countries borrow from each other. The arts, moreover, perpetually renew themselves by returning upon some previous form of expression. But still, we are hunting for the key that makes American Studies a special or unique academic discipline, and the idea of cultural borrowing proves to be like the idea

2. Neil Leonard, *Jazz and the White Americans* (Chicago: University of Chicago Press, 1962).

of an interdisciplinary program—it simply pushes the issue back one step. What does the debtor country do to, or with, what is borrowed, to give these lendings a special characteristic?

One can of course reverse the equation. America lends as well as borrows. In the nineteenth century other countries feared or desired to be in some degree Americanized—conservatives feared it, liberals desired it: you can find both attitudes richly expressed in French thought and literature. But if we put aside the political aspects of Americanization and come down to the present century, we note that "Americanization" now seems to imply a process of industrialization, or, since we did not invent industrialism, a process of adapting our peculiar variety of industrialization, which is, I suppose, a kind of managed capitalism. For more sensitive persons Americanization is tantamount to vulgarization—at least, it is not high culture but popular culture that seems to be most evident abroad. Baseball goes around the world. Italian roadsides burst out with signs for Coca-Cola. The jukebox invades Mexico. Television commercials barge in on British broadcasting. Tokyo nightclubs flaunt the striptease artist. Automobiles crowd the streets of Munich as they crowd the streets of Chicago. Moving pictures are displayed on remote islands in the South Pacific. Packaged foods invade Lebanon. It is probably true that accompanying these adaptations there is also in the country affected a subtle alteration in the tempo of life, a kind of new popularity for movement and speed, a growing restlessness that conservative nationals resent and that they attribute to Americanization. But is this the essentiality of American culture? Considering our art museums, our symphony orchestras, our national parks, our great foundations, some, at least, of our great buildings, and many of our geniuses in politics, science, the arts, and so on, few of us seriously think so. Most of us would rather be known as the nation that nourished Lincoln than as the nation that invented the singing telegram.

I suppose, whether we talk about the importation of European culture or the exportation of American culture abroad, the process commonly passes through four phases: importation (or exportation), imitation, rivalry, and conquest. That is, we first import the foreign article, custom, or value, whether it be Paris gowns or Scottish philosophy; we then seek to imitate it, as the Connecticut Wits tried to write imitation European epics; we then rival it, as when we establish symphony orchestras as good as the New York Philharmonic or the Boston Symphony; and then we somehow turn it to our own special use. What is that special use?

I earlier indicated that I was temporarily putting political considerations aside. I now return to them. In the course of his essay on Milton, Walter Bagehot remarks that the time of the Commonwealth was the only period in English history in which the fundamental questions of government were thrown open for popular discussion in England. In the same spirit I remark that during the century between the Seven Years' War, which ended in 1763, and the American Civil War, which ended in 1865, the American colonies at first and the United States afterwards were the one great area in Western society where fundamental questions of government were thrown open for continual popular debate. The Declaration of Independence, to which our courts and our Congress from time to time recur, and the Federal Constitution, which is the fundamental law of the land, are philosophical documents arising out of this discussion and occasioning its continuance. They make us the oldest nation in the world founded upon a set of a priori general principles.

Perhaps because of our easy familiarity with what Rufus Choate once called the glittering generalities of the Declaration, we do not always recognize the astonishing and radical novelty of the ideas thus expressed, nor are we always aware that the Constitution, which sought to apply general principles to a vast and novel experiment, was and is an amazing document. We try to get around this patent truth in all sorts of ways. Nothing, in this connection, is more characteristic than that the Fourth of July, which was once signalized by the reading aloud of the Declaration and by an orator of the day who discussed it, has become a great national picnic. We say that the Age of the Enlightenment is over, or that the Constitution was a pragmatic compromise among contending economic and political forces, or that American life, developing in this vast and empty continent, would have come out pretty much the same way whether these state papers existed or no. This seems to me an absurd assumption.

Doubtless there are both a theology and a philosophy behind a much older political concept, that of the Holy Roman Empire. Doubtless the apologists for monarchy like Sir Robert Filmer and for absolutism like Thomas Hobbes made out philosophical cases for forms of government other than the republican one. It is true that when Jefferson, in explanation of the Declaration, said he had put down only the common sense of the matter, he was summarizing tendencies that go back to Jewish lore and to Aristotle. Nevertheless I also think it true that until the rise of the Soviets the American nation was the only country of the Western World in modern times to be consciously shaped by philosophical principles. This is clear if one contrasts the thinking of Jefferson and Madison with that of Blackstone and Burke. Jefferson and Madison were calling a novel government into existence; Blackstone and Burke were trying to work out a conservative philosophy that would fit an inconsistent governmental pattern centuries old. I urge that the philosophical principles of the founding fathers not only have shaped national policy—on this we all tend to agree—but are also fundamental to an interpretation of American cultural studies, a proposition we do not all accept.

What was this philosophy? Its principal ideas are familiar to the point of weariness, and perhaps that is why specialists in American Studies seem so often to be trying to avoid them. This philosophy was an eighteenth-century philosophy. It was shared by men who believed in a rational deity, an orderly mechanical universe, the philosophy and psychology of John Locke, the existence of a moral sense as an innate characteristic of men, women, and children, a faculty called taste, and the equality of mankind. These are tremendous notions. They were applied a little later with explosive force by the French to a society medieval in structure, and the result was both innovation and confusion—we continue as a republic, but the French have gone through three monarchies, two empires, and five republics in the same period. They were applied with somewhat more moderate results to other European countries in 1830, in 1848, and later. They were adopted in Latin America. They have reached the ancient East. The radical meaning of some of these principles produced our own Civil War. They reappear, belligerent and vital, in our national effort to overcome racial prejudice, the problem of what to do about religion in the public schools, the rights of women, the so-called sexual revolution of our time, the concept of President Johnson's Great Society, and the endless debate over the question whether the impact of the United States upon the contemporary world is that of a liberalizing or an imperialistic power. These issues are what William James called live options, just as in the eighteenth and nineteenth centuries the question whether the American republic was a beacon light or a danger signal in a world of monarchies was a live option. I suggest that the governing philosophical concept for American Studies is whether in the twentieth century a culture consonant with these eighteenth-century generalizations is still possible in the United States.

For we no longer believe in the principles of the Enlightenment, but only in some of them. We no longer believe in the rationalistic deity of the eighteenth century, under the impact of modern physics we no longer believe in the Newtonian universe, we no longer accept either the philosophy or the psychology of John Locke, we no longer assume there is a universal faculty of reason, we do not hold that there is an innate moral sense, we have done queer things to the concept of taste as a universal faculty, and about the only element in the original pattern on which we tend to agree, at least emotionally, is the concept of the equality of mankind.

Inasmuch as our form of the state is the result of a philosophy and that philosophy is not a function of the form of the state, the American Studies specialist, when he inquires into the relation of American culture to this fundamental postulate, will of course not reduce inquiry to politics, but he will ask whether the accepted value system of the republic is aided or damaged by particular expressions of activity, past or present, in education, religion, science, technology, literature, the arts, and so on. He will also have at hand a useful measure in determining when and how imported cultural forms enrich or impoverish these American postulates. But as this may be too generalized for immediate understanding I conclude with two examples. One has to do with mass culture, and one with high culture.

The proponents of mass culture argue that they are giving the people what they want, that to do so is to operate democratically, and that those who do not like mass culture—from their point of view a highbrow minority—can let it alone. The critics of mass culture reply that mass culture is perpetually mediocre culture, that it is produced not for the public good but for profit only, and that there seems to be no halting its steady deterioration in the direction of vulgarity. From what standpoint should a specialist in American Studies approach this characteristic modern problem?

He will, in the first place, insist that mass culture is not the same thing as popular culture and try to distinguish between activities, whether vulgar or not, that arise from the people and activities that are imposed upon the populace. He will, in the next place, inquire not so much whether mass culture increases general intelligence, comfort, and pleasure as whether intelligence, comfort, and pleasure thus increased are consonant with the general welfare of a state which demands from its democracy a certain order of judgment. He will try to extract from it those elements that seem to express traditional values and those elements that are new, and ask whether the new values are consonant with traditional values, which, partly because they are traditional, are presumably consonant with the American value system. He may also compare and contrast the mass culture of the United States with the mass cultures elsewhere—say, in Russia or China—and thus sharpen his ability to discriminate between what we think of as democratic values. He will be both historian and critic, but his criticism and his history will continually recur to the philosophical postulates of the republic in order to determine whether the ideas, announced as absolutes in 1789, are viable in the United States of 1967. His analysis will be in no sense chauvinistic; it will rather be a critical estimate of an important American activity in the light of the Jeffersonian premises, which are themselves one of the four or five great statements of humanistic value.

In the area of high culture let me select American fiction as my example. It is commonplace that theorists demanded a mature and independent American literature from before the creation of the republic; and, despite early objection to fiction on the ground it was immoral, the novel soon became one of the important branches of imaginative writing in the United States. How has the novel dealt with the fundamental postulates of human nature and of society on which the republic is founded? Again reminding the reader that the question is not a political but a philosophic one and that the point at issue is less the aesthetic value of a book than its presentation of man as a social being—I dare not call him a political animal for fear of being misunderstood—I note that the assumptions made by American novelists about mankind tend more or less to coincide with the Jeffersonian view until we reach Mark Twain, who announced not once but many times that the moral sense in man was the cause of all the evil that he does. Oddly enough, American naturalists, never extreme pessimists, managed to argue for determinism and simultaneously to demand moral and social reform. But when we get fairly into the twentieth century, the leading novels are books from which God disappears—Hemingway's famous sentence: "I know only that what is moral is what you feel good after," demands an extraordinary power of foresight on the part of the doer. Under the influence of Freud and Jung American novels admired by critics and reviewers have tended consistently to deny virtually every premise of the Enlightenment except equality, and equality is defined as sympathy with human beings in proportion as they are unfortunate or abnormal. It comes out as scepticism in proportion as they are successful and well-adjusted. A political world in which the Snopes family secures control of county and state, a social world in which a leading novelist makes a good thing out of a set of unmotivated murders, a moral world in which Fitzgerald's Gatsby and Saul Bellow's Herzog are titular heroes, and Scarlett O'Hara of *Gone with the Wind* and Leonora Pendleton of *Reflections in a Golden Eye* are titular heroines differs radically from the world of Cooper, Hawthorne, William Gilmore Simms, and William Dean Howells.

If the object of American Studies were simply to study the novel in America, the inquirer might merely note that these variants are but the latest phase in a form of imaginative entertainment that runs all the way from Petronius to Erle Stanley Gardner. But the object of American Studies is not the novel in America but the American novel, and this can only mean a critical examination of the novel as responsible writing in the context of what responsible writing is supposed to be in this republic. The critical question is not whether the novel is now better or worse under Freud and Jung than it was when Cooper and Hawthorne wrote, but whether the image of American life in the novel endorses or questions or denies our two great original premises: first, that an enduring republic can be founded on human nature; and second, that the arts in this republic will support and nourish this particular representative system and this particular democratic society. If the novelists are now right about human nature, then the philosophic postulates on which we began may be wildly wrong; and if the philosophic postulates are right, the novelists may be, if not wrong, at the least obsessed with a wrong-headed value system.[3] Such an inquiry or something like it

3. I discuss this problem at greater length in *Jeffersonianism and The American Novel* (New York: Teachers College Press, 1966).

seems to me to differentiate American Studies from other branches of humane learning.

At the opening of the nineteenth century Jefferson said: "We have the same object, the success of representative government. Nor are we acting for ourselves alone, but for the whole human race." It is entirely possible he erred. He had said earlier: "I consider the people who constitute a society or nation as the source of all authority in that nation." If man is as irrational as he is pictured by many leading novelists, it is possible that Jefferson was mistaken. The object of American Studies seems to me to look into this kind of problem. They thus become more than an interdisciplinary gadget, they become a philosophic inquiry, testing the probable truth in Faulkner's Nobel Prize Speech when he remarked that the artist "must teach himself that the basest of all things is to be afraid; and, teaching himself that, forget it forever, leaving no room in his workshop for anything but the old verities and truths of the heart. . . . Until he does so he labors under a curse. He writes not of love but of lust, of defeats in which nobody loses anything of value, of victories without hope and, worst of all, without pity or compassion. . . . I decline to accept the end of man." If the United States is in any sense
what a great American said it was, the last, best hope of
man, American Studies must refuse to accept
the end of man and must agree with
Faulkner that man in the
republic will prevail.

SEVENTEENTH-CENTURY
PROLOGUE

Ola Elizabeth Winslow

Sheepscot, Maine

Except for possibly a scant dozen names, the writers of America's seventeenth-century generations are either unknown or forgotten. They were not men of letters in any version of the accepted sense, and had they remained in England most of them would never have published a page. However, transported into strangeness sometimes past belief, they had something to say, and said it. Not drama of the Elizabethan stamp, but drama of wonder and mystery; nature untamed for *mise en scène*, savages among the actors, adventures, dangers, deliverances that had appeared in no previous repertoire of English imagining. Later generations would use some of these details in poetry or romance, but conscious art would make something different of the atmosphere, the overtones of the earlier reports which were intended as truth unvarnished. There is only one first time, and the navigators, explorers, and first settlers who belonged to the vanguard of the greatest migration history knows wrote an artless story that defies translation. To read their first-hand reports as they wrote them is to see a New World as it could never be seen again.

As the calendar approached 1600, the three-century tract of time we call the Renaissance was coming to an end. In the thought of the men who began to write the American story, the universe had grown almost inconceivably more vast since the days of their grandfathers. Our earth was no longer flat but had become three-dimensional, and as time itself stretched farther back, the forward view was lengthening likewise. God's judgment day was postponed. Only ten years after the death of Columbus, Sir Thomas More published his *Utopia*, and as other utopias followed in rapid succession, America in popular imagination became part of this fabled hope. A better world than England might lie somewhere toward the west, whither ships in search of new trade routes were steering. Old patterns of thought were in flux, class distinctions (particularly middle-class) were growing less fixed, authoritarianism in both religion and government was loosening its hold, and a new spirit was stirring in the minds and hearts of Englishmen—the spirit of new conquest, new hope.

The distance from the Middle Ages, however, was as yet not far enough for the natural world to be other than a world of signs and wonders past literal explanation. There is not a seaman's log, narrative of a voyage, tour of exploration, or a personal diary in which direct observation and some scrap of folklore are not mingled on page after page. The line between fact and fable is continually blurred. St. Elmo's flame "about the bigness of a great candle" on the masthead to announce an approaching storm, one flame to give warning, two flames to promise hope of deliverance; spectral ships in the clouds, woods creatures that might have stepped out of the *Bestiaries*, invisible spirits for bane or blessing appearing from behind a bush or stepping forth from a rock or stream bed. The door to the invisible world always stood ajar.

Evidences are multiple. John Josselyn wrote in the record of his 1638 voyage,[1] "June the first day in the afternoon, very thick foggie weather, we sailed by an inchanted island . . . heard cawdimawdies, seagulls, and crowes (birds that always frequent the shoar), but could see nothing by reason of the mist. Towards sunset, when we were past the island, it cleared up" (p. 7). Why not an enchanted island? Men were still talking of the lost Atlantis, not as an idea but a place. John Josselyn also reported "a sea serpent or snake, that lay quoiled up like a cable upon a rock" at Cape Ann, mentioning it as literally as the "two mighty whales" spouting in the sea a few pages earlier. Similarly in the tale of one "Mr. Mittin" who had seen a Triton or a merman in Casco Bay. The creature put his hands (very like human hands) on the edge of the canoe, and when Mr. Mittin chopped off one of them with a hatchet, the merman disappeared, "dyeing the water with his purple blood." There was also report of one Foxwell, who when returning from Cape Ann in his shallop by night, heard a loud call from the shore: "Foxwell, Foxwell, come ashore" (pp. 23-24). Fearing to land, he put out a little farther to sea, watching from this safe distance. He saw a great fire on the sands, men, women, and children dancing around it hand in hand. After an hour or two they

1. John Josselyn, *An Account of Two Voyages to New England, 1638/9, 1663/71* (London, 1674).

vanished. Next morning, when he dared to investigate, he found burned brands, and the footprints of men, women, and children, shod in shoes, but met no one. Did the shoeprints make them human beings, or could they have been demons?

Possibly, since demons were sometimes visible even in daylight to seventeenth-century eyes. Once on the fourteenth of June in this same year John Josselyn reported sailing by an "island of ice, three leagues in length, mountain-high, in form of land, with bays and cliffs like high cliff land, and a river pouring off it into the sea. We saw likewise two or three foxes or devils skipping upon it." Fox or devil, one was as likely as the other.

There was nothing misleading to English readers in this mingling of fact and inherited tradition. To English eyes concrete reality was still transparent enough to suggest the intangible reality which lay behind and underneath all nature. Proofs were not asked, nor were they necessary.

Tragedy and near tragedy in these same voyage accounts fill many pages. In a furious gale on November 8, "After we had heard and felt a mighty sea break on our foreship," Colonel Norwood wrote in his 1649 *Voyage to Virginia*,[2] "The ship stood stock still, with her head under water, seeming to bore her way into the sea." The mate was walking up to his knees in water, "prayers in his mouth." "Assaulted with the fresh terror of death, we took a short leave of each other," then all hands fell to work while a chance for action lasted. That was only the beginning. With forecastle gone, anchors gone, topmost mast fallen into the sea, stays of all the masts gone, no rigging left to keep the ship steady, water in the hold and our supply of bread "greatly damnified," passengers and crew drifted for days, not knowing where they were or how much longer half a biscuit a day and rainwater would keep them alive. First for days, then weeks, until those who lived through the strain saw land on January 3.

"My dreams were all of cellars and taps running down my throat," Colonel Norwood wrote. Safe on land at last, and conducted to a fresh stream of water and lying prostrate beside it, "setting my mouth against the stream so that the water might run into my thirsty stomach without stop," I thought this "the greatest pleasure I ever en-

2. Col. Henry Norwood, *A Voyage to Virginia*, Force Tracts, Vol. III, No. 10, pp. 10 ff.

joyed on earth" (pp. 23-24). In such a detail out of the many in this "stroke of death" experience, this first-person account is from the inside of the experience of thirst, long endured. Similarly of hunger, of terror, of hopeless abandonment to the fury of the winds, of steady faith in God, and the sight of land after unnumbered days. The historian, generations afterward, writes perforce from the outside. He tells. The seventeenth-century writer does not merely tell; he reveals. He remembers how it felt and gives life to the experience from within. Similarly of many other unforgettable moments: of loneliness on the fringe of an apparently unending forest, the sense of being lost within it, the howling of wolves as they came nearer, the war whoop of Indians and the sound of an arrow just overhead. Such experiences take on imaginative reality in these first-person records. Almost no surviving record of our first century lacks them. They live long afterward in the reader's memory.

Accounts of early explorations on land are most numerous of all, and to the English reader for whom they were written, most determining. Most of these are little more than listings of bird, beast, fish, tree, plant, usually in the pattern of Thomas Hariot's *Briefe and True Report* of 1588. His divisions had been commodities that are merchantable, commodities that sustain man's life, and a longer section on Indians. Informational in motive, these reports were in great demand. Ship companies and colonial agents were eager to print experienced knowledge and the English reading public eager to read it. Anonymous broadsides promising extravagant advantages must be contradicted. Merchant hope of trade in the New World must be invited. For the prospective settler, the urge to come must be made compulsive.

For the lay reader there was much of marvel, with frequent spicing of legendary detail, especially in sections dealing with animal life. The porcupine attacks his enemy with a shower of quills. The wolf's eyes shine like lanterns in the night. Turtles weep tears and sob passionately, as if sensible they are about to die, when caught. Alligators roar hideously before foul weather. Only of the wood pigeons, darkening the sun in their flight of thousands past imagining, breaking great branches of mighty trees when they alight, has scientific investigation gone far beyond these early descriptions which passed for exaggeration in their time. Personal experiences of the explorer are often interwoven with these early inventories of tree, plant, animal, giving sprightly pages to a practical reference sheet. An encounter with a wolf, domestic habits of the bear seem at close hand, a miraculous escape from a snake, a lion, the sight of an eagle striking his prey, the running of the alewives in the spring. Many of these personal incidents presage the American tall story, even to the wink in the eye, the twist at the climax.

Records of early settlement are usually more literal, but always with something of marvel. The point of departure was naturally comparison with what was similar in England, with America usually proving the better. Compared to Virginia, "the most fertile part of England is but barren," said John Brereton in 1602. The colony is "interlined with seven most goodly rivers, the least whereof is equall to our River Thames," added Alexander Whitaker. Never have I beheld "a larger or more beautiful river." The Thames seems "a mere rivulet" in comparison with it, echoed Andrew White.[3]

Such statements are legion, and soon extravagance was part of each comparison. The lesser the detail the greater the extravagance. Jacob Steendam, in his *Praise of New Netherland*,[4] along with his mention of fish that

> The nets to loathing; and so many, all
> cannot be eaten,

sang of oysters

> So large, that one does overbalance three
> Of those of Europe; and, in quantity,
> No one can reckon.
> (p. 55)

In his *Prickel-Vaersen* of the following year (1663) he returned to oysters with equal extravagance,

> The fish swarm in the waters, and exclude the light;
> The oysters there, than which none better can be found;
> Are piled up, heap on heap, till islands they attain;
> And vegetation clothes the forest, mead and plain.
> (p. 71)

Jasper Dankaerts, perhaps unknowingly, outdid Steendam by asserting that New York oysters were sometimes not "less than a foot long,

3. John Brereton, *A Briefe and true Relation of the Discoverie of the North Part of Virginia* (London, 1602), p. 7; Alexander Whitaker, *Good Newes from Virginia* (London, 1613), p. 37; Andrew White, *Relatio Itineris in Marylandia, Force Tracts*, Vol. IV, No. 12, p. 18.
4. Jacob Steendam, *Praise of New Netherland* (New York, 1661); Henry C. Murphy, ed., *Anthology of New Netherland* (New York, 1865).

and they grow sometimes ten, twelve, and sixteen together, and are then like a piece of rock."[5]

There is much more of this from other pens. Not only are rivers wider and deeper, trees taller, plant life more lush, but the air itself restores the sickly to life. "Many that have beene weake and sickly in old England, by comming here have beene thoroughly healed and growne healthfull and strong." This from Francis Higginson,[6] who had cast away his cap and now dressed comfortably in breeches without linings. Unwisely perhaps, for he was gone before the year's end.

William Wood added to the marvel of climate by declaring that "In publicke assemblies it is strange to hear a man sneeze or cough as ordinarily they doe in old *England*; yet not to smother anything, sometimes they freeze their feet,"[7] although to be sure, this is through carelessness. Comparatives quickly became superlatives in ever more entertaining fashion. Such inconsequential details as the size of strawberries, walnuts, lobsters, the length of a wheat ear, the weight of a wild turkey were continual subjects for exaggeration and colony rivalry. Turkeys weigh thirty pounds, says South Carolina; they weigh forty-eight, says Massachusetts; forty to fifty, says Pennsylvania; fifty and upwards, says Maryland; sixty, says Virginia, as though in childish escalation.

But there is more than childishness in all this, if one reads discerningly, and samples more than one generation of such writings. Quite clearly the age speaks through them. As the range of man's experience widened, imagination responded. What had seemed impossible, now came within reach. Size, abundance, usefulness challenged the first settler on every side, and dilated his vision for the years ahead. The wilderness was wasteful. These abundant resources must be used. Francis Higginson was troubled by the "aboundance of Grasse that groweth everie where, both verie thicke, verie long and verie high in divers places; but it groweth verie wildly with a great stalke and a broad and ranker blade, because it never had been eaten with Cattle, not mowed with a Scythe, and seldome trampled on by foot."[8]

Yes, added Daniel Denton; it is "as high as a man's middle," and "serves for no other end except to maintain the Elks and Deer, who

5. Jaspar Dankaerts, *Journal of 1679-1680* (Long Island Historical Society, 1867), p. 123.

6. Francis Higginson, *New England's Plantation* (London, 1630), p. e.

7. William Wood, *New England's Prospect* (London, 1634, 1635, 1639), p. 5.

8. Higginson, *op. cit.*, B 2.

never devour a hundredth part of it." Denton observed also the woods in May curiously bedecked "with Roses and an innumerable multitude of delightful Flowers"; when their virtues were known, there would be "no disease common to the Countrey, but may be cured without Materials from other Nations."[9]

Usefulness always came first. This, too, is the age speaking, but to say that the emphasis on commodity (one of the favorite words in these descriptions) means that these early men were blind to beauty is not to read what they wrote. Truly enough, Niagara is "an insurmountable bar to all passage by water," the White Mountains yielded nothing worth the pains of the first men who climbed them, the "Pure and Chrystal Streams flowing from the Vales in Virginia" would make the "best Waterworks in the World at a very small Expence," but read also how many times these same writers were ravished (also a favorite word) at what their eyes saw. Let John Brereton speak for them all: "Comming ashore, we stood a while like men ravished at the beautie and delicacie of this sweet soile."[10] It should not be forgotten that a century later no less a poet than Thomas Gray wrote a letter characterizing the Apennines as "not so horrid as the Alps," and that some years later Goldsmith, Addison, and various of their contemporaries were still speaking disparagingly of mountains as compared with flat country. American imperviousness to rugged natural beauty must be thought of in connection with such parallels as well as with the ever-present colonial goal of practical advantage.

To read the record forward, decade by decade, is to be made aware that gradually a sense of possession was dawning. Not explorers, to whom America was a spectacle, and who had no intention of remaining, but residents were writing. After a few sowings and reapings, it is "*our* Turnips and Parsnips and Carrots [that] are here both bigger and sweeter than is ordinarily to be found in England." *Our* goodly cornfields, *our* woods and fields; the *our* is everywhere. It would be a long process, but already, unconsciously, and at the cost of unceasing labor, weariness, hardship, and always risk, a man's land was beginning to be his by more than a legal claim.

By the mid-century the first-generation leaders were slipping away, one by one: Thomas Hooker in 1647, John Winthrop and

9. Daniel Denton, *A Brief Description of New York* (London, 1670), p. 4.
10. Brereton, *op. cit.*, pp. 7-8.

Thomas Shepard in 1649, John Cotton and Nathaniel Ward in 1652, Edward Winslow in 1655, William Bradford in 1657. Even some of the younger ones had gone long before, and by the time another decade or two had passed, few original settlers of Jamestown, Plymouth, Boston, Hartford, Dorchester, Roxbury, and other early coast towns would still be active in leadership. A new generation had already moved into their places. Born to the wilderness, these new leaders and laymen had no personal knowledge or experience of the mother country for such comparisons as had shaped their parents' first impressions. They accepted the severity of New England winters, the summer caterpillars and mosquitoes, the danger of wolves, of warring Indians, and of now and then being lost in the woods. They belonged to what they still called "the wilderness," and the wilderness was beginning to belong to them. They did not have the formal education of their fathers. In fact, in the second half of this first century of American life, the level of culture was lower than at the first foundings and lower than it would ever be again. But these sons of pioneers willingly paid their peck of corn annually toward the support of Harvard College, and in due time some of their sons and more of their grandsons might be students there.

By this mid-century great things had already happened and were happening in the story of a new nation's life. Of this and to the great loss of later generations, no literary record exists. Instead, only the literal entry in town or church books and homemade diary volumes of lives lived, daily work done, votes passed, boundaries extended, towns settled, sermons preached, sinners forgiven, faith in God holding fast. Much appears on all these pages of which literature is made, but the alchemy to transmute it into art is lacking. The "swan on still St. Mary's lake" does not yet "float double, swan and shadow." The very stuff of life is here, but only rarely, in the very fact of being written down, does it take on something of art. More usually, the motive for literature was lacking.

Inevitably, it would come. Strangers, aliens, men of another heritage and training had first to tell of the strangeness all around them. Given time gradually to possess the new landscape through their own labors and the slow mastery of its secrets, and then to be able to assume it, not merely to describe what they saw, they would presently come to speak out of their own sense of possession, of belonging to the very land itself and being part of New World history. Obviously what they wrote would no longer be mere information.

By that time the earlier decades would have changed many things. Fixed convictions would have been reshaped by the new environment. Later generations would not state their goal as simply as John Winthrop had stated Boston's goal in his *Arbella* sermon, as his flagship neared the New England shore, but in far more complex terms the sense of high destiny ahead of those who came would still endure in dream and action.

To attempt to judge America's earliest writings, informative and promotional as they were intended to be, for literary merit is more often than not to write blank pages. But to read these first-person accounts, not in terms of a later literary ideal, but in their own seventeenth-century terms, as first impressions, first responses of the beginners who had left their own safe chimney corners and dared the Atlantic in sailing vessels, is to meet something in human hope and thrilling capacity for endurance which left a mark—indelible, we trust—in what we call the American character. The unliterary, if you please, chapter of the American story is a prologue to what has followed, and after all, a prologue is part of the story. For the understanding of America, these thousands of her earliest pages will answer many questions on many paths of inquiry, and their reward in human interest may astonish the modern reader.

THOMAS PRINCE, MINISTER

Theodore Hornberger

University of Pennsylvania

Most of the comment upon Thomas Prince (1687-1758) has centered either upon *A Chronological History of New-England* (1735-1753) or upon his passion for collecting Americana, which resulted in one of the most interesting of colonial libraries. The *Chronological History* is both impressively ambitious and pathetically absurd. So great was Prince's concern for accuracy that he has had the reputation of "an American pioneer in historical writing."[1] On the other hand, his devotion to the dating rather than the interpretation of events robbed his annals of literary interest, and his decision to begin with the Creation was, as Moses Coit Tyler kindheartedly observed, a "sad miscalculation of the time at his disposal."[2] Prince got no further with New England than the year 1633. His book-collecting was far more judicious. "The New-England Library," including manuscripts and now invaluable imprints of the colonial presses, was bequeathed to the Old South Church and stored for decades in a tower room. Although it suffered depredations, such as the disappearance for many years of Governor Bradford's manuscript history of Plymouth, its uniqueness was eventually recognized, and to the colonialist it is now one of the great attractions of the Boston Public Library.[3]

To present Prince again as historian or bookman is not the purpose here. He was, first of all, a minister, and a popular one, if one can judge by the fact that thirty-five of his sermons were printed,

1. Michael Kraus, *A History of American History* (New York, 1937), p. 89.
2. *A History of American Literature, 1607-1765* (New York, 1878), II, 147. See also Kenneth B. Murdock, "Colonial Historians," in *American Writers on American Literature*, ed. John Macy (New York, 1931), p. 11: "But there is no style, and the result, priceless for reference and an awful foretaste of much in later historical writing, is to be consulted, not read." Samuel Eliot Morison terms Prince's plan a "mistake" (*The Intellectual Life of Colonial New England*, New York, 1956, p. 182).
3. For a brief account of the Prince Library, see Hellmut Lehmann-Haupt, *The Book in America* (New York, 1939), pp. 302-303. Fuller information may be found through the references given by Edward H. Dewey at the end of his article in the *Dictionary of American Biography*, XV (New York, 1935), 232-233. "It is undoubtedly," wrote Dewey, "as bibliophile and student that he will be longest remembered."

twenty-nine of them in his lifetime.[4] He was frequently chosen to speak on important public occasions, and no fewer than eighteen of his discourses fall in the category of the memorial or funeral sermon, which was one of the most characteristic rituals in the Puritan tradition. The sermons in print are, of course, only a small fraction of those which he delivered in his forty years as minister at the Old South. They are enough, however, to suggest that he expressed to a remarkable degree the convictions, confusions, and visions of his times.

Clifford K. Shipton has confessed some wonder at Prince's popularity at the beginning of his ministry:

His sermons demonstrated unusual mental powers (even his enemies admitted that) but they were too learned for the common people, and most of his sermons, sooner or later, came around to his experiences in Europe. Moreover Mr. Prince read his sermons in a monotone from a small volume which, because of his near-sightedness, he held so close to his nose as to give him the appearance, appropriate enough, of having a book for a head. (p. 347)

His "learning" and his own experience do indeed get into Prince's sermons, sometimes in curious and surprising ways. He was not a run-of-the-mill New England clergyman.

The learning seems to have grown out of the experience which, while not unique, was unusual. Prince's preparation for the ministry did not follow the usual pattern.

He was graduated from Harvard College, to be sure, in 1707, but he apparently lacked the means to continue reading divinity in Cambridge and await his call to a pulpit. After a stint as a schoolmaster, he set out to see something of the world. He left New England on March 20, 1709, and did not return until July 17, 1717. About seventeen months of his eight-year absence were spent at sea or in Barbados, the remaining time almost wholly in England. There he probably acquired most of his learning, as well as tastes and predilections which he never wholly lost. He preached, moreover, both at sea and before a number of Dissenting societies. His most extended connection, of about four years with one interruption, was with a congregation at Coombes in Sussex. He could, had he wished to do so, have stayed permanently in England.

We know far too little about Prince's self-education in England

4. For bibliographical and biographical facts, this essay relies upon Clifford K. Shipton, *Sibley's Harvard Graduates*, V (Boston, 1937), 341-368.

between 1711 and 1717,[5] but he was obviously closely identified with English Dissent, which in these years was facing one crisis after another.[6] He was in London at the time of the trial of Henry Sacheverell, whose attack on toleration had aroused mobs to demonstrate against the Dissenters. He was in England at the time of the Occasional Conformity Act of 1711, which sought to end the accommodation by which the nonconformists, most of them Whigs, had attained political power in the middle years of Queen Anne's reign. He must have shared the alarm of his associates at the Schism Act of 1714, which was intended to destroy the Dissenting academies, where most of the ministers of the nonconforming sects were being trained.[7] He rejoiced, we may be sure, at the accession of George I in 1714 and in the suppression of the Jacobite rebellion in the following year.

One thing which Prince brought to his Boston congregation, therefore, would seem to be a renewed sense of the importance of religious freedom. He returned a staunch Congregationalist, and his ordination sermon contains a long passage on the necessity of the congregational election of ministers.[8] A lecture sermon of 1727, delivered before the General Assembly of Massachusetts and printed at the desire of the House of Representatives, compares George I to David and George II to Solomon.[9] A thanksgiving sermon of 1746 sees the hand of God in the defeat of Prince Charles and his forces at Culloden.[10] The "improvement" of *God destroyeth the Hope of*

5. A letter-book covering this period, once in the hands of the Reverend Chandler Robbins (1810-1882), has been lost. See Shipton, p. 361.

6. See such general histories as G. M. Trevelyan, *England under the Stuarts* (21st ed.; London, 1949), G. N. Clark, *The Later Stuarts, 1660-1714* (2nd ed.; Oxford, 1955), and Basil Williams, *The Whig Supremacy, 1714-1760* (2nd ed.; Oxford, 1962).

7. See Nicholas Hans, *New Trends in Education in the Eighteenth Century* (London, 1951), pp. 57-59. The standard works on the academies are Irene Parker, *Dissenting Academies in England; Their Rise and Progress, and Their Place among the Educational Systems of the Country* (London, 1914), and Herbert McLachlan, *English Education under the Test Acts, Being the History of the Non-Conformist Academies, 1662-1820* (Publications of the University of Manchester, Historical Series, No. LIX, Manchester, 1931).

8. See *A Sermon . . . at His Ordination* (Boston, 1718), pp. 15-16.

9. See *A Sermon On the sorrowful Occasion Of The Death Of His late Majesty King George of Blessed Memory, And The Happy Accession Of His present Majesty King George II. to the Throne* (Boston, 1727). Prince had seen both men "about 10 Years agoe" (p. 17). "And for my Part—I shall never forget the Joy that swell'd my Heart; when in the Splendid Procession at his *Coronation*, preceeded by all the Nobles of the Kingdom, and then his Son & Heir apparent, our other Hope, with their Ermine Robes & Coronets—That *Royal Face* at length appear'd, which Heaven had in that Moment sent to Save these Great Nations from the Brink of Ruin. Nor do I speak it as my case alone, but as what appear'd to be the equal Transport of the Multitudes round about me. The Tears of Joy seem'd to rise and swim in every' Eye: And we were hardly able to give a Shout, thro' the labouring Passions that were swelling in us" (p. 20).

10. See *A Sermon Delivered at the South Church . . . August 14, 1746. Being the*

Man! (Boston, 1751), a sermon on the death of Frederick, Prince of Wales, contains (pp. 19-25) a panegyric on the Hanoverian Succession.

Combined with religious and political views which Prince shared with the English Dissenters, and even less likely to be unpopular, was an unfeigned delight at returning to New England, whose history and institutions were to him almost as dear as the Bible itself. Pride and patriotism make his first published sermon, *God brings to the Desired Haven* (Boston, 1717), glow to this day; when, in addition, Increase Mather in "To the Reader" could find it "Judicious & Solid," one need not wonder about his call to the Old South. Prince's best effort in this strain, however, was his single election sermon, *The People of New England put in mind of the Righteous Acts of the Lord to Them and their Fathers, and Reasoned with concerning them* (Boston, 1730). The year, as he did not fail to observe (p. 22), was the centennial of the arrival of the *Arbella*, and the discourse is in essence a brief history of New England, bolstered by quotations from earlier election sermons. What he has to say about the founding fathers is most revealing of the affinity between Puritanism, Dissent, and the New England Way:

> For the Generality of them—They were the near *Descendants* of the first *Reformers* in ENGLAND. They were born of pious Parents, who brought them up in a Course of strict Religion, and under the Ministry of the most awakening Preachers of those Days. Like so many *Timothies*, they were from their Childhood taught to know the HOLY SCRIPTURES, to reverence them as the Inspirations of GOD, as the only Rule of Faith and Piety, and to aim at a pure scriptural way of Worship, and at the vital Power and Practice of Godliness. And they continued in the things they had learned and had been assured of, as knowing of whom they had learned them.
>
> Under such Means as these they became inspired with a Spirit of Piety, and with a growing Zeal to reform the *Worship* of GOD to the most beautiful and perfect Model of his own Institutions.
>
> In Points of *Doctrine*, they entirely held with the *Church* of ENGLAND, their Judgment of *Orthodoxy* being the very same: But they apprehended it to be the sole prerogative of GOD Himself, and a Glory that He would not give to another, To appoint the Orders of his own House, and the acceptable Ways of his own Worship: That RELIGION *is a free obedience to the known Laws of* GOD; and it is neither in the Power of Men or Angels, to make that Religion which He has not made so Himself: That his own Institutions ought not to be set on a Level, mixed or debased with the low Devices of Men; and that it is a plain, full and decisive *Rule*

Day of General Thanksgiving for . . . the Glorious and Happy Victory near Culloden (Boston, 1746).

of his own Injunction—*To the* LAW *and to the* TESTIMONY; *if they speak not according to* THIS WORD, *it is because there is no light in them.* (pp. 23-24)

For laboring after this pure religion, the founding fathers were "censured, pursued, seized, imprisoned, fined, and suffered a World of Hardship not now to be named" (p. 24).

However, thro' the infinite Mercy and Wisdom of GOD, it was well for our *Fathers,* and for *Us,* in the End, that they were thus afflicted. For had there been then a Succession of such indulgent PRINCES and *Bishops* in ENGLAND, as there have since the PRINCE of ORANGE ascended the Throne; there had never been such a Countrey as *This,* for Religion, good Order, Liberty, Learning and flourishing Towns and Churches; which have given us a destinguishing Name in the World, and have reflected a singular Honour to the Persons and Principles of it's original *Setlers* for this *Hundred Years.* But having a rougher Surface, a barrener Soil, a more inclement Air than the Southern Countries; it wou'd in all humane Prospect, have been at this Day as the wasts of NEW-SCOTLAND or the wilder Desarts between us, but abundantly fuller of barbarous Natives; or at most in no better condition than the bordering Plantations.

But the omniscient and sovereign GOD had espied and chosen this Land for our Fathers, for a Refuge and Heritage for them and their Children; that here they might set up his Worship and Churches according to the inspired Pattern, behold the Beauty of the Divine Appointments in their Scriptural Purity, & leave these inestimable Privileges, which they justly preferred above all things else in the World, as a Blessed Inheritance to their Posterity, as we see at this Day. (pp. 24-25)

In addition to reinforcing the convictions of his parishioners about the peculiar good fortune of New England, Prince gave them a taste of the new learning, both biblical and scientific, which was characteristic of English Dissent.[11] In presenting science as a bulwark of religion rather than as a threat to it, he had been preceded by Cotton Mather and others.[12] Like Mather, Prince larded his sermons with information and speculation which many of his hearers probably found none too relevant. The best-known examples of his method are the earthquake sermons of 1727, which so established Prince as an authority on earthquakes that in 1755 he published *An Improvement of the Doctrine of Earthquakes,* with somewhat disas-

11. An excellent example of the Dissenting community's examination of the Bible is the work of Nathaniel Lardner (1684-1768), *The Credibility of the Gospel History* (1727-1757) being most conspicuous. Williams, pp. 85-86, describes the "enlightened system of education" of the Dissenting academies, in which science played a remarkable role.

12. See Theodore Hornberger, "The Science of Thomas Prince," *New England Quarterly,* IX, 26-42 (March, 1936).

trous effects on his reputation.[13] Most important, however, is a thanksgiving sermon of 1749, *The Natural and Moral Government and Agency of God in Causing Droughts and Rains.* Dedicated to the Royal Society of London, this piece, which is extensively footnoted, reveals Prince's wide reading in the scientific and religio-scientific books of his day.

Much of his thinking, perhaps like that of his congregation, was an attempt to reconcile the new science with a profound belief in divine intervention or at least divine design in the natural world. There is therefore, as Shipton notes (p. 350), some "medieval other-worldliness" in his sermons. He had experienced special providences in his own life: the ship on which he had planned to return to New England sailed without him and was lost at sea; his daughter almost but not quite drowned in his arms; his prayer for the aid of the wind against the invading French fleet in 1746 had raised, he and his fellow Bostonians believed, such a storm as the North Atlantic had seldom seem (a deliverance memorialized, by the way, in Long-fellow's "A Ballad of the French Fleet").[14] The problem of providence crops up again and again in Prince's sermons, as it probably did in the minds of his congregation. *God brings to the Desired Haven*, already mentioned, extols the power of prayer, with implicit reference to his own experience. *Civil Rulers Raised up by God to Feed His People* (Boston, 1728), a lecture sermon after the arrival of Governor Burnet, argues for a providence "from the very nature of created Substances, and from the State and Order of things in these lower Parts of the Creation" (p. 12). The election sermon of 1730, previously quoted, compares the history of New England to that of Israel and argues that eminent leaders are raised up by the Lord in special favor to a people of God. *Extraordinary Events the Doings of God, and marvellous in pious Eyes* (Boston, 1745), a thanksgiving sermon on the taking of Louisburg, asserts "that some extraordinary Events, without being properly term'd miraculous, have such lively Characters of their being the Doings of GOD, as they are evidently so to unprejudic'd and careful Observers, and appear marvellous in their pious Eyes" (p. [7]). This last sermon is of

13. See Eleanor M. Tilton, "Lightning-Rods and the Earthquake of 1755," *New England Quarterly*, XIII, 85-97 (March, 1940).

14. For the poem, see *The Works of Henry Wadsworth Longfellow*, Standard Library Edition, III (Boston, 1886), 111-113. Shipton describes (pp. 345-346) the circumstances of Prince's failure to sail on schedule. Prince gives an account of his daughter's rescue in *The Sovereign God Acknowledged and Blessed* (Boston, 1744), p. 22.

special interest because it develops Prince's favorite argument that, although God does not work in a manner contrary to His usual ways, *"singly in themselves consider'd,"* His doings are discernible if one looks at a concatenation of events. One can see God's hand, therefore, (1) when in affairs of vast importance there is a wonderful continued train of timely coincidences; (2) when in the series there are many monumental and critical incidents; (3) when in desperate situations deliverance comes "beyond our Power and Thought"; and (4) when an extraordinary spirit of prayer is raised up in many. Needless to say, all of these appear in the fall of Louisburg. The same type of demonstration of divine intervention on behalf of New England appears in *The Salvations of God in 1746* (Boston, 1746), a thanksgiving sermon in which Prince lists a series of fourteen events, the climactic one being that the day of fasting and prayer was immediately followed by great storms—as his hearers doubtless remembered. The striking thing about Prince's preoccupation with providence is that he was apparently aware of the danger of interpreting isolated events teleologically. His concatenation argument preserved the traditional theory of God's care for his chosen people and yet gave it a flavor of rationality. If not convincing to a modern reader, it very probably seemed reasonable to Prince's contemporaries.

How much of Prince's sermon style may be attributed to his English training is a question which can be answered only after more careful study than has yet been made of the discourses of New Englanders and of English Dissenters. Possibly, however, he was somewhat more willing to vary the traditional doctrine-reasons-uses pattern than was, to take a single example, Jonathan Edwards. Prince always began, of course, with a biblical text, which he was fond of placing in its context. His explications vary in length, involving sometimes the analysis of single Greek or Hebrew words, with the help of biblical commentators, and occasionally even consideration of grammatical structure.[15] If he presented a "doctrine" it was generally little more than a paraphrase of the text; quite often he omits the doctrine altogether and contents himself with "observations," "propositions," "illustrations," or simply general "heads." There is usually an "improvement," but seldom any elaborate piling up of "uses." There are few passages which seem

15. His ordination sermon (cf. note 11, above), pp. 4-5, is a good example.

likely to have made his listeners uncomfortable about the state of their souls. The effect is often that of a lecture, rather than an exhortation, the tone urbane, sophisticated, and hopeful. Prince was on the whole a comforter, not a gadfly.

His appeal is nowhere better explained than by his treatment of death. The memorial sermon, most often delivered on the Sunday following the funeral and interment of a member of the congregation, was a form wherein Prince excelled, judging by the test of publication, presumably at the expense of the relatives or friends of the deceased. These sermons display considerable variety, and a few of them present a view of death which, if not unique, is decidedly rare.

To take death as a warning or a call to repentance is not uncommon. Prince, however, ventured only once into this kind of thing. After the unexpected deaths of three relatively young Bostonians he published *Morning Health No Security against the Sudden Arrest of Death before Night* (Boston, 1727). Taking as his text Psalms 90:5-6 ("In the morning they are like grass which groweth up. In the morning it flourisheth and groweth up; in the evening it is cut down and withered"), Prince touched lightly upon the transience of human life and the necessity of being as free from sin as possible. As a persuasive to reform, his sermon is surprisingly gentle.

Another familiar component of the Puritan and Dissenting funeral sermon is an account of the last days and deathbed conversations of the subject. Prince tried this more often, but most elaborately in *The Sovereign God Acknowledged and Blessed* (Boston, 1744), a funeral sermon on his daughter Deborah. The text is Job 1:21 ("The Lord gave, and the Lord hath taken away; blessed be the name of the Lord"), and the forty pages of the discourse are about evenly divided between reflections on the situation and feelings of Job, with whom Prince as the bereaved father implicitly compared himself, and an account of the religious experience and final illness of Deborah. This is the most personal and harrowing of Prince's funeral sermons. In several other instances he was able to provide similar although much shorter accounts of the last days of his subject.[16] The fascination which this kind of thing had

16. See *The Pious cry to the Lord for Help* (Boston, 1746), preached after the death of Thomas Cushing; *Be Followers of Them, who Through Faith and Patience Inherit the Promises* (Boston, 1755), a sermon occasioned by the death of Mrs. Hannah Fayerweather; and *The Case of Heman Considered* (Boston, 1756), on Edward Bromfield.

for Puritans of all periods is common knowledge, the best-known example being Jonathan Edwards's case study of Phebe Bartlett, in his *Faithful Narrative.*

Prince's fondness for analogy, evident in the treatment of the text from Job, got more elaborate and formal expression in four sermons wherein he chose to retell a biblical story in a way intended to lead his hearers to make their own comparisons with the subjects of his discourses. One has already been mentioned—the lecture sermon on the death of George I, in which that gentleman is treated as an eighteenth-century David. The text is 1 Chronicles 29: 26-28 ("Thus David the son of Jesse reigned over all Israel . . . And he died in a good old age, full of days, riches, and honour; and Solomon his son reigned in his stead"). Half of the sermon is devoted to David's accomplishments, the other half to those of King George. A roughly similar method is followed in *The Departure of Elijah Lamented* (Boston, 1728), delivered after the death of Cotton Mather, on 2 Kings 2:12-13 ("And Elisha saw it, and he cried, My father, my father, the chariot of Israel, and the horseman thereof. And he saw him no more: and he took hold of his own clothes, and rent them in pieces. He took up also the mantle of Elijah that fell from him"). Prince devoted three-fourths of his space to five "observations" on the importance of eminent ministers, the remainder to Mather himself. One wonders if he thought of himself as Elisha. If so, he had good reason, for in many ways Prince was more like Cotton Mather than was any other New England minister of the period. The fullest use of the analogical method, however, is *A Sermon at the Public Lecture . . . Upon the Death of . . . Samuel Sewall* (Boston, 1730). Prince must have seized upon his text with sheer delight; he found not only a parallel but the same name in 1 Samuel 7:16-18 ("And Samuel judged Israel all the days of his life. And he went from year to year in circuit to Beth-el and Gilgal, and Mizpeh, and judged Israel in all those places. And his return was to Ramah; for there was his house; and there he judged Israel; and there he built an altar unto the Lord"). The life of Samuel is dwelt on in great detail, with much discussion of "integrity" and its synonyms; only the last five of the thirty-six pages speak of Sewall directly. A similar method of indirect praise is used in *The Character of Caleb* (Boston, 1756), a sermon preached after the funeral of Josiah Willard. All of these four sermons required their hearers to use their biblical knowledge while thinking of the traits of the deceased. All four, it should be noted, dealt with prominent citizens.

By far the most interesting class of sermons dealing with death is, however, that in which Prince expounds the meaning of the promise of immortality. There are four such sermons, and so far as death can be made attractive they succeed in making it so. In them we find the latter-day Puritan version of the Beatific Vision.

Prince's ideas on this subject appear first in *The* GRAVE *and Death Destroyed, and Believers Ransomed and Redeemed from them* (Boston, 1728), preached after the death of his eighty-year-old father. A "spring of Consolation" came to him from Hosea 12:14 ("I will ransom them from the power of the grave; I will redeem them from death; O death, I will be thy plagues; O grave, I will be thy destructions; repentance shall be hid from mine eyes"). Christ's role in death is also alluded to in Hebrews 2:9, 10, 14 and in 2 Timothy 1:10. From these texts Prince derived three "Observations":

1. THAT the *Grave* and *Death* have a dreadful and destroying *Power,* even over those that are dear to CHRIST or are his Covenant People.
2. THAT this Almighty Saviour beholds his People under this dreadful Power, with a most tender *Pity* for them, and an holy *Indignation* at these devouring Enemies.
3. & lastly, THAT in this active Pity and Indignation, He is inflexibly resolv'd to *Ransom* and *Redeem* his People from their Power, & to *Destroy* those Enemies of theirs for ever. (p. 4)

Expanding the first observation is a somewhat macabre description of the mouldering of the body in the grave. Death and dissolution come to all; original sin and the Fall have placed men at the mercy of death and the grave.

And tho' CHRIST has purchased them a compleat Redemption from every Evil; yet He is pleased for wise Intentions to apply the Purchase and redeem them *by Degrees,* till He brings the Work to its design'd Perfection.
FIRST he rescues them from the moral Dominion of Sin and Satan at the very Instant of their true Conversion. He then delivers them more and more from their prevailing influence, as they are marching on to the Heavenly Places. At the Moment of Death, He compleatly redeems the Soul from Sin & Sorrow, and puts an utter End to the Polution and Influence of Sin in their Bodies. And then He suffers the Power of Death and the Grave to prevail, that He might bare his Witness against the Sin of his People, and that his almighty Power may the more appear and shine, in raising their dissolved Dust to Life, and forming so vile a Substance into Glorious Bodies. (pp. 8-9)

Under the second head Prince explores the relation of Christ to the bodies of believers. These bodies were once enlivened with rational and immortal souls, sanctified together by the Holy Spirit, and so God's temples. In them Christ resided; they were "Members of his mystical Body" (p. 9). Therefore their death is precious to Him.

> CHRIST must needs behold the struggling Contest [i.e., the affliction of His people] with great Concern. And when the *vile Body* is bereft of Life and Soul, He does not leave it: When 'tis carried to the Grave, He goes down with it Thither: His gracious Presence dwells with it there: and there He tenderly watches over it, that not a Dust may be lost that may be a convenient material to be put into the Building again. While the Carcase lies putrifying, in all it's Noisomenesse and Blackness, He does by no means despise it; but He Pities it, and accounts the Dust of his Temples to be precious while it lies in Destruction and Ruins. (p. 11)

The third observation is treated under two questions: (1) in what respect does Christ ransom and redeem His people from the power of the grave and death and destroy those enemies? and (2) when and in what manner will He accomplish this glorious work? Prince answers them by brief references to the "*sufficient* Purchase" Christ made while here on earth and the "*infinite* Power *of his Godhead*" and to the Second Coming. The resurrection of the body is not difficult, he says, "either to *Reason* or *Nature*." Consider what happens in the spring to a heap of vile and filthy earth, the mould perhaps of dead human bodies. It is soon covered with thousands of beauteous flowers.

> NOR does it in the least avail, to say, that these arose from *Seeds* which there lay hid, and now their Roots expanded and drew the Parts which were their proper Nourishment.— For what are *Seeds* but tender Plants already formed by the invisible Power of GOD, and infolded in proper Teguments to protect them from outward Injuries? And if you were to see their fine Materials running into the curious Form and disposing themselves along into every Part till they come to constitute a perfect living Plant in miniature, compos'd of a vast Variety of Coats and Vessels; would not this still be as wonderous as the other?
>
> AND is it not as equal with the Power of GOD to cause this Dust to run and form into an *humane Body*, as into a curious and beauteous *Vegetable*? And when he has form'd the Body, to inspire and unite the Soul, as He once has done in another way before? He that orders the Course of *Nature* as He pleases, can in a moment change the Course, and make it every whit as natural for the Bodies of Men to rise up out of the Dust as the Stalks of Plants, or as He used to form the Bodies of Animals out of earthy Substances in their Parents Bodies. And the one will then be as easily comprehended, and be no more wonderous or supernatural than the other. (p. 17)

Probably, however, the resurrection will be as described in Ezekiel's vision of the valley of dry bones (Ezekiel 37:1-14).

Christ abolishing Death (Boston, 1736), a sermon preached after the interment of Mrs. Mary Belcher, shows a new dimension in Prince's relatively cheerful speculation on the end of earthly life. His text was one of those mentioned in *The Grave and Death Destroyed*: 2 Timothy 1:10 ("... the appearing of our Saviour Jesus Christ, who hath abolished death, and hath brought life and immortality to light through the gospel"). This text, Prince says, presents "A great Variety of surprising Subjects," of which he will choose four: (1) death, (2) confusion about a future state, (3) the abolishment of death, and (4) immortality. He recurs to the analogy with plants, reviews the opinions of the ancient philosophers in some detail, and touches once more upon the role of Christ. In the discussion of immortality, however, Prince comes to the pleasures of Heaven, which he is to contemplate with greater fulness in two later sermons, the most remarkable, perhaps, to come from his pen.

The first is *A Funeral Sermon On the Reverend Mr. Nathaniel Williams* (Boston, 1738). Its text is Acts 7:59 ("calling upon God,[17] and saying, Lord Jesus, receive my spirit"). This verse comes at the end of Stephen's vision of the glory of God—a passage to which Prince referred elsewhere.[18] No doctrine is derived. Prince considers three things: (1) the case of a true Christian ready to expire; (2) the peculiar object of our believing view and application at such a season, which is Christ Himself; and (3) the great and comprehensive favor we are then to implore of Him, viz., to receive our spirits. The description of what it means for Jesus to receive our spirits is among the most eloquent passages in all his printed writings. What Christ will do is

to take it into his special, gracious, safe, and faithful Care, at the very Moment of its Separation: Interceeding effectually with the *Father* for it; applying the meritorious Virtue of his most precious Blood, by the agency of his *almighty Spirit,* to purify it perfectly from every Remain of Sin, and make it perfect like himself in Holiness. At that very Moment, he by the same *Agent* fills it with a Perfection of Life and Power: He makes it glorious like the *holy Angels* its new Companions: He makes it

17. Prince's citation significantly omits the word "God." It is the role of Christ which he found fascinating.
18. In *Be Followers of Them, who Through Faith and Patience Inherit the Promises* (Boston, 1755), p. 18. This is a sermon preached after the death of Mrs. Hannah Fayerweather. A footnote refers the reader to Prince's sermons on Acts 7:59 and Psalm 16:11, which appears to suggest that he regarded the sermons on Williams and Mrs. Stoddard (cf. below) the most considered statements of his views.

fit for their exalted Company: He opens its latent Powers to see its own Glory and the Glory of those illustrious Substances, as he once opened the Powers of *Elijah's* Servant: He in a Moment learns it their perfect Language: He commits it to their glad Embraces, their delightful Converse, their safe Protection (tho' all are comprehended in his own) and their certain and most speedy Conduct and Transportation, as his mighty and ready Instruments, to the heavenly World.

Their Spirits doubtless fly as swiftly as the inconceivably grosser *Rays of Light*, which in a *Minute* pass above *ten million Miles*: And the Joy and ravishing Desire of all the Company to reach the celestial Regions, will needs be as most active Wings to speed them thither.

Yea when he receives the separate Spirit, he no doubt receives it (as he did that of *Stephen*, even before its Separation) to the opening Prospect of that blessed World to which 'tis going: Tho' the higher it ascends, the brighter may the Glory still appear, the more distinct and clear the surprizing Objects open to the View, and the more capaciated may the Spirit grow for the more immediate Vision and Enjoyment of them.

If you ask me, *Where is this World of Glory?* I wou'd only answer, Do we not with our bare Eyes behold innumerable Multitudes of *dazzling Worlds* about us, enlighten'd with perpetual Day; some of which are found a *Million* times greater than the *Earth* we live on? And how much greater may others be we cannot yet discover. Or if these will not suffice; you may every clear Night by the Help of Glasses, look up and see several wondrous *Openings* in the Heavens over us; where immeasureable *Spaces of Light* appear, underived from any visible Bodies, and that seem to be beyond the starry Regions.

May not the GOD of Heaven allow us, from his Earth, to look unto the outmost Borders of his *upper World?* May not the *Light* appearing in those amazing *Chasms*, remote immensely from us, be the distant Rays of the heavenly Glory? Does not every one acquainted with the Laws of *Opticks* know, that these Rays may be so directed as to make those *Chasms* appear vastly nearer; yea, to open as large as Half the Firmament above us, and even represent the glorious *Objects* from whence they flow? And may not this be the surprizing *Vision* of the separate Spirit, when its visive Powers are freed, perfected and opened; whither as a Rebel to behold its awful Judge above, or as an Heir to be advanced to its design'd Inheritance? (pp. 13-15)

The spirit will have a joyous welcome from the angels and will join in the celestial chorus. At this point Prince's beatific vision becomes highly personal, as the mysteries of science, the frustrations of the historian, and the pains of the minister at the spectacle of human frailty are all cleared away.

Yea, what *new* and *surprizing* Scenes of *Visions* and *Enjoyments* will continually open to delight us there! What Discoveries of the divine Perfections, Designs and Works; both in the *Creation* of Heaven and Earth, with innumerable other Worlds, of different Constitutions and Inhabitants; the various Trains of *Dispensations* in them, with their admirable Harmony and Wisdom; the astonishing *Redemption* of an amazing Multitude of Sinners of the Race of Men, from their first Apostacy, thro'out all their various and successive Generations, in every Nation, Age, and Country, to the entire Accomplishment at the joyous Resurrection.

And O! how *perfect* and *perpetual* the *Blessedness* which CHRIST receives the Spirit to in those exalted Regions!

For *there* is no Degree of Darkness or Blindness; but perfect and perpetual Light and clear Discernment: No Death, Pain, Infirmity, or Faintness; but perfect and perpetual Life, Pleasure, Strength and Vigour: No Degree of Error or Mistake; but always a right Conception of every Thing exhibited: No Hatred, Envy, Ill-Will, or Enmity; but perfect and perpetual Love, Complacency in each other's Blessedness, Benevolence, and Friendship: No Contention, Discord, or disturbed Passions; but perfect and perpetual Peace, Serenity, and Harmony: No Sorrow, Doubt, or Fear; but perfect and perpetual Joy, and full Assurance of the Continuance of this Felicity to the Resurrection, and for ever after. (pp. 16-17)

To this exhilarating and comforting vision Prince returned again in *The Fulness of Life and Joy in the Presence of God* (Boston, 1748), a sermon delivered after the death of Mrs. Martha Stoddard. His text this time was Psalms 16:11 ("Thou wilt shew me the path of life: in thy presence is fulness of joy; at thy right hand there are pleasures for evermore"). Again there is no doctrine, only illustrations: (1) what is eternal life? (2) what may be intended by the presence and right hand of God; (3) from whence the joys and pleasures there arise; and (4) a survey of the fulness of joys and pleasures there forever. Eternal life means the perfection of both the natural and the moral powers of the sanctified spirit. To be in the presence of God is to dwell in the third or highest Heaven, represented in the Scriptures

in the highest Sense, as the *Kingdom,* the *City,* the *Palace,* the *Temple,* the *Sanctuary,* the *Holy of Holies,* and the *Throne* of GOD: as *the high & holy Place* wherein he *dwells, and the Habitation of his Holiness and Glory.* It is described as being full of Light; and the Light so dazzling, as no mortal Eye is able to approach and live. Nothing of Impurity, nothing of Unloveliness, nothing hurtful, nothing disagreable, nothing vain or mean, nothing but what is perfect in Holiness, and in every amiable Excellency, shall ever enter there.

In fine, this is the happy Receptacle of all the glorified *Saints* of all Nations, Countries, Worlds and Ages; to which they are constantly ascending. This is the glad Resort from Time to Time of all the holy and blessed *Angels:* Thence are they continually descending, with Pleasure to perform the Orders, accomplish the Designs and advance the Glory of their Creator: Thither are they constantly ascending with their glad Tidings and happy Charges of perfect Spirits, to increase the Joy of Heaven itself, receive fresh Discoveries, and join with all the heavenly

Hosts in their new Songs of Praise and Adorations. That is the holy Place whereinto CHRIST entered: There is the Throne of the SON of GOD in human Nature: There he shines perpetually in the Brightness of the FATHER's Glory, and the express Image of his Person: There both the perfect Saints and Angels are continually beholding, and adoring him: and that's the happy Place designed for the eternal Residence of all the Saints with their most illustrious HEAD, when they shall have received their raised and glorious Bodies, fashioned in a Likeness to his own, and presented to him in one vast Assembly arrayed in all their glittering Attire, as a Bride adorned for her Husband: Thither, after the Honours done them in the publick Judgment, shall they openly ascend together with him; and there admire and love, enjoy, praise and serve him, with supream and fresh Delight for ever. (pp. 12-13)

These pleasures and joys come, of course, from the infinite excellence of God. Sanctified spirits, finally, will perpetually delight in their freedom from sin and imperfection, the perfection of their powers, their perfect view of the heavenly world, their seeing of the saints, the angels, seraphim, and cherubim, their sight of Christ, their reviewing of the designs of grace and the steps of God's providence, their view of the history of Christ, their having the Scriptures opened to them, and having Christ reveal

the infinitely various *Histories* of their Fellow *Saints* and *Angels* from their Creation; their various Genius's, Capacities, Situations, Helps, Improvements, Employments; the various Trains of Dispensations towards them, the divine Contrivance and Perfections in them; and all subserving and advancing the Glory of their CREATOR, and the universal Joy and Blessedness of the heavenly World for ever. (p. 18)

Christ will "open" the Scripture promises and prophecies, especially the Book of Revelation, and the sanctified souls will adore, praise, and see the Father, Son, and Spirit.

And these are but some general Hints, which have risen in my Mind as I went along, and might easily be branched into numberless Particulars. Nor have I given the *Scriptures* which suggest them, least I had interrupted their Connection and left out many of great Moment to enlighten the Subject. (p. 19)

The "improvement" suggests, as one would expect, that Mrs. Stoddard is fortunate in dwelling in the third Heaven rather than in this world, by comparison "a mean, contemptible, dark and wretched Place" (p. 19) .

How horribly full of all Kinds of Corruption and heinous Wickedness are the *Hearts* and *Lives* of Men continually! of Impiety, Selfishness, Pride, Avarice, Sensuality, Deceit, and all other vile and hurtful Lusts, which drown them in Perdition! How full is this lower World of Idolatry, Profaness, Defiances of GOD and Enmities to one another! Tyrannies and Contentions; Drunkenness, Fornications and Adulteries; Stealing, Cheating, Lying and Defamations; Briberies and Partialities; Robberies, Oppressions, Persecutions, Cruelties, Murders, and all Kinds of Injuries and Violence! Multitudes a plundering, wounding and destroying each other—Distress of Persons, Families, Countries, Nations, and great Perplexities!—innumerable Crosses, Losses, Wants and Troubles—Diseases, Pains and Death afflicting and devouring all before them; filling our Houses with Griefs and Cries, and leaving the Survivors to expect soon to meet the same Fatality.

But now look up into the *heavenly World*—where none of these shall ever enter—and *There* is nothing but Perfection, Light and Glory, perfect Purity and Holiness—all the *Saints* and *Angels* eternally united with each other and with the blessed GOD in one common Interest and Desire—intirely, purely, fervently, and incessantly loving and delighting in each other—and *There* are surprizing, satisfying, and perpetual Visions & Enjoyments—the infinite GOD for ever filling, but not over-bearing their enlarged and growing Capacities, with such Views and Joys as he has Himself; eternally pouring the delightful Streams of his own undiminished Excellence & Blessedness into them, and eternally advancing them in their most joyous Likeness to Him. (pp. 20-21)

As has been suggested, Prince's portrayal of the intellectual and moral delights of Heaven was not unique. Much of Christian literature touches upon the Beatific Vision.[19] Such popular Puritan and Dissenting books as Richard Baxter's *The Saints' Everlasting Rest* (1649) and Isaac Watt's *Death and Heaven* (1722), and *The World to Come* (1739) show a similar pleasure in the promise of relief from the imperfections of the human mind and human condition, and more than one English funeral sermon can be cited as a parallel.[20] In New England, however, so far as the present writer's knowledge goes, no one else pursued this line of thought as far or as en-

19. See Joseph Hontheim, "Heaven," in *The Catholic Encyclopedia*, ed. Charles G. Herbermann and others (New York, 1910), VII, 170-175, and C. Harris, "State of the Dead (Christian)," in *Encyclopaedia of Religion and Ethics*, ed. James Hastings (New York, 1920), XI, 833-838.

20. See the Preface to William Bates, *A Sermon Preached at the Funeral of the Reverend & Excellent Divine Mr. David Clarkson* (1686), in *The Whole Works of the Rev. W. Bates, D.D.*, ed. W. Farmer (London, 1815), IV, 344: "The life to come extends beyond all possible number of ages; the felicity is so complete and sure, that the least shadow of evil shall never eclipse it; the soul shall be in a state of highest perfection and joy; the understanding illuminated with perfect knowledge, with no more study, than opening the eye and fixing it on the glorious objects, the will satisfied with the perfect loves and enjoyment of the blessed God: the body shall be clothed with light as with a garment, and shine with a beauty that never disflourishes and decays; the innumerable assembly of angels and saints always affords new and inestimable delights. . . ." Cf. also Thomas Amory, *The Character and Blessedness of those to whom to live is Christ, and to die Gain* (London, 1738) and *The Character and Blessedness of those who die in the Lord* (London, 1749), funeral sermons for James Strong and John Moore, as well as James Foster, *A Sermon . . . On Occasion of the Death of the late Reverend and Learned Mr. Thomas Emlyn* (London, 1741).

thusiastically as Prince did. He made death about as attractive as anyone could.

Thomas Prince's reputation was achieved, it would seem, by ideas which were the product of strong and rather enviable convictions. Whatever his shortcomings as a speaker, he spoke for a segment of the world which was still deeply religious, still proud of its past. He believed, as did his contemporaries, that it was still possible to reconcile the scientific order with divine direction. His sermons present a remarkable variety of form and of content. Most significantly, however, he believed in a real Heaven, where the moral and intellectual powers of men and women would be perfected to infinity. No wonder his congregation liked him, and no wonder that he was in demand when the ritual funeral sermon was required.

FORM AND SUBSTANCE IN
FRANKLIN'S AUTOBIOGRAPHY

A. Owen Aldridge

University of Illinois

James Madison once observed to James K. Paulding that Benjamin Franklin "has written his own life; and no man had a finer one to write, or a better title to be himself the writer."[1] This is a tribute to the literary quality of Franklin's autobiography as distinguished from its moral, historical, and practical value.

There is no question that Franklin was a skilful writer; the style of his autobiography as well as of nearly everything he wrote reflects the qualities of smoothness, brevity, and clarity, which he himself set forth as the criteria of good writing. But does this mean that his autobiography is a work of literature or one of the classics of the autobiographical genre? Those who grant it this eminence rarely present their reasons for doing so. And formalistic critics who apply arbitrary rules concerning style and form would have little difficulty in proving that for them the reminiscences of Franklin's life are beyond the pale of literature.

If we accept the premise that literature is fundamentally a matter of complex form or that it depends substantially upon symbol and myth, there is no need to try to make a case for Franklin—despite the efforts of some writers who have treated literary manifestations of Puritanism, capitalism, and the gospel of work as myth. As Simone de Beauvoir remarked about her own autobiography, very similar in spirit to Franklin's, "I most certainly do not pretend that it is . . . *a work of art*."[2] One must make the same admission about Franklin's *Memoirs,* but after doing so one must also go on with Mme de Beauvoir and point out that the label *work of art* has little to do with the spirit and real value of autobiography. "This word [a work of art] makes me think of a weary statue in the garden of a mansion;

---

1. April, 1831. Quoted by Adrienne Koch, ed., *The American Enlightenment* (New York, 1965), p. 480.
2. ". . . de toute façon je ne prétends pas qu'il soit . . . une œuvre d'art" (*La force des choses,* Paris, 1963, p. 8).

it is a word for collectors, a word for consumers and not for those who create. I would never dream of saying that Rabelais, Montaigne, Saint-Simon or Rousseau have produced *works of art,* and it makes little difference to me if people refuse to give my autobiography this label. No, it is not a work of art, but my life in its impulses, its distresses, its shocks, my life which seeks to express itself and not to serve as a pretext for niceties."[3] It is possible to argue that the vigorous expression of one's personality and ideas is a major quality of literature, and in embodying this quality Franklin's autobiography represents a high artistic achievement.

In form, Franklin's work is a virtual disaster. First of all, it is composed of four separate parts, written during four widely separated periods. Although there is no need of going into the elaborate history of Franklin's text, which has been covered in a number of recent books, some attention should be given to the aesthetic effects of its having been composed in stages. Franklin, for example, had in mind a set of readers for the first part completely different from those he had in mind for the other three. The first part was presumably written for the benefit of his family; the three others for the world at large. For this reason, I am unable to accept the theory that there is any kind of conscious art in Franklin's over-all structure as opposed to the separate parts, for example, the view of a recent critic that the narrative order of the work consists of two major divisions, the first, describing Franklin's education and character development, the second, his public career.

The work begins with the date and the salutation "Dear Son" as though it is in reality a lengthy letter of personal confidences from a father to his son, designed to serve the latter as a moral and practical guide through life. Since Franklin's son, William, at the time was over forty years old, the device of paternal counsel is certainly a fictitious one. If Franklin had a single potential reader in mind, it is more likely to have been William's son, William Temple, who was then eleven years old and under his grandfather's care. But it is more likely that Franklin was writing for his own amusement and gratification than for any particular external audience. Franklin's

3. "Ce mot me fait penser à une statue qui s'ennuie dans le jardin d'une villa; c'est un mot de collectionneur, un mot de consommateur et non de créateur. Je ne songerais jamais à dire que Rabelais, Montaigne, Saint-Simon ou Rousseau ont accompli des *œuvres d'art* et peu m'importe si on refuse à mes mémoires cette étiquette. Non; pas une œuvre d'art mais ma vie dans ses élans, ses détresses, ses soubresauts, ma vie qui essaie de se dire et non de servir de prétexte à des élégances" (*ibid.*).

stimulus for beginning his work at that moment was almost certainly the chance purchase during the previous month of "a curious collection" of bound pamphlets with manuscript notes of his own uncle in the margins of many of the pieces.

In the opening sentence of his memoirs, Franklin remarked, "I have ever had a Pleasure in obtaining any little Anecdotes of my Ancestors," a clear indication that he considered that he was engaging in the writing of family reminiscences—and a reminiscing tone, it is important to keep in mind, is the predominant one of Part I. The underlying didactic strain grew out of his subsidiary purpose of acquainting his posterity with the means he had used to emerge "from the Poverty and Obscurity" in which he was born, to rise "to a State of Affluence and some Degree of Reputation in the World." This moral strain is representative of Franklin's total personality and is reflected in virtually everything he wrote—in his light, good-humored pieces as well as in his obviously didactic ones. Although not dominant in Part I, it becomes somewhat obtrusive in the later parts.

Franklin admitted that he had undertaken his autobiography for a number of personal reasons: as a means of living his life over again through recollection, of indulging the natural inclinations of old men to talk of themselves and their past actions, and to gratify his vanity. After a few pages, he halted the narrative to recognize his "rambling Digressions" and to attribute them to his old age. He had formerly written more methodically, he affirmed, but "one does not dress for private Company as for a publick Ball. 'Tis perhaps only Negligence." This is the best evidence to indicate that at this time he had not intended his work for publication.

Eighteen years later, when he was working on the continuation of his memoirs, he appealed to one of his English friends, Benjamin Vaughan, to edit the manuscript carefully on the grounds that he was no longer able to judge whether it was suitable for the public eye. Paradoxically, in this very same letter in which Franklin questioned his own literary judgment, he gave Vaughan detailed criticism of the latter's writing. "Your language seems to me to be good and pure, and your sentiments generally just; but your style of composition wants perspicuity, and this I think owing principally to a neglect of method."[4] By *pure* and *good*, Franklin meant words in common usage. This we know because in 1760 he had admitted

4. A. H. Smyth, ed., *The Writings of Benjamin Franklin* (New York, 1907), X, 51.

to Lord Kames that he had erred in one of his pamphlets by choosing some words which were obscure and low and had agreed that it would not be correct to invent new words when old ones seemed inadequate. It was the subject of method, always considered by Franklin to be his own great weakness, on which he gave Vaughan the most detailed and specific advice. Essentially he recommended that Vaughan spend several days in considering his proposed subject, during which he should jot down notes or short hints of every thought. He was then to assign a number to each thought according to the order in which it could be logically presented to the reader. "In this mode," Franklin concluded, "you have a better chance for a perfect production; because, the mind attending first to the sentiments alone, next to the method alone, each part is likely to be better performed, and I think too in less time."

Evidence indicates that Franklin aspired to achieve this kind of "perfect production" in his memoirs since a copy of his original outline has survived. Apparently he wrote the introductory paragraphs dealing with his family background and childhood without prior planning and then prepared an outline for the rest of the work. The outline begins with the subject of the composition of the Dogood Letters and extends far beyond the point at which Franklin eventually gave up writing.

The time lapses between the four parts of the memoirs explain the repetitions, variations in tone, and other blemishes which Franklin's detailed outline should have prevented. Franklin wrote Part I in England in 1771, Part II in France in 1784, Part III in Philadelphia in 1788, and Part IV also in Philadelphia between November, 1789, and April, 1790. When he returned to Philadelphia in 1775 at the outset of the Revolution, he took with him the manuscript of Part I and the outline of the entire work, but left both in America when he embarked for France in the next year. Subsequently they came into the hands of a Quaker merchant in Philadelphia, Abel James, who copied the outline and sent it to Franklin in Paris accompanied with the earnest request that he complete his project of writing his life and publish it for the edification of American youth—in James's words, "to promote a greater Spirit of Industry and early Attention to Business, Frugality and Temperance with the American Youth." There can be no question that Franklin accepted this estimate of the function of his memoirs and that he wrote the last three parts in large measure to inculcate these practical virtues.

Franklin showed the outline and James's letter to Benjamin Vaughan, who was then in Paris.[5] Vaughan seconded James's appeal that Franklin carry out his design and predicted that in conjunction with another work which Franklin had projected, on the Art of Virtue, it would improve the private characters of all who would read it and consequently aid "all happiness both public and domestic."

Presumably these letters influenced Franklin to change his design in two ways: (1) to write for publication instead of for an intimate circle and (2) to emphasize moral concepts rather than family reminiscences. He incorporated both letters into his manuscript after Part I and indicated that what followed was accordingly "intended for the Publick."

Part II concerns only three subjects: Franklin's part in the establishment of the Philadelphia public library, his religious opinions, and his scheme for attaining virtue. The first of these appears in the outline; the other two do not. When Franklin returned to his memoirs in Paris, he did not have Part I in his possession, and he had forgotten that he had previously discussed the Philadelphia library. His subsequent treatment in Part II is therefore a repetition, although still interesting because of some new anecdotes. The brief section on religion sets forth Franklin's creed, and it is repeated almost verbally in Part III. It does not appear in the outline in either place.

More than half of Part II is devoted to Franklin's scheme for attaining moral perfection in his own life, almost certainly the same material he would have included had he published separately the "Art of Virtue," which Vaughan mentioned in his letters. It is based upon a pocket-sized collection of charts for checking infractions against rules of conduct which Franklin had devised in youth and still carried about with him in France. One of the thirteen virtues included in Franklin's scheme is order, a characteristic associated with nearly every phase of his life and which is symbolized in the moral scheme itself. Yet Franklin paradoxically confessed in Part II, "In Truth I found myself incorrigible with respect to *Order*; and

5. Details of the writing of Franklin's memoirs and the letters of James and Vaughan are to be found in Leonard W. Labaree, ed., *The Autobiography of Benjamin Franklin* (New Haven, 1964).

now I am grown old, and my Memory bad, I feel very sensibly the want of it." The insertion of this practical scheme for attaining virtue is indeed an infraction of the order of Franklin's outline and, as we have said, marked a decided change in tone from the informal recollections of Part I.

After returning to America in 1785, Franklin kept alive his project of continuing his memoirs largely because of the urging of two French friends, Louis le Veillard and the Duke de la Rochefoucauld. But because of external political activities he was unable to resume work until August, 1788. Reading over the first two parts, he concluded with some satisfaction "that the book will be found entertaining, interesting, and useful, more so than I expected when I began it."[6] Particularly significant here are the adjectives *entertaining* and *interesting*. The early parts, he confided to La Rochefoucauld, would be of particular "Use to young Readers; as exemplifying strongly the Effects of prudent and imprudent Conduct in the Commencement of a Life of Business." In similar vein, he explained to Benjamin Vaughan that he had omitted "all facts and translations, that may not have a tendency to benefit the young reader, by showing him from my example, and my success in emerging from poverty, and acquiring some degree of wealth, power, and reputation, the advantages of certain modes of conduct, which I observed, and of avoiding the errors which were prejudicial to me." From this perspective, the work has little to distinguish it from such pedestrian tracts as Franklin's *Advice to a Young Tradesman* and his *Hints for Those That Would be Rich*. But the self-revelations and realistic view of life in his memoirs, which his remarks take no account of, elevate his work to a higher plane than the didactic one he recognized.

"What is to follow," Franklin remarked to La Rochefoucauld, "will be of more important Transactions."[7] By this he meant that he would subsequently concentrate upon scientific, political, and diplomatic activities which belonged to the history of his nation and of mankind. Even though in fact he never described many of these historical moments because he failed to carry on the work much beyond the point of his arrival in London as Agent for Pennsylvania in 1757, the more objective and historical tone of Part III lacks the universal appeal of Part I. The outstanding sections in Part III are

6. Smyth, ed., *Writings*, IX, 676.
7. *Ibid.*, IX, 665.

the warm, self-revealing ones, particularly those describing his relations with George Whitefield, with the Quakers, and with the Indians. Part IV is so brief that its literary character hardly merits separate attention.

We have already mentioned as a violation of order in Franklin's narrative his two descriptions of the founding of the Library Company. Other obvious repetitions are found in duplicate statements of his religious creed and of the underlying philosophy of his written resolutions on conduct. These repetitions represent blemishes in Franklin's style and should be so recognized even though there are valid explanations to excuse them.

A similar imperfection exists in structure. If we assume that a biographical work should have a beginning, middle, and end, Franklin's is deficient in all but the introduction. Despite his outline, there is no dramatic conflict or sense of the unfolding or intensifying of a story. Some recent critics have, nevertheless, sought to establish a parallel between John Bunyan's *Pilgrim's Progress* and Franklin's memoirs as the pilgrimage of his life. To me, the parallel is dubious. It is true that Franklin himself commented on Bunyan's style in his memoirs, but solely on Bunyan's method of narrative, not on his theme. Since a realistic style of English narrative had not yet been established through the novel, Franklin percipiently observed that Bunyan was the first author to his knowledge "who mix'd Narration and Dialogue, a Method of Writing very engaging to the Reader, who in the most interesting Parts finds himself as it were brought into the Company, and present at the Discourse." As illustrations of practitioners of this style, Franklin cited Defoe and Richardson.

In the history of English biography, the method of "mix'd Narration and Dialogue" has probably been used most successfully by Franklin's contemporary James Boswell, whose *Life* of Samuel Johnson appeared in the year after Franklin's death. Franklin himself used the mixed method in a number of his essays and letters, but limited his memoirs to straight narrative. His expository method strongly resembles that of the picaresque novel—a rambling series of events joined together by a single protagonist, but with no unity of theme or purpose except for the announced motif of chronicling the author's rise from poverty to affluence. One could hardly argue that the work acquires distinction from this theme any more than from its structure. The only unity is psychological.

Franklin's literary style is characterized primarily by a natural, easy flow of words. In his autobiography, he rejected all "tropes" or artificial rhetorical devices and focused directly and simply upon each point as it came up. The most important adornments in the work consist of proverbs, some from *Poor Richard* and some from other sources. His friend Jean Baptiste le Roy remarked on the outstanding characteristic of his mind, his "always considering in any circumstance the most simple point of view."[8] This trait is reflected in the *Memoirs* along with Franklin's ability to see the relations between minor events and large ones. A forerunner of the autobiography which appeared in the *London Chronicle*, October 1, 1778, highlighted the concept of "great events from little causes," and a contemporary critic of the first publication of the *Memoirs*, Chamfort, was impressed by Franklin's tracing "the influence of minor events in youth upon the character, upon the ideas which determine the habits of a lifetime, and upon principles which eventually decide the role one plays in the most important circumstances."[9]

La Rochefoucauld, who read Franklin's work in manuscript, was struck by his objectivity: "He speaks of himself as he would have spoken of another. He traces his thoughts, his actions and even his errors and his faults. He depicts the development of his genius and of his talents with the sentiment of a clear conscience which has never had to reproach itself."[10]

Another stylistic feature of nearly all of Franklin's writings is axiomatic statement, an identifying mark of the entire age. In the autobiography, Franklin achieved an exquisite balance between reflection and anecdote. His delight in storytelling is strongly revealed in many of his personal letters and in his early journalism. One early reader of Franklin's memoirs found in it "too many trifling details and anecdotes of obscure individuals" for his taste,[11] but most readers, as Franklin anticipated, consider the anecdotes to be the brightest passages in the work.

8. A. O. Aldridge, *Benjamin Franklin and His French Contemporaries* (New York, 1957), p. 222.

9. *Ibid.*, p. 157.

10. *Ibid.*, p. 158.

11. Bruce Ingham Granger, *Benjamin Franklin: An American Man of Letters* (Ithaca, N. Y., 1964), p. 210.

One may adduce at least two plausible theories to account for the richness of anecdotal material in Franklin's memoirs. One is that he was consciously following a specific theory of the art of biography, first enunciated by Plutarch, a writer whom Franklin "read abundantly" in his youth and still highly valued in old age. At the outset of his life of Alexander, Plutarch had remarked that it is not "in the most distinguished achievements that men's virtues or vices may be best discerned, but very often an action of small note, a short saying, or a jest, shall distinguish a person's real character more than the greatest sieges, or the most important battles" [Langhorne translation]. Without any question, Franklin told some of the stories of his boyhood primarily for the light they shed on his character or to illustrate the influence of an event in early life upon mature development. Absolute proof that Franklin consciously related events to character in this manner exists in his well-known bagatelle "The Whistle." Here he traces the indelible impression upon his mind of an event in his life at the age of seven, showing how it remained sharp in his memory and guided his conduct throughout life. Although he does not always make the connection this precise in his *Memoirs,* there is little doubt that it exists. In my opinion, Plutarch is a much more likely source than "the Puritan tradition" to explain the quality of "symbolic anecdote, or parable" in Franklin's work.

Many of the anecdotes in Franklin's *Memoirs,* however, have nothing whatsoever to do with foreshadowing his brilliant career or with any didactic purpose. They are told for the sake of the story alone. The character sketch of the "odd Fish" Samuel Keimer, for example, and the description of Franklin's visit to the garret of a Catholic spinster of seventy years have no other function than human interest. These episodes, resembling the realistic touches in novels of a later period, are skilfully narrated. "You know everything makes me recollect some Story," Franklin wrote to his daughter, January 26, 1784, just about the time he was composing Part II of his *Memoirs.*[12] And he specifically confided to Benjamin Vaughan that he wanted the history of his life to be entertaining and interesting as well as useful.[13] It is even possible that Franklin included some of the entertaining material of Part I primarily to amuse the daughters

12. Smyth, ed., *Writings,* IX, 168.
13. *Ibid.,* IX, 676.

of Bishop Shipley, in whose country home Franklin composed it. On his return voyage to America in 1786, for example, he wrote his "Art of Pleasant Dreams" specifically to comply with a request of Catherine Shipley's.

Throughout his writing career, Franklin attained a degree of wit and imagination far beyond the standard set by his fellow citizens of Boston and Philadelphia—and his associates took it for granted that he could always produce some lively work. Even in the midst of his diplomatic mission to France, his daughter urged him to write something sprightly for a dull magazine, the *American*, which had just been established in Philadelphia. "Its want of entertainment," she wrote, "may induce you to send something that may make the poor man's [the editor's] Magazine more useful and pleasing."[14] In his *Memoirs*, Franklin was virtually forced to live up to his reputation as a diverting stylist.

When Vaughan wrote to Franklin urging him to continue his memoirs, he provided rather sophisticated arguments for his doing so—and these arguments in themselves illustrate the literary value of the work as completed. Vaughan recognized first of all that Franklin's activities had been so intimately connected with the development of the American nation that his personal history represented a valuable social document. As Vaughan expressed it, "All that has happened to you is also connected with the detail of the manners and situations of *a rising people*; and in this respect I do not think that the writings of Caesar and Tacitus can be more interesting to a true judge of human nature and society." The revelation of the intertwining development of an individual and a nation has almost as much artistic as historical significance.

We cannot be sure, however, that Franklin consciously considered himself as a prototype of his times and his country merely because Vaughan recognized the connection. What we are justified in observing is that Franklin's autobiography closely resembles several other works of the same kind written in virtually the same span of years, all of which are notable for incorporating considerable amounts of social background. Carlo Goldoni began his *Mémoires* in 1784, and they were published in French in 1787. Giovanni Casanova began his *Mémoires* in 1791—also in French, and they were published in 1820, twenty-two years after his death. Carlo Gozzi wrote the

14. October 2, 1779 (*Letters to Benjamin Franklin*, New York, 1859, p. 114).

major part of his *Mémoires* in Italian in 1780, and revised them for publication in 1797. These works are essentially as forthright as Franklin's in discussing intimate details and are filled with anecdotes and philosophic reflections. But most important of all, they reveal the inherent relationship between the author and the times. For this reason they were highly praised by Stendhal, a social realist, who contemplated including in his autobiography a contrast between his own amours and Napoleon's military campaigns.[15]

Benjamin Vaughan also believed that Franklin's emphasis upon the simple affairs of his daily life, his ordinary concerns and intimate thoughts, was something novel and refreshing in literature. "When we see how cruel statesmen and warriors can be to the humble race," he wrote, "and how absurd distinguished men can be to their acquaintance, it will be instructive to observe the instances multiply of pacific acquiescing manners; and to find how compatible it is to be great and *domestic*; enviable and yet *good-humored*." Even though judging merely from Franklin's outline and his own knowledge of the man, Vaughan recognized that Franklin's "affairs and management will have an air of simplicity or importance that will not fail to strike"; also that the "nearest thing to having experience of one's own, is to have other people's affairs brought before us in a shape that is interesting." Vaughan saw in Franklin's career an opportunity of establishing general principles concerning the fundamental motives of human conduct. Franklin's example, he felt, could serve to prove "that man is not even at present a vicious and detestable animal; and . . . that good management may greatly amend him."

At the time Vaughan was writing, three widely different types of autobiography were popular in England: political memoirs, represented by *The Life of Edward Earl of Clarendon* (first published 1759) ; detailed records of religious experience, represented by John Wesley's *Journals* (1739 ff.) ; and gossipy narratives of literary contentions, represented by Colley Cibber's *An Apology for the Life of Mr. Colley Cibber* (1740). The last two contained large elements of self-conscious posturing, and for this reason Vaughan predicted that Franklin's sincere self-revelation would reform the prevailing mode of autobiography, and would "make a subject of compari-

15. Henry Debraye, ed., *Vie de Henri Brulard* (Paris, 1913), I, xix.

son with the lives of various public cutthroats and intriguers, and with absurd monastic self-tormentors, or vain literary triflers."

As we have seen, Franklin began his memoirs in 1771 and wrote the last part in 1789, but he was by no means continuously occupied with them during the intervening eighteen years. As a matter of fact, his period of actual composition covered a few weeks instead of years. He composed all of Part I, nearly half of the entire *Memoirs* as they now exist, in the course of a vacation sojourn of less than two weeks at the country seat of an English friend. And even during this short period, he was not writing incessantly, but was participating in the family routine of his hosts. The evidence indicates that he wrote rapidly and painlessly, suffering very little of the agony of creation.

But even though Franklin spent only a relatively small amount of time in composing his *Memoirs*, this does not mean that he was not deeply concerned with what he said. The image he presented to the world he considered to be of major importance, and he took pains to see that it conformed to his desires. He wanted to put his best foot forward for posterity. A masterly study by Charles Coleman Sellers of the Franklin iconography reveals that few men of Franklin's milieu sat for artists more frequently than he, and his portraits were by no means all commissioned because of his historical importance.[16] In 1778, long before it was generally known that Franklin had any intention of writing an autobiography, John Adams made the following direct reference to Franklin's desire for favorable personal publicity:

A Man must be his own Trumpeter, he must write or dictate Paragraphs of Praise in the News Papers, he must dress, have a Retinue, and Equipage, he must ostentatiously publish to the World his own Writings with his Name, and must write even some Panegyrics upon them, he must get his Picture drawn, his Statue made, and must hire all the Artists in his Turn, to set about Works to spread his Name, make the Mob stare and gape, and perpetuate his fame.[17]

One might argue that the question of Franklin's vanity concerns his personality and not the literary aspect of his writings, but the two can hardly be separated. Jared Sparks is responsible for the common view that Franklin cared little for literary reputation and that he

16. *Benjamin Franklin in Portraiture* (New Haven, 1962), p. 5.
17. Adams to James Warren, December 2, 1778 (*Warren-Adams Letters*, Massachusetts Historical Society, 1925, II, 72).

was almost never motivated by "the fame of authorship."[18] James Parton in a virtual echo remarked that "except Shakespeare, no great writer has shown so little of the vanity of authorship. . . . And as to his Autobiography, when he had written the few pages which recorded the favorite, oft-told anecdotes of his youthful days, he had no heart in the work, and could not force himself to complete it."[19] This romantic view that Franklin was writing one of the world's greatest autobiographies without being aware of it—or without caring—is of course completely false.

The political ramifications of the work, to go no further, were of tremendous importance to Franklin. On this subject we have the opinion of Horace Wemyss Smith, grandson of Franklin's most bitter political and personal enemy, the Reverend William Smith. He charges that Franklin

was covering up with apparent calmness and candor, in the most careful of his writings, . . . the offenses of his early life, the intrigues of his trade, the aims and arts of his local politics in an autobiography which, by concealing, coloring, substating and overstating should make—upon the basis of generally admitted fact—whatever impression, whether a true one, or one false—it was the author's design to leave.[20]

Obviously, Franklin did not present himself as a perfect man. He exposed his errata (at least five of them) and admitted some of his shortcomings (particularly vanity and lack of order). Yet there is no question that he carefully selected the kind and degree of human frailty which he wished to reveal. This is not the place for a catalogue of the divergencies between the Franklin of real life and the self-portrayed man, but one example will serve as illustration. The autobiography portrays Franklin as an abstemious person, rigidly controlling his pleasures and amusements. But the evidence of his biography shows that he wined and dined lavishly throughout most of his life—certainly to the limit of his physical capacity after the age of forty. One cannot, of course, be sure whether Franklin's abstemiousness remained fresher in his memory than did his self-indulgence or whether he engaged in conscious shading. But he never maintained that he was presenting the full picture, and he never made a vain boast such as Rousseau makes in his *Confessions* that he had never silently passed over anything bad or added anything good.

18. *Works of Benjamin Franklin* (Boston, 1840), I, v.
19. *Life and Times of Benjamin Franklin* (New York, 1865), II, 651.
20. *Life and Correspondence of the Rev. William Smith* (Philadelphia, 1880), II, 651.

In alluding to the relationship between Franklin's actual life and his life as he imagined it or chose to portray it through selection or coloring, we are touching on what might be called the philosophy of autobiography. Literature—even autobiography—is not necessarily a literal statement of life. A writer may adopt a pose or consciously seek to disguise or even conceal events in his life, but at the same time either consciously or subconsciously present psychological truth—his emotions, intellectual processes, and personality. If a man makes an honest effort to portray himself and his life as they existed for him, he may quite legitimately depict an image more perfect than the life itself. Rather than attempting an exact equivalence between image and life—an impossibility no matter how much good faith is involved—he may present an image reflecting the dramatic essentials of that life. This would not be a literal statement, but an interpretation. This is what Franklin had in mind: to present a carefully selected series of events in his life in such a way that they could be of significance to every other human life. As Simone de Beauvoir remarks, the writer often "lacks the means of describing at the same time the facts of a life and its meaning. Neither one of these two aspects of reality is more true than the other."[21]

For an estimate of the place of Franklin's *Memoirs* in literature, one must give some attention to its reputation and influence. Its reputation is enormous if one judges by the number of editions and translations, but it is only moderate if one accepts the comparisons which have been made with other world-renowned autobiographical works. As a fair sample, one might take an essay on autobiography published in the *Reflector* (London, 1811), perhaps the earliest criticism ever devoted to the genre.[22] Here Franklin is mentioned along with a number of other writers, but not considered as by any means an innovator or outstanding practitioner of the art. He is presented chiefly as an instance that no one but the man himself—not even a close friend—is "able to relate those circumstances relative to the manner in which he passed his childhood and youth." Greater praise or attention is given to Rousseau, Lord Clarendon, Thomas Brown, Montaigne, Lord Herbert of Cherbury, Cardan, Cellini, and even Colley Cibber.

21. *La force des choses*, p. 523. "... l'écrivain n'a pas le moyen de dire en même temps les faits d'une vie et son sens. Aucun de ces deux aspects de la réalité n'est plus vrai que l'autre."
22. By J. A., II, 243-249.

Traditionally, critics have compared Rousseau's confessions with those of St. Augustine. It has become almost as traditional to consider Franklin's *Memoirs* as a virtually unique work. It is frequently said and accepted that he had no literary model. This view is misleading if it implies that no works of similar scope were previously conceived. The two most important elements in Franklin's *Memoirs* are the revelation of the author's character in the essential truth of nature, and the presentation of the man in relationship to the times in which he lived. We have already noticed three successful Italian autobiographies roughly contemporaneous with Franklin's *Memoirs* which embody these essential elements. One could also mention the autobiography of Lord Herbert of Cherbury, printed for the first time by Horace Walpole in 1768. Lord Herbert's ostensible purpose was virtually the same as that expressed by Franklin: "to relate to my posterity those passages of my life, which I conceive may best declare me, and be most useful to them."

Franklin's life story when considered solely from the perspective of its didactic intent has much in common with a forerunner in the Italian Renaissance, Luigi Cornaro's *Discorsi della vita sobria* [*Discourse on the Sober Life*] (*ca.* 1555), which explains the regimen which enabled the author after a sickly youth to attain a healthy old age. Cornaro's work, which Franklin probably knew, was frequently published in English during the eighteenth century and won the commendation of Addison for its "spirit of cheerfulness and good sense." Doctor Thomas Scott later drew a parallel between Cornaro's *Discourse* and Franklin's *Way to Wealth*, but the resemblance to Franklin's *Memoirs* is much closer.[23] Both are narrative records in the first person of genuine experience, and both expound a physical and psychological discipline in youth which leads to happiness and self-fulfilment in old age.

The recent Yale edition of Franklin's *Memoirs* correctly observes that the work "has had its greatest influence not as history or as a standard of style, but as a source book and text in the education of youth." The most exotic milieu of its penetration so far known is Japan, where it was translated in complete form in 1887 "under the title *Meika no Yokun* which means fragrance of a sweet flower."

23. Many editions of Cornaro's work were printed in England and America during the eighteenth century. Of special interest is *The Immortal Mentor: or Man's Unerring Guide to a Healthy, Wealthy, and Happy Life. In Three Parts. By Lewis Cornaro, Dr. Franklin, and Dr. Scott* ... (Philadelphia: Printed for the Rev. Mason L. Weems, 1802).

A few years earlier, the Empress of Japan converted twelve of Franklin's virtues into Japanese odes, for some reason omitting chastity.[24] Unquestionably many people have modeled their lives upon Franklin to one degree or another, but the influence of his *Memoirs* in literature seems minimal. To be sure, authors of biographies and autobiographies are less ready than authors of other literary types to admit to following models. Influence in these genres is an elusive quality. Yet I am not aware of any writer of an autobiography who acknowledges the influence of Franklin's self-portrait as, for example, Stendhal refers to that of Benvenuto Cellini. Goethe cites Franklin in his *Dichtung und Wahrheit*, but primarily as "a perfect man of business" addressing the people in weekly papers, not as a writer of his own life.[25] The strongest statement I know of concerning the influence of Franklin's *Memoirs* (as distinguished from his life itself) upon a man of letters is that of Domingo Faustino Sarmiento, Argentinian statesman, 1811-1888, in his *Recuerdos de provincia* (1850).

No book has ever done so much for me as this one. The life of Franklin was for me that which the lives of Plutarch were for him, for Rousseau, Henry IV, Mme. Roland and many others. I considered myself as Franklin. And why not? I was extremely poor like him, studious like him, and being clever and following his tracks, I could one day succeed in becoming like him, to be doctor *ad honorem* like him, and to make a place for myself in American letters and politics.[26]

Although this is very high praise of Franklin's autobiography, that which Sarmiento chiefly drew from it was merely a plan for succeeding in life. He was apparently not moved by the sense of pleasure which Franklin received through the communication of his personality. He missed the humor and good spirits which one also finds, for example, in the memoirs of Casanova or Cellini. The greatest and most enduring literary value of Franklin's memoirs is psychological rather than artistic—the delight and satisfaction in fulfilling and recording a life of superior achievement.

24. Katsuhiko Takeda, "Introduction of American Literature in Japan," in François Jost, ed., *Proceedings of the IVth Congress of the International Comparative Literature Association* (The Hague, 1966), II, 1394.

25. R. O. Moon, trans. (Washington, 1949), p. 527.

26. "... libro alguno no me hecho más bien que éste. La vida de Franklin fue para mí lo que las vidas de Plutarco para él, para Rousseau, Enrique IV, Mme. Roland y tantos otros. Yo me sentía Franklin; ¿y por qué no? Era yo pobrísimo como él, estudioso como él, y dándome maña y siguiendo sus huellas, podía un dia llegar a formarme como él, ser doctor *ad honorem* como él, y hacerme un lugar en las letras y en la politica americana" (John E. Englekirk, "Franklin en el Mundo Hispano," *Revista Iberoamericana*, XXI, 319-337 (Ehero–Diciembre, 1956).

WASHINGTON IRVING
AMATEUR OR PROFESSIONAL?
Henry A. Pochmann

University of Wisconsin

In recognition of Washington Irving's becoming the first American man of letters to win a wide international reputation, his grateful countrymen fastened upon him titles such as Inventor of the Modern Short Story, Ambassador of the New World to the Old, and Father of American Literature. Gratulatory admiration of this kind engendered a literary reputation that has suffered little diminution, comparable for example to Longfellow's or Holmes's. His fame and his honors, so the story goes, came unsought—the result of a happy conspiracy between fortuitous circumstances and innate talents; and with becoming modesty, he allowed them to rest lightly and gracefully on his slim shoulders.

Irving himself is as responsible as anyone for creating the atmosphere in which such a legend could grow. In his first writings he pictured himself as one of a knot of carefree young blades, who might have been known a generation earlier, in and about New York City, as bloods or macaroni whose primary concern, after wine-women-and-song, was literary dilettantism. In two series of periodical letters and essays appearing in 1802-1803 and 1807-1808 he represented himself as one of "the Nine Worthies," "the Lads of Kilkenny," or "the Ancient and Honorable Order of New York"—the others being his brothers William, Peter, and Ebenezer, Peter and Gouverneur Kemble, Henry Brevoort, Henry Ogden, and James Kirke Paulding. After exhausting the pleasures of the city, they often resorted to an old family mansion of the Kembles on the Passaic (Cockloft Hall in *Salmagundi*) for frolicsome entertainments befitting young bachelors with literary tastes. Sometimes they met for convivial suppers and literary powwows at a genteel public house known as Dyde's, and when their purse was low, contented themselves with "blackguard suppers" at a porterhouse on the corner of John and Nassau streets. Always they were in good spirits, and almost always their entertainment took a literary turn and concerned whatever social or political overtones the happenings of the day or the whims of the worthies suggested. So it was that the earlier series of letters by Jonathan Oldstyle, in which Irving masqueraded as a kind of nineteenth-century American reincarnation of Tatler-Spectator (of which he wearied after penning nine short epistles for his brother Peter's *Morning Chronicle*), developed into a joint production setting forth the opinions and whim-whams of the gay wags and making what they properly called a Salmagundi, a mixed dish, a medley, a potpourri of personal essays, poetical effusions, social satire, political innuendo, dramatic criticism, and editorial idiosyncrasy. Alternately grave and facetious, the youthful editors posed as "critics, amateurs, dilettanti, and cognoscenti," and proceeded merrily with cocksure insolence through twenty numbers, satirizing the ways of the fashionable world, inserting squibs on the theater, occasionally mixing a little political bastinade, waging war against "folly and stupidity," and teaching "parents ... how to govern their children, girls how to get husbands, and old maids how to do without them." It was Addison and Steele transplanted from London to New York. It was all good-natured raillery, and all the more welcome as a change of fare from the heavy bombardment of polemics since the days of 1776. The essays were read in coffeehouses and gentlemen's clubs, and they made their way to many a proper belle's toilet table. Many of the "characters" were recognizable, and while some shunned being identified, others were secretly envied. The "fascinating [Mary] Fairlie" was obviously the original of Sophie Sparkle; there was no lack of young ladies who coveted her notoriety; and the superficial disguises under the names of Ding Dong, Ichabod Fungus, and Dick Paddle provoked no affairs of honor. But fatuous theatrical critics, taking a glance at themselves in the mirror of 'Sbidlikens, found it advisable to hold their peace; fashionable upstarts shrank before the portraits of the Giblets; the small beer of politicians soured at the portrait of Dabble; and the feathers of carpet soldiers wilted when they saw themselves paraded in the regiment of the Fag-Rags. *Salmagundi* made no great fortune for the three editors, but it became the talk and the mild terror of the town.

So it came to pass that Irving became less and less regular in his attendance at No. 3 Wall Street, where he had gingerly hung his shingle underneath that of his brother John. Instead of drawing up legal briefs, he was entertaining vague ideas of turning author. To be sure, the law had never been a serious vocation, but as the youngest of five sons of a substantial merchant (all the others already fairly launched in business, medicine, or the law) it behooved him to prepare for a profession. It was expected of him. So for a number of years he harried his inveterate enemies, the fathers of the law, in several lawyers' offices and was duly admitted to the bar "by the grace of God" and Josiah Ogden, his latest mentor, who also served on his examining committee. It is said that at the conclusion of the examination, the other examiner said to Josiah Ogden, "Well, Jo, I guess he knows a little law." "Make it stronger," said Jo, "damned little." But Irving knew very well that not much was expected of him as an attorney. He might take a turn at representing the brothers' business interests, or lobbying for them in Washington, but neither he nor they regarded his commissions or his returns as very weighty. It had already been decided among them that they could afford to indulge their youngest, favorite, and gifted brother to the extent of making him a nominal but profit-sharing partner and so leave him free to cultivate his talents. He would be a proper ornament, and so he was. He had already considered Washington Allston's advice that he turn painter, only to have "doubts and fears gradually cloud over that prospect"; turning now to the opposite extreme, he took a turn at practical politics by participating in a municipal campaign, but one such assay left him and his "forlorn brethren, the Federalists" intolerably beaten and discomfited. While he labored manfully, "talked handbill-fashion with the demagogues, and shook hands with the mob," "was sworn brother to a leash of drawers," and "drank with any tinker in his own language," in the end he had to conclude: "Truly, this saving one's country is a nauseous piece of business, and if patriotism is such a dirty virtue—prithee, no more of it." This does not mean that Irving foreswore for all time any crumbs that might fall into his hands (and several later did) at the dispensation of loaves and fishes in Albany or Washington. Nor did he forget (long after he had given up all ideas of turning painter) his facility at sketching with his pencil a scene for his notebooks when the descriptive power of his words failed him. Keeping a detailed journal early became a confirmed habit, and eventually an inestimable aid to his writing. Emerson called his own journals his "penny-savings bank"; Irving's diaries were in many cases his entire stock-in-trade.

Relieved of business cares by the largesse of his brothers and unconcerned about politics by his own preference, he was free to indulge his tastes and to meet the right people, for whom he had a natural affinity. In Washington he barely arrived before he put on his "pease blossoms and silk stockings" and sallied forth to one of the levees of Dolly Madison, with whom and "half the people in the assemblage" he was "hand in glove" within ten minutes. For the rest he spent his spare hours hobnobbing as agreeably with a knot of "Frenchmen & Democrats" as with his compatriots, the Federalists; and he conducted the regular seasonal campaigns of "banquetry, revelling, dancing, and carousals" in Baltimore, Philadelphia, and "Gotham."

Of a piece with his dilettante pursuit of the law was what he called "the gentlemanly exercise of the pen." If there had been any considerable returns from David Longworth, the printer of *Salmagundi*, and if there had been among their acquaintances any poor-devil authors, he and his writing fraternity might have emulated Byron who, during his expansive youthful years, showed "the same blind contempt for pecuniary gains" and turned the profits of his writings over to his more impecunious scribbling friends. There persisted among them still something of the Renaissance gentleman's attitude toward the products of the pen as the fruits of idle hours, and their monetary gains as beneath a gentleman's notice. When, therefore, "Duskie Davie" volunteered some unsolicited editorial suggestions and voiced objections to the length of the twentieth number of *Salmagundi*, they summarily took their leave and turned to freer pursuits—Irving to another *jeu d'esprit*, a comic history of New York.

Begun with his brother Peter as an *œuvre de joie*, this first full-length book of Irving's turned out quite otherwise before it was finished. Soon after it was fairly begun, the sudden death of Matilda Hoffman threw a pall over the undertaking and a profound and unrelieved gloom over his spirit; but when Peter departed for England, leaving him to go on alone, he rallied, radically revised the plan, and set to a far more serious and prolonged stint of writing than he had ever dreamed possible. After many delays and unanticipated complications, when the book was finally done and the first printing lined his pockets with the tidy sum of three thousand dollars, the young author of twenty-six had learned some serious lessons regarding literary craftsmanship—including the need for painstaking research, meticulous checking of sources, sticking to the plan in hand before giving way to will-o'-the-wisps and vagaries that beckoned invitingly, reliance upon his own resources, however meager they might be, and above all, the necessity for keeping steadily at it, whatever the distractions. The result was a major contribution to the world's store of wit and humor, and its success caused the erstwhile amateur litterateur to have some serious second thoughts then and later, when the once abundant supply of funds from his family diminished. The success of *Knickerbocker* in 1809 confirmed his wish to embrace a writing career, but ten more years were to elapse before he was fully embarked on the road to professional authorship.

Until the War of 1812 began to cloud the horizon, Irving continued merrily as beau, reporter, essayist, satirist, detached politician, and occasional poet to sidestep every commitment that might have resulted in anything so time- and energy-consuming as another full-length book. He occasionally felt the "itching propensity to scribble which every man has who once appeared with any success in print," but did little for two years beyond editing the poems of Thomas Campbell, who then enjoyed in America a vogue nearly equal with that of Scott and Byron. His adulatory biographical sketch won him the friendship of Campbell but served notice that he was unlikely to win many plaudits as a literary critic or that he had as yet arrived at any firm critical principles of his own. Beyond that, it affords the first indication of a mild interest in romantic modes and motifs, of which his writings hitherto had been virtually innocent—an interest that burgeoned a decade later in *The Sketch Book* and made him henceforth a traveler in search of more romantic and picturesque literary provender.

To supplement his irregular education, he immersed himself for varying periods of time in the well-stocked library of his friend Brevoort, or took a turn at lobbying for his brothers' firm in Washington. Next, he devoted upwards of a year to the "irksome business" of editing the *Analectic Magazine*, did a tour of duty as a colonel during the closing years of the War of 1812, and for the rest dutifully slaved in the Liverpool branch of the Irving business but failed to forestall the inevitable collapse of the firm. So ten years clicked by with monotonous regularity while he did little more than form resolutions to resume his interrupted literary career. In the end it was mainly the stimulation of new alliances formed with the reigning literati of London (during brief periods snatched from the grub and grime of the Liverpool counting house), the encouragement of Sir Walter Scott (whom he visited twice at Abbotsford), and the all-too-evident necessity for relying on his pen as the only remaining means to an independent livelihood that led to that rededication of which *The Sketch Book* was born. Begun haltingly and beset by trials of composition and by complications of publication, it proved a greater success even than *Knickerbocker*, and Irving the professional was fairly launched.

Never a tyro in the art of progress through favor, he still dallied with the idea of accepting "some situation of a moderate, unpretending kind," if his friends could swing it; but increasingly his letters and journals put the emphasis on "adding to my literary reputation by the assiduous operations of my pen," on a determination "to win solid credit with the public," "establishing a stock of copyright property," and amassing "a literary estate." So he put by proffered posts in Washington and consular posts elsewhere; he refused the flattering offer of Scott and his friends to edit, for a handsome salary, an anti-Jacobin journal to be founded. He rightly gauged his talents as wayward and his mind too untractable for any regularly recurring task. Indeed, much of Irving's success henceforth was owing to his properly appraising his capacities, or rather his incapacities, and wisely steering his fitful career away from whatever he had learned he could not do well. He knew by now that the only instrument given him was the lowly lyre—that if he would play at all, he must learn to play well on its few strings; that there was little likelihood of swapping the lyre for the harp, or of learning to play variations on an instrument beyond his capacity.

Irving's turn from a devil-may-care scribbler to a circumspect author took place about the time he wrote the stories and essays that form *The Sketch Book*—his first book written specifically for profit. This conversion was accompanied by a more guarded and decorous selection and handling of materials. Heretofore he had not scrupled to paint what the Dutch of New York denigrated as a coarse and libelous caricature of their forebears, or to relate with evident gusto the free love-life of some of the old Dutch worthies—all without the least compunction or remorse. But about the time he turned to writing for a livelihood, he became cautious. In 1818, while preparing a new edition of *Knickerbocker*, he took care to delete certain earthy Elizabethanisms and to remove both anti-British and anti-Catholic passages. He hoped the new *Knickerbocker* and the forthcoming *Sketch Book* might attract readers in Britain as well as in Catholic countries—as, indeed, they did beyond his expectations. But this did not prevent his continuing to record in his journals, for his own edification, any choice morsels he came upon in his travels. Pretty young women continued to elicit near ribald comments, as when he noticed with evident satisfaction meeting a fresh young Irishwoman whom "a man would feel no compunction in begetting children on" (*Journal*, April 8, 1824). Conversely, he made note of "the fierce virtue" of an ugly older woman "who arrogates great merit in preserving what nobody was ever tempted to steal" (*Journal*, Sept. 13, 1822). At Marseilles he recorded with relish how the bootblacks of the town, who knew no English beyond what they had picked up from American sailors, pursued him and his traveling companion, and in an effort to attract their attention and custom, cried, "Monsieur, monsieurs, God dam, God dam son de bish, son de bish." In Syracuse, where he was shown "no less than five thigh bones of St. John the Baptist, three arms of St. Stephen and four jaw bones of St. Peter," he observed in the privacy of his diary, "these disciples must have been an uncommon bony set of fellows." Two months later he was relieved when in Rome, at the church of St. Paul, he was shown "the preserved body of St. Paul." "I was happy to find his bones at length collected together for I had found them in my travels scattered through all the convents of churches I had visited." On another occasion he calculated that if all known fragments of the Cross were collected, they would form "a tolerably stought [*sic*] ship of the line." Mark Twain made literary capital of all such titbits. Not Washington Irving! The sense of accommodation which prompted him to regard discretion as the better part of wisdom begat the resolution that whenever he could not get a dinner to suit his taste, he would endeavor to get a taste to suit his dinner. He became circumspect, then hesitant, and finally timorous—lest he give offence in quarters where it might hurt. And when, after seventeen years of schooling in European decorum, he returned to his native land in 1832, his sense of propriety was shocked and outraged at what he saw of Jacksonian democracy in high places or of the free-and-easy manners of a frontier society. To his trusted friends he complained that Americans had obviously gone "masking mad" during his absence, but in his public statements he measured out his critical and patriotic sentiments guardedly: he complimented his fellow countrymen on the great strides forward of "progress" that he saw on every hand, and, as for Andrew Jackson, he confessed to "rather liking the old cock of the walk." Within a year, this erstwhile Federalist became known as "a Jackson man," and was probably not very much surprised when Old Hickory did not overlook him at the next division of the spoils.

Unconcerned as he had been about arrangements with publishers, or the exacting requirements of seeing his earlier writings through the press, he began, while the last numbers of *The Sketch Book* were being published, to attend to such details, either for himself or through the competence of Brevoort, and to begin negotiations that were obviously designed to entice John Murray to become his publisher. He managed the matter so well that while Murray had refused *The Sketch Book* in 1819, by May of the next year "the Prince of Booksellers" capitulated. For his part, Murray (said Irving) conducted himself "in a fair, open and liberal spirit," while Irving was at great pains to supply Murray with successive successes. At one point, when Irving sensed a lukewarmness on Murray's part toward a new manuscript, he outfoxed him by suggesting a figure well above what he expected, only to find Murray taking the bait. The reception of *Bracebridge Hall* was a disappointment; yet he played his cards so well that even *Tales of a Traveller* (the composition of which had caused him no end of grief so that he knew it was a mishmash) got him surprisingly good terms from Murray. "Your offer," he wrote to Murray on March 25, 1824, "of twelve hundred guineas without seeing the mss. is I confess a liberal one and made in your own gentlemanlike manner, but I would rather you see the mss. and make it fifteen hundred" (see also *Journal*, May 29, 1824). In the meantime he had traveled on the Continent, formed countless new alliances with great and little men and women, indulged in a variety of literary undertakings, and learned the ins and outs of the publishing business as it was conducted in Paris, as well as the complications brought on by the non-existence of a satisfactory international copyright law. His letters directing his agents or publishers were businesslike and specific, so much so that when it is remembered how nonchalant he had been about the tiresome details of publishing his earlier works (possibly in emulation of Byron's affectations in this regard), he strikes one as following now the older Byron's advice to authors to practice "the good old gentlemanly vice of avarice."

The adroit dealings by which he maneuvered his literary products through various publishers until he made the mutually profitable arrangement with George P. Putnam is a long story, too long to be detailed here, but it betokens a lively interest in, and capacity for, business. Equally important is the care he exercised during 1848-1850 in giving his books a complete and meticulous overhauling for the "Author's Revised Edition" by which he wished the world to know him. Although he complained often and long about slaving at revisions and reading proof in a hot city, while foregoing the comforts of his Sunnyside retreat, he stuck with it to safeguard and enhance his "literary capital." Even after this long chore was completed, he kept touching up individual volumes. *Knickerbocker*, having by then already undergone three complete revisions, was hauled out again for toning-up here and there, and *The Sketch Book* was subjected to a similar refurbishing. A recently discovered copy of an 1854 issue (printed from the 1848 plates) contains extensive revisions on the printed pages and forty-one new interleaves in Irving's handwriting. The precise identification of this volume and the edition for which these alterations were intended awaits exhaustive collation with 1855 and 1857 impressions, but the evidence is enough to suggest that even while Irving was preoccupied with the five-volume *Washington*, he neglected no opportunity if so well-established a volume as *The Sketch Book* could be made to add another mite to his reputation and his income.

During his later years he sometimes allowed his real or fancied need for additional income to get the better of his aesthetic judgment. The compulsion to add "capital" led him to collect in volume form some of his earlier, more ephemeral periodical contributions that might better have been allowed to remain forgotten. It may also have blinded him to John Jacob Astor's motive in enlisting his pen to romanticizing Astoria. And there are other instances (related in detail by Stanley T. Williams in the second volume of his biography) that explain, though they do not entirely excuse, Cooper's saying that Irving always trimmed his sails to the prevailing winds: "What an instinct that man has for gold!" A more charitable man than Cooper might have observed that Irving's later potboiler writings represented simply the overanxious and perhaps ill-considered efforts of the oldest "pro" of the American writers' guild to sell what remained of his literary energy and ability to the best advantage in the popular market.

It may be doubted that when Irving wrote "Rip Van Winkle" and "The Legend of Sleepy Hollow" he was fully aware that he was inventing a new genre; but once it was done, he was not slow to realize what he had done or to understand the techniques of his storytelling art. Thenceforth, as he said, "I have preferred adopting a mode of sketches & short tales rather than long works, because I chose to take a line of writing peculiar to myself, rather than fall into the manner or school of any other writer. . . . I believe the works I have written will be oftener re-read than any novel of the size I could have written." And with true Irvingesque whimsicality he could point out that "if the tales I have furnished should prove to be bad, at least they will be found short."[1]

If in his stories about Rip and Ichabod, he wrote better than he knew, he was not slow to make an astute assessment of the short story's potentialities. By 1824 he recognized the sterility of the then current American novel as an art form, and said as much. In Cooper's case, for example, the format required that it be "In Two Volumes," and it did not matter much whether he strung together a series of short narratives or strung out a short narrative to make two volumes duodecimo. Hawthorne and Melville had not yet demonstrated what could be done in the genre by adapting it to the "romance," as they preferred to call their longer narratives. At any rate, by the end of 1824 Irving knew what he was about, and, possibly with an eye on Cooper, he said, "It is comparatively easy to swell a story to any size when you have once the scheme & the characters in your mind; the mere interest of the story too carries the reader on through pages & pages of careless writing and the author may often be dull for half a volume at a time, if he has some striking scene at the end of it, but in these shorter writings every page must have its merit. The author

1. *Letters of Washington Irving to Henry Brevoort*, ed. George S. Hellman (Library ed., 2 vols. in 1, New York, 1918), pp. 398-400.

must be continually piquant—woe to him if he makes an awkward sentence or writes a stupid page; the critics are sure to pounce upon it. Yet if he succeed, the very variety & piquancy of his writings, nay their very brevity, makes them frequently recurred to—and when the mere interest of the story is exhausted, he begins to get credit for his touches of pathos or humour, his points of wit or turns of language. I give these as some of the reasons that have induced me to keep on thus far in the way I have opened for myself. . . ."

It may be useless to conjecture whether or not he could have written a novel. Certainly he never did (though he started at least one), and there is reason for believing he did not possess the requirements for writing a good play—sustained concentration, searching analysis of character, strict construction of plot, and fine adjustment of numberless details into a continuous fabric of thought. *The Sketch Book* is precisely what the title implies—a collection of sketches, odds and ends, many of them good enough in themselves, but without cohesion, one with another. *Bracebridge Hall* is a collection of stories gleaned from various sources and held together by the mechanical device, as old as *The Arabian Nights*, of having them all related by members of a hunting party marooned in Bracebridge Hall. By the time he wrote *Tales of a Traveller*, he was encountering real difficulty managing his heterogeneous materials, and the result is a hodgepodge in four parts, none of which has any relationship to the others. Irving resented the severity of the critics who took the book apart, but he was fully aware that he had exploited the sketchbook vein to the limit. The result was another change of climate and scene—a trip to and residence in Spain, where once more, under the stimulus of romantic surroundings, he produced something akin to *The Sketch Book's* excellence. Among the productions of his middle and more creative period, *The Alhambra* comes near being a book, in the sense that it is all of a piece, so far at least as atmosphere and tone could make it so. Thereafter he wisely limited himself mainly to biography (interwoven with history) or to the literature of exploration and adventure, chiefly as associated with the western United States. But in any case, the materials for these later works came ready to hand, and except for that inimitable style that was Irving's, he did little more than transcribe what lay before him. When he tried for more, as he did in *Goldsmith*, it was his basic sympathy for the man, in so many ways like himself, that made it an engaging biography. *Washington*, his most ambitious undertaking, is better in details than in conception. It exhibits no great structural skill; the incidents crystallize more around the man than around principles. For the method of the philosophical historian or the critical biographer he had little aptitude; he was at his best when he grasped his subject by his sympathies rather than by rationalization from causes to effects. All in all, his first book, properly so-called, namely *Diedrich Knickerbocker's History of New York*, came nearest to meeting the Aristotelian requirements of unity—in inception, in organization, and in execution; but cold analysis reduces even it to what is basically an aggregation of tales told in chapters and books rather than a continuous story or history.

However readily Irving composed his first literary efforts, he began to encounter trouble about the time he wrote *The Sketch Book*. Congenitally a man of moods, he was given to feelings of indolence, indirection, ineffectuality, melancholy, self-depreciation, insecurity, enervation, sterility, and despair. For months he did little more than register the state of his personal thermometer ten times daily. This preoccupation with the moody state of his mind first, last, and all the time becomes positively torturous for the reader of his journals, and belies the reputation he had of being habitually and by nature the soul of gaiety and geniality. If he managed to show the world the brighter side of himself, it was because he instinctively and consciously withdrew from social intercourse when he felt the dark moods coming on. So he carefully watched himself and nursed his oversensitive disposition. Following the great success of *The Sketch Book* he confided to his friend Leslie, "Now you suppose I am all on the alert, and full of spirit and excitement. No such thing. I am just as good for nothing as ever I was; and, indeed, have been flurried and put out by these puffings. I feel something as I suppose you did when your picture met with success—anxious to do something better, and at a loss what to do."[2]

"What to do next" became from now on a haunting worry and the natural cause for many ill-conceived plans, misdirected efforts, or false starts. At the time he refused Scott's offer to turn editor, he confessed, "My whole course of life has been desultory, and I am unfitted for any periodically recurring task, or any stipulated labor of body or mind. I have no command of my talents such as they are,

2. Pierre M. Irving, *The Life and Letters of Washington Irving* (New York, 1862-1864), I, 415.

and have to watch the varyings of my mind as I would a weather cock. Practice and training may bring me more into rule; but at present I am as useless for regular service as one of my own country Indians or a Don Cossack. I must, therefore, keep on pretty much as I have begun—writing when I can, not when I would. I shall occasionally shift my residence and write whatever is suggested by objects before me, or whatever runs in my imagination, and hope to write better and more copiously by and by."[3] He probably never wrote better than he did just then. This much is certain: whenever he wrote "more copiously," he did not compose as well. Often he gave way to distractions, if only to avoid the ordeal of sitting at the table unable to do more than chew his pen; and so he spent as much time preparing to write as in writing. These hesitations and doubts and the variety of uncongenial works undertaken, always with little satisfaction to himself, give evidence of the uncertainty of mind that never ended but did subside somewhat after he was fairly launched on the routine work of his biographical and historical research in Spain—that is, after he turned from composition to compilation. Routine proved a good wall to which to retreat. Even so, writing remained for him hard, agonizing work, and he had to drive himself mercilessly. During his last illness, when he was given the fifth and last volume of *Washington*, just arrived from the printer, he said with obvious and heartfelt relief, "Thank Heaven! Henceforth I give up all tasking with the pen!" Under these circumstances, the dilettante or tyro would never have produced the stout twenty-seven volumes that comprise Irving's literary output; only Irving the professional could pull it off. And the wonder is, as Dr. Samuel Johnson might have said, not that he did it so well, but that he did it at all.

We need not quarrel with Irving for not attempting what he could not and *knew* he could not do well. It is enough if we are to appreciate his doing so well with so little. His success is owing largely to his husbanding his slender store of genius and measuring out carefully his slim stock-in-trade. This studied procedure bespeaks the craftsman who knows his business rather than the divine amateur who expects a miracle. He believed he could do his countrymen a greater service chronicling Hudson River legends and bringing to them a touch of merry England and romantic Spain than by overtaxing his talents and tiring his readers' patience with moral or

3. *Ibid.*, I, 441-442.

philosophical disquisitions; he calculated correctly that as an inter-mediary between old-world culture and new-world rawness and as a romancer in the sphere of belles-lettres he would speak to better purpose than as politician or preacher. "I have attempted no lofty theme, nor sought to look wise and learned, which appears to be very much the fashion among our American writers at present. . . . I seek only to blow a flute accompaniment in the national concert, and leave others to play the fiddle and French horn."[4] This careful calculation of his own potential labels him less the amateur toying with esoteric aspirations beyond his reach than the canny professional gauging his grasp by his reach.

4. *Ibid.*, I, 415, 416.

POE'S "THE CITY IN THE SEA" REVISITED

Wilson O. Clough

University of Wyoming

Textbooks for survey courses in American Literature, almost without exception, include Poe's "The City in the Sea," with or without editorial comment. Notes, if any, customarily refer to Sodom and Gomorrah or to certain biblical passages prophesying general destruction to Babylon, or to the fact that earlier versions of the poem bore other titles: "The Doomed City," or "The City of Sin." Students left to their own devices, and noting further the presence of "a thousand hells" in the last lines, are likely to take Poe's poem as some sort of handmaiden to Jonathan Edwards's most famous sermon. It seems to occur to few that Poe, with his passion for "unity of effect," must have discarded the earlier titles precisely because they interfered with his final conception of the poem's possibilities.

I

Thus ancient guesses meander down through the textbooks, with small bows to "sources" and "influences," but with all too rarely an original judgment or a serious attempt to approach the author's creative intent. Such is the fate of many a poem or tale, until in due time critical explication arrives at a more satisfactory reading.

In Bradford, Beatty, and Long's *The American Tradition in Literature*[1] we read, for example, the unsupported statement: "The meanings of this poem are emphasized by its earlier titles"—an echo, perhaps, of Norman Foerster's widely used *American Poetry and Prose*:[2] "The earlier titles Poe used for this poem indicate aspects of its meaning." While the former text is thus led to limit the poem to the "theme of the dominion of evil," Foerster adds: "Poe now carried the 'Gothic' poem to perfection through his selective, constructive imagination and his verse technique. He was concerned

1. *The American Tradition in Literature* (New York, 1961), p. 750.
2. *American Poetry and Prose* (Boston, 1957), p. 372.

with a purely aesthetic effect uncomplicated by any moral or religious aims." The "effect" is not further defined.

Professor J. B. Hubbell, in his excellent *American Life and Literature*,[3] after the familiar references, suggests that certain lines dropped from "Al Aaraaf" may have furnished the incentive:

> Far down within the crystal of the lake
> Thy swollen pillars tremble—and so quake
> The hearts of many wanderers who look in
> Thy luridness of beauty—and of sin.

So go the standard texts, with obvious indebtedness to two major predecessors: Killis Campbell's invaluable edition of Poe's poems, with notes and variant readings, and a brief paper by Louise Pound entitled "On Poe's 'The City in the Sea.'"[4] Miss Pound followed Campbell's lead in her references to certain apparently relevant biblical passages; for example, Isaiah 13:10, which reads: "For the stars of heaven and the constellations thereof shall not give their light; the sun shall be darkened in his going forth, and the moon shall not cause her light to shine." But this type of language, along with Ossianic prose, seems the common property of Romantic poets, though the parallels are of interest. Further, a closer examination will reveal more differences than likenesses. The Old Testament prophet predicts doom for a literal Babylon and neighboring cities, in terms of wrath and violent destruction; and the desolation of their sites, far from being sunk beneath the sea, is marked by "the wild beasts" which "shall cry in their desolate houses." But no life invades Poe's city; nor is the biblical hell of a later verse the same as Poe's, for it rises to receive Babylon, not to reverence, and further "stirreth up the dead" to rejoice also in the city's discomfiture. Nor do the passages of Revelation, Chapters 16–18 accord with Poe's conception, though the seas and rivers therein do, indeed, become "as the blood of a dead man," in retribution for those who "shed the blood of saints and prophets." Neither saints nor prophets appear in Poe's poem, nor is there any spirit of vengeance.

Though Miss Pound also takes note of "Al Aaraaf" as foreshadowing something of Poe's city, she finds the resemblance "not very close." "It seems clear," she adds sensibly, "that neither Babylon nor Gomorrah accounts adequately for Poe's phantom city"; and again, "We have to do here with poetic echoes, merely, not plagia-

3. *American Life and Literature* (New York, 1949), p. 425.
4. *American Literature*, VI, 22-27 (March, 1934).

rism." Though venturing that "His sea surely owes features to the Dead Sea," she notes that Poe's city is not sunken at the outset of the poem, nor razed, nor even disturbed by fire or earthquake, being thus distinguished from legendary cities of doom. There is as much of Europe as of biblical lore in this poem, she concludes. "One of the most original and imaginative of his poems," she remarks. "It owes very little to the work of his predecessors or his contemporaries." Yet Miss Pound fails to explicate further.

Among pertinent lines in "Al Aaraaf" we may select the following:

> Friezes from Tadmor and Persepolis—
> From Balbec, and the stilly, clear abyss
> Of beautiful Gomorrah! O, the wave
> Is now upon thee—but too late to save!

Or again Poe's own footnote to the line "Unguided here hath fallen—mid 'tears of perfect moan' ":

> There be tears of perfect moan
> Wept for thee in Helicon—*Milton*[5]

or these from "Tamerlane":

> Of a high mountain which look'd down
> Afar from its proud natural towers.[6]

Yet "The City in the Sea" shows little more than echoes of such lines from Poe's youthful work, all done before he was twenty. Indeed, "Al Aaraaf" is echoed frequently in Poe's later work.

Poe's notes to "Al Aaraaf" have also been cited, especially his mention there of the five cities in "the valley of Siddim": Adrah, Zeboin, Zoar, Sodom, and Gomorrah; and the characteristic flourish of learning in his: "It is said [Tacitus, Strabo, Josephus, Daniel of St. Saba, Nau, Maundrell, Troilo, D'Arvieux] that, after an excessive drought, the vestiges of columns, walls &c. are seen above the surface. At *any* season, such remains may be discovered by looking down into the transparent lake."[7] But Poe in no way later linked such notes with "The City in the Sea"; and their relevancy would seem to be chiefly the evidence that engulfed cities fascinated Poe as they did his contemporaries.

Where did Poe come by the learned authors? It is quite possible

5. Edgar A. Poe, *Al Aaraaf*, ed. T. O. Mabbott (New York, 1933), pp. 26-27, 34 n.
6. *Ibid.*, p. 50.
7. *Ibid.*, p. 27. The brackets are Poe's. The five cities appear in Genesis 13:2, 3, and 8.

that he adapted them from some convenient encyclopedia or magazine article, a suggestion more plausible than the assumption that he had read them all. In this connection, I reach on an impulse for my copy of Constantin Volney's *The Ruins: or Meditations on the Revolutions of Empire*.[8] Volney had studied Oriental languages and visited the Near East, as well as America in 1797. His book, a favorite with Jefferson and Abraham Lincoln, first published in 1791, was put into English in London in 1797, again in Philadelphia in 1799, and underwent, with the personal encouragement of Jefferson, a new translation by Joel Barlow and its author in 1802. New editions appeared in Albany in 1822, in Boston, 1833, etc.

The book opens with an invocation: "Hail solitary ruins, holy sepulchres and silent walls!" The narrator resolves on visiting Palmyra—the ancient Tadmor. "Having traversed the Valley of Caves and Sepulchres, on issuing into the plain," he writes, "I was suddenly struck with a scene of the most stupendous ruins. . . . The earth [was] everywhere strewed with fragments of cornices, capitals, shafts, entablatures [Poe used "entablatures" in "The Doomed City"], pilasters, all of white marble, and of the most exquisite workmanship." Again, at evening, when "through the dusk could only be discerned the pale phantasms of columns and walls," the narrator reflects: "Where are those ramparts of Ninevah, those walls of Babylon, those palaces of Persepolis, those temples of Balbec and of Jerusalem?" Note that five of Poe's cities have already appeared. Yet there is no need to propose Volney's book as a "source," though it must have been in Jefferson's University of Virginia, for its purpose was political utopianism by means of a "vision" which outlines the future of mankind. All it points up is the popularity and prevalence of ruins in the literature of Poe's milieu.

Poe, as we know, was an inveterate reviser of his own poems. Revisions between "The Doomed City" and "The City in the Sea" are in the direction of a more subtle music and a greater consistency within the poem. The early version appeared in his *Poems* of 1831, when Poe was but twenty-two. It was reprinted as "The City of Sin" in the *Southern Literary Messenger* of August, 1836; in the *American Whig Review* (April, 1845) as "The City in the Sea: A Prophecy"; and in its present form in the *Broadway Journal* of August, 1845, and in *The Raven and Other Poems* in 1845. The

8. *The Ruins* . . . (New York, 1890), based on the 1802 text. Quotations from pp. 1-6, *passim*.

Preface to the last made a point of each poem's being "as I wrote it."

We need not trace each single change; but how right Poe was in the following shift:

There shrines, and palaces, and towers	There shrines and palaces and towers
Are—not like anything of ours—	(Time-eaten towers that tremble not!)
O! no—O! no—*ours* never loom	Resemble nothing that is ours.
To heaven with that ungodly gloom!	
Time-eaten towers that tremble not!	

Or compare:

Whose entablatures intertwine	Whose wreathéd friezes intertwine
The mask—the viol—and the vine.	The viol, the violet, and the vine. . . .
There open temples—open graves	There open fanes and gaping graves
Are on a level with the waves. . . .	Yawn level with the luminous waves. . . .
While from the high towers of the town . . .	While from a proud tower in the town . . .
The wave! there is a ripple there!	The wave—there is a movement there!
As if the towers had thrown aside. . . .	As if the towers had thrust aside . . .
As if the turret-tops had given	As if their tops had feebly given
A vacuum in the filmy heaven.	A void within the filmy heaven.[9]

In each case Poe has made poetry of semi-prose. Note, too, how he dares risk seven t's in one line ("Time-eaten towers that tremble not") ; and how, against all pedagogical advice, he repeats the single syllable *up* nine times in seven lines, yet counts on the reader's unawareness because of the unstressed syllable and the subtle variations in the words which follow.

II

So far we have concerned ourselves with matters of sources, influences, and revisions. It is time to heed Poe's warning in "The Poetic Principle" to turn our attention to "this poem *per se*, this poem which is a poem and nothing more, this poem written for the poem's sake." There is a profound rightness in such insistence, since critical comment is justified by one major consideration, that it should lead *to* the work under discussion, and that it be finally con-

9. Poe, *Poems*, 1831, ed. Killis Campbell (Fac. Text Soc., 1936), pp. 49-51; and *The Raven and Other Poems*, 1845, ed. T. O. Mabbott (Fac. Text Soc., 1942), pp. 21-22.

sistent with the evidence within that work itself. Yet even here we must consider the larger problem of the mind of Poe; and here, though dealing with this one poem only, we may turn to three recent critics, and in the order below, because each had the advantage of his predecessor.

Mr. Allen Tate has written two papers on Poe, to be found in his *Collected Essays* (1959), though both appeared earlier.[10] In the first of these Poe is seen as "with us like a dejected cousin," one of those romantically determined relatives who never quite manage a conventional adjustment; yet also with us because, like many a modern man, he wrote as if the older traditions had been lost. Indeed, says Tate, "Had Poe not written *Eureka*, I should have been able, a man of this age, myself to formulate a proposition of 'inevitable annihilation.'" The reference is better explained by the second essay, to which one sentence in the first leads: "The great mythologies are populous worlds, but a cosmology need have nobody in it."[11] For it is Poe's cosmology which concerns us for the moment.

This topic Tate approaches through an examination of several of Poe's prose works: "The Conversation of Eiros and Charmian," "The Colloquy of Monos and Una," "The Power of Words," and above all *Eureka*, in all of which Poe envisions a cataclysmic end to the world. Admitting that Poe proceeds with "ingenuity rather than complex thinking," if not with some faked science, Tate argues that Poe, nevertheless, wrote seriously, and to a unique, if incompletely resolved, cosmic view. Poe unquestionably conceived of his *Eureka* as a bid for intellectual fame. He wrote it in the year before his death, and title and style indicate his inner excitement.

The germ of Poe's idea lies in an early sentence in *Eureka*: "In the original unity of the first thing lies the secondary cause of all things, with the germ of their inevitable annihilation." The concept of a beginning, out of a nameless unity before matter, involves, we may say, a return to that prebeginning, the original unity and material non-existence from which all emerged. (And, indeed, does not Genesis say: "In the beginning . . . darkness was upon the face of the deep?" God sat in darkness; and Poe, by a resolute and cyclic logic, returns all to the original darkness, which is yet mind, imagination.)

10. *Collected Essays* (Denver, 1959), the text used here. "Our Cousin, Mr. Poe" appeared originally in the *Partisan Review*, XVI, 1207-1219 (Dec., 1949). "The Angelic Imagination: Poe and the Power of Words" (later "Poe as God") appeared first in the *Kenyon Review*, XIV, 455-475 (Summer, 1952).
11. *Collected Essays*, pp. 470, 465-466.

Poe's supernatural discoursers in the three essays which precede *Eureka* (and especially in "The Power of Words") imply that by thought (by the "word") they create, even if but for brief duration. Thus the poet, though earthy, is nearest the heavenly creation. Yet all is doomed to the return to the eternal Silence. Poe "*means* the destruction of the world," says Tate.[12]

Whereas Melville's Ahab confronts the "mask" of nature with a frontiersman's unaided will, Poe attempts the more difficult task of reconciling that enigma with the science of his time—a mathematical, Newtonian universe, pre-Darwinian, static, plus the astronomy of Laplace and the speculations of von Humboldt. Drawing his analogy from the diffusion of light from a single beam, and the Newtonian and Lucretian atomistic composition of all things, Poe retains a vaguely pantheistic God who sits in lonely thought, to which all returns, in a solitude surely the most harrowing in American literature; or, as Mr. Tate puts it, "the non-spatial center into which the universe [and as well, the poet's internal world], by a reverse motion of the atoms, will contract." Poe's unity thus ends in zero, or well-nigh that, and he ends by "taking God along with him into a grave which is not smaller than the universe." "Poe's center," says Tate, "is that place—to use Dante's great figure—'where the sun is silent.'" Or again, "It is the Pascalian center which is everywhere and no-where, occupied by nothing." Thus, in the end, "Poe as God sits silent in darkness."[13]

Such, according to Mr. Tate, is Poe's *tour de force* (in the original sense of an exercise demanding great physical or mental vigor), the effort of a poet rather than of a scientist or philosopher, a defense of the supremacy of intuition and the passion for "supernal beauty" over science or logic alone. Poe, the anti-transcendentalist, is thus strangely linked with other American figures, Jonathan Edwards, Captain Ahab, Twain's Mysterious Stranger, even with Emerson, though Poe's central thesis is aesthetic rather than moral. Even Poe's critical insistence on aesthetic unity becomes but the poet's faint share in the cosmic urge toward a universal oneness.

Edward Davidson, in his *Poe: A Critical Study* (1957), examines *Eureka* to a similar conclusion. In it, Poe treats matter, he says, as dominated by the contending forces of attraction and repulsion, which individualize matter into special forms, the highest of which

12. *Ibid.*, p. 439. Italics Tate's.
13. *Ibid.*, pp. 452-454, *passim.*

may lie beyond our knowledge, as "conscious and intuitive intelligence," but from which the diffused spirit will in time withdraw, returning all to the original center. In other words, says Davidson, Poe has clothed in transcendental meaning Newton's "Every atom, of every body, attracts every other atom . . . with a force which varies inversely as the squares of the distances between the attracting and attracted atom." A kind of "electric force" thus unites matter and thought, for "thought in man is the same as the mechanism of the universe."[14] All is determined by the "supremeness of symmetry"; but harmony, symmetry, demand unity both as source and end.

Thus Poe dreams that by the power of aesthetic intuition, imagery, symbolism, the poet may bridge the gap between the empirical world and the mind that contemplates that world; and art becomes, in Davidson's words, "man's one instrument for making some order out of the infinitude of empirical formlessness."[15] Yet art, as we know it, is doomed to incompleteness, and leaves the world of "reality" as chaotic as before; and the poet, striving for a world after his dream, risks the loss of "reality," the absorption into a cosmic void.

Davidson had earlier touched on Poe's prose poem, "Silence: A Fable." In that sketch, silence is the one thing the solitary human observer cannot endure, and from which he flees in terror. "What Poe was trying to express by the mystic word 'Desolation,'" says Davidson, "was the presently observed state of total disunity, and by the term 'Silence' the inevitable coalescence of all substance."[16] This comment brings Poe's "Silence: A Fable" within Poe's cosmology; yet the validity of such an observation must rest finally on how far Poe can be assumed to have modified all poems and sketches to be consistent with *Eureka* (which means *"At last* I have found it"). To insist that a poet be logically consistent from start to finish would be a form of the "heresy of the didactic."

Richard Wilbur, like Mr. Tate a practicing poet, edited the Poe portion of a textbook entitled *Major Writers of America* (1962), and was thus brought to comment on "The City in the Sea" as follows:

14. Edward Davidson, *Poe: A Critical Study* (Cambridge, Mass., 1957), p. 230.
15. *Ibid.*, p. 252.
16. *Ibid.*, pp. 131-132. Hubbell, *American Life and Literature*, p. 383, found in "Silence: A Fable" echoes of DeQuincey and of Byron's "Darkness," and possibly an element of parody of such literature.

Whatever this poem may owe to Byron's "Darkness," Shelley's "Lines Written Among the Euganean Hills," or Flavius Josephus' account of the engulfment of Gomorrah in the Dead Sea, it is very much Poe's own, and amounts to a vague and eccentric apocalyptic vision. The sleeping inhabitants of the city are not, as line four makes plain, the wicked dead alone. Perhaps they are the dead in general, awaiting Judgment and the destruction of the symbolic Babylon. More likely still, they may be that race of dreamers described in "Al Aaraaf" who in life and after-life prefer their dreams and beauty to any "truth," human or divine, and must therefore pay the price of a final annihilation.[17]

This is ingenious; yet, had Mr. Wilbur stopped here, he, too, would seem to have groped among textbook annotations for significance. That is, "apocalyptic" is not precisely the word; nor is Poe vague in details, nor do any sleeping inhabitants lie within Poe's city, nor must the city be a symbolic Babylon, since only Babylon-like walls are mentioned; nor is a Judgment Day in any way necessitated. The poem, again, is finally less "eccentric" than original.

But Mr. Wilbur has also edited Poe's poems for a paperback series (later, if we may judge by internal evidence); and in the process he wrote an Introduction which imposed a closer examination, in the course of which "The City in the Sea" became a central exhibit.[18] As a setting for Poe as poet, Mr. Wilbur felt obliged to consider his prose at some length. Without going into detail, we may say that Wilbur discovers in Poe "all one story of the mind's escape from corrupt mundane consciousness into visionary wholeness and freedom,"[19] and a tendency to reject the common experience for this visionary search for the ideal realm. Wilbur, too, arrives at a consideration of Poe's "cosmic myth," treated with somewhat more aesthetic content than by the others. Man's fall from the supernal unity, so Wilbur reads Poe, left man with only glimpses from childhood's innocence or from the poet's vision of what he has lost.

From this consideration of Poe's cosmic view, Wilbur turns to "The City in the Sea." After the now familiar references to scholarly "sources," he comments: "But it is impossible to imagine that Poe's poem is merely a Gustave Doré illustration of certain apocalyptic passages in the Bible.... Poe's mind was not so submissively orthodox." "My suggestion," says Mr. Wilbur, "is that 'The City in the Sea' is simply a version of the star Al Aaraaf; that its residents are not

17. *Major Writers of America*, ed. Perry Miller (New York, 1962), pp. 386-387.
18. *Complete Poems of E. A. Poe*, ed. Richard Wilbur (New York, 1959), Introduction, pp. 7-39.
19. *Ibid.*, p. 23.

the wicked dead but dreamers, poets, and other refusers of 'Truth'; that the main body of the poem represents their entranced afterlife, and the close their annihilation."

Poe's star, it may be recalled, was borrowed from one observed by Tycho Brahe, a star which flashed into brilliance, then gradually faded. Poe made of it the abode of certain spirits who had chosen love and the intoxication of beauty and the senses as their highest good, and who, in consequence, were doomed to fade with the star. His footnote read: "Sorrow is not excluded from 'Al Aaraaf,' but it is that sorrow which the living love to cherish for the dead.... The passionate excitement of love, and the buoyancy of spirit attendant upon intoxication, are its less holy pleasures—the price of which, to those souls who make choice of 'Al Aaraaf' as their residence after life, is final death and annihilation."[20]

Nevertheless, Mr. Wilbur's "simply" cannot go unchallenged, plausible as this reading is. The injection of "passionate excitement" and intoxication into Poe's City in the Sea is quite out of tune with its "eternal rest" and its utter motionlessness of silence, and the atmosphere can only be that of post-annihilation of the dreamers.

Mr. Wilbur himself is not satisfied, and comments further: "The poem, if my reading is correct, employs biblical material to present, and at the same time to disguise, an unorthodox or 'Satanic' idea: the idea that the poet will refuse any heaven save that of his own dreams ... that special afterworld which Poe reserved for those devoted, in this world and the next, to 'visions that the many may not view.' "

This comment would surely limit the poem too narrowly to biblical material, even to "orthodox" criteria of some sort; and is Poe's refusal of any heaven save that of his dreams a sufficient motivation for this poem? It would seem that the poem is at least a representation of the landscape of dreams without a future. Mr. Wilbur, still not content with his reading, adds a further confession of difficulties unresolved: "The poem is so thoroughly pictorial, so lacking in narrative or argumentative structure, that all evidence of Poe's true meaning must be drawn from external sources: largely from prose pieces of later composition."[21] Do we detect here an echo of Mr. Tate's analysis of Poe's later prose pieces? And must we not

20. *Poems*, 1831, ed. Campbell, p. 104 n.
21. Quotations from Wilbur are from his Introduction to *Poe*, pp. 30-32, *passim*.

hesitate at "all" evidence as from external sources, surely an odd suggestion from a poet of Mr. Wilbur's talents?

We have touched upon the published commentary on Poe's poem; if, indeed, we have not loaded it with a considerable burden of cosmological complication. Neither Mr. Tate nor Mr. Davidson applied his reasoning to this specific poem as such; and Mr. Wilbur almost alone appears to have wrestled with the application of Poe's prose speculations to this particular poem. Yet these three critics have greatly aided us toward a final statement on the poem.

What, then, has been accomplished? We have, in the first place, freed the poem from the conventional annotations and made clear that it is an "unorthodox" poem, without concessions to the conventional pieties of Poe's time. We see the poem as Poe's own, and not a mere hash of legendary or biblical lore. We see more clearly the importance of Poe's effort to evolve a cosmology for his own age, a compound of the science of the time and his own predilection for aesthetic unity. We are prepared to accept Mr. Tate's insight that Poe was quite capable of *meaning* what he wrote, whether in a single poem or in a theory of a universe of atoms uniting into special forms, endowed at their highest with intelligence of a transcendent sort, yet destined to disunite in cosmic time and to return to the original silence, in a literal sinking of all material substance, with the intelligences dependent on the same, into a cosmic sea; that, indeed, whereas the great mythologies are populous worlds, a cosmology need not have people in it. It is this uncompromising acceptance of a Lucretian, Newtonian, and Einsteinian world without concession to human hopes that led Paul Valéry to see Poe as a forerunner of the twentieth century.

With such premises in mind, we may now see "The City in the Sea" as consistent within itself and within Poe's peculiar genius. The poem falls into perspective. Unorthodox that city is, for in it there are, indeed, neither good nor bad, no literal Babylons, no sleeping souls awaiting a personal Judgment, no trite "lessons" to be gleaned. There are but the dissolving atoms, embodied in the last symbols of human pomp and circumstance when the human life has departed from them; and the slow sinking into the waiting void, that void which the bodiless airs cannot replace when the towers slightly yield, and in which the dead waters cannot even spill over into the open graves, nor even remind us of the "far-off" happier seas of our own ephemeral world. There Death itself, in its proud tower, sinks with the rest, for there is no more death where nothing lives. It is this unchanging silence which humanly conceived hells on a thousand imaginary thrones must reverence, for they are populous worlds, less terrifying than this eternal void.

It is an error, then, to seek the poem's meaning in external sources alone, much as those sources may contribute to our understanding. For this poem must be read *per se*, accepting its pictorial detail as it is, its pitiless landscape wherein all is sculptured ivy and stone idols, where the melancholy waters lie in an eternal serenity, and the light comes from the waters only, the cosmic sea of its origin and its return, for the sun indeed is silent. That city's final engulfment is without sound and without the fanfare of the trumpets of Judgment, and its sinking takes place so slowly that Time is of no consequence. It is a city of Death, but Death without palliatives. What has handicapped the reading of this poem has been the reader's reluctance to accept it for what it literally says. Poe has not disguised its meaning; and far from lacking structure, it is a masterpiece of inner consistency, a rejection of earlier versions toward a final "unity of effect" that has its parallels in his later excursions into metaphysics and contemporary science.

Poe's works, it has been noted, often possess a curious realism within their farthest reaches, a consistency of the factual with the imaginative concept. Poe's "Dream-Land," for example, has too hastily been taken as fanciful only. Dreams have literally no geography, no spatial maps, no clocks to mark off the time. We do each of us literally enter our land of dreams alone, going and returning by a route which no psychologist has as yet unraveled. It is a factual statement that the landscape of dreams will not conform to the waking knowledge, and that in dreams remembered figures may "start and sigh" and pass us by. And, according to psychoanalysis, it is equally true that we cannot and dare not openly confront our most vivid dreams; and that the open eye of daylight cannot see them as they were, but only as a fleeting memory permits, a memory that, as all tests show, quickly distorts the dream content to satisfy the protective censor. Thus we do, indeed, behold dreams "but through darkened glasses." Poe's poem on dreams becomes thus consistently factual, only its detailed landscape being perhaps that of his own peculiar vision.

Thus "The City in the Sea" may have originated in its earlier versions in lines from "Al Aaraaf," with biblical and Ossianic echoes, such as appear also in "Silence: A Fable." But Poe's talent showed a progressive maturing; and as his mind engaged in prose speculations, critical or metaphysical, he saw within this poem, I believe, an opportunity to revise it toward a purer consistency within itself, one that unflinchingly imaged the cosmos that the later prose works treated by abstractions. Who more than Poe has insisted on the differing functions of prose and poem?

Should some space traveler one day come upon a planet dead and uninhabitable, yet find thereon some last evidence of a lost civilization, a few towers shining faintly in the cosmic darkness, would not his sober reflection recall "The City in the Sea"? Yet his experience would be factual, neither visionary nor apocalyptic, though possibly suggesting earthly parallels. And if there be no such planets, habitable now or ever, then, indeed, we may be humanly alone in a cosmic silence, unrelieved by any guarantee that our own little world may not sink in time into the same soundless sea.

Yet for those who rebel against seeing Poe's poem in such a grim frame, we may propose a parallel symbolizing of the slow, inevitable engulfment of memory, individual, communal, or even human, as it sinks without sound into the lengthening past, until it, too, is swallowed in the eternal silence. Who today can recover the complex symbolism of the ancient Egyptian tombs, or recover the thoughts of Stonehenge men or those of the caves of Dordogne? There, too, only the stone image remains, subjected, so long as we and the stone remain, to our imaginative reconstructions, and then silence. For the proud creations of our imaginations, in the words of a poet greater than Poe, may, indeed, be "melted into air, into thin air," and all— towers, palaces, temples, yea, "the great globe itself"— be dissolved and "leave not a rack behind."

Even so, Poe's towers refuse still to melt like airy imaginings,
but stand unique in literature for
their grim realism.

THE MORALS OF POWER
BUSINESS ENTERPRISE AS A THEME IN MID-NINETEENTH-CENTURY AMERICAN FICTION*

Henry Nash Smith

University of California, Berkeley

Few nations have ever undergone such rapid and far-reaching economic change as did the United States during the middle and later decades of the nineteenth century. It was the period when the use of steam power in transportation and manufacturing was transforming an agrarian into an urban economy, establishing the main outlines of the society we live in today. The new energies made available by mechanization multiplied many times over the capacity of the working force to perform physical labor. But this was only the beginning of the social transformation. For the use of steam favored large-scale enterprises in the basic industries, and thus required the investment of capital in staggering amounts. Railway transportation and the electric telegraph broadened the geographical scope of business enterprise. The industrial corporation, comparatively rare in the first half of the century, became the dominant form of economic enterprise. The creation of these larger administrative units concentrated power in the hands of an emergent business elite of managers and financiers, a "democratic plutocracy" whose power exceeded that of government itself in the days of Jefferson or Jackson, and perhaps in the days of Grant as well.

The new captain of industry was far too powerful to be scorned or patronized by novelists, yet he could not be made a hero because he was too much of a philistine and above all too ruthless. Thus for a long time he proved baffling to the literary imagination. At the very turn of the twentieth century, in 1898, Henry James declared that although this formidable character was "the typical American

---

*This is the second of two lectures delivered in January, 1966, at the University of Toronto, under the sponsorship of the Program in American Studies.

figure," he had still hardly been touched upon by the serious novelist and dramatist.[1] For this reason, the first gropings toward literary treatment of the forces released by the industrial revolution have a special interest.

As early as the 1840's Emerson had a prophetic half-glimpse of the contours of the future world of really big business. He recognized that its most appropriate symbol would not be Poor Richard, but Napoleon, whom he described as the representative of "the class of business men in America, in England, in France, and throughout Europe. . . ."[2] These men strove, to be sure, for wealth, but not primarily as a means of attaining respectability or even a luxurious mode of living. They sought wealth because it conferred power. Such a craving could never be satisfied; it would become in the end a kind of tropism, an irrational compulsion. Emerson quotes a significant remark of Napoleon's: "My power would fall, were I not to support it by new achievements. Conquest has made me what I am, and conquest must maintain me." There is a similar suggestion of impersonal forces controlling the representative man's actions in Napoleon's styling himself "the creature of circumstances" and even the "Child of Destiny." Yet the dominant feature of such a leader is his egotism. He has relentless will-power, at once personal and impersonal. As Emerson says of Napoleon, "He is firm, sure, self-denying, self-postponing, sacrificing everything to his aim,—money, troops, generals, and his own safety also . . . . His victories were only so many doors, and he never for a moment lost sight of his way onward, in the dazzle and uproar of the present circumstance."

Nevertheless, Emerson did not realize all the implications of his portrait of Napoleon. He failed to see that a transcendental universe of absolute harmony could not contain a centrifugal force of the magnitude he ascribes to "the spirit of commerce, of money and material power" in the nineteenth century. The shrewd Montaigne-Emerson (to use Lowell's phrase) could recognize the tendency of the new era, but the Plotinus-Emerson who maintained that the universe is moral from center to circumference refused to take this per-

1. "The Question of the Opportunities" (1898), in *Henry James: The American Essays*, ed. Leon Edel (New York, 1956), p. 202. One of Howells's fictional spokesmen had declared in 1889 that a certain crude, ruthless new millionaire represented "the ideal and ambition of most Americans" (*A Hazard of New Fortunes*, New York, 1960, p. 190).

2. The essay "Napoleon; or, The Man of the World" appears in *Representative Men* (1850), but the contents of this volume had first been delivered as a series of lectures in 1845-1846. I quote from the text in *Works* (5 vols.; Boston, 1880), II, 179-205.

ception seriously. As a result, the essay on Napoleon ends in a striking anti-climax. Napoleon was after all only an "experiment":

He did all that in him lay, to live and thrive without moral principle.
It was the nature of things, the eternal law of man and the world, which
balked and ruined him; and the result, in a million experiments would
be the same. Every experiment, by multitudes or by individuals, that
has a sensual and selfish aim, will fail.

Emerson's confidence in the operation of moral laws was so
strong that he could feel a comic disdain for Napoleon. He endorses
the self-crowned emperor's scorn of "the born kings, . . . 'the hereditary asses' " generally. Yet for all his immense natural abilities, Napoleon is vulgar. Viewing him from above, Emerson renders a judgment not unlike Cooper's attitude toward Aristabulus Bragg in *Home
as Found*:

. . . when you have penetrated through all the circles of power and
splendor, you were not dealing with a gentleman, at last; but with an
impostor and a rogue; and he fully deserves the epithet of *Jupiter Scapin*,
or a sort of Scamp Jupiter.

The subversive threat of commercialism could wear a quite different aspect for an observer not supported by Cooper's aristocratic
self-confidence or Emerson's metaphysical optimism. And Nathaniel
Hawthorne had neither of these resources. In *The House of the
Seven Gables*, published in 1851, he gives a central position to a
character endowed with many of the traits that Emerson attributes
to Napoleon, such as "hard, keen sense, and practical energy," an
"immitigable resolve," and a "hot fellness of purpose, which anni-
hilated everything but itself." Judge Jaffrey Pyncheon, says Hawthorne, was "powerful by intellect, energy of will, the long habit of
acting among men": he was "bold, imperious, relentless, crafty; lay-
ing his purposes deep, and following them out with an inveteracy of
pursuit that knew neither rest nor conscience; trampling on the weak,
and, when essential to his ends, doing his utmost to beat down the
strong."[3] Since we actually see the Judge in action only within a very
limited theater of operations—"a rusty wooden house" in a by-street
of the town of Salem—his career lacks the epic grandeur of Napoleon's military campaigns on three continents. But the Judge's lust
for money and power identifies him with the rising commercialism
of which Emerson declares Napoleon to be the type.

3. *The Complete Works of Nathaniel Hawthorne*, ed. George P. Lathrop (13 vols.;
Boston, 1898), III, 34, 277, 159, 287, 151-152.

The Judge's activities on the specimen day for which Hawthorne gives us a detailed program were to be primarily concerned with business matters. He would have spent some time in an insurance office exchanging gossip with men of financial influence; he was to preside at a meeting of bank directors; and later he was to meet "a State Street broker, who has undertaken to procure a heavy percentage, and the best of paper, for a few loose thousands which the Judge happens to have by him, uninvested." To be sure, these business activities are not developed with the documentary detail we have come to expect in realistic fiction. Hawthorne disdains them, and evidently conceives of them in terms of clichés. Of the bank directors' meeting, he remarks in scorn, "Let him go thither, and loll at ease upon his money-bags!" But the intention is to depict the Judge as being deeply involved in financial transactions.[4]

Hawthorne places further emphasis on the lust for wealth as a force of evil in his references to the past. The "legend" presented in the romance, "prolonging itself, from an epoch now gray in the distance, down into our own broad daylight,"[5] begins with the crime of the founder of the family, the seventeenth-century Colonel Pyncheon who caused Matthew Maule to be executed for witchcraft so that he might seize Maule's property. The same ruthless greed has appeared in an eighteenth-century Pyncheon, and the pattern has been repeated once again in the early career of the nineteenth-century Judge. We are to understand that in his youth Jaffrey Pyncheon contrived to have his cousin Clifford sent to prison for thirty years for the alleged murder of a wealthy uncle who actually died of natural causes. The motive was Jaffrey's desire to secure for himself the inheritance originally destined for Clifford. At the climax of the plot of *The House of the Seven Gables*, Judge Pyncheon attempts to force the enfeebled Clifford to reveal to him the hiding place of certain documents that the Judge believes will enable him to lay claim to valuable lands "to the Eastward" acquired by the Pyncheon family at some remote point in the past. To this end he threatens to have Clifford, only recently released from prison, confined in an insane asylum; and he is prevented from executing his threat only by a mysterious stroke which kills him as he sits waiting for an interview with Clifford in the old family mansion.

This material is essentially melodramatic; it has the stereotyped

4. *Ibid.*, pp. 319-320.
5. *Ibid.*, p. 14.

air of popular "sensation fiction." Not only are the crimes ascribed to Judge Pyncheon so outrageous as to be unbelievable; Hawthorne makes no effort to provide a plausible motivation for the character's behavior, and seems to be concerned only with making him a totally repulsive villain. Hawthorne's undisguised hatred rises to a climax in the remarkable chapter called "Governor Pyncheon." The only actual character on stage is the Judge, and he is dead: his corpse sits upright in a great oaken armchair. No action is performed and no word spoken by anyone except the author, who is so completely mastered by a savage, Old Testament exultation that he devotes pages on end to taunting his dead enemy and even executes a kind of verbal dance of triumph around the corpse.

Hawthorne's portrayal of Judge Pyncheon is too strongly colored by emotion to be accepted as merely an abstract denunciation of greed. Cooper, for example, evidently disliked commercialism as much as Hawthorne did. Yet there is nothing in Cooper's treatment of this theme that even approaches the intensity of Hawthorne's feeling toward Jaffrey Pyncheon. A significant difference is the element of fear in Hawthorne's attitude. To be sure, he says that Clifford might have been able to withstand the shock of contemplating unbridled greed, "the worst and meanest aspect of life," if he had had a tragic power of scornful laughter.[6] And there are moments of grim comedy in Hawthorne's taunting of the Judge's corpse. But the basic emotion of the chapter is more accurately expressed in his exclamation toward the end: "Yonder leaden Judge sits immovably upon our soul. Will he never stir again? We shall go mad unless he stirs!"[7]

Frederick Crews proposes to read *The House of the Seven Gables* as an act of exorcism in which the Judge, as a father figure, must be destroyed in accord with the imperatives of an Oedipal pattern.[8] This view seems to me persuasive. It accounts not only for the intensity of Hawthorne's feeling, but for the elaborate symbolism with which he surrounds the Judge's death, such as the sudden appearance of a Golden Bough in the Pyncheon Elm, and the unexpected blooming of flowers among the plants growing in roof angles of the old house. Most important of all, Mr. Crews's interpretation makes sense of the whole peripeteia of the fable, the release of vital energies in all the

6. *Ibid.*, p. 198.
7. *Ibid.*, p. 332.
8. "Homely Witchcraft," chap. x of *The Sins of the Fathers: Hawthorne's Psychological Themes* (New York, 1966), pp. 171-193.

surviving characters and the declaration of love between Holgrave and Phoebe that provides a comic resolution for the plot.

The Freudian view can readily accommodate the economic and in the broad sense political meanings that I have pointed to in the characterization of Judge Pyncheon. Even if we do not wish to go so far as to note that money often stands for libido in Freudian constructions, we can recognize that Hawthorne links the Judge's relentless drive to amass wealth with sexual tyranny. The close association between the two themes appears with especial clarity in one of the most fully worked out emblematic episodes in the book. An Italian with a barrel-organ and a monkey stops in the street under the windows of the old house. While he turns the crank, the monkey capers about, begging coins from the onlookers. Hawthorne moralizes the scene with emphasis:

The mean and low, yet strangely man-like expression of his wilted countenance; the prying and crafty glance, that showed him to be ready to gripe at every miserable advantage; his enormous tail (too enormous to be decently concealed under his gabardine), and the deviltry of nature which it betokened,—take this monkey just as he was, in short, and you could desire no better image of the Mammon of copper coin, symbolizing the grossest form of the love of money.[9]

In this passage, as elsewhere in the story, Hawthorne associates a voracious love of money with suggestions of gross sexuality: the monkey's deviltry is evident both in his greedy snatching of coins and in the repulsively phallic tail. Mr. Crews notes a number of references to Judge Pyncheon's "fleshly effulgence," his "great animal development"; and Hawthorne also hints darkly at outrageous sexual behavior that hastened the death of his wife.[10] The overt indictment of the Judge as a man dominated by a craving for wealth gains force from the partly explicit sexual symbolism. The author's hostility toward a single character tends to become a repudiation of all forms of established authority.

It must be added, however, that this subversive emotion finds only indirect and muffled expression: the force of inhibition is too strong. Although Holgrave is the most formidable adversary of the Judge, Hawthorne does not manage to bring them face to face in open conflict. Instead, Holgrave is represented as being an economic and political radical. He cherishes rather vague doctrines about the

9. Hawthorne, *Works*, III, 198.
10. *Ibid.*, pp. 144, 151.

need to tear down "the moss-grown and rotten Past" so that a golden
era may be inaugurated for mankind.[11] Like Hawthorne, he has even
"spent some months in a community of Fourierists"; and Hawthorne
expresses a considerable sympathy for Holgrave's "enthusiasm" in
the very act of declaring it to be a "crude, wild, and misty philosophy."[12] It is true that the young man renounces his radicalism in
order to marry Phoebe and take possession of the Judge's inheritance, but there is a certain hang-dog air about his recantation, and
the conclusion of the story is notably lacking in imaginative power.

For our purposes, the most significant aspect of the implied
antagonism between Judge Pyncheon and Holgrave is Hawthorne's
identification of commercialism and wealth with official status in the
community. Business interests are already in control of society. The
young man, the archetypal son who is hostile to the Establishment,
is indifferent to the profit motive. This pattern contradicts Emerson's conception, which associates "the spirit of commerce, of money
and material power" with "the democratic classes," "the young and
the poor who have fortunes to make" and are "recruiting their
numbers every hour by births," and opposes this group to the "idle
capitalists"—a class that is "continually losing numbers by death."[13]
With some forcing of the issue, we might say that Emerson regards
the typical businessman as being self-made, like Napoleon, whereas
in using Jaffrey Pyncheon to represent the commercial spirit Hawthorne moves toward the Jacksonian contention that the business
system was an aristocratic money power hostile to the plain people.

This would perhaps be an oversimplification of Hawthorne's
complex vision of his materials. Nevertheless, on one point Hawthorne is quite clear and recognizably Jacksonian. Judge Pyncheon
is a Whig (he even has a few traits suggesting Daniel Webster) [14] and
he is eager to continue his political career as the corrupt servant of

11. *Ibid.*, pp. 215-216.
12. *Ibid.*, pp. 212, 216-217.
13. *Ibid.*, II, 179-180.
14. "It was he, you know," remarks Hawthorne, "of whom it used to be said, in
reference to his ogre-like appetite, that his creator made him a great animal, but
that the dinner-hour made him a great beast" (*ibid.*, p. 325). Theodore Parker asserted in his "Discourse Occasioned by the Death of Daniel Webster" (1852) that
Webster "became over-fond of animal delights, of the joys of the body's baser parts;
fond of sensual luxury; the victim of low appetites. He loved power, loved pleasure,
loved wine" (*Additional Speeches, Addresses, and Occasional Sermons*, 2 vols., Boston,
1855, I, 275). Henry James wrote: "It is difficult to say whether Hawthorne followed a
model in describing Judge Pyncheon; but it is tolerably obvious that the picture is an
impression—a copious impression—of an individual. It has evidently a definite starting-
point in fact, and the author is able to draw, freely and confidently, after the image
established in his mind" (*Hawthorne* [1879], Ithaca, N. Y., 1956, p. 102).

conservative economic interests. Hawthorne tells us that on the day he did not live to see, the Judge was supposed to attend a dinner,

the most important, in its consequences, of all the dinners [he] ever ate! The guests were to be some dozen or so friends from several districts of the State; men of distinguished character and influence... practised politicians, every man of them, and skilled to adjust those preliminary measures which steal from the people, without its knowledge, the power of choosing its own rulers. The popular voice, at the next gubernatorial election, though loud as thunder, will be really an echo of what those gentlemen shall speak, under their breath, at your friend's festive board. They meet to decide upon their candidate. This little knot of subtle schemers will control the convention, and, through it, dictate to the party. And what worthier candidate,—more wise and learned, more noted for philanthropic liberality, truer to safe principles, tried oftener by public trusts, more spotless in private character, with a larger stake in the common welfare, and deeper grounded, by hereditary descent, in the faith and character of the Puritans,—what man can be presented for the suffrage of the people, so eminently combining all these claims to the chief-rulership as Judge Pyncheon here before us?[15]

In this parody of a nominating speech at a political convention we can feel the weight of experience in a writer who had held a patronage appointment as a "Loco-Foco Surveyor" in the Salem Customs House, and would presently write a campaign biography of his college classmate and friend Franklin Pierce. Hawthorne knew what he was talking about when he urged the Judge, "Be present at this dinner!—drink a glass or two of that noble wine!—make your pledges in as low a whisper as you will!—and you rise up from table virtually governor of the glorious old State! Governor Pyncheon of Massachusetts!"[16]

The ironic allusions to "safe principles" and to the stake-in-society theory of politics are an attack on the conception of government as an instrument of the wealthiest men. The pledges that the Judge would have made in return for the nomination are left ominously vague, but their general nature can be inferred. When he fails to appear at the dinner, the diners are unperturbed; they are "warm and merry; they have given up the Judge; and, concluding that the Free-Soilers have him, they will fix upon another candidate."[17] The actual man in office is a matter of indifference, since the real control is exercised by business interests behind the scenes.

During the two decades following the publication of *The House*

15. Hawthorne, *Works*, III, 324.
16. *Ibid.*, pp. 324-325.
17. *Ibid.*, p. 325.

of the Seven Gables, the subservience of political to economic power became the most conspicuous feature of American government. It took many forms, but was most significant in the new operations forced on the federal government by the Civil War and the policy of land grants and other subsidies for the construction of Pacific railroads. The gigantic corruption in and out of Congress and the scandals created by revelations of bribery and graft during the decade following the war have made this era a byword in American history.

It is called the Gilded Age from the title of a collaborative novel by Mark Twain and Charles Dudley Warner published in 1873 at the peak of postwar inflation and just on the eve of a major financial collapse. As if by contagion from its subject, the novel is a chaos of incompletely developed fragments of plot, many of them lifted straight out of sensation fiction and popular melodrama. But the most fully developed material is a satiric attack on the universal craze for getting rich quickly through speculation, and the corruption of Congress by business interests. The theme of Judge Pyncheon's whispered pledges to the political bosses of Massachusetts is here transferred to the larger arena of Washington and portrayed as the dominant pattern in American public life. Although some contemporary reviewers protested against caricature and exaggeration in the novel, the prevalent opinion then and subsequently has been that it makes even excessive use of directly observed fact.

The Preface to the novel announces ironically that it will be a description of an "ideal commonwealth," "a State where there is no fever of speculation, no inflamed desire for sudden wealth, where the poor are all simple-minded and contented, and the rich are all honest and generous, where society is in a condition of primitive purity and politics is the occupation of only the capable and the patriotic...."[18] Warner makes the same points without irony in describing one of the characters, Philip Sterling, who is more or less a self-portrait of the author:

... he was born into a time when all young men of his age caught the fever of speculation, and expected to get on in the world by the omission of some of the regular processes which have been appointed from of old. And examples were not wanting to encourage him. He saw people, all around him, poor yesterday, rich to-day, who had come into sudden opulence by some means which they could not have classified among any of the regular occupations of life. A war would give such a fellow a

18. Mark Twain and Charles Dudley Warner, *The Gilded Age: A Tale of Today* (1873), ed. Justin D. Kaplan (New York, 1964), p. 1.

career and very likely fame. He might have been a "railroad man," or a politician, or a land speculator, or one of those mysterious people who travel free on all railroads and steamboats, and are continually crossing and re-crossing the Atlantic, driven day and night about nobody knows what, and make a great deal of money by so doing.[19]

What is really alive in the novel, however, is Mark Twain's character of Colonel Beriah Sellers. Except for the fact that he provides another variation on the theme of speculation, the Colonel seems out of place amid the stereotypes from popular fiction and journalistic exposés. He exists in a different literary mode. He is not a novelistic character at all, but a composite figure incorporating several major themes of American folklore. To introduce such a character into a novel was to court disaster; and Sellers does destroy whatever coherence *The Gilded Age* might have had as a straightforward satire of political corruption. Yet no reader will regret Mark Twain's decision, for the portrait of Sellers is not only a comic masterpiece but also a profound and suggestive commentary on American attitudes toward business enterprise.

To the end of his life Mark Twain insisted that Sellers was modeled closely on an actual person, an uncle for whom he had a high regard.

The real Colonel Sellers [he declared in his Autobiographical Dictation], as I knew him in James Lampton, was a pathetic and beautiful spirit, a manly man, a straight and honorable man, a man with a big, foolish, unselfish heart in his bosom, a man born to be loved; and he was loved by all his friends, and by his family worshiped. It is the right word. To them he was but little less than a god.[20]

In a curtain speech on the opening night of the play based on the novel—which was virtually a monologue pronounced by Sellers—Mark Twain complained only half-humorously that the actor John Raymond had left all the pathos out of the scene of the Sellers family dining on raw turnips.[21] It is certainly true that Mark Twain makes much of the warmth of feeling within the impoverished Sellers household. And the Colonel is undeniably generous: when the workers on the navigation project are cheated of their wages by the big operators back in New York and Washington, he

19. *Ibid.*, p. 350.
20. *Mark Twain's Autobiography*, ed. Albert B. Paine (2 vols.; New York, 1924), I, 89-90.
21. DeLancey Ferguson, "Mark Twain's Lost Curtain Speeches," *South Atlantic Quarterly*, XLII, 263 (July, 1943). Here and elsewhere I am greatly indebted to the full documentation of the biographical and historical circumstances surrounding the composition and publication of the novel provided by Bryant M. French in *Mark Twain and* The Gilded Age: *The Book That Named an Era* (Dallas, 1965).

divided with them the money he still had in the bank—an act which had nothing surprising about it because he was generally ready to divide whatever he had with anybody that wanted it, and it was owing to this very trait that his family spent their days in poverty and at times were pinched with famine.[22]

At this point, it is worth remarking, Sellers is the victim of the real speculators, not their accomplice.

Nevertheless, he is a character in a book rather than an actual man, and there was never a clearer case for trusting the tale rather than the teller. As he appears in *The Gilded Age* Beriah Sellers has several traits more conspicuous than his generosity. Some of these may also have been drawn from James Lampton: the question is of little moment. What is beyond dispute is the close similarity between Sellers and the character of Ovid Bolus created by Mark Twain's predecessor in the humorous tradition, Joseph G. Baldwin. The important point about both characters is their gift of improvisation, their mastery of tall talk. Baldwin introduces Bolus with a disquisition on lying as a fine art. Some men, he says, are liars from interest, some from vanity, some from "a sort of necessity, which overbears, by the weight of temptation, the sense of virtue." But "Bolus was a natural liar, just as some horses are natural pacers, and some dogs natural setters." "What he did in that walk, was from the irresistible promptings of instinct, and a disinterested love of art." Indeed, "Bolus's lying came from his greatness of soul and his comprehensiveness of mind. The truth was too small for him. Fact was too dry and common-place for the fervor of his genius. . . . His world was not the hard, work-day world the groundlings live in: he moved in a sphere of poetry; he lived amidst the ideal and the romantic."[23] Baldwin relates in paraphrase many of Bolus's feats of lying which closely resemble those of Sellers, especially the practice of dignifying commonplace objects by fictitious associations—a book that he declares was given him by Van Buren, a walking stick that was a present from General Jackson, whiskey that was the last remnant of a distillation of 1825 smuggled in from Ireland.

With a sounder artist's instinct, Mark Twain allows Sellers to reveal himself in his own words. Since the sheer torrential outpouring of words and images is essential to the effect of these monologues, they can not be represented adequately in brief quotation, but a few

22. *The Gilded Age*, p. 176.
23. *Flush Times in Alabama and Mississippi* (1853), in Walter Blair, ed., *Native American Humor (1800-1900)* (New York, 1937), pp. 356-357.

sentences may give some idea of the Colonel's speech. Sellers is explaining to young Washington Hawkins the dazzling future he has in mind for him:

"I intend to look out for you, Washington, my boy. . . . I'll put you in a way to make more money than you'll ever know what to do with. You'll be right here where I can put my hand on you when anything turns up. I've got some prodigious operations on foot; but I'm keeping quiet; mum's the word; your old hand don't go around pow-wowing and letting everybody see his k'yards and find out his little game. But all in good time. You'll see."

He describes "an operation in corn" and a "hog speculation" that is bigger still: an investment of only six millions will yield "whole Atlantic oceans of cash, gulfs and bays thrown in." Hawkins, feverishly excited, pleads with him not to throw away these chances, but Sellers quiets him with a "sweet, compassionate smile":

"Why Washington, my boy, these things are nothing. They *look* large—of course they look large to a novice, but to a man who has been all his life accustomed to large operations—shaw! They're well enough to while away an idle hour with, or furnish a bit of employment that will give a trifle of idle capital a chance to earn its bread while it is waiting for something to do, but—now just listen a moment—just let me give you an idea of what we old veterans of commerce call 'business.' Here's the Rothschild's proposition—this is between you and me, you understand—"

Washington nodded three or four times impatiently, and his glowing eyes said, "Yes, yes—hurry—I understand—"

—"for I wouldn't have it get out for a fortune. They want me to go in with them on the sly—agent was here two weeks ago about it—go in on the sly" [voice down to an impressive whisper, now,] "and buy a hundred and thirteen wild cat banks in Ohio, Indiana, Kentucky, Illinois and Missouri—notes of these banks are at all sorts of discount now—average discount of the hundred and thirteen is forty-four per cent—buy them all up, you see, and then all of a sudden let the cat out of the bag! Whiz! the stock of every one of those wildcats would spin up to a tremendous premium before you could turn a handspring—profit on the speculation not a dollar less than forty millions!"

When the Colonel discovers that Washington has only eighteen dollars to his name, he shifts gears downward with admirable poise:

"Well, all right—don't despair. Other people have been obliged to begin with less. I have a small idea that may develop into something for us both, all in good time. Keep your money close and add to it. I'll make it breed. I've been experimenting (to pass away the time) on a little preparation for curing sore eyes—a kind of decoction nine-tenths water and the other tenth drugs that don't cost more than a dollar a barrel . . . before many weeks I wager the country will ring with the fame of Beriah Sellers' Infallible Imperial Oriental Optic Liniment and Salvation for Sore Eyes

—the Medical Wonder of the Age! Small bottles fifty cents, large ones a dollar. Average cost, five and seven cents for the two sizes. The first year sell, say, ten thousand bottles in Missouri, seven thousand in Iowa, three thousand in Arkansas, four thousand in Kentucky, six thousand in Illinois, and say twenty-five thousand in the rest of the country. Total, fifty-five thousand bottles; profit clear of all expenses, twenty thousand dollars at the very lowest calculation."

And this is only the beginning:

"Why, Washington, in the Oriental countries people swarm like the sands of the desert; every square mile of ground upholds its thousands upon thousands of struggling human creatures—and every separate and individual devil of them's got the ophthalmia! . . . Three years of introductory trade in the orient and what will be the result? Why, our headquarters would be in Constantinople and our hindquarters in Further India! Factories and warehouses in Cairo, Ispahan, Bagdad, Damascus, Jerusalem, Yedo, Peking, Bangkok, Delhi, Bombay and Calcutta! Annual income—well, God only knows how many millions and millions apiece!"[24]

Sellers's fantasies are obviously a compensation for the squalor of actual life in the remote backwoods community of Hawkeye, Missouri. On other occasions he makes it plain that he has invented for himself a composite identity. As the self-conferred title of Colonel implies, he conceives of himself as a Southern gentleman of the old school. When he is far enough away from Hawkeye, he refers grandly to his plantation, and intimates that he is accustomed to a way of life represented by a non-existent basket of champagne he meant to send to the railroad surveying crew at their camp. In Washington he rises to the sublimity of remarking, "The President's table is well enough . . . for a man on a salary, but God bless my soul, I should like him to see a little old-fashioned hospitality"—back at the Colonel's place in Missouri.[25]

But if Sellers is a Southern gentleman he has moved far enough West to have acquired the Western taste for land-speculation and town-building. He has conceived a metropolis called Napoleon that is to be brought into existence on the site of a miserable handful of log huts on the bank of Goose Run. Goose Run is to be renamed Columbus River and dredged so that it will be navigable to the Mississippi; and Napoleon is also to be served by the proposed Salt Lick & Pacific Extension Railway. These are the schemes for which the Colonel solicits (and secures) the interest of Senator Dilworthy.

24. *The Gilded Age*, pp. 56-57.
25. *Ibid.*, p. 272.

The scene in which Sellers describes for his discouraged wife the route of the proposed railway, representing by means of salt cellar, pincushion, candle snuffers, and inkwell the thriving cities that are certain to spring up along the route, is one of the comic triumphs of both novel and play. Few of Mark Twain's inspirations are more charming than the choice of names for the way stations along this pathway to the stars: Slouchburg, Doodlebug, Brimstone, Belshazzar, Catfish, Babylon, Hail Columbia, Hark-from-the-Tomb, and so on.[26] The names may belong to Nevada more clearly than to Missouri, but the gap between backwoods reality and Sellers's millennial vision is nowhere more brilliantly established.

The Colonel as speculator—or, to be more accurate, as the laureate of land-speculation and town-building—is thoroughly in the American grain. As early as the 1830's Tocqueville had exactly described the situation of Sellers:

Nothing conceivable [wrote Tocqueville] is so petty, so insipid, so crowded with paltry interests—in one word, so anti-poetic—as the life of a man in the United States. But among the thoughts which it suggests, there is always one that is full of poetry, and this is the hidden nerve which gives a vigor to the whole frame.

The hidden vein of poetry amid the tedium and the squalor is the vision of America's destiny, of the triumphant future:

In Europe people talk a great deal of the wilds of America, but the Americans themselves never think about them; they are insensible to the wonders of inanimate nature. . . . Their eyes are fixed upon another sight: the American people views its own march across these wilds, draining swamps, turning the course of rivers, peopling solitudes, and subduing nature. This magnificent image of themselves does not meet the gaze of the Americans at intervals only; it may be said to haunt every one of them in his least as well as in his most important actions and to be always flitting before his mind.[27]

This is the larger context within which Sellers's fantasies must be viewed. Michel Chevalier provided a more mundane theory of what speculation meant in the post-frontier period:

Public opinion and the pulpit forbid sensual gratifications, wine, women, and the display of princely luxury; cards and dice are equally prohibited; the American, therefore, has recourse to business for the strong emotions which he requires to make him feel life. He launches with delight into the ever-moving sea of speculation. One day, the wave raises him to the clouds; he enjoys in haste the moment of triumph. The next day he dis-

26. *Ibid.*, pp. 186-188.
27. *Democracy in America*, trans. Henry Reeve, ed. Phillips Bradley (2 vols.; New York, 1954), II, 78-79.

appears between the crests of the billows; he is little troubled by the reverse; he bides his time coolly and consoles himself with the hope of better fortune.[28]

It will be noticed that neither Tocqueville nor Chevalier refers to a merely mercenary motive: they saw speculation as a psychological necessity and a consequence of boundless faith in the American destiny. Colonel Sellers's grandiose schemes represent the national habit of living in a continually more glittering future. But there was a chronic element of fraud in this booster spirit. One remembers Cooper's scornful allusion to "the great game of brag that most of the country had sat down to."[29] Sellers is representative in this respect also. His Optic Liniment sounds a good deal like the "article to take the tartar off the teeth" that the *soi-disant* Duke of Bridgewater, in *Huckleberry Finn*, has been peddling in the Mississippi River towns just before he finds it expedient to take refuge on Huck Finn's raft. That is, besides being a Southern gentleman and an orator of Manifest Destiny in the manner of Thomas Hart Benton, the Colonel is also something of a rascal. In a later novel called *The American Claimant* Mark Twain reveals that Sellers believes himself to be the rightful heir to an English earldom—a trait that allies him even more closely with the disinherited Duke and his crony, the long-lost but rightful heir to the French throne. He is cousin both to P. T. Barnum and to the traveling medicine man with a spiel capable of enthralling credulous yokels like Washington Hawkins.

Were it not for this touch of the picaresque in the Colonel, Mark Twain's decision to transport him from the Missouri hinterland to Washington would be thoroughly incongruous. Even so, the Colonel seems to have undergone a drastic change in character when he reappears as the assistant (no longer the victim) of Senator Dilworthy. They are lobbying for a federal appropriation to buy certain Tennessee lands belonging to the Hawkins family at an outrageous overvaluation, on the pretext of founding there an Industrial University for freed Negroes. Sellers writes to his friend Harry Brierly:

28. *Society, Manners, and Politics in the United States* (first published 1836; trans. 1839), in Edwin C. Rozwenc, ed., *Ideology and Power in the Age of Jackson* (Garden City, N. Y., 1964), p. 27.
29. *Autobiography of a Pocket-Handkerchief* (1843), ed. George F. Horner and Raymond Adams (Chapel Hill, N. C., 1949), p. 148.

"I don't care . . . so much about the niggroes. But if the government will buy this land, it will set up the Hawkins family—make Laura an heiress —and I shouldn't wonder if Beriah Sellers would set up his carriage again. Dilworthy looks at it different, of course. He's all for philanthropy, for benefiting the colored race."[30]

And presently Sellers is explaining to Washington Hawkins the rituals through which Congress regularly purifies itself of corruption by investigating charges against its members and even in extreme cases passing resolutions of reprimand. Mark Twain has begun using the character as a mere mask, a device for satirizing Congress:

"There is no country in the world, sir, that pursues corruption as inveterately as we do. There is no country in the world whose representatives try each other as much as ours do, or stick to it as long on a stretch. I think there is something great in being a model for the whole civilized world, Washington."[31]

Of course, no member is ever expelled. "That," declares the Colonel in accents that would be repeated a few years later by Tom Sawyer, "would not be regular." Like Tom Sawyer, he is now maintaining a willed illusion. The self-deception is charming as a boy's game, but in a man lobbying a fraudulent bill through Congress it is cynicism.

Mark Twain's later comments suggest that he did not notice how this use of Sellers compromised the sound moral core he had ascribed to him in the beginning. But contemporary critics not only saw that Sellers had been depraved by Washington, they proclaimed him as a representative American type. Looking back from our own perspective, we can see here perhaps a more accurate account of the general American experience in the postwar years than Mark Twain intended or realized. The war and the postwar economic boom had destroyed the innocence of the American Adam, who could retain his pristine virtue only so long as he remained in an agrarian environment. The New York *Tribune*, for example, said that "the tribe of Sellers" included both an honest and a dishonest "division," but at this distance the distinction does not seem very sharp. The editorial continues:

At Washington, . . . Sellers is ubiquitous and influential. He has held a score of seats in every Congress within the memory of man, while in the lobby he is always in a majority. . . . His bill fails of passage for want of three minutes' time on the morning of the Fourth of March, and is

30. *The Gilded Age*, p. 210.
31. *Ibid.*, p. 358.

knocked on the head by the blow of the speaker's mallet which declares the Congress ended; or his project is referred to a Committee whose Chairman, he finds to his disgust, is virtuous. He inaugurates Pacific Railroads and lays the foundations for vast fortunes on which others build.... Many a man is a ... Sellers who would be astounded if you dubbed him so ... foolish fellows who think that real success is a thing to be stolen or bought or snatched out of the hand of Fate—these are representative Americans and representative of much that is raw and worthless in our civilization....[32]

A similar judgment underlies William Dean Howells's comment on *The Gilded Age* written in 1901, almost three decades after the book was published:

[Sellers] embodies the sort of Americanism which survived through the Civil War, and characterized in its boundlessly credulous, fearlessly adventurous, unconsciously burlesque excess the period of political and economic expansion which followed the war. Colonel Sellers was, in some rough sort, the America of that day, which already seems so remote, and is best imaginable through him.[33]

If "boundlessly" and "fearlessly" point here toward Sellers's generosity and improvidence as well as to his soaring fantasy, "credulous" and "unconsciously" point toward an element of self-deception in his enthusiasm.

To Howells, the mood represented by Sellers already seemed remote. But has not some of it survived into the present in American attitudes toward big business? Perhaps we are dealing with a trait deeply implanted in our popular culture. It is true that the shock of the Depression, World War II, and then the pieties of the cold war have banished much gaiety from public life. Most of the time we take business very seriously indeed. Although we may deplore the bluntness of Charlie Wilson's remark that what is good for General Motors is good for the country, almost everyone knows in his heart that Charlie was right. Recent popular fiction in the style of *Executive Suite* assures us the only good life is that of the Organization Man secure in the embrace of his corporation. Yet some aspects of the contemporary attitude toward big business still show more than a trace of what Mark Twain expresses in his portrayal of Beriah Sellers. As customers and consumers, at least, we suspect there is a joke in business somewhere: perhaps a joke on us, and a practical joke at that, but even so one that is rather amusing. How else explain our tolerance for the preposterous round-the-clock medicine show staged

32. Quoted in *Mark Twain and* The Gilded Age, pp. 210-211.
33. "Mark Twain: An Inquiry," in *My Mark Twain* (New York, 1910), p. 173.

for us, at our expense, by Madison Avenue? Neither Colonel Sellers nor his listeners—except perhaps a few hopeless innocents like Washington Hawkins—actually believe his marvelous improvisations. They are not intended to be, in the literal sense, either believed or disbelieved; they are meant to be enjoyed as works of art. The equivalents in our day are the productions of the advertising men and the "images" manufactured by public-relations experts. The fact that Sellers's gorgeous rhetoric nearly always has something to do with a swindle does not make it less enjoyable: and the same is true of television commercials. What I am trying to suggest is that we do not expect cast-iron facts from business, either in its advertising or in its pronouncements about policy. Fortunately, we do not swallow everything we are told, either by advertising men or by politicians.

Nevertheless, even though we do not believe in it, we seem to be enthralled by the fictive world they maintain for us with such immense expenditure of talent, energy, and money: that gleaming world in which everyone is happy, or soon will be, or at any rate can readily become so by a visit to his neighborhood drugstore or automobile agency. It is Tocqueville's master poetic idea in undiminished vividness. And it is still, as it was a hundred years ago, a function of innocence. This is all right as long as we are only playing. But it is dangerous for an innocent man, or society, to be like Beriah Sellers in Washington, carrying a childish innocence into a real world of power and responsibility.

MRS. STOWE'S CHARACTERS-IN-SITUATIONS AND A SOUTHERN LITERARY TRADITION

Richard Beale Davis

University of Tennessee

Although Edmund Wilson has recently admired Harriet Beecher Stowe's characterization in *Uncle Tom's Cabin* and Edward Wagenknecht has commented with approval on her theory of fiction as represented in this and other works, little has been said of her two anti-slavery novels as marking the definite beginnings of a literary tradition. Francis P. Gaines sees *Uncle Tom's Cabin* (1851) and *Dred* (1856) as belonging definitely to the plantation novel genre. But Jay B. Hubbell observes that the Negro has been treated by the twentieth-century Southern writer much more in the manner of Mrs. Stowe than in that of Thomas Nelson Page.[1] What these sometimes casual comments suggest is that in her two anti-slavery novels Mrs. Stowe presented a peculiar variety of characters and their unusual tragic situations with such force as to indicate to later writers the potentialities of the plantation novel as a vehicle of depth and complexity and moral seriousness. In other words, though there was to continue from Kennedy's *Swallow Barn* (1832), and a few other novels before it, through the works of John Esten Cooke, Thomas Nelson Page, and Margaret Mitchell a popular sentimental novel

---

1. F. P. Gaines, *The Plantation Novel* (New York, 1925), pp. 37 ff.; Leslie Fiedler, *Love and Death in the American Novel* (New York, 1960), p. 261; Edmund Wilson, *Patriotic Gore* (New York, 1962), pp. 3-58; Edward Wagenknecht, *Harriet Beecher Stowe: The Known and the Unknown* (New York, 1965), p. 160 and *passim*; Jay B. Hubbell, *The South in American Literature* (Durham, N. C., 1954), pp. 115-116, 387-392. Among other useful studies of Mrs. Stowe's life and work are Forrest Wilson, *Crusader in Crinoline: The Life of Harriet Beecher Stowe* (Philadelphia, 1941); Charles H. Foster, *The Rungless Ladder: Harriet Beecher Stowe and New England Puritanism* (Durham, N. C., 1954); Alexander Cowie, *The Rise of the American Novel* (New York, 1948), pp. 447-463 and *passim*; Charles E. Stowe, *Life of Harriet Beecher Stowe Compiled from Her Letters and Journals* (Boston, 1890); and H. R. Brown, *The Sentimental Novel in America, 1789-1860* (Durham, N. C., 1940), *passim*. See also Kenneth S. Lynn, Introduction to the John Harvard Library edition of *Uncle Tom's Cabin* (Cambridge, Mass., 1962). The Riverside edition of the *Writings of Harriet Beecher Stowe* (Boston, 1896) has been used for quotations from *Uncle Tom's Cabin* and *Dred*.

with perennially entertaining characters and situations, the use made by Mrs. Stowe of the same or similar scenes and even characters was to enlarge the dimensions of the form, particularly on its darker and moral side. And it is interesting and certainly significant that the principal writers who appear to have developed the suggestions incipient in Mrs. Stowe's novels have all been Southern-born, from Mark Twain and George W. Cable to Paul Green, William Faulkner, and Robert Penn Warren, among dozens of others since World War I.

What *Uncle Tom's Cabin* and *Dred* brought forth from the South immediately upon their appearance was a flood of vituperation and dozens of feeble tractarian novels attempting to prove the falsity of her pictures of the South. In the three decades after the Civil War came the moderately tempered, saccharine depictions of life in a paradisiacal South that never was. Even then, a few natives of the region, who could view without nostalgia and prejudice and sometimes with a real sense of the richness and tragic complexity of what the South had been and was, were creating art, sometimes with a tinge of didacticism, out of the materials and somewhat in the manner which Mrs. Stowe had employed. Chief among these were Cable and Twain. Louis Rubin has seen "The Road to Yoknapatawpha"[2] leading straight from one novel of Cable's, but the present writer would suggest that it broadens out also from a path plotted by Twain, and that both Twain's and Cable's paths are extensions, consciously and unconsciously, of certain qualities in the work of Harriet Beecher Stowe. Every one of the Southern authors whose works are mentioned below is intrinsically a better writer, in artistic achievement and vision, than the author of *Uncle Tom's Cabin*. But she set patterns or gave hints—and a weight of moral passion—they have in varying degree followed and developed.

I

For purposes primarily of convenience, Mrs. Stowe's white characters will be first considered. Both whites and blacks are remarkably varied because some of them act partly as mouthpieces for their creator and at the same time are genuine individuals, and simultaneously some of them represent the many facets of slavery and the Southern way of life as Mrs. Stowe saw them. One must agree with Edmund Wilson that most of her figures "leap into being with a

2. *The Faraway Country: Writers of the Modern South* (Seattle, 1963), pp. 21-42.

vitality that is all the more striking for the ineptitude of the prose that presents them."[3] She hardly knew the South firsthand, but she spent her life observing character, and through her reading and experience in Cincinnati had developed an almost uncanny perception of what the Southern nature was, especially in its relations between the two races. In the Preface to the first edition of *Uncle Tom's Cabin* she remarked that "In the Northern states, these representations may perhaps, be thought caricatures; in the Southern states are witnesses who know their fidelity." The Southern witnesses to the faithfulness of her portrayals did not appear at once, but, as we have noted, they did appear, and in the form of the principal prose artists of their time.

There is no stereotype of the Southern planter in *Uncle Tom's Cabin* and *Dred*, for he is represented by at least three or four distinct individuals in each. In *Uncle Tom's Cabin* Mr. Shelby of Kentucky, the first introduced to the reader and Tom's first owner, is a well-meaning, kindly man who must sell some of his slaves to pay his debts from mismanagement and gambling. He is simply a man of weak and shallow feeling, led into a crime against humanity by the laws and social institutions of his time and region. So also with Simon Legree, the Vermont-born villain of the novel, who is likewise a plantation owner. Though Mrs. Stowe for fairly obvious reasons gave him Yankee origins, his lust, his sadism, his cowardice, his drunkenness—she is careful to point out—might be found in man anywhere. But it is only in the slaveholding Deep South, the novelist insists, that he can fully exercise these qualities that lead to the tragedies of which he is the overt agent.

The pair of Louisiana brothers, Augustine and Alfred St. Clare, are a study in contrasts. Hearty, country-living Alfred scoffs at Augustine's reminder that "All men are born free and equal." Yet Mrs. Stowe endows Alfred with strong and in many respects likable qualities and shows the strong bond of affection between the brothers.

It is on Augustine St. Clare among the plantation owners that the novelist focuses most of her attention. Reared partly by paternal relatives in Vermont, Augustine imbibed his notions of justice and equality among men and hypocrisy among religionists not from his Northern kin or early environment but from himself, his reading

3. *Patriotic Gore*, p. 5.

and his observation. Quiet, compassionate, deeply attached to his one child "Little Eva," and resigned to a hypochondriac wife (of whom more below), he looks at the South with clear eyes and even at his confinement within its system with a wry sense of humor. He is at once Mrs. Stowe's mouthpiece and the voice of the Southern conscience she believes exists. But it is significant that he can do and tries to do nothing to right the wrongs organic in the system itself. Once he thought he might have been an emancipator, but then he "got the despair of living Solomon did." And he takes it out in talking, especially to his New England relative Miss Ophelia, who has come to New Orleans to supervise his household.

Augustine St. Clare looks behind, around, and beyond at his native region. He loves music, and he sings the *Dies Irae* and plays Mozart's *Requiem* both for himself and his land and people. He never becomes a mere symbol of conscience or a conscience in the South, yet like his creator he is a moralist.

In the better organized but less effective *Dred* Mrs. Stowe's gallery of portraits of planters continues. Here her setting is North Carolina, which she then knew absolutely nothing about from personal experience. In Supreme Court Judge Clayton, father of the hero, appears the upright, troubled, legal-minded planter and jurist who must decide against human right in his son's first case (prosecution of a white man who had beaten the slave Milly) on purely legal grounds. When he gives his decision, a reversal of a lower court's finding in favor of punishment, he discourses at length on the evils of the slave system but points out that slaves are legally only property, and that he can do no more than decide in favor of the right to retain—and discipline—that property. Dignified and strong, he puts the law before the individual. The whole case is a dramatic and telling point in Mrs. Stowe's attack upon the institution which has compelled such a decision from a good and intelligent man.

John Gordon, the jovial uncle of the heroine, habitually fleeced by overseers, poor whites, and Negroes in his vicinity and hectored by his wife, is an intriguing picture of the Southern aristocrat of democratic behavior. He abhors the so-called educated democracy of the North and believes that contentment will come in the South when the poor white has been put in his proper place beside the Negro.

In the heroine Nina Gordon's brother Tom, Mrs. Stowe paints

in broad strokes her most devastating picture of the Southern land-owner. Tom is the aristocrat at his worst. He has thrown away an education, gambled away a fortune, brutally beaten or killed his own and other people's Negroes, lusted after his half-brother the octoroon Harry's nearly white wife and tried to take her by force, and after his sister's death instituted a reign of terror in her plantation household. Evil he would have been anywhere, but slavery has allowed him to create worse tragedy than he ever could have in the free world.

Edward Clayton, son of the Judge, is in some respects another Augustine St. Clare. He believes as sincerely as the Louisianian in the moral, economic, and social evil of slavery. He is as "literary" as —perhaps even more so than—St. Clare, for he reads and broods deeply on the world in which he lives. But Clayton is a man of much more force. Among his reasons for studying law was his belief that it might be a means of proving openly that slavery was a *guardian*, not a *chattel-holding* institution. He believes that there was no more use in trying to make the Negroes Anglo-Saxons than in "making a grapevine into a pear tree. I train the grapevine." In long conversations with his father after the lost legal case he continues his arguments against slavery on moral grounds. Clayton, said his usually cynical friend Frank Russel, "is as radical and impracticable as the Sermon on the Mount, and that is the most impracticable thing I know in literature."

In her minor white males in *Uncle Tom's Cabin* and *Dred* the author suggests other patterns of characters-in-situations. In the former three slave traders present variants of evil evolving from the antebellum traffic. Young George Shelby, son of the weak, well-meaning sire and strong mother, hunting Uncle Tom to free him and finding him dead, speaks as another awakened conscience of the South.

In *Dred* there are several well-drawn minor characters. Repulsively alive is Mr. Jekyll, a lawyer and Calvinist church elder, who connives with Tom Gordon to recover quadroons set free by a relative. Jekyll's favorite subject is the nature of true virtue. Here are developed a whole gallery of clerical types, ranging from the humble and simple Father Dickson and his more expedient brother Father Bonnie to the sophisticated city preachers, such as Dr. Cushing, "moral effeminacy," Dr. Calker, a Presbyterian who loved his church better than Christianity, and the Reverend Shubael Pack-thread, the fence-straddler whose words were always capable of double interpretation.

Of the four major female characters of *Uncle Tom's Cabin* little need be said here of Evangeline St. Clare, "Little Eva," for a century now a figure of folk and popular romance. Miss Ophelia, righteous New Englander who comes to look after her cousin Augustine's household because his wife is incapable of doing so, is a significant study of the Yankee in a Southern setting and of a certain kind of Northern attitude toward the Negro. Mrs. Stowe grants her piety, moral opposition to slavery, and goodness of motive, but then points out her personal dislike of the Negro as an individual.

Most interesting, most exasperating, and most familiar to readers of Faulkner, for example, is Marie St. Clare, Augustine's wife. Once a reigning New Orleans belle, she has faded into a querulous, self-pitying, monstrously egocentric, cruel hypochondriac who would in-stitute order among her servants by the lash. She complains about everything and everybody, including her husband and child, who look after her with extreme solicitude. Marie St. Clare's opposite is Mrs. Shelby, the "woman of a high class, both intellectually and morally," who had to be her husband's conscience as well as her own. Uncle Tom's first mistress manages her multitudinous affairs unobtrusively and efficiently, and she voices again and again her opposition to the whole slave system.

Five plantation chatelaines grace the pages of *Dred*, or at least four of them *grace* the tale. Aunt Nesbit, who acts as a sort of chap-erone for the heroine, Nina Gordon, has so little concern for her Negroes that she hires out a faithful personal maid to a man she knows will treat her brutally. The other four ladies Mrs. Stowe treats with respect as she emphasizes their differences.

Aunt Maria, Mrs. John Gordon, is a woman whose "bright, keen, hazel eyes, fine teeth, and the breadth of . . . ample form attest the vitality of the old Virginia stock from which she sprang." Lines of anxiety crease her brow, however, for plantation household manage-ment was for her something of a burden, because, the author tells us, she was a penny-pincher by nature. She tolerated her Negroes only because she felt that supervising their labors was a little better than not having them. Mrs. Clayton, the hero's mother, dark-eyed and imaginative, again a fine figure, concurring heart and soul in her husband's and son's feelings for the Negro, is Mrs. Gordon's opposite in most ways. Yet even Mrs. Gordon is portrayed not unsympathetically.

Mrs. Clayton's beautiful daughter Anne, the hero's favorite sister, has at twenty-seven never married because her noble father and brother spoiled her possible taste for other men. Possessed of an estate of her own in South Carolina, she rules her slaves *with love* in an harmonious household, as visiting Nina Gordon is quick to note.

The heroine of *Dred*, Nina Gordon (at one time the author used her name as the title for the novel), is at the beginning of the tale the kind of coquette and heartless flirt best known today in Scarlett O'Hara. Nina is engaged to three men at once (including Edward Clayton) and is resolved above all else to have a good time. Thanks to Clayton's patience and love and counsel, Nina's character deepens and broadens; she awakes to the moral obliquity of slavery, and falls deeply in love with Clayton. Nina is vividly drawn, but is not quite real enough in her development.

Certainly many of Mrs. Stowe's people of color owe something of their comic characters to the minstrel show popular in her day. And they may owe a great deal to the comic and semi-comic faithful sable retainers created by her countrymen Cooper and Simms, as well as to a number of white servants in the work of her favorite girlhood author, Sir Walter Scott. The Shelby's Sam, for example, in his hilarious fun-loving semi-roguery, is kin to his brethren in the work of these three novelists. But he probably develops beyond any other fictional Negro before his time as a real individual, and he constitutes an insult to the white traders' intelligence.[4] Sam, more than Cooper's or Simms's or the early backwoods humorists' scapegrace black servants, anticipates some of the traits of a dozen twentieth-century Southern characters.

Topsy, whatever she may have become on the stage, is in the novel, as Kenneth S. Lynn has pointed out, a bundle of perversities reflecting the guilty consciences of her owners and finally tamed, as was Hawthorne's Pearl, by an overt acknowledgment of love. Perhaps the shock of recognition from the reader of the twentieth-century novel is strongest as he gets brief glances at two minor characters, Lucy and Cassy. The former, sold down the river with her last baby, is tricked out of the child and leaps from the riverboat to her

4. Lynn, Introduction to *Uncle Tom's Cabin*, p. xii.

death. Even more powerful a story potentially is that of Cassy, nearly white mistress of Simon Legree, who is sent to the fields for disciplining. She aids and nurses Uncle Tom and tells him her story. Educated in a convent, she came at fourteen to her white father's funeral. Though the parent had always meant to set her free, he had never done so. She was sold in turn to two young planters, to each of whom she was passionately devoted, and with whom she lived in style. The first sold her to pay for gambling debts, and the second died. Then she came into the hands of Simon Legree. Here are the materials of a complex and poignant story.

Uncle Tom's character has in the public mind, because of its debasement in play and musical, become synonymous with fawning and complaisance. But the broad-shouldered black man Mrs. Stowe actually drew, perhaps still unbelievably pious, has convincing strength because his undeviating gentleness is clearly undeviating defiance of the kind his race at its best was to represent from his time on.

The beautiful quadroon stereotype of earlier and later fiction is certainly suggested in Eliza as it is in Cassy (who turns out to be her mother). But Eliza and her equally nearly white husband George Harris are individualized. Not nearly so aggressive as her husband, Eliza yet rises to her child's danger and flees with him across the floating ice to the Ohio, shown in a scene long since incorporated into American folklore as well as into drama and painting.

Eliza's husband George Harris is intensely devoted to his family, but he also looks beyond it to the problem of the Negro as individual and as a potential equal of the white. His hard master withdrew him from the factory (where he was producing a neat income for that brutal and incompetent man) because he heard that George's inventive genius had resulted in certain remarkable improvements, and the master wanted no Negro to be too much or think himself too much. Thus George was returned to heavy field labor. His bitter question to his wife, "Who made this man my master?" is preceded by a comparison of abilities of the slave and his owner. Who made me what I am, why am I what I am, become haunting questions in the fiction of later generations.

The Negroes in *Dred* are almost as varied in character as those in *Uncle Tom's Cabin*. Again lesser characters like the mulatto boy Tomtit, the coachman Old Hundred, and the musician Dulcimer are close to comic stereotypes. Harry's beautiful Louisiana-born wife, the Creole-of-color Lisette, is scarcely more than the conventional beautiful quadroon.

But four others, while most show kinship with some of the personae of Mrs. Stowe's earlier novel, are original enough to be noticed. Dred himself, certainly inspired by, if not modeled upon, Nat Turner of the famous Virginia rebellion bearing his name, is an elusive and therefore not entirely convincing figure. Partly noble savage, partly mystic, partly the semi-biblical avenger, he is apparently meant to be some sort of symbol of the release of his race from bondage. That he does not successfully dominate the novel, even in the author's mind, is evidenced by the fact noted above, that the book was published at one time under the title *Nina Gordon.*

Old Tiff is held by some critics to be merely a variant, by others to be a superior version, of Uncle Tom. Actually his situation is entirely different from Tom's, and what he shows primarily is attachment to the children of the blue-blooded mistress who had married a poor white, a resourcefulness in time of need, a tendency to giggle, and withal a genuine, quiet dignity.

Aunt Milly, selfish Mrs. Nesbit's "tall, broad-shouldered, deep chested African woman, with a figure approaching corpulence," is the offspring of African royalty captured in war. Inherent dignity she had, a penchant for picturesque habiliments, a depth of tropical passion, and a generosity which equaled the passion. Her drollery and abundant mother wit are contrasted with the real tragedy of her situation, her lost children and her painful beating when she was protecting a child at the time she had been hired out by her unfeeling mistress. Mrs. Stowe lets Milly tell dark tales of her life, and Milly does it well. She was one who had endured.

By far the most carefully drawn of the Negro figures is Harry, quadroon elder half-brother of Nina and Tom Gordon. In some respects he is the George Harris of this novel, but his situation is more subtle and more dangerous. He is actually the male protector and manager of estates for his sister Nina, who does not know of their relationship, but to whom he is devoted. His white brother Tom, who presumably does know of the blood relationship, tries, as we have noted, to seduce Harry's wife. Proud, handsome, well-educated, tender, Harry is forced to feel pressures of white-black blood in a number of ways George Harris never did. To his wife he observes bitterly: "Lisette, I'm just like the bat in the fable; I'm neither bird nor beast. How often I've wished that I was a good honest, black nigger . . . ! Then I should know what I was; but, I'm neither one thing nor another. . . ."

This may be Mrs. Stowe speaking, but it is also the voice of the later Southern writer as he and his region's mind become more introspective.

II

By 1880 the flood of local color in fiction was full. No section contributed to its development more than did the South in the next two decades. The Northern reader who had a generation before devoured Mrs. Stowe's pages with fascination, horror, and indignation now found himself pleasantly entertained by these new portraits of gracious or quaint ways of life which were pouring forth from the conquered region. In most of the new tales, Uncle Toms had been replaced by Uncle Remuses, and Marie St. Clares had been forgotten behind the new bevy of plantation belles. The black had returned where he belonged, with the faithful retainers of the pre-Stowean plantation novel.

Perhaps, as has occasionally been suggested, a certain feeling of guilt at the rascality and harshness of Reconstruction treatment of the South was in a measure responsible for Northern readers' easy acceptance of this perfumed picture of a people and a region with which they had too recently been in mortal combat. The harsher Reconstruction politicians had by 1880 been publicly repudiated for the most part. The feeling in journalistic and publishing circles at least was that this new-old portrait of the smiling South must be accepted at face value. They were all for peace, and profit.

In the generation after the war there were naturally in the North a few literary dissenters who declined to accept the portrait as authentic, though today John W. DeForest seems the only one among them of any real artistic stature. What is most interesting is that from 1880 to the present, the major writers who have denied the authenticity of the happy-South-under-slavery portrait or the later free-Negro-happy-in-his-place overlay of the Stowe picture have been Southern-born, and in their writing have developed a fairly distinct tradition of character-in-situation to show *how it was* and *what it is* in the South. Every reader of twentieth-century fiction is aware of the work of some of these Southerners, but he may not be aware that their kind of work goes back at least to 1880, and that they seem direct heirs—not imitators—of Mrs. Stowe in her slavery novels. Actually, there are dozens if not scores of these Southern writers—playwrights and poets as well as fictionists. But there is room in this essay to cite only a few, and even then to suggest their methods only in selected instances.

In the late nineteenth century George W. Cable and Mark Twain traveled the lecture circuits together, and each wrote at least two novels about the regions in which they were born. Cable wrote primarily of the lower South and Twain of the upper and middle Mississippi region. In quite different ways they depicted the relation of Negro and white as the South's great moral problem.

Cable's *The Grandissimes* (1880) is a *Kulturroman* set in New Orleans at the period when the United States was taking over the Louisiana Territory from the French. It is essentially a representation of the clash of two white "races" between and among themselves, especially in their attitude toward a third "race," the Negro-quadroon. Cable's biographer comments that despite its glamorous and remote scene, and its study of moral problems existing in a particular social order, "it is first of all a novel of character."[5] Like Mrs. Stowe, the author insisted his personae were copied from living models. And like hers, his moral problems are presented in terms of character, each in a particular situation.

The Creole mother and daughter Nancanou are as charming Southern belles as Nina Gordon, but they are poor and speak a form of English with a delightful disregard for its structural cadences. The Fusiliers, De Grapions, and Grandissimes may be city gentlemen of mercantile or professional interests, but they also have plantations. Yet it is in the closer contacts of city life that Cable presents his comedies and tragedies of alien Anglo-Saxon, native and aristocratic Creole, the free man of color, and the pure black African.

Frowenfeld the newcomer and Dr. Keene represent a sort of detached Anglo-Saxon consciousness and conscience, highly appreciative of the good and bad qualities of the changing society in which they find themselves. Agricola Fusilier is as inflexible a champion of the old order as was Alfred St. Clare or Uncle John Gordon. But the primary racial moral problem in *The Grandissimes* is somewhat different from that of Mrs. Stowe's novels. Here the quadroon-octoroon characters in whom the tragedy centers are f. m. c.'s (free

5. Arlin Turner, *George W. Cable* (Durham, N. C., 1956), p. 91.

men of color), emancipated by their white fathers long before. What Cable is telling us is that their problems remain tragic. The beautiful octoroon sorceress Palmyre la Philosophe is hopelessly in love with the white Honoré Grandissime, and his quadroon half-brother of the same name hopelessly in love with Palmyre. Here both white and colored brothers Grandissime are sympathetic characters. Both possess a high sense of honor and both some business acumen (the darker Honoré more). It is the white Honoré who, like St. Clare and Clayton, ponders the place of the man of color in the South. In defiance of tradition and family threats, he makes his half-brother a full partner in the family business. But he realizes that he has no more solved the problem of a place for the free man of color in Southern society than St. Clare or Clayton had solved it for the slave.

Chapters XXVII-XXIX present "The Story of Bras-Coupé," the tale of a giant one-time African prince somewhat reminiscent of the chained-chieftain of Melville's "Benito Cereno" and of Faulkner's Sam Fathers and his mighty Negro ancestors. The dramatic story is too long and involved to repeat here. But the dark tragedies of Bras-Coupé's involvements are among the powerful elements of the novel.

Though Cable sets his tale at a significant historical moment in the slavery era, it is quite clear that he is thinking strongly of the intensified problem of the free man of color's place in a Southern society after the Civil War. In *John March, Southerner* (1894) the same author brings his scene-in-time up to the Reconstruction age. Since this was a period of peculiar old and new problems with which Mrs. Stowe never dealt, both character and circumstance diverge more widely from her patterns than they did in *The Grandissimes*. But many of them remain, and others grow out of characters-in-situations of the actual slavery period.

By this date even Richard W. Gilder, the Northern editor who had praised *The Grandissimes*, objected to the unpleasant things Cable had to say about the South in *John March*.[6] Gilder did not want depicted at all, much less dramatized in fiction, such matters as the education of the Negro and the evils and problems arising from the industrial expansion of the South. Here Cable deliberately chose a different milieu, north Georgia, where the problems were archetypically indigenous to the whole South and not noticeably

6. Rubin, *The Faraway Country*, pp. 28-29.

differentiated even in part, as were lower Louisiana's problems. His tainted and tarnished Confederate heroes anticipate some of Faulkner's, and are presented far more satirically. John March himself is fully in the traditions of St. Clare and Clayton in his pondering of regional problems and of the latter in his attempt to do something about them.

Mark Twain, "first and always a Southerner,"[7] with greater art and less obvious reformist tendencies than Cable, through a whole gallery of personae in short and long fiction presents Southern life, and certainly with a moral bias as firm as his whilom platform partner's. Two of his novels, *The Adventures of Huckleberry Finn* (1884) and *Pudd'nhead Wilson* (1894), are perhaps our best cases in point. Their familiarity to most readers will necessitate only a brief recapitulation of their place in our tradition. Two major Southern themes run through these books, the false standards of the aristocracy and the problem of liberation of the Negro, spiritually as well as physically. Connected with and perhaps a part of the latter is the special problem of the near-white, suggested only in *Pudd'nhead Wilson*.

In *Huckleberry Finn*, Twain depicts in ironic satire the ridiculous and tragic in the Grangerford-Shepherdson feud and in cynical Colonel Sherburn's murder of the poor wretch who reflected upon "his honor." Even the Duke and Dauphin are travesties upon Southern notions of chivalry. But the story is principally about Huck and Jim, and what one Southern boy will do, when faced with the dilemma of going against the law and mores of his region, and his developing sense of moral responsibility to another human being, albeit a black one. In the famous meditation in Chapter XXI on what to do with Jim, ending with "All right, then, I'll go to Hell," Huck makes his final decision on the basis of humanity, as Mrs. Stowe insisted the Southern white should.

In *Pudd'nhead Wilson* (by no means as successful a book as *Huckleberry Finn*) Twain tries too hard on the farce and not hard enough in creating believable characters, though he succeeds in at least two. The town of the setting, Dawson's landing, has as its chief citizens York Leicester Driscoll, proud of his Virginia ancestry, his manners, and his hospitality, and a few others also of impeccable Virginia ancestry. Into the village wanders David Wilson, college-

7. Kenneth S. Lynn, *Mark Twain and Southwestern Humor* (Boston, 1959), p. 143.

bred New Yorker seeking his fortune. His nickname—in the book's title—derives from the town's stupidity in failing to understand a deadpan remark of his and then putting him down as a fool. Wilson goes his serene way, which includes finger-printing all the town's inhabitants.

Then appears Roxy the slave, fifteen-sixteenths white and possessed of a baby thirty-one of thirty-two parts white. Roxy is drawn with discernment and humor. Unlike Cassy and Eliza, she is sexually promiscuous from choice, aggressive, greedy. Afraid that her child may be sold down the river, she exchanges him with her white master's baby of the same age. The sale down the river does not occur, and the white child grows up as an uncouth clown and play-mate-servant to his bad-tempered and cowardly nearly-white presumed master. Many years later, in a moment of pique, Roxy reveals to her son his true origin. Afterwards he thinks as he tosses sleepless:

"Why were niggers *and* whites made? What crime did the first uncreated nigger commit that the curse of birth was decreed for him? And why is this awful difference made between white and black? . . . How hard the nigger's fate seems, this morning!—yet until last night such a thought never entered my head."

Through Wilson's glass-plate finger-printings made when the two boys were infants, the truth comes out at last, but not before Twain throws in a few more gibes at the South's notions of aristocracy and honor. The gibes also continue to the last page. For the impostor child of Roxy, sentenced as a white man to life imprisonment for murder, is declared a Negro and is therefore such valuable property that the governor pardons him at once so that he can at last be sold down the river. The restored white boy and rightful heir finds himself, presumably for life, acutely embarrassed by his gait, his manners, and his lack of education. He feels at ease only in the kitchen, and even in church casts longing glances towards the "solacing refuge" of its "nigger gallery" which is now closed to him forever.

The twentieth century has produced in the Southern Flowering a galaxy of writers who have re-examined, with probing care and moral anxiety, the nature of their region past and present. Most of them have seen, as Hawthorne did for his New England, the presentness of the past as well as the past itself. The Southern social structure, town and country, Negro and white, has been expressed in terms of characters enmeshed in environment. Paul Green in *In Abraham's*

Bosom (1926), Erskine Caldwell in *Kneel to the Rising Sun* (1935), and Lillian Smith in *Strange Fruit* (1944) are among those who have been concerned with miscegenation and Negro longings and their consequent tragedy for individuals of both races. One might go on with the roll call, but space permits only a glance at the fiction of two of the most distinguished mid-twentieth-century writers, Robert Penn Warren and William Faulkner.

Warren, Kentucky born, has from his first book *John Brown: The Making of a Martyr* displayed a persistent interest in the Southern white's problems as they relate to the Negro and vice versa. *World Enough and Time* (1950), his fictional version of the Beauchamp-Sharp affair, has as its central figure in the closing chapters a kind of debased and deformed Dred, the outlaw Louis Caddo, "La Grand' Bosse." In his verse-novel *Brother to Dragons* (1953), Warren's inciting situation is the brutal murder of a slave by two of Thomas Jefferson's Kentucky nephews, leading to a series of dramatic dialogues with Jefferson himself as the protagonist and a principal speaker and including "R. P. W." as a persona. It is a study of the fallibility of the dogma of man's perfectibility, and it is presented in terms of characters caught in a Southern situation, most of them Southern aristocrats. Though Warren is concerned here as elsewhere with man's search for self-definition and its concomitant, the meaning of humanity, it is a tale of Southern idealism which leads to individual and family tragedy, a tragedy springing directly from the state of Southern society.

In *Band of Angels* (1955) Warren took up the brief story of Cassy from *Uncle Tom's Cabin*, or from some of its sources or derivatives, and developed a full-length analysis of a person like Cassy in blood and education, a careless white father who meant to free her, and a remarkable gallery of men who come into her life. The heroine's name is Amantha Starr, and she tells her own story. A student at Oberlin, she did not know of her slight touch of Negro blood or that she was a slave until she was seized at her father's funeral. This is melodrama that is history, for Warren read the source documents much as Mrs. Stowe had done.[8]

This is a development of Cassy in an intricacy and complexity of situation Mrs. Stowe could never have imagined. But like Mrs. Stowe, Warren insists, by means of his Yankee captain protagonist and his

8. Charles H. Bohner, *Robert Penn Warren* (New York, 1964), p. 128, and Leonard Casper, *Robert Penn Warren: The Dark and Bloody Ground* (Seattle, 1960), p. 188.

treatment of Negroes in the West and in Chicago, that Amantha's is a *national* problem. The most unusual twist is Amantha's husband Yankee Tobias Lear's self-satire, his constant weighing of his own and others' motives, the quality which makes him tell "Manty" in anger at an exorbitant sum she has paid a worthless Negro: "It was for this we bled and died. Hooray for William Lloyd Garrison, Harriet Beecher Stowe, Abe Lincoln and me."

The microcosm of Yoknapatawpha County, owned and peopled by William Faulkner, presents all of Mrs. Stowe's characters and problems directly or indirectly and a plenitude of others she never imagined. His characters do *not* leap into vital being through inept prose, but emerge gradually from the graceful and extended rhythms of his words into enduring life. They in their situations ponder the South to a depth she never plumbed, and act in passion, including the sexual, as she would never have thought of having them do. Lubricity and ambition and fears and hopes drive them into actions of grotesquerie and horror and despair and, in a few cases, into serenity. For Faulkner has not needed to iterate that he presents people in predicaments in time and place who represent all humanity.

The plantation aristocracy appears in all the rich variety of its weakness and strength. When his settings are antebellum or when his personae are allowed to tell their tales of those days, the planters are often as noble as the best of Mrs. Stowe's. One gathers that the earlier generations of Sartorises, Compsons, even Beauchamps and McCaslins and De Spains and Carotherses (if these latter were then aristocrats) were in most respects the equals of the St. Clares, the Gordons, or the Claytons.

But we see the decline in successive generations of Sartorises. The Compsons, founders of the town of Jefferson and always among its leading citizens, begin and end as plantation aristocrats but can be traced in a steady decline of body, mind, and spirit from the first Jason to the monstrous money-mad Jason IV and his idiot brother and nymphomaniac sister. The De Spains descend into mere urban bankers and philanderers. The McCaslins and Edmundses and Beauchamps live on only in their Negro-blooded descendants.

The women are frequently as tragic as their menfolk. Even the Aunt Jinny of *Sartoris* and Rosa Coldfield of *Absalom, Absalom!* are not faded roses of old romance, but resolute women, often

Cassandras prophesying but not preventing the doom of their race. Mrs. Jason Compson III (née Caroline Bascomb) of *The Sound and the Fury* is neurotic self-pitying Marie St. Clare brought down to the twentieth century, surrounded by an alcoholic brother, four self-destroying children, and a family of black servants. Joanna Burden, though hardly of plantation stock, a daughter of the New England Puritans and fanatic "uplifter" of the Negro by whom she is fascinated and repelled, is in a sense Aunt Ophelia reincarnated on a ruined Mississippi plantation.

Miscegenation has brought literally upon scores of Faulkner's characters, black and white, a Gothic night of agony and judgment. The tragic train of events in *Absalom, Absalom!* begins its accelerating movement when the mountaineer-born plantation owner Sutpen refuses to recognize, even by a single word or gesture, his octoroon son Charles. Incipient incest, actual fratricide, bloody murder, and fiery death are among the retributions Sutpen brings down upon himself and his family.

Light in August, in the plot-thread concerned with Joe Christmas and his mistress the Joanna Burden mentioned above, is equally a tale of miscegenation, or alleged miscegenation, for the tragedy behind the tragedy is that Christmas never knows whether he has Negro blood or not. And Faulkner forgets the clergy no more than did Mrs. Stowe, for in the Reverend Gail Hightower and the quasi-preacher of Calvinism "Doc" Hines are two of the memorable, and perhaps most perplexing, creations of modern fiction.

In *The Bear* (the longer version) Faulkner tells the story of the McCaslins and their kin and the last of the white McCaslins, who achieves peace only as a humble carpenter. But in this story, too, is the tragic dignity of Sam Fathers, part Negro and part Indian, mighty hunter, and symbol of the white man's sin against the two races. In the same tale a white McCaslin tells a Negro of the curse on the land which is the South, and a few pages later, summarizes the qualities of the Negro race. After admitting some of their weaker qualities, he concludes that they are "a people who have learned humility through suffering and learned pride through the endurance which survived the suffering."

The principal "voice" in Faulkner on racial and other moral problems is Gavin Stevens, by no means always Faulkner himself. But certainly in his musings on the nature of Southern good and evil and his will to do good, he is a recognizable descendant of Augustine St. Clare and Edward Clayton.

On the individual Negro, near-white and coal-black, small land-owner, migrant worker, slave, or servant, Faulkner has focused much of his attention. Joe Christmas and Charles Bon we have already mentioned. But there are the memorable Lucas Beauchamp of *Intruder in the Dust,* proud of his descent from an old white family and willing to be lynched for a crime he did not commit; the two Nancys of *Requiem for a Nun* and "That Evening Sun Go Down," each waiting for death as retribution; and Dilsey, the cook of the Compsons who has seen what the Lord giveth and what he taketh away. "They endured."[9]

One of Faulkner's last public appearances was at West Point in 1962. There, as earlier at Virginia and Princeton, intensely interested students interrogated him about his own books and characters, his theories of fiction, and his opinions of other writers past and present. In answer to a query as to why he thought Mrs. Stowe wrote one of her novels, he replied:

> I would say that *Uncle Tom's Cabin* was written out of a violent and misdirected compassion and ignorance of the author toward a situation which she knew only by hearsay. But it was not an intellectual process, it was better than that; it was out of her heart. It just happened that she was telling the story of Uncle Tom and the little girl, not telling the story—not writing a treatise on the impressions of slavery. . . . She was simply writing a story that moved her, seemed so terrible and so hot to her that it had to be told. But I think she was writing about Uncle Tom as a human being—and Legree and Eliza as human beings, not as puppets.[10]

Cable and Twain and Warren and Faulkner likewise knew of their Southern situations partly by hearsay, but more than Mrs. Stowe they knew by experience. What they followed her in, if they did not learn it from her, was the writing of a story of their own land that moved them, a story told by placing human beings in situations. Consciously or not, they were moved by the same story that moved her, and in their loftier and more sophisticated perspective, and with greater abilities, they raised it from moral sentimentalism to the moral art which is a major Southern tradition.

9. Faulkner, "Appendix" [Foreword] to the Random House ed. of *The Sound and the Fury* (New York, 1929), p. 22.
10. Joseph L. Fant and Robert Ashley, eds., *Faulkner at West Point* (New York, 1964), p. 104.

UNCLE TOM'S CABIN *IN ITALY*

James Woodress

University of California, Davis

When William Dean Howells arrived in Italy in 1861 to take up his duties as American consul in Venice, he found that Harriet Beecher Stowe was as well known to Italians as to Americans. In *Italian Journeys* he writes of an evening spent in Padua in the company of several professors from the university: "Then we began to talk of distinguished American writers, of whom intelligent Italians always know at least four, in this succession,—Cooper, Mrs. Stowe, Longfellow, and Irving. Mrs. Stowe's *Capanna di Zio Tom* is, of course, universally read."[1]

At the time Howells made the observation, the novel had existed only ten years. Cooper, who had been translated in Italy as early as 1828, had twenty-four years' headstart. His popularity rested on sixteen of his novels available in Italian editions at the time Howells went to Italy; yet not one of Cooper's novels went through as many editions between 1828 and 1852 as *Uncle Tom's Cabin* did in a single decade. Then, as now, no other American book ever has been so widely distributed and read in Italy as *La capanna dello Zio Tom*.

Mrs. Stowe's popularity continues today despite the tremendous Italian interest in later American authors. A current list of American writers well known in Italy would contain a score of names, mostly contemporary and many as recent as Saul Bellow or Philip Roth; but even the enormous popularity of Faulkner and Hemingway has failed to eclipse the long and continuing acquaintance that Italians have had with *Uncle Tom's Cabin*. Italian interest in American literature, which began as a trickle in the last century, grew to a stream in the early twentieth century, and swelled to a torrent after World War II, has continued to carry Mrs. Stowe along the flood with her belletristic betters. The chief difference between the novel's nineteenth-century status and its present standing lies in its emergence as a child's classic and its gradual decline as a novel for adults.

Uncle Tom's Cabin has enjoyed continuous popularity in Italy

1. (New York, 1867), pp. 212-213.

since it first was published both in Milan and Turin in 1852.[2] Apparently, the novel has never been out of print, and a hundred editions and reprintings have supplied the steady demand. Initially, nine Italian editions were brought out between 1853 and 1854 when the book was new; the demand still was great enough in 1953 to warrant six more editions in a single year. As a standard child's book, it is to be found in all bookstores in abridged and illustrated editions; but it is also available in adult editions ranging from careless abridgements to adequately translated complete texts. It is probably safe to say that every Italian with a high school education has read the book.

In view of the novel's vogue in Italy, it comes as a surprise to Italians to learn that the book is not so well known in the United States. An American professor is fortunate if half of the students in his undergraduate survey course in American literature have read *Uncle Tom's Cabin,* and it is a rare college course in which the novel is required or collateral reading. The book is one that Americans know about but have little experience with directly. They use "Simon Legree" and "Uncle Tom" as nouns without having a sure knowledge of the source of the terms.

When the Modern Library edition of the novel appeared in 1948, *Uncle Tom's Cabin* had been out of print in the United States for a number of years. Interest in the book had steadily diminished in the decades after the Civil War. Apparently the novel had seemed an artifact of the anti-slavery struggle made obsolete by the war. The postwar neglect of it was perhaps due to the strained relations between the North and the South. "The Northerners," as one observer put it, "embarrassed by the memory of the war and not without feelings of guilt, did not care to be reminded of the issue which had given rise to so much bitterness." And in the South, "where before the war any public discussion of slavery had by general tacit agreement been banned, nothing afterwards was wanted less than Northern criticism of pre-war conditions."[3] Whatever the reason, it was possible to grow up in the United States in the early decades of this century without ever having seen a copy of *Uncle Tom's Cabin.*

The Library of Congress catalogue reflects this neglect of the

2. The pioneer study on this subject is Frederick H. Jackson, *"Uncle Tom's Cabin* in Italy," *Symposium,* VII, 323-332 (1953), which surveys the reception of the novel in 1852-1853 with particular reference to the controversy it aroused in the Italian press and the various dramatizations of the novel on the Italian stage.

3. Edmund Wilson, *Patriotic Gore* (New York, 1962), p. 4.

novel. The copyright protection of a book published in 1852, the year *Uncle Tom's Cabin* appeared, lasted forty-two years, from 1852 until 1895; then the book passed into the public domain. Between 1895 and 1955, when any publisher could have reprinted the book, only nineteen editions came out in the United States. During this same period Italian publishers issued forty-five new editions. What is even more striking is the contrast during the years from 1930 to 1955. In this quarter of a century Italian publishers brought out twenty-two editions while American publishers were bringing out only three.

When the novel first appeared in 1852, however, it was extraordinarily popular everywhere. While it was selling 300,000 copies in the United States alone during the first year, Italian translators lost no time making their versions. The novel appeared in March in the United States, and by the end of the year two Italian publishers in the North, Fontana in Turin and Borroni and Scotti in Milan, had issued it. Italians who could read English had the opportunity also to read the novel in a Tauchnitz edition, published in Leipzig in 1852 and distributed throughout the Continent. Subscribers to Cavour's newspaper, *Il Risorgimento*, in Turin followed the adventures of Zio Tommasso in installments that began on November 10, 1852, though they did not learn until December 20 that the author's name was not "Harrier Beegher Howe." Two other newspapers, *Il Mediterraneo* in Genoa and *Gazzetta uffiziale di Venezia*, also serialized the novel.

The success of the first translations evidently spurred on other publishers. In 1853 five more editions appeared, including one version published in Naples that had been turned into Italian from a French translation. Three of the other four editions of that year came out in Milan, which then, as now, was the publishing capital of Italy. The fifth edition of 1853, also printed in Milan, was an English language edition with Italian notes issued by John Millhouse, an English writer of school books. Two more editions appeared in 1854 before the initial excitement over *Uncle Tom's Cabin* wore off, one in Turin and one in Milan; but after 1854 the market apparently was glutted, for there were no further editions until 1868.[4] Yet before the first flurry of interest abated, the tradition

---

4. Jackson, *op. cit.*, p. 331, lists an additional edition published in Naples in 1853 and editions published in Venice and Florence in the same year. I did not find these editions in any of the libraries or catalogues I consulted, and I have not listed them in my bibliography.

of *Uncle Tom's Cabin* as a child's book began. One of the 1854 editions was translated by "Sacerdote L. G.," who retold the story for children with the purpose, as he explains in his introduction, "of instilling in them sentiments of fraternal love and religion."[5]

The book's continuous popularity in Italy may be documented in any city public library or any branch of the national library. The novel obviously has captured and held the Italian imagination in a way not duplicated in the United States. Not only has the book been edited and reprinted with monotonous regularity, but it has also generated a sizable amount of critical comment. Whereas Cooper's translators and publishers felt little need to provide introductions, a great many of the translators of Mrs. Stowe prefaced their versions with small sermons. The editions published before the Civil War saw the novel much as anti-slavery advocates in the United States did. Those published afterwards regarded it as a poignant and permanently useful illustration of man's inhumanity to man. Even today, while contemporary introducers may apologize for the novel's limitations, they still present it as a significant work.

The most ambitious and interesting of the early editions was one of those issued in Milan in 1853, translated and introduced by B. Bermani. In an extensive and flowery introduction Bermani delivered an impassioned polemic on behalf of the novel. He applauded the cosmopolitan popularity the book already had enjoyed and presented it to his readers as a noble appeal to the generous instincts of human nature. The book's value, he felt, far transcended narrow questions of literary aesthetics. New England abolitionists could not have praised the novel more highly as an instrument that would end slavery than did Bermani.

Then Bermani went on to make invidious comparisons between the contemporary European novel and *Uncle Tom's Cabin*: "European readers were sadly resigned to a conventional and generally emasculated literature, obliged to submit to the utmost of vacuous declamation.... The European novel with its insipid and pernicious exaggerations ... inflated with bad taste ... diet of hypocrisy and charlatanism ... eternal and shameless lying ... had finally lost its vogue." The weariness and nausea produced by this "asthmatic and

5. See Bibliography, item 10. For an excellent study of the polemics aroused by the novel in the Catholic and liberal press in Italy, see Joseph Rossi, *"Uncle Tom's Cabin and Protestantism in Italy," American Quarterly*, XI, 416-424 (Fall, 1959). The Catholic press saw the novel as a threat and attacked it, while the liberal press in Piedmont, where religious freedom was allowed, praised it extravagantly.

paralyzing literature made it desirable that the novel . . . be revitalized in the waters of truth, of good sense, of respectable art as a goddess and not as a courtesan." Mrs. Stowe's work was a "revelation and a lesson." Then he added significantly that the sympathy that the book aroused in Europe stemmed in part from its "applicability to certain conditions and certain facts which make up our sick social state." He concluded that while slavery *per se* did not exist in Europe, the importance of the novel lay in its depiction of "the struggle between pleasure and suffering, the clash between right and power, the collision between passion and duty, the battle between property and the proletariat."[6]

The political overtones of this commentary invite reflection. At the time the novel reached Europe the abortive revolutionary year 1848 was still vividly remembered. Already the flow of emigrants from Europe to America, many seeking political asylum, had begun in earnest, and what is most important for Italy is the fact that the *Risorgimento* was moving towards its climax. Bermani's introduction published in 1853 precedes by only eight years the establishment of the Kingdom of Italy. The events for which Italian patriots had been working for decades were close to fruition when *Uncle Tom's Cabin* appeared with the explosive power of a new weapon. Thus the political situation in Europe made Mrs. Stowe's novel important regardless of its aesthetic value. Bermani's attitude is similar to that of Francesco Guerrazzi, novelist-patriot of the *Risorgimento*, who declared that his books were works of siege and that it did not matter to him whether they lasted, just so long as they furthered his cause.[7]

The nine editions of the novel published in Italy between 1852 and 1854, plus the Tauchnitz edition, satisfied the demand for the next fourteen years. After the unification of Italy there was no new edition until 1868, and during the balance of the century five additional editions kept the book alive in Italy. Between the turn of the century and World War I there were nine more. After the war, when the novel was going out of print in the United States, it took on new life in Italy. Since 1920, *Uncle Tom's Cabin* has averaged more than one Italian edition or printing per year.

During the peaceful years that lay between the final unification of Italy in 1870 and World War I, the fortunes of *Uncle Tom's Cabin* declined. Fourteen editions of the novel during this span of forty-four

6. See Bibliography, item 4, pp. iii-xvi.
7. Quoted by Howells in *Modern Italian Poets* (New York, 1887), p. 3.

years represent statistically the lowest point it ever reached in Italy. One edition every three years in this era contrasts sharply with the average of almost two editions every three years during the rest of its Italian history. The aims of the *Risorgimento* accomplished, the novel no longer was needed as a work of siege.

The translators, however, continued to praise the novel with undiminished enthusiasm. Typical is the introduction to the Hoepli edition, first issued in 1912, which has been reprinted or reissued five times since and is still in print. The translator, Fulvia Saporiti, wrote that Mrs. Stowe's palette did not contain "paint but blood and tears." The novel "is one of those books of faith that move men and produce great consequences." Even though the slaves had been freed long before, this translator ascribed to the novel "the life-giving power which sprang from the gospels and regenerates the spirit."[8]

Also in this period the novel moved out of the arena of polemical journalism and began to find its place in the commentaries of academic critics and literary historians. The first important Italian critic of American literature, Enrico Nencioni, referred briefly to *Uncle Tom's Cabin* in an essay on Whitman and the Civil War. Nencioni observed that "the dramatic picture of the suffering of millions of human creatures, picturesquely and pathetically described in the simple and eloquent book of Beecher Stowe, moves all of Europe."[9]

A more extensive comment than Nencioni's and one not very flattering to Mrs. Stowe's accomplishment appears in the first Italian history of American literature. Here Gustavo Strafforello takes a longer view of the novel and puts Mrs. Stowe in context with her literary compatriots. He notes caustically:

Who has not bathed in tears the pages of *Uncle Tom's Cabin*...of which a million copies have been sold. That novel was the battle cry... against slavery, although it does not have exceptional literary merits. Having one day become famous, like Byron, Stowe published successively *Dred, The Minister's Wooing, The Pearl of Orr's Island*, and that *Agnes of Sorrento*, which bored the readers of Thackeray's *Cornhill Magazine* by being so tedious and colorless.[10]

Italian readers have always felt the vitality of *Uncle Tom's Cabin*, while American readers have had to rediscover the book. From Bermani's introduction in 1853 through the eighteen editions published

8. See Bibliography, item 24.
9. *Saggi critici di letteratura inglese* (Firenze: Le Monnier, 1897), pp. 205-206.
10. Gustavo Strafforello, *Letteratura americana* (Milano: Ulrich Hoepli, 1884), p. 125.

in Italy between 1951 and 1955, Italian commentators repeat in substance the views of the translator previously cited who described *Uncle Tom's Cabin* as a "book of faith" and a work of "life-giving power." In contrast, one records Edmund Wilson's experience in rereading the novel in the 1950's. He was startled to find that Harriet Beecher Stowe had written a great book:

It is a much more impressive work than one has ever been allowed to suspect. The first thing that strikes one about it is a certain eruptive force.... The story came so suddenly to Mrs. Stowe and seemed so irresistibly to write itself that she felt as if some power beyond her had laid hold of her to deliver its message.... This is actually a little the impression that the novel makes on the reader.... characters leap into being with a vitality that is all the more striking for the ineptitude of the prose that presents them.[11]

While Wilson was making his discovery, the Italians were celebrating the centennial of *Uncle Tom's Cabin* with new editions and commemorative essays. One of the centennial essayists wrote: "As art it is weak. As apostolic work for a great cause, it is one of the greatest books ever written."[12] Another commentator at the same time argued that novels exist solely for their human values. They may be written with more or less art, but they must communicate the author's passionate view of life.

Uncle Tom's Cabin is not precisely a work of art ... more the work of a propagandist than a novelist ... as Lincoln repeated, this book did more than he did for the liberation of the Negroes.... This is, I believe, the ideal type of 'protest novel.' ... And the lasting glory of Harriet Beecher Stowe is in having succeeded in defending her thesis with direct and simple methods.[13]

This is also much the view of the introducer of one of the 1953 editions: "... it presents a living, interesting, and convincing picture of the society of the time and of the social, economic, and political problems which disturbed it.... the power undoubtedly is the great and generous social passion which gushes from it"; but naturally the work "is not without faults." This writer concludes that it remains "one of the most important books of its time."[14]

Although most of the criticism of *Uncle Tom's Cabin* deals with the novel as a social document, there are enough literary judgments

11. Wilson, *op. cit.*, p. 5.
12. Luisa Banal, "Il centenario d'un libro celebre," *La Parola e il Libro*, XXXV, 323-325 (Nov.-Dec., 1952).
13. Paul Vialar, "Lo Scrittore e responsabile," *La Fiera Letteraria*, VIII, 1 (Feb. 26, 1953). This article was originally published in French in *Nouvelles Littéraires*.
14. See Bibliography, item 56, pp. 6-9.

scattered about to be worth noting. The writer quoted above, for example, makes the same point that Edmund Wilson develops nine years later: Mrs. Stowe's novel invites comparison with the work of Dickens and Thackeray. The similarities between Dickens and Mrs. Stowe, in particular, are frequently observed in the Italian criticism —both by the academic critics and the literary journalists. One of the former, Salvatore Rosati, in his able history of American literature, treats Mrs. Stowe kindly. He admits that the characters in her novels are either too white or too black but adds: "However, when one thinks that the same observation can be made about Dickens's novels, one becomes more cautious in hanging the cross on Harriet Beecher Stowe's back." Of course, he continues, she is no Dickens, "but her Puritanism gives her a sense of misery and a reserve which in her better moments almost make one think of Hawthorne."[15] Yet few of the Italian critics would go so far as Giacomo Prampolini, who inserted this judgment in the American portion of his seven-volume history of world literature: "One does not wish to date from *Uncle Tom's Cabin* the birth of the modern American novel, but it remains a fact that its appearance marked the beginning of a study more attentive to man and reality and precurses by more than a decade the advent of regional realism introduced by the humorists."[16] Prampolini is more in step with his compatriots when he summarizes: "Antiquated in technique, lachrymose, didactic, the book compels attention for its knowledge of the Negro heart, the power with which it depicts the conflict between two civilizations, and for the intensity of certain episodes."

After World War I, *Uncle Tom's Cabin* took on renewed life in Italy. Fifteen editions and reprintings appeared between 1920 and 1937. All but two of these years, one notes, fall within the span of Mussolini's regime. The surge of interest in *Uncle Tom's Cabin* during the Fascist era parallels the general interest in American literature that developed in Italy between the two wars. As Italian intellectuals felt increasingly alienated from Mussolini's government, they turned towards America. Mrs. Stowe's novel rose on the tide of this new interest in American literature.

During the Fascist regime many Italian writers, especially Elio Vittorini and Cesare Pavese, discovered America. Their discovery

---

15. *Storia della letteratura americana* (Torino: Edizioni Radio Italiana, 1956), p. 70.
16. *Storia universale della letteratura* (Torino: Unione Tipografica Editrice Torinese, 1951), V, 385.

resulted in a great flood of translations, chiefly of American books never before rendered into Italian. What the United States meant to Italian writers in this period has been summed up by Pavese:

Toward 1930, when Fascism commenced to be "the hope of the world," a lot of young Italians looked in their books and discovered America; an America pensive and barbaric, blissful yet quarrelsome, dissolute, fecund; burdened with all the past of the world, yet youthful, innocent. For several years these young people read, translated, and wrote in a mood of joyful discovery and revolt that scandalized the official culture.[17]

It seems reasonable to speculate that *Uncle Tom's Cabin*, for all its defects, struck sparks in Italian hearts opposed to Fascism, as it formerly had moved patriotic Italians during the *Risorgimento*.

Later, when World War II blacked out the aspirations of European liberals, the book must have taken on even more poignant significance. One of the most interesting editions of the novel was published in Turin in 1943 and reprinted in 1944 and 1945. This is the time and place that Pavese describes vividly in *La casa in collina* [*The House on the Hill*]. It was a time when bombs were falling nightly on Turin, the Nazis and their Fascist collaborators were hunting out the partisans, and the allied armies were painfully making their way north through the Apennines. Published by Paravia, this edition contains only a one-page, unsigned introduction, but that brief headnote passionately urges the reading of this book, whose author raised her voice fearlessly against slavery, risking "calumny, even prison" to speak out "for the triumph of the good cause."[18] Significantly, the title page contained a circle of chain as an ornamental device. It was appropriate that this edition appeared in Turin, which had been a center of anti-Fascism during Mussolini's era.

The same connection between *Uncle Tom's Cabin* and anti-Fascism was made again in one of the centenary essays that appeared in 1953. The writer concluded his praise of the novel with these words: "... from 1936 to 1945 we have seen the Nazi regime throw the Jews into concentration camps ... inflict on them a torture still more dreadful. ... It is necessary at all costs [for writers to speak out] ... Beecher-Stowes are necessary. Uncle Toms are necessary."[19]

In summarizing the reception of *Uncle Tom's Cabin* in Italy

17. "Yesterday and Today," first published in the Turin *L'Unita'* (Aug. 3, 1947), here quoted from the appendix to Donald Heiney, *America in Modern Italian Literature* (New Brunswick, N. J., 1964), p. 245. Not my translation.

18. See Bibliography, item 38. This is the only edition of *Uncle Tom's Cabin* that was reprinted between 1940 and 1945.

19. Paul Vialar, *op. cit.*

over a hundred and fourteen years, one finds that interest in the book has remained fairly constant from 1852 until the present. There are, however, three periods of maximum popularity, and these three coincide with the emergence of major political crises. During the *Risorgimento* the book swept over Italy so that Howells could report that in the early 1860's it was universally read. During the Fascist era it took on renewed life and went through almost annual editions and reprintings. And finally, after World War II, when liberty returned to Italy, the flood of new editions testified to the continued relevance of the novel for Italian readers.

As long as there is injustice in the world Harriet Beecher Stowe seems destined to be honored in Italy. As one introduction written in 1952 notes, her book will serve its purpose "if it helps to advance understanding among men in all the world, regardless of color."[20] Another recent preface states the belief that the novel still has "a power to inspire all categories of readers,"[21] and a third points out that it has "survived its century, conserving a freshness and a flavor already lost from many other so-called classics."[22] And finally, an anonymous commentator, who introduced the novel in 1920 between the end of World War I and Mussolini's march on Rome, describes *Uncle Tom's Cabin* as a "vital work of art which already has outlasted many fugitive literary fashions and will live beyond the vicissitudes of our day because the pain, the piety, and the hope it inspired are universal and eternal."[23]

BIBLIOGRAPHY

Italian Editions of Uncle Tom's Cabin

The following bibliography lists sixty-seven editions of *Uncle Tom's Cabin* published in Italy between 1852 and 1961. Eight of them I have not been able to see but have listed from reliable bibliographical sources: Attilio Pagliaini, comp., *Catalogo generale della libreria italiana dall'anno 1848 a tutto il 1899* (Milano, 1901) ; *Primo supplemento dall 1900 al 1910; Secondo supplemento dall 1911 al 1920; Library of Congress Catalogue of Printed Cards* (1945) ;

---

20. See Bibliography, item 50.
21. See Bibliography, item 56.
22. See Bibliography, item 63.
23. See Bibliography, item 27.

Catalogo dei cataloghi del libro italiano (1922). In one instance I have listed a book described in the catalogue of the Biblioteca Nazionale Universitaria in Turin, though the librarians were unable to locate it. All items not seen have been starred. In addition I have noted, *passim*, 35 reprintings of various numbered editions. These, if added to the separate editions, would make the total number of editions and reprintings come to a hundred.

The definition of an edition for this bibliography has posed a problem. It is impractical to list as a new edition every issue in which the type was reset from an earlier edition. Italian publishers usually did not make plates but reset type whenever a new printing was needed. Thus many issues of the same translation appear with slight variations in pagination. A case in point is Hoepli's Fulvia translation (see item 24). I have listed as new editions only those which vary significantly in pagination or format from their predecessors or appeared a good many years after the original edition.

Except in the cases where the information is included on the title page, I have not recorded whether or not the text has been abridged or adapted for children. Perhaps as many as half of the editions are abbreviated, a fact usually not noted on the title page or in the occasional introduction that accompanies the text. The standards of translation vary widely. There has been such variation that one editor, Ettore Fabietti (see item 36), complains in a note to his readers about the errors of other translations. The various editions, he laments, are not complete when they say they are and often contain grave errors in translation. There ought to be some system for warning the public, he concludes, so that "we would save ourselves from the shame of masterpieces rendered unrecognizable by mutilations and disgraces of every type" (p. 6).

1 *La capanna dello Zio Tom.* Racconto. Milano: Borroni e Scotti, 1852.*

2 ————. Torino: Fontana, 1852.*

3 *La capanna di Papa Tom; ovvero, vita de' negri in America.* Libera versione dal francese di Luigi Lo Gatto. Napoli: G. Nobile, 1853.*

4 *La capanna dello Zio Tommaso, ossia la vita dei negri in America.* Traduzione di B. Bermani. Milano e Lodi: presso La Tipografia di Claudio Wilmant e Figlio, 1853.

5 *La capanna dello Zio Tom.* Milano: presso L'Editore Luigi Cioffi, 1853.

6 *Uncle Tom's Cabin.* With Italian Notes by John Millhouse. Milan: Millhouse, 1853.

7 *La capanna dello Zio Tom.* Traduzione di Giuseppe Lazzaro. Milano: Tramater, 1853.*

8 ———. Torino: Società Editrice Italiana, 1854.

9 ———. Torino: Società Editrice Italiana, n. d. [A later edition of the same anonymous translation issued in double-column magazine format.]

10 *Lo Zio Tom.* Narrato ai fanciulli. Versione del Sacerdote L. G. Milano: 1854. [No publisher listed.]

11 *La capanna dello Zio Tom.* Milano: 1868. [No publisher listed.]

12 ———. Volume unico. Milano: presso Serafino Muggiani e C., 1871.

13 ———. Volume unico. Milano: Francesco Pagnoni, Editore, 1877. [Reprinted in 1890, 1893, 1898, and 1904.]

14 ———. Firenze: Adriano Salani, 1885. [Reprinted in 1891 and 1896.]

15 ———. Narrato ai fanciulli. Per cura di C. Grolli. Milano: Liberia di Educazione e d'Istruzione, Paolo Carrara, Editore, 1888.

16 ———. Milano: Premiata Casa Editrice di Libri d'Educazione e d'Istruzione di Paolo Carrara, 1894. [Reprinted in 1905.]

17 ———. Milano: Società Editrice "La Milano," 1900.

18 ———. Milano: Antonio Vallardi, 1902.

19 ———. Volume unico. Milano: Casa Editrice Cesare Cioffi, 1902.

20 ———. Nuova versione di Palmiro Premoli. Milano: Società Editrice Sonzogno, 1903. [Reprinted in 1909, 1929, and 1939.]

21 ———. Riduzione dall'inglese sull'edizione completa. Firenze: R. Bemporad e Figlio, Editori, 1910.

22 ———. 4 volumi in uno. Milano: Casa Editrice Bietti, 1911.

23 ———. Adattato per i fanciulli da Mario Corsi. Roma: Voghera, 1911.*

24 ———. Nuova traduzione italiana e introduzione di [Rachele] Fulvia [Saporiti]. Milano: Ulrico Hoepli, Editore, 1912. [Reprinted with shortened introduction in 1922, 1928, 1940, 1950, 1955. These editions vary from 384 pp. in 1912 to 377 in 1923

and 1928, 437 in 1940, and 377 again in 1950 and 1955. Only the last two are identical.]

25 ———. Racconto della vita dei negri nell'America del Nord prima dell'abolizione della schiavitù. Tradotto e ridotto per la gioventù da Luigi di San Giusto. Torino: G. B. Paravia e C., 1912. [Reprinted in 1921 and 1923.]

26 ———. A cura di Maria Fabietti. Milano: Federazione Italiana delle Biblioteche Populari, 1919.

27 ———. In due volumi. Milano: Fratelli Treves, Editori, 1920. [Reprinted in 1929 and 1935.]

28 ———. Firenze: Adriano Salani, 1921.

29 ———. Firenze: Adriano Salani, 1922.

30 ———. Nuova edizione. Volume unico. Milano: Casa Editrice Cesare Cioffi, 1922.

31 *Uncle Tom's Cabin.* Con note italiane. Milano: F. Bracciforti, Editore, c. 1922.*

32 *La capanna dello Zio Tom.* Riduzione dall'inglese sull'edizione completa. Quarta ristampa. Firenze: R. Bemporad e Figlio, Editori, 1924. [Although listed on the title page as fourth printing, this edition differs from item 21. The second and third printings have not been seen. Fifth and sixth printings appeared in 1930 and 1937.]

33 ———. Milano: Casa Editrice Bietti, c. 1926. [Reprinted in 1934 and 1935.]

34 ———. Firenze: Adriano Salani, 1927.

35 ———. Nuova traduzione. Firenze: Nerbini, 1928. [Only fascicles no. 1, 2 (32 pp.) noted.]

36 ———. Traduzione integrale dell'inglese di Mara [*sic*] Fabietti. Sesto San Giovanni (Milano): Edizione "A. Barion" della Casa per Edizioni Populari, 1928. [Reprinted in 1933 and 1935.]

37 ———. Milano: Sonzogno, 1931.

38 ———. Riduzione di Luigi di San Giusto. Torino: G. B. Paravia e C., 1935. [Reprinted in 1940, 1943, 1944, 1945, 1950, 1952, 1954, and 1958.]

39 ———. Romanzo. Milano: Aurora, 1937.

40 ———. Firenze: Adriano Salani, 1939.

41 ———. Riduzione dal racconto inglese. Firenze: Adriano Salani, 1940.

42 ——. Versione italiana di Filippo Faber. Milano: Genio, 1947.

43 ——. Riduzione di Lucia Petrali Castoldi. Milano: Antonio Vallardi, 1949.

44 ——. Traduzione di Anita Chelini. Torino: Società Editrice Internazionale, 1951.

45 ——. Traduzione di Anita Chelini. Torino: Editrice Salvatore, 1951.

46 ——. Traduzione di G. Tenconi. Milano: Carroccio, 1951.

47 ——. Traduzione di Paolo Reynaudo. Firenze: Marzocco, 1952.

48 ——. Traduzione di Aldo Novi. Brescia: La Scuola, 1952.

49 ——. Traduzione di Hans B. Vicenza: Editrice Paoline, 1952.

50 ——. Traduzione di Pina Ballario. Milano: Arnoldo Mondadori, Editore, 1952.

51 ——. Traduzione di Maria Surra. Roma: Società Apostolato Stampa, 1953.

52 ——. Romanzo. Milano: Tipografia Editoriale Lucchi, 1953.

53 ——. Romanzo. Versione di A. Natasi. Milano: La Sorgente, 1953.

54 ——. Traduzione di Carla Bonetti. Milano: Orlando Cibelli, 1953.

55 ——. Traduzione di G. Tenconi. Milano: Carroccio, 1953.

56 ——, *ovvero la vita dei negri negli stati schiavisti d'America*. Traduzione di Beatrice Boffito. Milano: Rizzoli, Editore, 1953.

57 ——. Torino: Società Apostolato Stampa, 1953.

58 ——. Traduzione di Liana Trozzi. Bologna: Editrice A. e G. M., "Nettuno Omnia," 1954.

59 ——. Traduzione di Egidio Modena. Milano: Editori Fratelli Fabbri, 1954.

60 ——. A cura di Aldo Novi. Brescia: La Scuola, 1955.

61 ——. Traduzione di Giovanna Biasotti. Milano: Editori Fratelli Fabbri, 1955.

62 ——. A cura di Nino da Pergola. Milano: Edizioni Piccoli, 1956.

63 ——. Introduzione di M. C. Pittaluga. Traduzione a cura di Anna Maria Noli. Torino: Unione Tipografico Editrice Torinese, 1958.

64 ——. Traduzione di Simonetta Palazzi. Torino: W. E. T., 1958.

65 ——. A cura di Aldo Novi. Brescia: La Scuola, 1958.

66   ———. Traduzione dall'inglese di Maria Surra. Nuova edizione riveduta e corretta. Torino: Società Azionaria Internazionale Editrice, 1960.

67   ———. Traduzione di Annamaria Ferretti. Bologna: Editrice Capitol, 1961.

FREDERICK GODDARD TUCKERMAN
Edwin H. Cady

Indiana University

The literary criticism of recent decades has been much given to self-esteem. One's steel is taken to be too fine for any but "the great," if, indeed, there is not something a bit fraudulent about even them. On the other hand, any writer one is moved to discuss becomes "great" or at the least "of major significance." Though the temptations to debase the currency of language have been obvious, one need not yield. It is possible to discuss the neglected and "minor" without shame if one comes at the task from a humbler angle.

There are of course the few, towering, absolutely first-class literary artists of the world and the ages, the "great." And there are the far more numerous authors, excellent artists of wide implication and significance but clearly not of the highest class, who are "major." But then there is a third class, the singers of one song, tellers of one tale—or of a few. Some art rises seldom but truly. It keeps the power to move or sway, to open the eyes of our imaginations and print on our ears the sounds of sense we cannot forget and are delighted to hear again. No matter how few or narrow the achievements of such art, it legitimately commands attention, respect, and elucidation. If "minor," it is the real thing; and a dram of it is worth a pound of criticism.

I

When the accidents of literary history have served to make a "minor" poet also obscure, it will be his fate to be rediscovered repeatedly. Thus the recent edition by N. Scott Momaday of *The Complete Poems* discovers again the Yankee elegist and sonneteer Frederick Goddard Tuckerman. The history of Tuckerman's long non-existence as a reputation is worth recalling. His *Poems* were published in American editions of 1860, 1864, and 1869, and a British edition of 1863. Tennyson was his friend, Jones Very his Harvard tutor, Emerson an acquaintance; Hawthorne and Longfellow responded kindly to gift copies of his works. Emerson liked

Tuckerman's "Rhotruda," which made cautious fun of Charlemagne and his court in a manner not unlike the more Chaucerian pieces of Longfellow's *The Golden Legend*. Emerson got "Rhotruda" republished in the *Atlantic* in 1861, and anthologized it in *Parnassus* (1880). Nevertheless, Tuckerman became definitively unknown to the nineteenth century. It is perhaps not so surprising that Emerson was silent about the "Sonnets, Part I, Part II" which constitute Tuckerman's best achievement. They celebrated as they recorded the lives of grief, distraction, and of flight to art for refuge from which Emerson himself had escaped only by stern courage.

In 1866, the Roberts brothers, Boston publishers, issued in two volumes *The Book of the Sonnet*. Its editors were officially Leigh Hunt, who had died in 1859, and S. Adams Lee. As the survivor, Lee dedicated the volumes to George Henry Boker but was supercilious toward American sonneteers generally. The quality of their work "has embarrassed me," he confessed. "Had I exercised a severe critical judgment," said Lee, there could really have been no American section in *The Book of the Sonnet*. Upon Lee's list of forty-six mildly honored Americans appeared the names of Percival, Willis, Stedman, Saxe, Piatt, and Shillaber, but only the "wrong" Tuckerman: Henry Theodore. Whatever the explanation,[1] the right Tuckerman's bad luck held through the end of his century. E. C. Stedman omitted him from both the canonical *An American Anthology* (1900) and the huge *Library of American Literature* (1890). Not, indeed, until Witter Bynner published his rather arbitrarily edited[2] volume of *The Sonnets* in 1931 did Tuckerman achieve a place in the canon of minor American poets.

II

It is, however, less important that Tuckerman is "minor" than that he is a true poet. His powers are narrow in scope, but they are intense, distinctive, and at many points perfect of realization. As I

1. Lee's selections seem rather rusty as of 1864. Possibly he had stopped searching for American sonnets before Tuckerman's appearance in 1860.

2. By recent standards of textual editing, I think it is fair to say that there remains a need to have Tuckerman definitively done. No bibliographer, Bynner airily re-created Tuckerman to his own taste. What might have been expected to be a thorough treatment, *The Complete Poems of Frederick Goddard Tuckerman*, edited with an introduction by N. Scott Momaday (New York, 1965), leaves something to be desired. Momaday does not provide enough information on textual variants to permit his reader to judge the validity of his editorial decisions; but he does tell enough about certain of his procedures to raise doubts; further, I am not sure he has consulted all the relevant data.

have said, the testing ground for Tuckerman's powers lies in the sonnet sequence of his *Poems* (1860). The sources here of poetic power are four: the implied drama of the *persona*, the speaking voice, the figure observed or observing, sometimes the "I" of the sonnets; the diction; the beautifully controlled tonalities; the often superb imagery.

As S. Adams Lee would have been surprised to know, Tuckerman wrote sonnets in the Petrarchan tradition, fulfilling the technical requirements of the form with apparent ease, sometimes virtuosity, and in a voice not only transatlantic but Yankee. Perhaps the least predictable achievement of the sonnets as Tuckerman published them, however, was the fact that they constituted a sonnet sequence in a fashion as ancient as Petrarch but immediate to the poet's experience, in one aspect utterly conventional to the Wertheresque-Byronic clichés of international Romanticism but in another aspect decidedly American.

Tuckerman's sequence consisted of 55 sonnets balanced between 28 in the first part and 26 in the second, with an unnumbered, final prayer to serve as envoi. Part I depicts a sensitive youth seeking in nature the meaning of all the "dim fancies, cares, and fears" which haunt his life with intimations of disaster but finding in faith the resolve to defy "the Opposer's anger, arms, or art." Regardless, he is struck by nameless sorrow and estrangement until (in Sonnet v) he stands in desolation:

> And so the day drops by; the horizon draws
> The fading sun, and we stand struck in grief;
> Failing to find our haven of relief,—
> Wide of the way, nor sure to turn or pause;
> And weep to view how fast the splendour wanes,
> And scarcely heed, that yet some share remains
> Of the red after-light, some time to mark,
> Some space between the sundown and the dark.
> But not for him those golden calms succeed,
> Who, while the day is high, and glory reigns,
> Sees it go by,—as the dim Pampas plain,
> Hoary with salt, and gray with bitter weed,
> Sees the vault blacken, feels the dark wind strain,
> Hears the dry thunder roll, and knows no rain.

One could notice the adumbrations in Sonnet v of poets like Santayana, Robinson, even Eliot, without embarrassment—except that Tuckerman's poem has, after all, its own firm character and strength without need to lean or borrow.

Aging, the poet of these sonnets possesses his imagination of disaster in a wilderness of lost innocence:

IX

Yet wear we on; the deep light disallowed
That lit our youth,—in years no longer young,
We wander silently, and brood among
Dead graves, and tease the sun-break and the cloud
For import. Were it not better yet to fly,
To follow those who go before the throng,
Reasoning from stone to star, and easily
Exampling this existence? or shall I—
Who yield slow reverence where I cannot see,
And gather gleams, where'er by chance or choice
My footsteps draw,—though brokenly dispensed,—
Come into light at last? or suddenly,
Struck to the knees like Saul, one arm against
The overbearing brightness, hear—a Voice?

The image taken from the story of Saul on the road to Damascus is not irrelevant. When disaster strikes at last, it comes like the wine of astonishment and strikes him dumb:

X

An upper chamber in a darkened house,
Where, ere his footsteps reached ripe manhood's brink,
Terror and anguish were his cup to drink,—
I cannot rid the thought, nor hold it close;
But dimly dream upon that man alone;—
Now though the autumn clouds most softly pass;
The cricket chides beneath the doorstep stone,
And greener than the season grows the grass.
Nor can I drop my lids, nor shade my brows,
But there he stands beside the lifted sash;
And, with a swooning of the heart, I think
Where the black shingles slope to meet the boughs,
And—shattered on the roof like smallest snows—
The tiny petals of the mountain-ash.

Then he knows tragic truth, and in imagery strangely Melvillean:

XIII

As one who walks and weeps by alien brine,
And hears the heavy land-wash break, so I,
Apart from friends, remote in misery,
But brood on pain, and find in heaven no sign:
The lights are strange, and bitter voices by.
So the doomed sailor, left alone to die,
Looks sadly seaward at the day's decline,
And hears his parting comrades' jeers and scoffs;
And sees, through mists that hinder and deform,

The dewy stars of home,—sees Regulus shine
With a hot flicker through the murky damp,
And setting Sirius twitch and twinge like a lamp
Slung to the mast-head, in a night of storm,
Of lonely vessel labouring in the troughs.

Having confessed so much, the poet of these sonnets must now tell more: the fulfilment of those youthful intimations of grief comes as what Poe had supposed the most poetic of all possible subjects, the death of a beautiful woman. Tuckerman, however, can see and tell the story as not Poe, nor Byron, nor Coleridge, Wordsworth, even Goethe himself could do. As poems of love and grief in love's loss the two key sonnets of revelation are, so far as I can think, unique in romantic poetry: the love had been whole, complete, achieved, utterly genuine. As Yankee Emerson could be surprisingly frank about the love of his dead wife Ellen, so Tuckerman (for his poet-persona) :

XIV

Not proud of station, nor in worldly pelf
Immoderately rich, nor rudely gay;
Gentle he was, and generous in a way,
And with a wise direction ruled himself.
Large Nature spread his table every day;
And so he lived,—to all the blasts that woo,
Responsible, as yon long locust spray
That waves and washes in the windy blue.
Nor wanted he a power to reach and reap
From hardest things a consequence and use;
And yet this friend of mine, in one small hour
Fell from himself, and was content to weep
For eyes love-dark, red lips, and cheeks in hues
Not red, but rose-dim, like the jacinth-flower!

XV

And she, her beauty never made her cold,—
Young-Oread-like, beside the green hill-crest,
And blissfully obeying Love's behest,
She turned to him as to a god of old!
Her smitten soul with its full strength and spring
Retaliating his love: unto that breast,
Ere scarce the arms dared open to infold,
She gave herself as but a little thing!
And now,—to impulse cold, to passion dead,—
With the wild grief of unperfected years,
He kissed her hands, her mouth, her hair, her head;
Gathered her close and closer, to drink up
The odour of her beauty; then in tears,
As for a world, gave from his lips the cup!

This is one poem of paired sonnets, and its most striking feature is made of what does not appear. Here is the supreme lyric of Romantic egotism—the death of a beautiful woman—and it omits sin (no seduction, no incest, no necrophilia), Satanism (no defiance of God, mores, or law), and misogyny (the dead wife was modest but beautiful, humbly devoted, sexually vital, triumphant in self-giving). The grief is only for "unperfected years," and it implies for the ego in the poem not outraged self-pity but recognized unworthiness.

Succeeding sonnets flow full of images wherein nature reflects the poet's grief:

> The morning comes; not slow, with reddening gold,
> But wildly driven, with windy shower, and sway
> As though the wind would blow the dark away!
>
> (SONNET XXII)

But mere brooding, however picturesque, will not finally do; and Part I closes with an eloquent turn, not to theology but faith:

XXVIII

> Not the round natural world, not the deep mind,
> The reconcilement holds: the blue abyss
> Collects it not; our arrows sink amiss;
> And but in Him may we our import find.
> The agony to know, the grief, the bliss
> Of toil, is vain and vain! clots of the sod
> Gathered in heat and haste, and flung behind
> To blind ourselves and others,—what but this
> Still grasping dust, and sowing toward the wind?
> No more thy meaning seek, thine anguish plead;
> But, leaving straining thought, and stammering word,
> Across the barren azure pass to God;
> Shooting the void in silence, like a bird,—
> A bird that shuts his wings for better speed!

Lover, seer, and sayer struck down by the griefs of time and human fate, Tuckerman's poet became a figure of rebellion against Romantic conventions. He was revolutionary because he was conservative. The unblasphemous, legitimate, *married* lover inscrutably chastised, he became a Romantic paradox: Byron as Job. Seeing New Englandly, he stood in contraconvention to Poe. Since the discovery two generations later by Sculley Bradley of Boker's *Sonnets on Profane Love*, one may grasp by opposites how very New Englandly, conservatively, Americanly, Tuckerman saw his poet. In Part II of the Tuckerman sequence a major question becomes: what shall be done for the children?

In Part II there is striking imagery. Like Thoreau, Melville, and Whitman, Tuckerman was pioneering with figures from the new technology:

XI

Still pressing through these weeping solitudes,
Perchance I snatch a beam of comfort bright,—
And pause, to fix the gleam, or lose it quite,
That darkens as I move, or but intrudes
To baffle and forelay: as sometimes here,
When late at night the wearied engineer
Driving his engine up through Whately woods,
Sees on the track a glimmering lantern-light,
And checks his crashing speed,—with hasty hand
Reversing and retarding. But, again!
Look where it burns, a furlong on before!—
The witchlight of the reedy river-shore,
The pilot of the forest and the fen,
Not to be left, but with the waste woodland.

And with deepening perspectives the poet's grief connects to subtler, more poignant associations:

XVI

Under the mountain, as when first I knew
Its low dark roof, and chimney creeper-twined,
The red house stands; and yet my footsteps find
Vague in the walks, waste balm and feverfew.
But they are gone: no soft-eyed sisters trip
Across the porch or lintels; where, behind,
The mother sat,—sat knitting with pursed lip.
The house stands vacant in its green recess,
Absent of beauty as a broken heart;
The wild rain enters; and the sunset wind
Sighs in the chambers of their loveliness,
Or shakes the pane; and in the silent noons,
The glass falls from the window, part by part,
And ringeth faintly in the grassy stones.

But the whole sequence ends in a prayer of startling mythological erudition to accentuate the force which has been required to subdue the poetic ego to resignation. In his 1860 edition, Tuckerman gave this last sonnet no number:

As Eponina brought, to move the king,
In the old day, her children of the tomb,
Begotten and brought forth in charnel gloom,—
To plead a father's cause; so I, too, bring
Unto thy feet, my Maker, tearfully,
These offspring of my sorrow; hidden long,

And scarcely able to abide the light.
May their deep cry inaudible, come to Thee,
Clear, through the cloud of words, the sobs of song,
And, sharper than that other's, pierce thine ears!
That so, each thought, aim, utterance, dark or bright,
May find thy pardoning love; more blest than she
Who joyful passed with them to death and night,
With whom she had been buried nine long years!

The richness and density of Tuckerman's poetry at its best may be realized in even brief consideration of this poem's interlocking patterns of resonance. Eponina[3] was a Plutarchan heroine who during nine years visited her condemned rebel of a husband in the cave where he hid, bearing him two sons. When at the end she appealed to the king her father for pardon, all were executed. Tuckerman's poem is a masterpiece of multivalence, presenting simultaneously a series of dramas with meanings both like and different.

"Eponina," for instance, suggests a number of womanly figures: the heroine of historical myth; an archetypal Lady of Love and Sorrows; the lost lady of the poetic persona; Tuckerman's lost wife; either Tuckerman's or "the poet's" muse. The "children" of the sonnet are ambiguously real, fictional, analogically Eponina's. But they are also, still ambiguously, the children of the brain or the muse—poems—in need somehow of forgiveness, atonement. Correspondingly, the "I" becomes the rebel Julius Sabinus; a doomed lover and father seeking grace; a lost poet seeking grace, especially the grace of acceptance (public?) for his poems; Tuckerman seeking religious consolation. I suppose all of these readings, and perhaps more, may be both simultaneously and serially correct. The effect of this last, climactic sonnet is to make us look back through the whole set and perceive that, in short, Tuckerman's best was a sequence of moral, idealistic, romantically anti-Romantic poems, the widower's sonnets, a sonnet sequence on sacred love.

III

As the "Eponina" sonnet shows, when it became poetically useful to do so, Tuckerman never hesitated to make full use of the legitimate American heritages from classical lands and ages. He would have thought Santayana's qualms about "the genteel tradition" absurd. He was equally natural, however, in use of American reference and speech. The handling of language, for instance, in Sonnet

3. See Momaday, p. xxvii.

XIII (above) seems beyond mere praise. What begins sounding like a quite conventional *Book of the Sonnet* piece—"As one who walks and weeps by alien brine"—ends in the realized originality of that marooned sailor's eye which

> . . . sees, through mists that hinder and deform,
> The dewy stars of home,—sees Regulus shine
> With a hot flicker through the murky damp,
> And setting Sirius twitch and twinge like a lamp
> Slung to the mast-head, in a night of storm,
> Of lonely vessel labouring in the troughs.

The proportion of one-syllable words in Sonnet XIII is overwhelming. Yet not one is bathetic; they rap and sting like hailstones. At the same time, they provide perfect settings for exotic "Regulus" and "Sirius." It takes a bold, true ear to let Sirius "twitch and twinge"—homely, craven, physical words. But the sharp, hard words prepare elegantly for the dying, feminine sounds of "lonely vessel labouring," just as the exact, Yankee-sailor last word, "troughs," answers and denies the threatened gentility of the first line's "alien brine." Learned and homely, international and regional at will, Tuckerman's diction at its best has the essential poetic qualities of fitness which becomes inevitability while it preserves strangeness. It exacts of the reader that astonishment which recognizes unpredictability in precise use.

Tuckerman's imagery ranges from Eponina to Pampas grass salt with alkali, from the frightened engineer in Whately's woods to a recondite botanical reference. One of its most interesting manifestations, however, comes in Sonnet x (above). Of this poem Yvor Winters, qualifying high praise with a charge that the conclusion is "obscure," said: "There have been a few occasions when I almost thought that I understood the grammar and syntax of this passage, but I do not understand them now."[4] Professor Winters is by far the most distinguished of Tuckerman's critics, but it must be confessed that there are aspects of his criticism hard to understand: his huge over-evaluation of "The Cricket"; his conviction that somehow the right touchstone for Tuckerman is Verlaine. Though differing from Yvor Winters is known to be perilous, I think that, as Tuckerman himself printed the poem, Sonnet x is in fact syntactically not notably difficult but is a prime instance of his finest poetic genius.

In Sonnet x the poet has a vision of a man about whom sugges-

4. In Momaday, pp. xii-xiii.

tions of Christ cluster: "An upper chamber in a darkened house"; "Terror and anguish were his cup to drink." Obsessed, he "cannot rid the thought nor hold it close" but must "dimly dream upon that man alone." He does so, says the sonnet, through seasons of time—in season and out. Now in autumn he cannot escape the vision, though somehow, as we shall see, spring is essential to it. The troublesome lines are:

> Nor can I drop my lids, nor shade my brows,
> But there he stands beside the lifted sash;
> And, with a swooning of the heart, I think
> Where the black shingles slope to meet the boughs,
> And—shattered on the roof like smallest snows—
> The tiny petals of the mountain-ash.

These lines form the sestet of the sonnet, which of course must somehow answer to the octet. I do not believe that the difficulty in them is either syntactical or permanent. In the first two lines there is no trouble: the "I" of the poem cannot be rid of his vision; any least interruption of ordinary outward sight turns the eye of his mind to the man who stands smitten and afflicted "beside the lifted sash" and looks out the window. So visualizing, and with swooning heart, he lets his vision switch empathetically to become that of the figure. The difficulty is not linguistic but one of perspective. When the perspective shifts from the narrator's view to that of the subject, what occurs is a sharp dissociation, a blocking. Suddenly to the mind's eye it is very exactly spring, with the white on black paradox of blossoms like snow on the roof.

One suspects symbolism in the sharp image of the last three lines, but I do not see a clue to warrant saying just what the symbolic reference might be. Indeed, the significance of the lines may not be symbolic in any of the usual ways. Two other things are quite clearly indicated by the strategies of the poem. One is that the poem is confessional for its speaking narrator. Because he cannot be rid of the smitten sufferer lost out of time in his moment of terror and anguish, and because he can unite his vision with that of the sufferer, the two are one. His memory is projective, but he is the sufferer. The technique is the same as that of the more directly confessional Sonnets xiv, xv, where it was "this friend of mine" who lost a perfect wife. It is of course essential to the effect of all three poems that the reader should penetrate the disguises.

Finally, moreover, what is there ever to say of grief? Only perhaps that, while tyrannically overwhelming, it has no meaning. One sees, exactly, irrelevantly, beyond comprehension, how time, nature, beauty, and all the rest merely go on. Perhaps the poem is not mysterious because it is not symbolic at all. It is only a perfect way of saying something about the emotionally ultimate.

PARKMAN, RED FATE,
AND WHITE CIVILIZATION

Russel B. Nye

Michigan State University

Francis Parkman could not remember exactly when his interest in Indians first began. As a boy he was deeply stirred by a Sac and Fox ceremonial dance on Boston Common, and like others of his generation he immersed himself in James Fenimore Cooper, becoming "so deeply identified with the novelist's red heroes," one of his biographers wrote, "that he talked of them more than anything else, and emulated them in woodcraft on his walks." At fifteen, he remarked of himself later, "his thoughts were always in the forests . . . , whose features possessed his waking and sleeping dreams."

During six years at Harvard as undergraduate and law student, he read constantly about the Indian and the frontier; he also planned a history of North America, to be built about the Indian wars and the conquest of the forest. "My favorite backwoods were always in my thoughts," he wrote in his journal. "My theme fascinated me, and I was haunted with wilderness images day and night. . . . I wanted to paint the forest and its tenants in true and vivid colors." By his sophomore year his plans crystallized into writing "the story of what was known as the 'Old French War,' that is, the war that ended with the conquest of Canada."[1]

A friend said of him during these youthful years that Parkman "had Injuns on the brain," and there was some truth in the exaggeration. He spent his summers visiting Indian settlements, examining collections of artifacts, and observing tribal remnants in New England and Canada. By the time of his graduation in 1846 he had seen most of the Indian tribes east of the Mississippi and had visited nearly all of the important sites from Maine to St. Louis connected with the early history of French and English settlement. He

---

1. Charles E. Farnham, *A Life of Francis Parkman* (Boston, 1905), pp. 142-143; letter to George Ellis, June 3, 1864, in Wilbur Jacobs, ed., *Letters of Francis Parkman* (Norman, Okla., 1960), I, 177; "Autobiography," *Proceedings of the Massachusetts Historical Society*, N.S. VIII, 351 (1894).

had also, apparently, exhausted the library resources of Cambridge and Boston.[2] A year earlier, in 1845, he published some "blood-and-thunder chronicles of Indian squabbles and massacres" in the *Knickerbocker Magazine*. In these tales Parkman considered for the first time some of the implications of the Indian-white and wilderness-civilization conflicts he had found in Cooper.[3]

Parkman's interest in Indians was not unusual among young intellectuals of his time. The search by admirers of Scott for native literary materials and a national past guided them to the forest and the red man; the cult of natural nobility, inherited from the eighteenth century, led in the same direction; the sentimental concern of the Romantics for this "vanishing race" settled on the Indian too. The publication of a number of important works about the Indian during the early nineteenth century drew further attention to his position in the American past and present. Father Heckewelder's *Indian Nations of Pennsylvania* (1822), which proved invaluable to Cooper; Albert Gallatin's pioneer study of Indian ethnography, *Synopsis of the Indian Tribes* (1836); McKenney and Hall's three-volume *History of the Indian Tribes of North America* (1836-1844); Schoolcraft's *Algic Researchers* (1839) and his *Oneonta* (1844-1845); George Catlin's magnificent drawings and his *Letters and Notes on Indians* (1841); Benjamin Drake's *Life of Tecumseh* (1841)—these and other publications captured the interest and imagination of artists and scholars throughout the period. The newly founded state and local historical societies of the 1820's and '30's produced hundreds of articles on Indian languages and customs; the discovery and excavation of Indian mounds proved especially fascinating and led to all sorts of speculations about the Indian's past.[4]

Nearly two centuries of contact between Indian and white man produced theories of race, centered on the Indian, which when com-

2. The amazing range of Parkman's youthful knowledge of Indians is not usually appreciated. Before he was twenty Parkman had made on-the-spot studies of the Abenaki in Maine, the Iroquois in New York, and the Ojibwa of the Great Lakes area. Wilbur Schramm, *Francis Parkman* (New York, 1935), cxvii-cxviii, summarizes these trips; even after his return from the Oregon Trail Parkman immediately took a walking tour of Pennsylvania.

3. See Mason Wade, *Francis Parkman: Heroic Historian* (New York, 1942), pp. 198-199, concerning the place of these tales in Parkman's development. In one of them, a narrative poem titled "The New Hampshire Ranger," Parkman wrote: "I love the savage war-whoop/And the whistling of the ball;/The woods, the rocks, the boiling streams,/I love them, one and all."

4. See, for example, Josiah Priest's *American Antiquities and Discoveries* (Albany, 1833) or the essays on Indians in Caleb Atwater's *Writings* (Columbus, Ohio, 1833).

bined with the American experience with Negro slavery provided a rationale for white superiority. By Parkman's time Americans held a wide variety of views toward the Indian. Some hardly regarded him at all. Tocqueville in 1831 noted in American society, "so policed, so prudish, so sententiously moral and virtuous . . . a complete insensibility, a sort of cold implacable egoism" where "the American indigenies" were concerned. Some, looking at the Indian through the rosy glasses of Romanticism, saw him as a cultural primitive who illustrated the theories of sensibility, social simplicity, and natural wisdom derived from the eighteenth-century philosophers. Many more, however, saw the Indian as "inferior in reason and moral qualities," a childlike, cruel, and dangerous savage.

The idea of the Indian as irremediably primitive was the commonly accepted basis for thinking about him for the first half of the nineteenth century; he was assumed to be inherently different from and inferior to civilized peoples, incapable of any betterment. The article "America," written by Jedidiah Morse for the *Encyclopaedia Britannica* in 1793 and widely reprinted over the next fifty years, noted the Indian's "propensity to violence," the "surprising contrasts" of his nature, his "perfidy combined with cruelty," and his "weak understanding" and morality.[5]

Whether or not such primitives could ever be raised from a savage state, whether they possessed sufficiently strong human qualities ever to be absorbed into civilized society—these were debatable questions in Parkman's times. It was generally agreed by contemporary anthropologists that each race contained inborn characteristics which could be influenced only superficially by education and environment. The Indian's racial inheritance made it impossible to civilize him without changing his ways. If his race had already determined that his ways were unchangeable, it followed that he could not be integrated into civilization and thus must disappear. Benjamin Lincoln, writing in 1793, believed that "If the savages cannot be civilized . . . , they will, in consequence of their stubbornness, dwindle and moulder away . . . until the whole race shall become extinct."[6]

5. *Encyclopaedia Britannica*, American edition (Philadelphia, 1798), I, 541-553. The best study of the idea of the Indian in American culture is Roy Harvey Pearce, *The Savages of North America* (Baltimore, 1953); see also the excellent summaries in David Levin, *History as Romantic Art* (Stanford, Calif., 1954), pp. 126-136.

6. Pearce, *op. cit.*, p. 69. The eighteenth-century philosophers were divided on the question of the Indian's adaptability. Montesquieu believed the Indian incapable of

And thus, concluded Josiah Clark Nott more than a half century later, "A full-blooded civilized Indian is a contradiction in terms."[7]

Widely read, familiar with Indians both in books and in actuality, Francis Parkman knew all these things and wanted to study all he could about them. He wanted especially to observe Indians yet unaffected by white civilization; the Indians of the Eastern tribes he visited were decimated by years of war and disease, their culture tainted or destroyed by too much contact with white society. Although he learned much from them, they did not represent Indian life as the seventeenth and eighteenth centuries had known it. The Plains Indians of the West, touched for the most part only by white traders and hunters, possessed a quite different culture from that of the Eastern tribes, but Parkman believed that the psychology of the Indian in his aboriginal condition was much the same throughout. He, therefore, left St. Louis for the Oregon Trail in April, 1846, he wrote, "almost exclusively with a view of observing the Indian character"; or, as he wrote in the foreword of the first edition of his subsequent book, "with a view to studying the manners and characters of Indians in their primitive state."

Neither his readings nor his previous observations adequately prepared him for the actuality of Indian life on the plains. The Indians he saw near the settlements—chiefly Kaws and Shawnees—disillusioned him; they were "irrepressible beggars," living in "mere vacancy, lying about . . . with nothing to do or think of." He had seen lazy and shiftless Indians before, of course, but as he continued the trip he saw much more that repelled him. A strain of disgust runs through his accounts of Western Indians—their repulsive sanitary habits, their irresponsibility, cruelty, and most of all their utter and debased savagery. The contrast between the preconception and the reality of Indian life in the West was a source of constant shock to him, though some of it he had expected. He spent nineteen days with the Sioux, observed them carefully, and concluded that

---

civilization; Locke, more optimistic, thought he could be educated and absorbed. See Paul Honigsheim, "The American Indian in the Philosophy of the English and French Enlightenment," *Osiris*, X, 91-108 (1952). Jefferson thought that no matter what was done, Indians would "always relapse into barbarism and misery," as he told John Adams in 1812.

7. Nott, *Types of Mankind* (Philadelphia, 1856), 461-464. Nott, a phrenologist, found Indian skulls showed overdeveloped organs of "animal propensity" and underdeveloped organs of intellect; Samuel Morton's *Crania Americana* (Philadelphia, 1839) previously made the same conclusion. For a study of racial attitudes toward the Indian, see Thomas F. Gossett, *Race: The History of an Idea in America* (Dallas, 1963), chap. x; and Jack D. Forbes, *The Indian in America's Past* (New York, 1964).

"They were thorough savages. Neither their manners nor their ideas were in the slightest degree modified by contact with civilization. ... They were living representatives of the Stone Age." Only war saved them from "utter lethargy and debasement," for like animals, they found only aggressiveness meaningful.[8]

Yet the blunt and even repulsive fact of the Indian's savagery attracted Parkman's scholarly interests. To study the pure aborigine and to experience some of the "danger and charm" of a primitive society was what he wanted. He was fascinated by the picturesque quality of Indian life, by its barbaric, colorful violence, by the close relationship of the savage to the equally savage land. Many of his descriptions in *The Oregon Trail* were done as paintings; he saw a Dacotah encampment at evening in terms of Salvator Rosa, and even quoted Benjamin West.[9]

The experience of the Oregon Trail convinced Parkman that the red man was neither child of natural simplicity nor forest philosopher, but plainly a savage and nothing more—yet Parkman also perceived in that experience something of the power and majesty of Indian life, and of the pathos of the destiny of this proud, doomed race. The color and vitality of this primitive society appealed to his sense of the romantic; its implicit, subdued sense of evil and danger was to him attractive and exciting. But when he was involved directly with its detail—dirt and disease, wanton cruelty, feasts of boiled puppies, and promiscuous sexual habits—he found it repulsive, squalid, without meaning or purpose. Parkman could see Indian life in terms of a West painting or a Cooper novel; he could see it also as a half-animal, crude, and cruel Stone Age culture.[10] This is the central bifurcation of the book—the Indian is a savage, but at the same time the confrontation of civilization with savagery captivates the imagination and stirs the intellect. Parkman half accepts Indian life while he rejects it, and whatever the loss of illusion reflected in the book, there remains still in *The Oregon Trail* the strong, repressed attrac-

8. *The Oregon Trail* (New York, 1849), especially chaps. xiv, xv. The book was first serialized by the *Knickerbocker* in 1847; of great interest is his trail journal, reprinted by Mason Wade, ed., *The Journals of Francis Parkman* (New York, 1957), II, 383-511. Parkman observed and took notes on the Kaws, Shawnees, and Delawares in Missouri; later on the Kickapoos, Sioux (whom he called Dacotahs), Cheyennes, and Arapahoes in the West.

9. See particularly chap. ix, "Scenes at Camp."

10. Melville and Theodore Parker, among others, objected to Parkman's view of the Indian as barbarian. See Melville's review of *The Oregon Trail* in the *Literary World*, March 31, 1849; and Parker's letter to Parkman, reprinted in Farnham, *op. cit.*, pp. 374-375.

tion that the young New England aristocrat felt for the wild society of the Sioux.

Parkman refined his concept of savagery in *The History of the Conspiracy of Pontiac* (1851) which he began to write in 1848. Though he seems once to have planned an entire history of the North American Indian, he decided before his trip to the West that he would accomplish much the same purpose if he wrote instead about the impact of the Indian on American history. A study of Pontiac, "one of the most remarkable men that have appeared among the Indians," he said in 1846, afforded "the best opportunities for representing the Indian character and modes of life, a sort of focus, moreover, in aboriginal history—where the relations and position of the tribes may be conveniently located."[11] His opening chapter, "Indian Tribes East of the Mississippi," was a long and erudite consideration of Indian life, reflecting the tremendous scope of his research. From its tone it is evident that Parkman was well aware he was writing a book about the conflict of Indian savagism with encroaching civilization, and that he had concluded that savagery could not survive it. He composed this opening chapter, therefore, with great care, since on it would rest his conclusions about the significance of Indian life and culture, and about the Indian's position in the stream of American history.

He explained first that the real Indian was not yet in the books— that there was no truth to the "counterfeit image" of the red man found in "the rhapsodies of poets, the cant of sentimentalists, and the extravagances of some who should have known better." The Indian of popular fancy bears "no more resemblance to the original than the monarch of tragedy and the hero of the epic poem bear to their living prototypes."[12] All were purely literary creations. What, then, was the real Indian like?

There was no mystery about him; the Indian was a savage, an irretrievably barbaric savage. "Ambition, revenge, jealousy, are his

11. Letter to C. C. Trowbridge, March 7, 1846, in Jacobs, *op. cit.*, I, 35. Writing to the Abbé Cosgrain, forty years later, he said of *Pontiac:* "The truth is that I had a taste for the woods and Indians, and it was this that turned my attention to forest themes. At one time I thought of writing the history of the Indians, with the Iroquois as a central point, but on reflection I preferred the French colonies, as equally suiting my purpose while offering at once more unity and more variety, as well as more interest to civilized readers" *(Letters, II, 213)*.

12. *The History of the Conspiracy of Pontiac* (New York, 1888), I, 39-43. Parkman's use of his sources, and some critiques of his acceptance of oral tradition, may be found in Howard H. Peckham, "The Sources and Revisions of Parkman's *Pontiac,*" *Papers of the Bibliographical Society of America*, xxxvii, 1-15 (1943).

ruling passions . . . , a wild love of liberty, an utter intolerance of control, lie at the basis of his character." Because in Indians "the powers of perception preponderate over those of reason and analysis," they are essentially irrational, incapable of intelligent choice; their wayward impulses make them "unstable as water, capricious as the winds . . . , like ungoverned children fixed with the instincts of devils." Indians are "as infirm of purpose as a mob of children, and devoid of providence or foresight."

Pontiac, the center of Parkman's drama, served as his primary example, for he illustrated in "strongest light and shadow, the native faults and virtues of the Indian race." Of "commanding and magnanimous nature," he was a creature of "uncurbed passions"; proud and brave in battle, yet "marked with blackest treachery"; generous in thought and deed, yet "filled with craft and cunning . . . , stained with the odious vice of cowards and traitors." Pontiac represented "the thorough savage," the barbarian of barbarians that Parkman conceived the Indian inherently to be.

The static rigidity of the Indian character, Parkman concluded, sealed Pontiac's fate and that of all Indians with him. Fated to remain savages, forever so, they were doomed to disappear before the advance of a civilization into which they could never be absorbed. The Indian, wrote Parkman, by reason of his "lethargy of mind" and his rudimentary mental qualities, could neither improve his state, nor adapt himself to a higher one. He could not conceive of change or of progress; lacking "powers of expansion and assimilation," he could never "open up his mind to the idea of improvement," nor find any "strong principle of cohesion" with which to organize his culture. "To reclaim the Indians from their savage state," he concluded, "has again and again been attempted, and each attempt has failed. Their untractable, unchanging character leaves no other alternative than their gradual extinction, or the abandonment of the western world to eternal barbarism."[13]

Inflexibility, incapacity for change, Parkman suggested, have always characterized man and nature in their primitive states. The

13. *Ibid.*, I, 39-46, 191-193, 216; II, 17. The most important of Parkman's remarks occur in chapters i and viii of Volume I. See also his novel, *Vassal Morton* (1856): "Take a savage from the woods and prairies, and, school him as you will, the ingrained savage will still declare himself." O. W. Holmes, who was interested in anthropology, considered the Indian an incomplete human being, a "half-filled outline of humanity," whose *"ferae naturae* instincts" would inevitably lead to his extinction. William Gilmore Simms's novel *Oakatibbe*, built about the conflict of savage and civilized values, showed how even admirable Indian principles simply hastened the race's extinction.

American Indian and the American wilderness existed in a kind of natural symbiosis which could not survive intrusion. Both wild, both primitive— "savage scenery and savage men," wrote Parkman of the American wilderness—the organic relation of red man to forest in the original state was balanced and harmonious. "Imbued with the spirit of the wilderness," the Indian mind was but an extension of the environment which shaped it; he was a "true child of the forest and the desert," a product of "the wastes and solitudes of nature," sharing in its "wild sublimity." In this interaction and interdependence of wild nature and wild human nature, Parkman believed, lay the ultimate and tragic fate of both. For as he perceived the intimate natural connection of wilderness and Indian, so he perceived the inability of either to survive the impact of civilized society. The Indian is "hewn out of rock," said Parkman, "and it is this fixed and rigid quality which has proved his ruin." The advance of civilization, which neither could assimilate or control, doomed both the Indian and his primitive world. "He and his forest," wrote Parkman, "must perish together."[14]

Parkman's concept of the self-destroying qualities of savagism, as he explained it in *Pontiac*, was in effect both a statement and a rationalization of the pre-Darwinian principle of survival of the fittest. To say that the Indian's doom was sealed by the touch of civilization, and that the advance of civilization into his wilderness was inevitable, was to put into different terms the later Darwinian view that the weak disappear before the strong, the ill-adapted before the better-adapted. This inevitable, mutual death of savage and wilderness Parkman, despite his aversion to romantic sentiment, found it possible to regret. The historical narrative matter of the book concerned Pontiac's desperate attempt to turn back the advancing tide of English civilization. But its larger, implicit theme was the ultimate death of the Indian and his wilderness world, personified in Pontiac, whose "conspiracy" was simply the vehicle of its exposition. At the beginning of the book Parkman prepared the Indian's destiny; at the close, in Pontiac's personal fate, he encompassed that of the race. Parkman made his point clear in the closing image of the book, in which the modern city has quite literally erased the forest, and white civilization has overwhelmed the Indian. The burial place of the murdered chief, Parkman noted, was marked by neither monument

14. *Ibid.*, I, 1-3, 44-45.

nor memory; "For a mausoleum, a city has risen above the forest hero; and the race he hated with such burning rancor trample unceasing footsteps over his forgotten grave." Pontiac, buried beneath the bustle of St. Louis, served as the symbol of lost savagery buried beneath civilization.

The Oregon Trail was observation; *Pontiac* was generalization. The one was a narrative journal; the other historical writing. In *Pontiac* Parkman established a position for Indians in his historical system, a reason for their being, a rationale for their destruction. If neither Indian nor wilderness could survive the advance of a higher and more energetic culture, it seemed in the nature of things that both should perish as victims of inexorable progress. If the Indian were not equipped to survive, his elimination was therefore justifiable; the logic of events, as Parkman wrote, made the passing of the race "a foregone conclusion."[15]

Pontiac, however, was Parkman's first attempt at formal history, and his only book dealing wholly with an Indian theme. Over the fourteen years that separated it from his next one, he evolved the plan of his "great history" of *France and England in North America*, subtitled "A Series of Historical Narratives," the first of which appeared as *Pioneers of France in the New World* in 1865 and the last as *A Half-Century of Conflict* in 1892. He intended to construct his multi-volumed narrative about the central conflict of ideologies which the contest for North America symbolized, that is, the struggle between French authoritarianism and English freedom, between France's "barren absolutism" and the "crude, chaotic, vitality" of English liberty for mastery of the continent. When he came to the second volume of his series, *The Jesuits in North America in the*

15. Parkman's review of Cooper's collected novels reflected the conclusions already reached in *Pontiac*. Published in the *North American Review*, LXXIV, 147-161 (Jan., 1852), the review had praise for Cooper's ability to create character and sustain narrative, but none for his Indians, who were "for the most part either superficially or falsely drawn." Uncas, Cooper's Indian hero in *The Last of the Mohicans*, to Parkman "does not at all resemble a genuine Indian," whereas the deceitful and villainous Magua is "a less untruthful portrait." The contrast between Cooper's intent and the reality of Indian character makes Parkman's judgment dryly ironic. Parkman also published two more long reviews in the *North American*, which became the basis for the introductory chapter of *The Jesuits in North America* (1867). These were "The Manners and Customs of Primitive Indian Tribes," CI, 28-64 (July, 1865); and "Indian Superstitions," CIII, 1-18 (July, 1866). His earlier review of Squier's *Aboriginal Monuments* and Lewis Morgan's *League of the Iroquois*, while tremendously erudite, said little about the Indian mind or character: see the *Christian Examiner*, L, 417-478 (May, 1851). His review of Stone's "Life and Times of Red Jacket," *Atlantic Monthly*, XIX, 383-384 (March, 1867), noted once more the Indian's inability to adapt to civilization.

Seventeenth Century (1867), he had to fix the Indian and his presence in the wilderness within the framework of the Anglo-Gallic struggle, and to explain his role and assess his meaning in terms of the larger historical context.

The Jesuits marked the third and final stage in Parkman's concept of the Indian. In *The Oregon Trail* he drew the Indian as savage; in *Pontiac* he concluded that the Indian's savagery insured his ultimate extinction; in *The Jesuits* he suggested the meaning and function of that savagery in American history.

The introduction to the book, a ninety-page essay on Indian history, customs, government, religion, and the nature of Indian life, represented the fruit of years of study and reflection.[16] As before, Parkman's account reeks with repugnance for many of the details of Indian life, concluding that "to make the Indian the hero of a romance is mere nonsense."[17] The "noble red man of popular song and story" is only a "dream of poets, rhetoricians, and sentimentalists." Instead, he is a thorough savage whose mind is "hopelessly stagnant," in whose culture "the idea of moral good has no part," and whose God is merely a reflection of his own "barbarous and degraded humanity." Even the Iroquois, for whom Parkman had a grudging respect, was only a "finished and developed savage . . . ,— an Indian of Indians," true, but still "a thorough savage . . . , inveterately attached to savagery," incapable of civilization. Indians "melted away," he wrote, echoing *Pontiac*, "not because civilization destroyed them, but because their own ferocity and intractable indolence made it impossible that they should exist in its presence." But this time Parkman found no tear to shed at their passing.

In *The Jesuits* Parkman was writing part of the story of how an "ordered democracy" developed with God's help out of English (not French) origins in North America in the eighteenth century; therefore the capture of French Canada by the English was the decisive factor in that development. What role had the Indian played in this

16. "It is the result," he wrote Charles Eliot Norton, "of a very careful study of every thing—I speak literally—of the least value which has been written on or near the subject in early or recent times" (Jacobs, *op. cit.*, I, 174).

17. *The Jesuits in North America in the Seventeenth Century* (rev. ed.; Boston, 1874), especially his accounts of Indian torture (pp. 80-83); the Huron Feast of the Dead (pp. 71-79); the life of Indian women (pp. xxxiii-xxxv); and Indian cannibalism (pp. xl-xli). In a review of Bancroft's *Native Races of California*, *North American Review*, CXX, 44 (Jan., 1875), he came perilously close to the "good Indian is a dead Indian" theory, writing that the only man fitted to deal with Indians was "an honest, judicious, and determined soldier."

mighty drama of conquest? In Parkman's estimation, an unexpected and vital one.

Had the Jesuits succeeded in Christianizing and civilizing the Indians, he explained, the tribes would have multiplied, prospered, and spread over the Great Lakes and Mississippi Valley during the seventeenth century, occupying the area for New France and providing her with a lucrative source of revenue. The French would have settled and organized the West, making it a stronghold against which English arms could never have prevailed. In the eighteenth century the British armies would have been confronted not by "a depleted antagonist, still feeble from the exhaustion of a starved and persecuted infancy, but by an athletic champion of the principles of Richelieu and Loyola." There would have been in the American West a strong New France, "formed on the ideas and habits of a feudal monarchy, and controlled by a hierarchy profoundly hostile to freedom of thought ... , a hindrance and a stumbling block in the way of that majestic experiment of which America is the field."[18]

But because the Indian was irretrievably savage, none of this came about. The Jesuits' attempt to Christianize him failed, ruined "by the guns and tomahawks of the Iroquois." Again Parkman detailed in the book the nature of Indian barbarity—cruelty, deceit, and sensuality—and most of all its irrationality. The Indian intelligence was simply not rational; he could not be civilized and was swept aside; France could not hold the West; North America became English. Thus, Parkman could write, "Liberty may thank the Iroquois, that, by their insensate fury, the plans of her adversary were brought to naught, and a peril and woe averted to her future." The fact of savagery therefore had clear and direct historical effects. France lost an empire while the Jesuits tried to save unsavable souls and to civilize the uncivilizable—"the Providence of God seemed in their eyes dark and inexplicable, but from the standpoint of liberty, that Providence is as clear as the sun at noon."[19]

That the Indian could not be civilized, Parkman concluded, was

18. *Ibid.*, chap. xxxiv, pp. 447-449.

19. *Ibid.*, pp. 74, 76, 86-87, 66-68, 226, 448. Since the remainder of Parkman's historical writings were less directly concerned with the Indian, he found no reason to revise or expand his view. When the occasion arose, he repeated in substance what he had already said about savagism; for example, see *The Old Regime in Canada* (Boston, 1874), p. 376; *Frontenac and New France* (Boston, 1877), pp. 77-78; and *A Half-Century of Conflict* (Boston, 1892), I, 216.

one of the decisive facts in making the United States possible; had he been less of a savage, more adaptable to change, American history might have been different. And therein, to Parkman, lay the irony and the tragedy of the Indian's historic role. Ironically, his "inveterate barbarism" insured the final victory for the forces of freedom; tragically, for by reason of his own "intractable savagery," he was "destined to melt and vanish before the advancing waves of Anglo-American power." By thus perceiving and explaining the part played by the Indian in the unfolding drama of North America, Parkman found a way to give order to the red man's past, purpose to his presence, and tragic meaning to his fate.

PERSON, PLACE, AND THING IN JAMES'S THE PORTRAIT OF A LADY

Charles R. Anderson

Johns Hopkins University

Henry James's *The Portrait of a Lady* enjoyed the advantage of being his first major novel. It has the spontaneity that is possible only when an author lets himself go for the first time, unaware of the full extent of his powers. It was also his first artistic success with a subject and a theme that had occupied him increasingly during his long apprenticeship: the American girl involved in the international situation. Now in 1881, after many years abroad (the last six in continuous residence), James was able to record the observed reality of Europe with precision and to discriminate it from various American preconceptions and "myths." More important was his shift of focus from the sociological to the humanistic in handling the international theme—from the argument of a thesis to the creation of characters. By placing his emphasis on the "education" of Isabel Archer through her experience of Europe, he makes the cultural contrast merely a means to this end. Such are the attractions of this novel in theme and subject matter. Previous commentary has concerned itself with them almost exclusively, as if the *method* of rendering were of no importance. But *The Portrait* also marks James's first real break with the traditional novel and his pioneering of new techniques. It is with these problems of fictional art that the present essay is concerned.

A basic problem for the creator of fictions is how to put his characters in relation with one another so they can achieve communication and understanding. As long as the convention of the omniscient author prevailed, this problem was sidestepped. For the novelist who assumed he was able to penetrate the secret chambers of his characters' minds and hearts, as well as their houses, could simply pass on this knowledge to his puppets, who were then able to understand each other easily—almost at sight. But this assumption (never really made by serious authors, of course) has gone by the board in the last century. As the modern conviction has gained ground that in real life every individual is a kind of "isolato"—imprisoned in the capsule of his own self and only with the greatest difficulty able to penetrate the capsule of another self—so the responsible novelist has assumed the same difficulty for his fictional characters in their struggle to make meaningful relations with one another.

Henry James began his career just when this issue was coming to loom as crucial for the writer of fictions. He accepted the challenge as one that could be met only by developing adequate techniques. His most famous device is the use of a narrator, both as the voice for telling the story and as the point of view through which all is seen and understood. As a character who is involved in the action, as well as detached from it, he is capable of special insights; by being endowed with a detective's passion for exploring, he can circle around the character-situations and grope for all possible clues; and since he is a character rather than the creator, he can even confess in the end quite convincingly that this is all of the truth he has been able to discover, leaving much still unknown or ambiguous—something the reader might well resent in an author, who ought to *know*. As James experimented with this technique during a quarter century, he brought the novel a long way from the chronicle-fiction of his predecessors to the tighter forms we know today. The kind of loosely constructed novel likely to be written under the convention of an omniscient author—by Balzac, Dickens, George Eliot,[1] to mention only a few of his acknowledged masters— was developed in *The Ambassadors* into a marvel of dramatic structure. And the control of fictional materials made possible by a Lambert Strether, whose narrating voice virtually creates the world of this novel, was carried still further by Conrad with his ubiquitous Marlowe and by the compact first-person narrations of Hemingway—to name only acknowledged disciples of James. The narrator as point of view has

1. George Eliot was very much in James's mind during the composition of *The Portrait*, since her second marriage (to his friend John Cross) and her death a few months afterward came during the spring and summer of 1880. He had been an ardent reader of Dickens since childhood, and in the autumn of 1880 was contemplating writing a study of him. And all during the 1870's he was struggling to get out from under "the great shadow of Balzac" (Leon Edel, *Henry James*, New York, 1962, II, 371 and 420; Preface to *Roderick Hudson*, New York Edition, p. xiv).

several advantages over the novelist speaking in his own person, but this device does not solve all the technical problems. How can the other characters, whose story is being told, really achieve communication and understanding, how can they penetrate the appearances, façades, masks, and masquerades by which people conceal their secret selves from each other?

It has been a commonplace of Jamesian criticism to say that his characters exist only in their relations with each other. But the crux of the matter is, how do they arrive at any real relations at all? I propose to show that they do so only indirectly, and that the process of their doing so is the whole of their story. To put it in an oversimplified formula: character a does not understand character b until he comes to understand object x, which he assumes is symbolic of character b—the inherent ambivalence of the symbol being a chief complicating factor. I use the term "object," for convenience, to include a multitude of things: a house, estate, or rural landscape; the façade of a boulevard, the interior of a favorite cafe, an opera box, or a street scene; a painting, statue, or other work of art—and so on. This technique is particularly effective in *The Portrait of a Lady*, James's first masterpiece, published in 1881. This novel does not employ the device of a semi-detached narrator in any strict sense, but uses a similar point of view by "seeing" the whole story (or most of it) through one character's viewing consciousness, only occasionally "going outside." Isabel Archer, who lacks a rational and analytical mind, chiefly understands by what she *sees*—places and things which she takes to be symbolic.

The Portrait is pervaded by an elaborate system of imagery—the objects that fascinate the heroine as possible keys to the meaning of Europe and its people, those used by her friends when characterizing one another in their conversations with Isabel, and occasional symbols offered unobtrusively by the author himself. For example, her uncle is pictured as an old man contentedly drinking his tea (that is, what life had brewed for him) from an "unusually large cup, of a different pattern from the rest of the set and painted in brilliant colors." Madame Merle is compared to a rare and lovely piece of porcelain, but with a crack in it. Isabel's newspaper friend, Miss Stackpole, appears to her cousin "as crisp and new and comprehensive as a first issue before the folding and with no misprints." A large number of images are applied to the four men who center their lives on the heroine: Ralph Touchett, Lord Warburton, Gilbert Osmond, and Caspar Goodwood. The most elaborate series is inspired by Isabel herself, used by friends and suitors as they try to characterize what she means to them. All this richness is justified on the naturalistic level (and so is not mere ornament) by the fact that these characters are unusually sensitive to their milieu, especially Isabel Archer. In addition to normal desires for love and marriage, she also wants an education. She has come over to observe the "great lighted scene of Europe," to absorb the beauty and knowledge it has to offer: its art treasures, its storied past, its traditions, cities, and institutions, as well as its people and way of life. On a larger scale are four important houses: the family home back in America, her cousins' English house, Osmond's Tuscan villa, Isabel's Roman palace. All are described in great detail, and two of them undergo considerable change in the developing perspectives through which the heroine and the reader see them. They come to symbolize not only the characters who live in them and the events that take place there but the several stages of Isabel's education, thus forming the thematic structure of the novel.

Narrative structure is another matter entirely. Whether the span of time to be covered in a fiction is long or short—the entire life of the hero, or the events of a single day—there is always a temporal problem for the novelist. He must decide which parts of his story to elaborate and which parts to skimp, or to skip altogether. That is, he must proportion the time scheme he has chosen to the space at his command. In *The Portrait* James limited himself to a six-year period in the life of his heroine and allowed himself the maximum spread of the Victorian two-volume novel, but still he ran into trouble. As he warned himself in *The Notebooks*, during the process of composition, he had allowed himself so much space for elaborating Isabel Archer's initial experience of Europe that he would have to foreshorten dramatically at the end.[2] But in solving this strictly technical problem he created the climactic scene of the novel, Isabel's midnight vigil. Put in specific terms of proportioning, this means that two-thirds of the book (thirty-five chapters out of fifty-five) are given over to her European "education" during the first two years abroad, ending with her marriage in June, 1873. Then, skipping

2. *The Notebooks of Henry James*, ed. F. O. Mathiessen and Kenneth B. Murdock (New York, 1947), pp. 15-16.

nearly four years, the next few chapters take up the story of her married life in Rome during the winter of 1877 with a series of incidents culminating in a recognition scene, revealing the sinister relation between her husband and Madame Merle. This leads swiftly to the midnight vigil in Chapter 42, three-fourths the way through the book, in which Isabel reviews the high hopes and tragic outcome of her life. For the author it was a brilliant device for evoking in a symbolic vision the long years of her ordeal by marriage, instead of having to spell them out in discursive narrative. For the reader, who follows the heroine sympathetically in her exploration, it opens a door into the novel's full significance. And for the critic, faced with the impossible task of explicating a novel of more than eight hundred pages, it offers a single compact chapter for close reading.

It has been suggested previously that the characters in James's fictions arrive at meaningful relations only when they come to understand the objects—places or things—which they think of as symbolizing each other. It is in keeping with the basic techniques of this novel that now at last understanding comes to Isabel also through imagery, much of it being inversions of the same images she had failed to grasp earlier. Remarkable as it may be for so much significance to be contained in one brief chapter, it is even more remarkable that the key revelation comes from a single image. This is achieved by an elaborate play on the ambivalent meaning of vista— from the Latin *videre*, "to see," the controlling word in the novel. At strategic points throughout the story of Isabel's education a *vista*, in the Italian sense of a panorama, has been used as symbolic of the opportunities her European experiences were spreading out before her for art and knowledge, for love and marriage. But in English "vista" is normally used in the very different sense of a long *allée* whose lines seem, by perspective, to converge on some object—happily some object of beauty. Now in Chapter 42, four years after marriage, the image is used in both opposed meanings simultaneously, with startling effect. As she takes stock of her life in this midnight meditation, aware at last of her husband's subtle villainy, she suddenly finds "the infinite vista of a multiplied life to be a dark, narrow alley with a dead wall at the end." To follow the transformations of this image through the novel is to discover much of its meaning.

The first of the panoramas of opportunity that had opened up for Isabel Archer came in Chapter 1. At Gardencourt, the fine old country house of her aunt and uncle, she literally walked onto the lighted stage of Europe. The scene was at tea time on the lawn, as the "flood of summer light had begun to ebb." Since Isabel had just arrived she was still indoors, and it was from this vantage point she got her first glimpse of the park outside:

> Her uncle's house seemed a picture made real; no refinement of the agreeable was lost upon Isabel; the rich perfection of Gardencourt at once revealed a world and gratified a need. The large, low rooms, with brown ceilings and dusky corners, the deep embrasures and curious casements, the quiet light on dark, polished panels, the deep greenness outside, that seemed always peeping in, the sense of well-ordered privacy in the center of a "property"—... these things were much to the taste of our young lady. (I, 73)[3]

As she emerged, the ample doorway framed the world that awaited her: guests assembled on the lawn for tea, great oaks making a shade like velvet curtains, tables and cushioned seats furnishing the place as if it were an outdoor living room. This was her first English vista: "Privacy here reigned supreme, and the wide carpet of turf that covered the level hill-top seemed but the extension of a luxurious interior" (I, 3). Later on she explored the grounds with her cousin Ralph Touchett all the way to their boundary at the river, "where the opposite shore seemed still a part of the foreground of the landscape" (I, 87-88). But on this first afternoon it was the figures in the nearer landscape that caught her eye, especially the handsome Lord Warburton, booted and spurred, who had just ridden over from his neighboring estate. "Oh, I hoped there would be a lord," Isabel exclaimed characteristically as her cousin led her forward to be introduced: "it's just like a novel!" (I, 18).

On later occasions, as related in Chapter 7, she pursued the charming English vista far beyond Gardencourt, driving with Ralph over the surrounding country "through winding lanes and byways full of the rural incidents she had confidently expected to find; past cottages thatched and timbered, past ale-houses latticed and sanded, past patches of ancient common and glimpses of empty parks, between hedgerows made thick by midsummer" (I, 88). So the picture book of England, as American visitors preconceive it, was turned page

3. Volume and page references, in parentheses following the quotations, are to the New York Edition (Scribner's, 1907-1917) of *The Portrait of a Lady*, James's revised text. (The same references also apply to the more accessible Modern Library Edition.) Chapter locations have been added both to facilitate reference to all editions and also to indicate the wide diffusion throughout the novel of the images in the vigil scene.

by page before her eyes. What she saw there was just the opposite of what she had left behind. By contrast the American landscape seemed bare of the picturesque, without history or art to relieve its monotony. The Archer home in Albany was particularly bleak, as pictured in a flashback to that cold rainy afternoon in spring when Isabel was awaiting the arrival of her aunt, Mrs. Touchett, in a shabbily furnished room behind a permanently bolted front door: "She knew that this silent, motionless portal opened into the street; if the sidelights had not been filled with green paper she might have looked out upon the little brown stoop and the well-worn brick pavement. But she had no wish to look out" (I, 30). Life in America seemed to offer her little more prospect than was afforded by this house; even marriage to Caspar Goodwood, her persistent American suitor, would have meant only a more prosperous version of the same bareness. It was to rescue Isabel from this that her aunt touched her with a magic wand and brought her to Europe, where the opportunities were infinitely richer. Yet the possibilities of the first panorama offered by England failed to materialize for her, though not through any fault of its own. The dashing Lord Warburton had actually proposed marriage—"just like a novel"—but she turned him down, determined to see the broader vistas promised by the Continent before considering her education complete.

Meantime Ralph had arranged for a large part of the Touchett fortune to be settled on her so that she could "soar and sail," as he put it. Her first flight was across France to Italy, where the next great panorama was to open out for her (Chapter 21). Pausing just over the border at San Remo, "on the edge of this larger adventure," she looked with yearning eyes along the eastward curve of the Italian riviera:

> The charm of the Mediterranean coast only deepened for our heroine on acquaintance, for it was the threshold of Italy, the gate of admirations. Italy, as yet imperfectly seen and felt, stretched before her as a land of promise, a land in which a love of the beautiful might be comforted by endless knowledge. (I, 320)

This generalized prospect came to focus almost immediately in the view from Gilbert Osmond's villa on the outskirts of Florence, as elaborated in the next five chapters (22-26). The meanings of the two vistas for Isabel are given in identical terms, but the preliminary description of the latter differs in one curiously interesting detail. As one approached Osmond's villa from its little rural piazza, "its imposing front had a somewhat incommunicative character. It was the mask, not the face of the house. It had heavy lids, but no eyes; the house in reality looked another way—looked off behind, into splendid openness and the range of the afternoon light" (I, 325). When Isabel was taken there by Madame Merle, to meet her future husband, she walked straight through this façade—the blank-looking brown wall with its small doorway—to the terrace at the rear with its expansive view of Tuscan hills and valleys. The sequence here is exactly the reverse of the key image used in her midnight vigil: "she had suddenly found the infinite vista of a multiplied life to be a dark, narrow alley with a dead wall at the end" (II, 189).

Once inside Osmond's villa, Isabel discovered that it was a kind of miniature museum of the art and history of Italy, and presumably a symbol of its owner, who had devoted his life to high connoisseurship. As he showed her through the numerous apartments filled with his treasures, she felt almost "oppressed at last with the accumulation of beauty and knowledge to which she found herself introduced." But this had been her avowed purpose in coming to Italy, of course, to pursue her education in such matters. And when she was led to the garden terrace at the rear, the panorama there opened out to her eyes complemented what she had seen inside:

The sun had got low, the golden light took a deeper tone, and on the mountains and the plain that stretched beneath them the masses of purple shadow glowed.... The scene had an extraordinary charm. The air was almost solemnly still, and the large expanse of the landscape, with its gardenlike culture and nobleness of outline, its teeming valley and delicately-fretted hills, its peculiarly human-looking touches of habitation, lay there in splendid harmony and classic grace. (I, 379-380; chap. 24)

As Isabel returned to Florence at the end of the day, landscape and villa and owner tended to fuse into one picture:

She had carried away an image from her visit to his hill-top ...: the image of a quiet, clever, sensitive, distinguished man, strolling on a moss-grown terrace above the sweet Val d'Arno .... The picture had no flourishes, but she liked its lowness of tone and the atmosphere of summer twilight that prevaded it ..., of a lonely, studious life in a lovely land; ...of a care for beauty and perfection so natural and so cultivated together that the career appeared to stretch beneath it in the disposed vistas and with the ranges of steps and terraces and fountains of a formal Italian garden. (I, 399-400; chap. 26)

Since Osmond had deliberately "staged" this meeting with Isabel, as the first move in his cunning suit for her hand and fortune, he would have been gratified to know how perfectly he had achieved the effect aimed at. But he was a long time finding out his success. Though his proposal of marriage followed quickly, she delayed her response for a year, meanwhile restlessly seeking out the romantic in travels all over Europe. Returning to Florence, she put her experiences under review in order to reach a decision:

She had ranged, she would have said, through space and surveyed much of mankind, and was therefore now, in her own eyes, a very different person from the frivolous young woman from Albany who had begun to take the measure of Europe on the lawn at Gardencourt a couple of years before.... If her thoughts just now had inclined themselves to retrospect, instead of fluttering their wings nervously about the present, they would have evoked a multitude of interesting pictures. These pictures would have been both landscapes and figurepieces. (II, 32; chap. 31)

When she finally accepted Osmond, in the face of strong family opposition, he put the proper figures in the proper landscape, clinching his courtship by a dramatic appeal to the scene of their first meeting at his Tuscan villa that had so impressed her. He did this by making a new metaphor out of the vista from his terrace and applying it to their future married years:

My dear girl, I can't tell you how life seems to stretch there before us— what a long summer afternoon awaits us. It's the latter half of an Italian day—with a golden haze, and the shadows just lengthening, and that divine delicacy in the light, the air, the landscape, which I have loved all my life and which you love today.... It's all soft and mellow—it has the Italian colouring. (II, 81-82; chap. 35)

The one striking point all these vistas have in common is that they are set in a waning afternoon, or in actual twilight. This seems strange indeed since, as images, their function is to suggest the possibilities unfolding for a beautiful young lady on the verge of maturity and on the threshold of marriage. Their twilit aspect is clearly intended by James to be prophetic. Though first seen by the romantic Isabel as a "golden haze," in the end it is recognized by the disillusioned Isabel as a portent of the night that is closing about her life. In her midnight vigil, Chapter 42, imagery of light is replaced by imagery of darkness, and the expansive panorama opening out horizontally is replaced by a vertical shaft looking down into a kind of dungeon. The key passage about the "infinite vista of a multiplied life," which is first changed to a "dark, narrow alley," continues:

Instead of leading to the high places of happiness, from which the world would seem to lie below one, so that one could look down with a sense of exaltation and advantage, and judge and choose and pity, it led rather downward and earthward, into realms of restriction and depression where the sound of other lives, easier and freer, was heard as from above, and where it served to deepen the feeling of failure. It was her deep distrust of her husband—this was what darkened the world.... Then the shadows had begun to gather; it was as if Osmond deliberately, almost malignantly, had put the lights out one by one. The dusk at first was vague and thin, and she could still see her way in it. But it steadily deepened, ... [until] there were certain corners of her prospect that were impenetrably black. (II, 189-190)

Six chapters and several months earlier, when the Osmonds' married life in Rome is first presented, similar images of dark-light and dungeon-palace should have prepared the reader for what was to come, but the passage was so phrased as to be immediately discounted. Little Mr. Rosier, formerly a hanger-on of Isabel's and now a hopeless suitor of her stepdaughter Pansy, was on his way to one of the Osmonds' celebrated *salons*. As he approached Palazzo Roccanera, "a dark and massive structure . . .—a palace by Roman measure, but a dungeon to poor Rosier's apprehensive mind," it struck him as living up to its name (*Roccanera* meaning "black rock," or less literally black castle-keep) :

It seemed to him of evil omen that the young lady he wished to marry ... should be immured in a kind of domestic fortress, a pile which bore a stern old Roman name, which smelt of historic deeds, of crime and craft and violence.... Rosier was haunted by the conviction that at picturesque periods young girls had been shut up there to keep them from their true loves, and then, under the threat of being thrown into convents, had been forced into unholy marriages. (II, 100-101; chap. 36)

To be sure, this is too melodramatic for anyone to take stock in other than the immature Mr. Rosier. Even he dismissed it as soon as he entered Mrs. Osmond's "warm, rich-looking reception rooms" and saw her, dressed in black velvet, looking "high and splendid . . . yet oh so radiantly gentle!" His appreciation of her was based partly on "his eye for decorative character," but he was sure the years had touched her only to enhance her "lustre." "Now, at all events, framed in the gilded doorway, she struck our young man as the picture of a gracious lady" (II, 105; chap. 37) . This is the scene that gives the novel its title. But it was ironically a false portrait of Isabel behind which she hid her suffering, her true portrait being turned to the wall as her devoted cousin Ralph realized.

Rosier's gloomy foreboding as he approached Palazzo Roccanera, romantic and unfounded though it seemed, was a truer picture of the actual situation inside Isabel's Roman palace than what met his admiring eye. At first her new home had promised to combine all that had impressed her at Gardencourt and at Osmond's villa, with the added note of grandeur. She was to be the great lady, surrounded by beauty and knowledge, mistress of a house with a storied past that yet offered the present opportunity of elegant privacy or a richly patterned social life, as one chose. Instead, during her midnight vigil, it is revealed as a house of gloom with no light of love or even humanity:

> She could live it over again, the incredulous terror with which she had taken the measure of her dwelling. Between those four walls she had lived ever since; they were to surround her for the rest of her life. It was the house of darkness, the house of dumbness, the house of suffocation. Osmond's beautiful mind gave it neither light nor air; Osmond's beautiful mind indeed seemed to peep down from a small high window and mock at her. (II, 196)

The meaning of this phrase, "Osmond's beautiful mind," has ironic repercussions back through the novel. It will be remembered that she had first thought of Italy as the land of promise, where "a love of the beautiful might be comforted by endless knowledge." And when she first met Osmond he seemed the very embodiment of this conception of Italy: "There had been an indefinable beauty about him—in his situation, in his mind, in his face" (II, 192). At last, during her midnight vigil, the paradox is made clear to her:

> She had not been mistaken about the beauty of his mind; she knew that organ perfectly now. She had lived with it, she had lived *in* it almost—it appeared to have become her habitation. . . . A mind more ingenious, more pliant, more cultivated, more trained to admirable exercises, she had not encountered; and it was this exquisite instrument she had now to reckon with. (II, 194)

"Osmond's beautiful mind" has become both her prison and her torture chamber. At this point one remembers that when she had first approached the rather forbidding façade of his Tuscan villa, "it looked somehow as if, once you were in, you would need an act of energy to get out" (I, 364; chap. 24). This whimsical fear, fleetingly entertained, materialized after marriage in something far more subtly cruel than physical imprisonment:

The real offence, as she ultimately perceived, was her having a mind of her own at all. Her mind was to be his—attached to his own like a small garden-plot to a deer-park. He would rake the soil gently and water the flowers; he would weed the beds and gather an occasional nosegay. It would be a pretty piece of property for a proprietor already far-reaching. (II, 200)

This image of being "owned" by Osmond, which comes to Isabel during her midnight meditation, suggests exactly the opposite of what marriage to Lord Warburton had offered early in the novel. Dedicated to the service of his country, he would have respected her right to an independent and happy life. As the mistress of Lockleigh she could have enjoyed the romance of presiding over "a castle in a legend" and, far more importantly, her proud function as the wife of a liberal peer in the forefront of reform.

Another image of Osmond's cruelty is cast in terms of his owner-ship of Isabel not as a piece of property but as an *objet d'art* to add to his collection. When his suit for her hand and fortune had proved successful, he thought of his good fortune in an elaborate metaphor that brands him unmistakably as an exploiter. She was to be "a silver plate" that reflected his thoughts on its "polished, elegant surface." Further, she was to be "a plate that he might heap up with ripe fruits ... so that talk might become for him a sort of served dessert." Thus she would be useful as well as ornamental. His final elaboration of the image seems to encompass the use he intended to make of her fortune of £70,000 sterling: "He found the silver quality in this per-fection in Isabel; he could tap her imagination with his knuckle and make it ring" (II, 79; chap. 35). Though the reader overhears this scheming meditation, it never reaches Isabel's ears, of course. Yet she was not without ample warning. Ralph, in trying to dissuade her from marrying, had branded her fiancé as a "sterile dilettante," and though she defended him blindly she did confess to herself that he lived too much by his sensibility, "in a sorted, sifted, and arranged world." But his egotism was so skilfully masked she was slow in penetrating to it.

As long as Isabel remains under the spell of Osmond's calculated charm she misunderstands both him and Ralph. Seeing each one for what he truly is comprises the resolution of the novel, and her con-stant comparison of them forms a major pattern of her story's de-velopment. Her cousin and her husband are natural foils, since they stand for opposite values in James's moral code. One is the "appreciator," one the "exploiter," of other people. It is true that many aspects of their lives seem parallel: both are expatriates and bachelors who find themselves in mid-career drawn into Isabel's orbit; both are cosmopolites whose interests have centered on art and history. Yet it is in these apparent similarities that their differences are most dramatically revealed.

The characterizing image for Ralph Touchett occurred early in the novel, Chapter 10, when he was showing the art gallery at Gardencourt to a guest. He singled out one of the pictures, a small Lancret, as symbolic of his tastes: "[It] represented a gentleman in a pink doublet and hose and a ruff, leaning against the pedestal of the statue of a nymph in a garden and playing the guitar to two ladies seated on the grass. 'That's my ideal of a regular occupation,' he said" (I, 124-125). Similarly it was in terms of painting that he saw Isabel. When he showed his pictures to his beautiful cousin, he found himself looking at her more than at them, and thinking: "a character like that is the finest thing in *nature*, it is finer than the finest work of art." At the end of the novel, after he knows the tragedy of her life, he reflects: "She was meant to be original, to be natural, to be the full portrait of confident zestful life." This was the ideal portrait of a lady Ralph would have liked to paint.

Isabel was not privy to these inner thoughts, of course, but everything about her cousin's behavior from the beginning had bespoken the same dedication to beauty—to appreciating and serving her—the same selfless love. But she remains blind to all this—as well as to her husband's exploitative hatred—for a long time. It is not until she comes to understand the images characterizing both Ralph and Osmond that she understands the two men who mean most in her life, for good and for ill. By the time of the midnight vigil, however, her vision of the true nature of her husband has brought with it a much clearer view of her cousin. As she returns once again to a comparison of the two men, she first becomes aware of the latter's superiority of mind and then of something far more important:

It was simply that Ralph was generous and that her husband was not. There was something in Ralph's talk, in his smile ... that made the blasted circle round which she walked more spacious. He made her feel the good of the world; he made her feel what might have been. (II, 203; chap. 42)

The rest of the novel is given over to a resolution of this last phrase, though until she has come to terms with her actual present situation she cannot conceive "what might have been."

The many images that over the years have provided Isabel with clues to Osmond's cold egotism reach their culmination in the scene of his final appearance in the novel. She has received a telegram that Ralph is dying and wants her to come to him in England. When she goes to her husband's study to ask his "permission," she finds him seated at a table with an old folio propped in front of him:

This volume was open at a page of small coloured plates, and Isabel presently saw that he had been copying from it the drawing of an antique coin. A box of water-colours and fine brushes lay before him, and he had already transferred to a sheet of immaculate paper the delicate, finely-tinted disk. (II, 352; chap. 51)

He not only refuses his assent, saying that her request flouts the proprieties of marriage; he even refuses to divert his attention from his work. In the dialogue that follows she makes an open break, declaring that his opposition to her desires is "malignant." What makes this scene memorable is not the argument but the characterizing image of Osmond copying the antique coin. It symbolizes his concern with the form of art, the faultless imitation, rather than the creative spirit; his treatment of marriage as an institution rather than an affair of the heart; his cold metallic nature, calculating values either in terms of the rarity of an old coin or the current purchasing power of Isabel's fortune. Thus the image of Osmond as cold and hard in the midnight vigil, Chapter 42, is both prospective and retrospective—linking the image of the silver plate with that of the antique coin (Chapters 35 and 51).

When Isabel returns at the end of the novel to Gardencourt, the scene of her European launching, she is prepared to understand all. Wandering alone through the great drawing room and the deserted art gallery, she meditates yet once more on her tragic career: "She might have had another life and she might have been a woman more blest" (II, 404). One version of what might have been comes in the revelation at Ralph's bedside. With his death imminent, they are determined to be open and frank with each other. She confesses the failure of her marriage—Osmond's villainy, her own suffering—and her blindness to Ralph's love. His last words drop the pretense of cousinly devotion: "And remember this ... that if you've been hated you've also been loved. Ah but, Isabel—*adored!*" (II, 417; chap.

54). These words merely confirm what she had already learned from a sequence of images. What looms from the whole scene is a vision of the life they might have had together, at least for a few years. Gardencourt could have been transformed from a house of death into a house of sweetness and light. The glow of Ralph's love and the lambent play of his mind would have made it the opposite of Palazzo Roccanera, "the house of darkness and suffocation."

The final possibility of "another life" she might have had materializes after the funeral when Caspar Goodwood comes to press his case for the last time. Of all her suitors he is the wholly masculine one—in contrast to Ralph the invalid, Osmond the aesthete, Warburton the romantic nobleman. Since the field is now clear before Goodwood, he begins with a challenge she cannot refute— "You're the most unhappy of women, and your husband's the deadliest of fiends"—then folds her in a passionate embrace, an "act of possession" she admits he is justified in. But though she feels "that she has never been loved before," her resistance suggests she is still afraid of sexual love, still essentially virginal in spite of her years of marriage. She flees from him back to Rome and duty, back to the house of darkness. Goodwood's first preparation for his bold attempt at a rescue came from what he learned at first hand during a visit to Isabel in Rome a few months earlier. There Osmond, in a kind of perverse humor, put on a genial show of friendliness with him, pretending to be very confidential about "the conjugal harmony prevailing at Palazzo Roccanera." The curiously paradoxical image he used was only vaguely understood by Goodwood at the time: "We're as united, you know, as the candlestick and the snuffers" (II, 309; chap. 48). The real fiendishness of the double meaning here becomes apparent to him only after the dying Ralph reveals the truth about Isabel's marriage. "Snuffers" normally refers to an instrument for extinguishing candles. But "to snuff" can also mean to trim the carbon from a candlewick, hence "to make clearer or brighter, to purge." This is the perfect image for an exploiter. Osmond's idea of marriage was that it gave him the right to trim Isabel's flame in order to make it burn for his pleasure, then when he tired of her to put it out. Ralph had known this about him intuitively from the beginning, and so had tried to dissuade her from marrying him. Goodwood found it out late and tried to dissuade her from going back to him.

The revelation comes to Isabel herself during the midnight vigil in an image that foreshadows the candlestick and snuffers: "It was as if Osmond deliberately, almost malignantly, had put the lights out one by one" (II, 190). The key chapter itself, in keeping with the fine artistry that controls the whole of *The Portrait*, is framed by similar imagery. It begins as she leans back in her chair, closes her eyes, and for a long time ("far into the night and further still") sits in the deserted drawing-room given up to her meditation: "A servant came in to attend to the fire, and she bade him bring fresh candles and then go to bed" (II, 186). Then, after she has explored the meaning of her life through the intricate system of images and counter-images analyzed in this essay, the chapter concludes: "When the clock struck four she got up; she was going to bed at last, for the lamp had long since gone out and the candles burned down to their sockets" (II, 205). Isabel remains in the house of darkness, but she has seen the light. Like many of James's novels the story ends not in a resolving action but in a clarifying awareness, a new understanding that comes from self-knowledge. What gives *The Portrait* its special distinction is the brilliant new technique by which this is rendered in the midnight vigil.

It would be absurd to claim that the "retrospective meditation" was invented by Henry James. Novelists for a long time had made use of this convenient device, either to speed up the narration by using the faster pace of exposition, or to comment on the story through the mouth of a character and so avoid author-intrusion. Two examples will illustrate, drawn from Jane Austen and Hawthorne, predecessors he knew and admired. At one of the numerous minor crises in *Pride and Prejudice*, Elizabeth Bennet abruptly terminated a conversation with Mr. Darcy's cousin and withdrew to the Parsonage, where "shut into her own room . . . she could think without interruption of all she had heard" and try to apply it to understanding the conduct and character of the man she was eventually to marry; but her brief review of recent events (less than two pages) only "brought on a headache" and one more true-false estimate of Darcy. In *The Scarlet Letter*, for a second example, there is Dimmesdale's meditation as he returned alone from his rendezvous in the forest with Hester Prynne; in an effort to bring back some sense of reality after this dreamlike experience, "he recalled and more thoroughly defined the plans which [they] had sketched for their departure," their guilty flight, and so in a brief expository flashback (again less than two pages) we are given an episode that would have filled a chapter or more if rendered in dramatic dialogue between the conspiring lovers.

Examples could be multiplied, but these are probably representative of the retrospective meditation as used by novelists before James. It tends to be brief in itself, and it has reference to only a short past episode in the story. Furthermore, the expository manner in which it is presented seems more suited to the rational and analytical powers of the author than to the emotionally tense state of the character sunk in the reverie. As a consequence the reader simply accepts it as a useful plot summary rather than as a convincing part of the fiction. The midnight vigil in *The Portrait of a Lady* is something different altogether. In the first place it is a full-scale meditation, elaborated through a twenty-page chapter, and it refers to the entire novel—retrospectively to all that has gone before, prospectively to all that follows. More important than the scope of reference, however, is the mode of presentation. By having Isabel explore the meaning of her whole life through a labyrinth of images, James is as psychologically right as he is poetically effective. In the reverie-under-stress, as in dreams, the mind understands in pictures rather than by logically ordered recapitulation. Finally, a dramatic dimension is added by making the disillusioned heroine use for her self-exploration a cluster of images that are the reverse of those by which, as a romantically impressionable young lady, she had trapped herself in a tragic marriage.

James had been fully aware from the start that he was striking out in a new direction with *The Portrait of a Lady*. Early in 1880, when Thomas Sergeant Perry wanted to write an article on his works to date—some ten volumes of fiction, including *Roderick Hudson*, *The American*, and his one popular success *Daisy Miller*—he was told to wait until the novel-in-progress (*The Portrait*) came out: "It is from that I myself shall pretend to date—on that I shall take my stand."[4] A quarter of a century later, summing up his life work in the famous Prefaces, he placed his early masterpiece second only to *The Ambassadors* in its "architectural competence." Its success, he concluded, was due to the "technical rigour" with which the fictional materials had been given their formal structure, and he singled out as "obviously the best thing in the book" Isabel's "extraordinary meditative vigil." He had chosen to write a drama of the "inward life," as he phrased it, rather than "of the moving accident, of battle

4. Virginia Harlow, *Thomas Sergeant Perry* (Durham, N. C., 1950), p. 305.

and murder and sudden death." So he was convinced that this searching self-analysis furthered the plot better than twenty incidents would have done:

It was designed to have all the vivacity of incident and all the economy of picture . . . . It is a representation simply of her motionless *seeing*, and an attempt withal to make the mere still lucidity of her act as "interesting" as the surprise of a caravan or the identification of a pirate.[5]

The very extravagance of James's figurative language here indicates the importance he assigns to the vigil scene. What Isabel sees and *how* she sees—through colored or distorting glasses at first, with the clarity of a sharply focused lens at the end—these are essential to any understanding of her story, as the present effort has tried to demonstrate.

In conclusion, as an example of the possibilities for fiction opened up by such techniques, one may point out an interesting parallel between James's vigil scene and the last third of *Absalom, Absalom!*, written a half century later. There Faulkner also uses a midnight meditation to explore for meaning. Having failed to understand Thomas Sutpen's story by rational analysis and factual research, Quentin Compson and his Canadian roommate one cold January night at Harvard allow themselves to sink into a reverie. Gradually they fix their attention on the image of two half-brothers riding away from Sutpen's Hundred on that Christmas day long ago, project themselves backward in time, then identify imaginatively with Charles Bon and Henry Sutpen. By the end of their long and intricate vigil they have found the human love that was buried under a saga of inhumanity. This is not to suggest that Faulkner was directly influenced by *The Portrait of a Lady*, a novel utterly different in subject matter and theme, but that Henry James was one of the masters who showed him what miracles could be performed by experimenting with fictional techniques.

At any rate, it is such original devices as the midnight vigil that mark *The Portrait* as a new departure from preceding novels. Indeed, the boldness with which James staked all on technique is what makes him one of the fathers of modern fiction. For example, in *The Awkward Age* he tried writing a novel "straight as a play," by casting it almost exclusively in dialogue. In "The Turn of the Screw" he fused the modes of symbolism, allegory, and fable so closely as to

5. Preface to *The Portrait of a Lady*, New York Edition, p. xxi; the phrases quoted above are from pp. xvi-xxi.

raise an unending storm of controversy over its meaning. In *The Golden Bowl* he extended a single metaphysical conceit into an outsized two-volume novel. These are some of the brilliant experiments that enabled fiction to break away from the conventional realism of Howells and Trollope, even Flaubert, and that paved the way for the bolder new departures of Joyce and Faulkner. For the most part they came late in the master's career. But James's first triumph as a technical innovator came early, with *The Portrait of a Lady* in 1881.

LANIER AS POET

Edd Winfield Parks

University of Georgia

Sidney Lanier hoped to become a major poet, and desired that his work be judged on that basis. Overpraise of regional literature disgusted him; as early as 1869 he attacked the "insidious evil . . . of regarding our literature as *Southern* literature, our poetry as *Southern* poetry, our pictures as Southern [*sic*] pictures. I mean the habit of glossing over the intrinsic defects of artistic productions by appealing to the Southern sympathies of the artist's countrymen."[1] He was confident that his own work did not need this uncritical partiality. After the rejection of "Corn" by *Scribner's* and the *Atlantic,* and after much agonized introspection, he wrote to his wife "I *know,* through the fieriest tests of life, that I am, in soul, and shall be, in life and in utterance, a great poet" (IX, 105).

He did not achieve that goal. He never became even a major American poet, in the sense that Poe or Whitman or Emily Dickinson is. There are valid, often tragic, reasons. Throughout his adult life he suffered from tuberculosis to an extent that almost every time he completed a major or extended work he was incapacitated by severe hemorrhages of the lungs. His early death cut short work on three projected volumes of verse. For these, he left numerous poem outlines that rarely got much beyond the note-taking stage. A third factor was the precarious state of his personal finances, ranging from downright poverty to, at best, an insufficient and unstable income. Poverty forced him into literary hackwork, sometimes good, as in his redactions for boys of Froissart and of Malory; sometimes respectable, as in the erratic but occasionally brilliant guide and travel book *Florida;* sometimes degrading, as in the magazine sketches on India, a country which he had never seen. Yet even the best of these sapped energy from a man who had little vitality to spare.

Lanier himself was in part to blame. He had no sooner partially

1. *Centennial Edition of the Works and Letters of Sidney Lanier,* ed. Charles R. Anderson *et al.* (10 vols.; Baltimore, 1945), V, 260. Hereinafter cited internally by volume and page number. References to Aubrey H. Starke's *Sidney Lanier* (Chapel Hill, 1933) will be given as Starke, followed by the page number; when Starke is clearly identified, only the page number will be given.

recovered from a tubercular attack than he was planning grandiose projects, many of which he was poorly equipped to carry out. His application for a fellowship in the newly established Johns Hopkins University is almost unbelievable, for it was beyond the ability of a young, vigorous, well-trained man; in September, 1877, Lanier was thirty-five years old, in poor health, and with a decidedly sketchy academic background: "My course of study would be: first, constant research in the physics of musical tone; second, several years devotion to the acquirement of a thoroughly scientific *general* view of Mineralogy, Botany and Comparative Anatomy; third, French and German Literature" (IX, 474). President Gilman would have none of what Lanier admitted "may seem a nondescript and even flighty process," although some justification can be found in his belief that good poetry could not be written in his time "unless that poetry and your soul behind it are informed and saturated with at least the largest final conceptions of current science." Even more disruptive and irrelevant was the plan, growing out of his lectures in Baltimore, to edit an extensive series of anthologies of English poetry and (when established publishers rejected the projects) to publish them himself, although he had little experience as an editor and none as a publisher. At the time when he most needed to husband his energies and concentrate on his major talent, Lanier was spreading himself dangerously thin.

Two other stumbling-blocks he threw in the way of the reader. One was his incessant moralizing and didacticism; it may be justifiable to believe, as Lanier firmly did, that in literature morality is more important than artistry, but it is irritatingly quite another thing to "forgive" writers like Homer, Socrates, Dante, and Shakespeare (among many others: see "The Crystal") because they sometimes did not live up to his intransigent moral tone, or to dismiss Fielding and Smollett because their works seemed to him prurient. Too frequently Lanier lost all critical perspective, and this loss of perspective vitiates many of his own poems, as it does in "The Crystal." Less important is his fondness for archaic words and phraseology, his propensity in images to mix the concrete and the abstract, and his use of musical devices to such an extent that many readers consider his poems artificial and contrived.

These defects may be freely admitted, and some of them will be examined later, but there remains a residue of work that is excellent and germinal. Too often Lanier has been praised or condemned for the wrong reasons, and the sane commentaries of Aubrey Starke and Charles R. Anderson have been glided over.

The extant poems written when he was at Oglethorpe College, few in number and deficient in quality, are of value mainly in revealing the great if transitory influence of Poe, Byron, and Coleridge, and the quieter but more enduring influence of his "dearest friend" Keats (I, 228). Sidney's brother Clifford remembered the college poems, many of them no doubt lost, as being *"Byronesque*, if not *Wertheresque*, at least tinged with gloominess" (Starke, p. 37). But the gloomy introspection of Byron and Poe was soon replaced by the bracing saneness of Tennyson and, mainly through his favorite essayist Carlyle, by the romantic sentimentalism of the German writers Richter and Novalis. These men had direct formative influence on Lanier's thoughts, and on his writings. Even more direct because it was personal was the influence of Professor James Woodrow, who aroused in Lanier an interest in German lyric poetry and idealistic philosophy, and a continuing interest in trying to reconcile evolutionary thought with Presbyterian theology.

His tentative writings and, possibly more important, his plans to study in Germany were abruptly terminated by the outbreak of war. He returned briefly in 1863 to writing poems (inspired mainly by his love for Virginia Hankins) and to translating lyrics by Heine and Herder, but in the main, during this lull in his military activities, such literary energy as he could summon forth was devoted to his projected novel, *Tiger-Lilies* (1867). Somewhat oddly, it is in this prose rather than in his verse that Lanier has his best-sustained image, that of the blood-red flower of war (Book II, chap. 1).

Lanier's work, in this novel as well as in his poetry, is a curious mixture of nineteenth-century thought and antique vocabulary. He was at once a high-hearted if belated Romantic and a devout Medievalist. Shakespeare and Chaucer seemed beyond question the greatest of English poets, if not indeed the greatest of poets. He advised Paul Hamilton Hayne that to develop properly as a poet he must "drink much of Chaucer and little of Morris"; and he made such extensive use of Shakespearean imagery that Aubrey Starke credited him with so developing "the use of the Shakespearean imagery in description of nature as to develop what is almost a distinct genre" (p. 283).

In spite of his fascination with medievalism and his late, symbolic use of Bishop Aldhelm as "the Father of English Poetry," he belonged essentially to his own time. To Lanier, poetry had improved primarily by becoming more ethereal, more spirit-like. This seemed good; it led him at times, rather disconcertingly, to place Tennyson above Milton: "To discover the process of spiritualization which poetry has undergone, one has only to compare Tennyson with Milton. . . . Milton's is the strength of the sea in its rage; Tennyson's is the potential force of the sea in its repose" (V, 296-297).

Closely allied with his theory that as time flows on "sensuous things constantly etherealize" was his concept of metaphor. It was true that a metaphor was "always a union of two objects," but he also believed that metaphors "come of love rather than of thought." One object was normally abstract, the other concrete, so that the "nature-metaphor is a beautiful eternal bridal of spirit and matter . . . this harmonious union of soul and body, of spirit and nature, of essence and form, is promoted by the nature-metaphor" (V, 306-321).

It was not poetic theories but Reconstruction that aroused him to an authentic if brief lyricism. The best of these poems, "The Raven Days," states with precise power the hopelessness of men who felt themselves betrayed into such "hatred and bitterness as even the four terrible years of war had entirely failed to bring about." The poem ends with a question: will these dark raven days of sorrow be replaced by a warm light that will "gleam across the mournful plain?" More complex in structure and therefore indirect in statement is "Night and Day." Othello personifies night, but he also stands for the Civil War and for Reconstruction; the dark Moor (night) has murdered Desdemona (day), and at the same time he (as the dual strife of warfare and of reconstruction) has slain peace—and Lanier could see little hope that the "Star-memories of happier times" would soon return to his harassed region. The Shakespearian imagery is not merely a literary device; it is integral to the meaning of the poem (I, 15, 160).

Intermittently in the period from 1868 through 1874, Lanier devoted much of his poetic time and thought to a projected "novel in verse, with several lyric poems introduced by the action. The plot is founded on what was called 'the Jacquerie,' a very remarkable popular insurrection wh. happened in France about the year 1359, in the height of *Chivalry*" (VII, 397). This never-completed work was meant to be an attack on trade and a plea for the restoration of chivalry; from the surviving fragments, it seems unlikely that it would ever have become his *magnum opus*. But one lyric deserves to rank with his best: "The Hound was cuffed, the hound was kicked." The revolting peasants are symbolized by the hound which kills its master, and for once Lanier works entirely through his image. It is necessary to know the first twenty-four lines of the narrative for the lyric to become clear, but with this background the clean-cut imagery reinforces the tragic situation (see IX, 121-122).

An intensely personal poem, "Life and Song" (first entitled, significantly, "Work and Song") describes the ideal union of life and art, a fusion that would result in wholeness. Indirectly, the poem expresses a bitter realization that Lanier himself, in those poverty-stricken, troubled days, could not attain this harmony. The affirmation of faith in poetry and music is curiously balanced, yet enriched, by the note of personal renunciation (I, 16).

These seem the best of his early lyrics. Aubrey Starke (p. 147) preferred "Nirvâna," reading into Lanier's quest for spiritual contentment an epithalamium for Mary Day Lanier: "marriage to her more than anything else in his life brought to Lanier the enraptured ecstasy and the sense of escape from the terrors of contemporary events which he so subtly conveys to us in this poem." This is an attractive reading, although it hardly jibes with Lanier's explanation to Virginia Hankins that "Of course it is a rapt Hindu who speaks" (I, 335). But the erroneous conception of Nirvâna as the "Highest Paradise of Buddha, attainable only by long contemplation, and by perfect superiority to all passions of men and all vicissitudes of Time" (instead of a state of non-existence) has proved a stumbling-block to many readers. Possibly the didactic, declamatory tone harms it even more as a poem (I, 19-21).

The most popular of his early poems was "Thar's More in the Man than Thar Is in the Land," published in the *Macon Telegraph and Messenger*, February 7, 1871, and widely though often anonymously reprinted. It is written in the dialect of a Georgia Cracker, and it has humorous overtones and poetic trickeries (Lanier rhymes hum- with cum and sum, and begins the next line with Ble). But the poem is fundamentally serious. It was in fact the best of several dialect poems using the thesis that a plantation economy based on cotton had harmed if not ruined the South financially, and that the region must change the pattern to one of small farms and diversified agriculture. Unlike Henry Grady, he did not want an industrialized South; in direct contrast with the early war poems of Henry Timrod, Lanier had no faith in "the snow of Southern summers." Cotton was a money crop, dependent on trade—and he had come to hate everything connected with his conception of trade. In the narrative poem the Cracker Jones, who "lived pretty much by gittin' of loans," goes bankrupt first in Georgia and five years later in Texas, but Brown revitalized the run-down, eroded Georgia farm and made it pay by hard work and by planting wheat and corn. Lanier extends the diversification in "The Homestead" (which is not in dialect) to include fruit, cattle, chickens, hogs, and pastures, so that the farm becomes almost self-sustaining. But the major symbol of this diversification, in his mind, was corn, as cotton was the major symbol of the one-crop, money economy (I, 22-23, 25-28).

The poems in Negro dialect were primarily humorous. "The Power of Prayer," written in collaboration with his brother Clifford, is the story of an old blind Negro and presumably his young granddaughter who mistake for the devil the noise of the first steamboat coming up the Alabama River. When the boat rounds the bend and with diminishing noise proceeds upstream, the old Negro is convinced that through prayer he has foiled "the debble." There are primitive though authentic religious overtones, but these are subordinated to the humor. The poem was published in *Scribner's* (which also published the collaborative "Uncle Jim's Baptist Revival Hymn") and widely reprinted, but Lanier was doubtful of the validity of dialect poetry. He wrote to Charlotte Cushman: "Tell me, *ought* one to be a little ashamed of writing a dialect poem?" Although Fred L. Pattee called him "a pioneer in a rich field," he seems to have abandoned dialect with a feeling of relief (I, 215-217).

Perhaps these poems should have freed Lanier from his fondness for archaic and sentimentalized phraseology. They did not. Instead, his growing absorption in music led to a discontent with conventional rhythm and meter. When in March, 1874, he sent his wife "My Two Springs," he apparently was content with such phrases as "And home-loves and high glory-loves/And science-loves and story-loves," and in the last stanza he reduces the otherwise excellent imagery by explicitly describing the springs as the eyes of Mary Day Lanier. His discontent took another form: "since I have written it to print, I cannot make it such as I desire in artistic design; for the forms of to-day require a certain trim smugness and clean-shaven propriety in the face and dress of a poem, and I must win a hearing by conforming in some degree to these tyrannies, with a view to overturning them in the future" (I, 32-34; IX, 39-40).

His first rather mild attempt was in the Pindaric or Cowleyan ode, "Corn." The lines are of irregular lengths, but the prevailing pattern is iambic, and most lines fall into normal two-feet to five-feet accentual lengths; ordinarily, three consecutive lines have perfect end-rhymes, usually monosyllabic, but these triple rhymes are carefully interspersed with contrasting rhyming couplets. "Corn" represents an advance in his command of metrical effects to some extent in a freer, more easily flowing verse, but primarily in a longer, sustained, unified effort.

The structure of the poem has less unity. His friend Logan E. Bleckley complained that Lanier presented four landscapes, the first two in an Italian vein and painted "with the utmost delicacy and finish . . . . When you paint in Dutch or Flemish you are clear and strong, but sometimes hard." William Dean Howells in rejecting it for the *Atlantic* thought it was basically two poems but that "neither was striking enough to stand alone" (both quoted in Starke, p. 189). There is some justice in these statements. The poem begins with the poet wandering through a forest and describing the beauties of the trees and the undergrowth, although there is also a hint of his developing pantheism and fondness for personification in the lines, "I pray with mosses, ferns and flowers shy/That hide like gentle nuns from human eye/To lift adoring perfumes to the sky." The poet wanders to a zigzag fence separating the forest and a cornfield; he takes an aesthetic delight in its beauty: "without theft, I reap another's field." One tall stalk of corn is completely out of line; again personifying, Lanier reads into this "corn-captain" a kinship with the poet. The stalk is rooted in earth, yet reaches toward heaven; similarly, the poet should be rooted in the local and the particular, but should give to other men universal values by marrying the new and the old, by uniting earth and heaven, and by reconciling the hot and the cold, the dark and the bright in human lives.

Then Lanier shifts to his harshest direct attack on cotton as symbolic of agricultural trade. Cotton has been responsible for soil erosion; worse, it has been responsible for unstable, discontented lives. The cotton farmer is a "foolish Jason on a treacherous sea,/Seeking the Fleece and finding misery." Instead of secure, self-contained farming, he "staked his life on games of Buy-and-Sell,/And turned each field into a gambler's hell," until he became a "gamester's cats-paw and a banker's slave."

The final section is addressed to the eroded old hill. Once again, Lanier's indifference to the logic of his images is only too readily discernible, along with his fondness for literary personifications. The hill becomes a "gashed and hairy Lear," but his daughter Cordelia becomes the rejuvenating, pitying Spring. Perhaps Lanier considered this a union of matter and spirit, but it seems at best a strange yoking-together of a father and daughter. Spring and corn will revitalize the worn-out land. Perhaps Lanier thought of corn as symbolic of diversified farming; perhaps he oversimplified because of the beauty of the cornfield; but within the framework of the concluding section there is no hint that corn by itself will not enrich eroded land (I, 34-39).

In spite of defects in structure and in logical development, "Corn" remains the first of Lanier's major poems. The forest and the corn-field are vividly described, the attack on cotton sharp and readable. The nature-personifications are effective, although they only indicate a way that Lanier was to explore more fully in later works. When "Corn" was published in *Lippincott's Magazine* (February, 1875) and enthusiastically praised by the discerning Gilbert Peacock, it justifiably earned for Lanier a reputation as a poet of national importance.

In 1875 he wrote and published in *Lippincott's* one of his most ambitious poems, "The Symphony." The title may be an unfortunate one. It has led various commentators to object that the poem does not have the form of a symphony, thus implying that Lanier failed to achieve his objective. This is a misreading. The poem is meant to be a part (not all) of a performance or rehearsal; rarely, and then only for a few consecutive lines, does the entire orchestra play together. It is mainly a series of solo performances, by six different instruments.

As he noted, the poem treated "various deep social questions of the time," and it had in the writing taken possession of him "like a real James River Ague" (IX, 182). But the work was no hasty im-provisation; on the contrary, it was carefully wrought and its effect premeditated. For the first time Lanier attempted freely to make words do the work of music. Drawing on a Shakespearean sonnet for an allusion, he noted that "In my 'Symphony' Love's fine wit—

the love of one's fellow-men—attempts (not to hear with eyes, but precisely the reverse) to see with ears" (IX, 319). For this purpose he used many and varying devices of versification. In the opening section, the prevailing four-beat iambic line is broken with short lines, one with a truncated foot: "Trade is trade." There is a skilful use of two- and three-line end-rhymes, but there is also an occasional use of internal rhymes. More noticeable, and reflecting his recent study of Anglo-Saxon poetry, is the heavy monotone of alliteration. Both of these can be illustrated by one couplet:

> Of what avail the rigorous tale
> Of bill for coin and box for bale?
> (I, 46)

Later in the poem, when the knight promises to do battle for the lady, Lanier uses the form of a traditional medieval song, with its insistent refrain of "Fair Lady." The concluding sections contrast with this fixed pattern by their deliberate irregularity. He declared that he had "dared *almost* to write quite at my ease in the matters of rhythm, rhyme, and substance, in this poem," and he had largely succeeded (IX, 203).

In spite of the intricate metrical effects, Lanier seems to have been even more interested in the message than in the form. Yet the subject is not simple, but complicated with a series of related and intertwined ideas. The primary one, an attack on trade and materialism, had obsessed him since he had started struggling with "The Jacquerie," seven or eight years earlier. There is also a statement of his newly found belief that God reveals himself through nature, and this revelation must be translated for most men not through the Church but through art: "Where Nature spreads her wild blue sky/ For Art to make into melody!" More clearly stated is the demand for a restoration of chivalry in the world. But the overriding message, not in fact economic, is for a broader and deeper human love, supported by a more intense, deeply felt (if unorthodox) religion.

The poem develops through personifications. The violins and, quickly, the other strings, personify art; the flute, nature; the clarionet, the lady; the horn, the knight; the hautboy, the child (almost equated with Christ); the concluding bassoons, wise old age. The violins begin the attack on trade, but immediately suggest Lanier's metaphysical solution: "O Trade! O Trade! would thou wert dead!/ The time needs heart—'tis tired of head." Love has been overcome by greed that has degenerated into swinehood at the expense of humanity. Men have for too long disregarded Christ's words, "Man shall not live by bread alone." For trade has no mercy. The mistreated and the underpaid can easily be replaced, since the poor are prolific. Trade has become only "war grown miserly," but the solution is not in economics but in love: "Vainly might Plato's brain revolve it;/Plainly the heart of a child could solve it."

After a brief interlude by the orchestra, the flute is introduced with what seems to me Lanier's finest, best-sustained poetic image:

> But presently
> A velvet flute-note fell down pleasantly
> Upon the bosom of that harmony,
> And sailed and sailed incessantly,
> As if a petal from a wild-rose blown
> Had fluttered down upon that pool of tone
> And boatwise dropped o' the convex side
> And floated down the glassy tide
> And clarified and glorified
> The solemn spaces where the shadows bide.
>
> (I, 48-49)

The flute states precisely its own function in the poem: "I hold/ Full powers from Nature manifold" to speak for the great and the small, for the "no-tonguèd tree," the lichens, mosses, ferns. This power extends also to animate birds, animals, and insects, and even to the sound of the wind through the trees. The flute holds that man had once been in harmony with nature, but this equilibrium had been upset in ancient times by false mythologies and pagan religions—"cold creatures of man's colder brain." This separation from true nature continued until Christ proclaimed "Love thy neighbor . . . . *All men are neighbors.*" Then men briefly could understand nature and be at peace with mountains, rivers, trees, and with each other. But trade had again distorted this harmonious relationship, and it could be restored again only through love.

The clarionet blames trade for debasing the purity of womanhood and introducing prostitution into the world, and the horn promises through the revivification of chivalry to restore her to her rightful place in the world. As trade has warped our relations with religion and with nature, so it has warped our relations with each other. The hautboy, speaking for the child, quotes Christ after introductory words that suggest Lanier had given up his earlier faith in Christ's divinity: "Once said a Man—and wise was He—/*Never shalt thou the heavens see,/Save as a little child thou be.*"

The bassoons conclude the poem. Life itself is like a fugue, from birth to death (east to west), but the musical score is not freshly made; it is a continuum with "harsh half-phrasings,/Blotted ere writ," a "weltering palimpsest" dimly recording all that has gone before. Only through love can the discords be resolved. As early as *Tiger-Lilies* Lanier had written that "Music means harmony, harmony means love, and love means—God" (V, 31). At the end of "The Symphony" he returned to that theme. Drawing on his belief that man and nature steadily etherealize, he closed on a note of optimism, with an allusion to the biblical flood: "O'er the modern waste a dove hath whirred:/Music is Love in search of a word" (I, 46-56).

"The Symphony" won him new friends in Philadephia, most notably Bayard Taylor. Mainly through the intercession of Taylor, Lanier was commissioned to write the verses for a cantata to be sung at the Centennial Exposition in Philadelphia, the music to be composed by Dudley Buck. Although Taylor cautioned him to "make the lines simple and strong" and to make the poem representative rather than individualistic, Lanier disregarded his advice. As a musician himself, he felt that he had "to compose for the musician as well as the country" not in clearly stated lines but in *"broad bands of color"* (IX, 297). The poem, entitled "The Centennial Meditation of Columbia," celebrates America as a haven for those oppressed by religious or economic tyranny; names like Mayflower, Plymouth, Jamestown, Puritan, and Huguenot become in themselves symbols. There are eight contrasting stanzas in words mainly of Saxon derivation, beginning with the early difficulties of colonization and concluding with "the Triumph of the Republic over the opposing powers of nature and of man." Although he complained that limitations of space allowed him to devote only one line each to the philosophies of art, science, power, government, faith, and social life, he thought that he had made it "absolutely free from all melodramatic artifice, and wholly simple and artless" (II, 271; IX, 300, 311, 353).

When the poem was published without the music, it was immediately attacked as obscure and vague, with archaic words and stilted hyphenations, as in the lines "Toil when wild brother-wars new-dark the Light,/Toil, and forgive, and kiss o'er, and replight." Lanier defended the work vigorously: it was meant to be sung rather than to be read. He felt vindicated when, sung by a chorus of eight hundred voices to the accompaniment of one hundred and fifty instruments, the cantata was a dramatic success (I, 60-62).

Lippincott's commissioned Lanier to write a centennial ode for its July, 1876, issue. "Psalm of the West" is his longest complete poem, but it is also his most disjointed one. There is some excuse. It was written hurriedly, at a time when he was ill. Yet the good qualities in the poem are typical of Lanier, and so are the defects. As Aubrey Starke has noted (p. 248), Lanier had attempted "to compose a poem which should carry or create its own musical accompaniment." The beginning is conventional enough. America is the "Tall Adam of Lands, new-made of the dust of the West," from whose side Eve (Freedom) is carved. It is freedom that gives power to friendship, marriage, law, and other human attributes:

> And Science be known as the sense making love to the All,
> And Art be known as the soul making love to the All,
> And Love be known as the marriage of man with the All.
> (I, 63)

God will help this All-lover, the prophet and poet, the "lark of the dawn," by revealing to him the past and the future. Disregarding the Indians, Lanier celebrates in a ballad-like interlude the coming of the Norsemen, and in eight Miltonic sonnets the first voyage of Columbus (cast in the form of a dramatic monologue and narrated by Columbus himself). After the discovery, the colonization is symbolized in the poem by the *Mayflower*, and the war for independence is worked mainly around the battle at Lexington. Lanier notes in passing that Jefferson had told "the rights of man to men" and that "Deep-rooted Washington" had won final success at Yorktown. In his haste, and perhaps also because he did not wish to mar the unified nationalistic tone of the ode by discussing the issues and differences involved, Lanier incorporated a much earlier poem as an allegory of the Civil War. If "The Tournament: Joust First" was written, as Charles Anderson thinks, in 1865 as a peace-offering to the estranged Mary Day, this conflict between heart and brain may have been appropriate; as an allegory of the war, it is both absurd and insipid. Wisely, Lanier hastens on to the prophecy, as revealed by the artist's God: in this reunited land freedom will drive out the beasts of war, oppression, murder, lust, false art, and false faith (I, 62-82).

"Psalm of the West" is not a philosophical poem, but a series of pen-pictures that its author thought to be representative and tried to make symbolic. He succeeded best with the sonnet sequence. But he failed to impose an artistic unity on his diverse, unconnected forms and incidents, and his enthusiastic paean of over-optimistic prophecy is difficult to read seriously. But the poem solidified his reputation. This was further consolidated when later that year Lippincott issued in book form ten of his poems that had appeared in *Lippincott's Magazine*, including "Corn," "The Symphony," and "Psalm."

Temporarily abandoning his theories of musical versification, Lanier wrote in blank verse a long poem, "Clover." It embodied his artistic creed, and he later planned to use it as the title poem of a projected volume. It grew, he wrote, "out of a mood of solemn protest against the doctrine of 'Art for Art's Sake,' which has led so many of our young artists into the most unprofitable and even blasphemous activities" (IX, 398, n. 135). But it grew also out of his wrathful memories of the attacks on the Centennial Cantata, and he twice gives a list of fellow-artists who had likewise been mistreated: Dante, Keats, Chopin, Raphael, Lucretius, Omar, Angelo, Beethoven, Chaucer, Schubert, Shakespeare, Bach, and Buddha. As the materialistic ox destroys the clover, so the Course-of-things destroys the artist. Only faith that we are all part of God's plan will save us, with the realization that "The artist's market is the heart of man." It is a troubled, uneven poem, yet it is easy to see why Lanier overvalued it (I, 84-87).

That same year he wrote the most beautiful of the many lyrics to his wife, "Evening Song" (set to music by Dudley Buck under the title "Sunset"). Lanier's love poems rarely measure up to his best lyrics, but this dainty, tranquil poem is an exception. However, Lanier's poetic well was, temporarily, almost dry. Of the poems written in 1877, only two can be considered even reasonably successful. In "The Stirrup-Cup," death becomes a rare cordial handed to the horseman just before he sets out on a long journey. The appropriate metaphor, the literary allusions, and the gallant courage of a sick man willing to drink the "rich stirrup-cup ... right smilingly" give the lyric an enduring if somewhat personalized appeal. The second poem is more important and has become his best-known poem. The "Song of the Chattahoochee" marks Lanier's extreme use of personification, for, throughout, the river is the narrator; the onomatopoeia and the heavy use of the refrain testify to Poe's continuing influence; and the interlocking vowel and consonant sounds, the alliteration, and the internal rhymes indicate a desire for musicality at the expense of idea. The poem does have a lulling motion that has a narcotic effect on many readers. But the objection that the personification is a pathetic fallacy overlooks the fact that only this justifies Lanier in giving the Chattahoochee a moral duty to water the fields and turn the mills, before it at last becomes a part of the ocean (I, 88, 90, 103-104).

Lanier had become increasingly fascinated with the running or logaoedic dactyllic measure, which in his definition allowed a free admixture of iambics and spondees. "The Revenge of Hamish" he considered frankly "an experiment" in this meter (X, 72). The subject was derived practically without change from Chapter 2 of William Black's novel, *MacLeod of Dare*; the four-line stanza form and the rhyme scheme of this narrative poem suggest the medieval ballad, but the long, looping lines, the free meter, and varying rhythms are Lanier's own additions. It is a quick-moving, interesting story in verse of a brutal punishment and an even more brutal revenge, but it is quite uncharacteristic of Lanier's other poetry (I, 112-116).

Time spent in or near Brunswick, Georgia, alongside the Marshes of Glynn, revived his poetic imagination. He planned a series of Hymns of the Marshes, to be either a separate book or combined with related (and mainly unwritten) Hymns of the Fields and Hymns of the Mountains. Easily the best of these—in fact, his best long poem—is "The Marshes of Glynn." The form illustrates an even freer use than in "The Revenge" of the logaoedic dactyl—so free that at times the pattern disappears, ranging from the prevailing pentameter rhyming couplets to a one-syllabled line. It is also the most intricate musically, for as Norman Foerster has perceptively pointed out,[2] it is "not one melody artfully varied, but a bewildering succession of winding and darting melodies." The effect is orchestral rather than harmonic. Lanier begins with the feeling of ecstasy aroused by the live oaks and the marshes; he almost equates the oak with the Holy Ghost, as he was to equate the marsh with what he could accept of the primal beginning in the theory of evolution. It is evening, but he has secured a spiritual release from the finite world:

2. *Nature in American Literature* (New York, 1923), p. 235.

Ay, now, when my soul all day hath drunken the soul of the oak,
And my heart is at ease from men, and the wearisome sound of the stroke
  Of the scythe of time and the trowel of trade is low,
  And belief overmasters doubt, and I know that I know,
  And my spirit is grown to a lordly great compass within,
That the length and the breadth and the sweep of the marshes of Glynn
Will work me no fear like the fear they have wrought me of yore.
(I, 119)

In the enormously long first sentence, nature personified in the live oak is good, the essence of spiritual comfort; trade and finite time are evil. To the east is the ocean, to Lanier a symbol of infinity; in the east, also, was the beginning of the world. The recognition of this gives him faith, and a new-found freedom from doubt. The marsh now seems to him like the catholic man who has won "God out of knowledge and good out of infinite pain/And sight out of blindness and purity out of a stain."

In another of his curiously mixed metaphors in which he tried to weld together the concrete and the abstract, Lanier continues: "As the marsh-hen secretly builds on the watery sod,/Behold I will build me a nest on the greatness of God." This simile, widely and disconcertingly praised by many high school teachers, is the low point in the poem. Fortunately, Lanier soon recovers from this illogical sentimentality. The incoming tide serves a triple purpose: literally, the ocean floods the marsh, but figuratively the infinite floods the finite, and thus floods the soul of man so that he attains union with God. Yet the poem ends on a note of doubt. The high tide brings with it night and sleep, with its suggestion of death:

But who will reveal to our waking ken
The forms that swim and the shades that creep
    Under the waters of sleep?
And I would I could know what swimmeth below when the tide comes in
On the length and the breadth of the marvellous marshes of Glynn.
(I, 122)

This probing into the subconscious is uncharacteristic; so, too, is the element of doubt. "The Marshes of Glynn" is the final complete poem in the sequence. He planned to open the Hymns with "Sunrise" (written later), but it seems unlikely that he intended to close on this note. There is no way to know, but I am convinced that one of his most complete "Poem Outlines" (I, 276) at least indicates the direction the concluding poem would have taken:

The courses of the wind, and the shifts thereof, as also what way the clouds go; and that which is happening a long way off; and the full face of the sun; and the bow of the Milky Way from end to end; as also the small, the life of the fiddler-crab, and the household of the marsh-hen; yea, and more, the translation of black ooze into green blade of marsh-grass, which is as if filth bred heaven:
This a man seeth upon the marsh.

That the marsh had become a symbol in his mind of the condition from which man had developed (not evolved) is indicated by a passage in a letter about another poem in the sequence: "For whatever can be proved to have been evolved, evolution seems to me a noble and beautiful and true theory. But a careful search has not shown me a single instance . . . of an actual case of species differentiation" (X, 205).

A man was free to make his own choices; he was not a biological pawn in a predetermined game. In fact, Lanier was developing a theory of opposing forces in nature. All the motions in nature resulted from this opposition or antagonism of forces, and from this opposition came rhythm. This seemed to justify his belief in a freer form for poetry and music; following Herbert Spencer's *First Principles*, he believed evolution to be "a process from the uniform and indefinite to the multiform and definite." It did not justify formlessness: he quoted with approval and worked changes on the aphorism of the poet Hervé that "He who will not answer to the rudder, must answer to the rocks." Aubrey Starke has neatly phrased Lanier's principle of opposition as "Form against Chaos, of Good against Evil, of Love against Selfishness, of Design against Accident, of Belief against Scepticism" (p. 372). This "fundamental principle of creation" he embodied in the poem "Opposition." It is through the conquest of these adverse forces that man's will, his moral sense, and his art develop:

> Of fret, of dark, of thorn, of chill,
>   Complain no more; for these, O Heart,
> Direct the random of the will
>   As rhymes direct the rage of art.
>   (I, 130-131)

It is an abstractly philosophical idea which Lanier developed in *The Science of English Verse*, but which he nowhere stated more appealingly than in this lyric.

Although he shied away from theology, Lanier's mind was engrossed by religious problems. Out of this preoccupation came the long, humorless poem "The Crystal," with its odd spectacle of a minor poet forgiving, among many others, Dante, Shakespeare, and Milton. True, this recognition of their fallibility leads up to the infallibility and perfection of Christ the man. It is Lanier's clearest statement that he had come to regard Christ as symbol of divinity, but not divine. The conflict in his mind between religion and science resulted in the kindred poem "The Cloud," with its strong affirmation that while a cloud might be evolved, an artist could not be: he was a free and responsible being, yet answerable to himself, to mankind, and to God for the work he produced. The earlier title, "Individuality," better describes the idea that Lanier stressed; apparently he changed the title when he decided to incorporate the poem into the "Hymns of the Marshes" (I, 136-141).

He was to write two more magnificent lyrics, and a long, fevered poem. "Marsh Song—at Sunset" depends on a reasonable familiarity with *The Tempest*, but once again, as in "Night and Day," the Shakespearean imagery serves as a springboard to lead to his essential idea. It is an Ariel-cloud and a Caliban-sea, but it is not the brother or the man Antonio who has injured Prospero; rather, it is Antonio as man who has committed the injustice, and it is man in general (not a specific person) who must be pardoned. He followed this with the quickly written, intricately musical "Ballad of Trees and the Master." Ironically, with apparently no attention to what it says, the poem is included in a Methodist hymnal, and frequently sung. For it is Lanier's finest yet most extreme statement that God reveals himself to man not through the church but through nature. On the eve of his crucifixion, a disturbed and "forspent" Christ goes into the woods, and it is the olive trees that console Christ and give him strength to endure his ordeal. Like the live oak in "The Marshes of Glynn," the trees become synonymous with the Holy Spirit. It is Lanier's most beautiful lyric, one that we could not easily spare from our scant number of nearly perfect poems (I, 142, 144).

He had no chance to revise his last poem, "Sunrise." He intended it to be the first poem in "Hymns of the Marshes," and it is properly optimistic about the place man has attained in the world. Before he awakes, the poet is conscious of three major symbols: the live oak, the marsh, and the main. The live oak brings God to man; the marsh is that from which man has evolved; and the ocean is immortality. In this sense the marsh is indeed a "Reverend Marsh," a menstruum that dissolves and re-creates all matter. But a fourth major symbol, even more important than the earlier three, is added. The sun is equated with Christ; it is the life-giving force that makes the "sacramental marsh one pious plain." Before the rising of the sun there is the quiet stillness of dawn, the "ante-reign of Mary Morning." Then the sun, rising, gives to man a strength that even the live oak can not give: "I am strong with the strength of my lord the Sun." And the sun more even than the main gives us conviction of immortality: after death, "yonder besides thee/My soul shall float, friend Sun,/The day being done." It was the last, fitting testament of an unorthodox but deeply religious man (I, 144-149).

Any re-evaluation of Lanier as poet might well start with his admitted weaknesses. These can be listed briefly: (1) a strong tendency toward moralizing and didacticism, sometimes combined with an excessive, lushly-phrased sentimentalism, especially when these elements are not part of the texture of the poem but are added rather obtrusively; (2) a frequent use of over-fervid rhetoric as a substitute for imagination, as in the Sun-Bee passage in "Sunrise"; (3) a strained imagery that grew out of his desire to yoke together in one metaphor the concrete and the abstract; (4) the use of archaic words and constructions that, although characteristic of his thought, give a quaint, artificial character to many poems.

Such handicaps are severe. Yet they do not ruin, even if they do vitiate, his positive accomplishment. The best of the long poems have sufficient intellectual and philosophical content and enough musical form to lift them above their inherent defects. At their best, they have also a strong sense of locale, derived from exact and sympathetic observation. "Corn" is a spirited economic protest against the agricultural money-crop cotton, and a strong plea for diversified agriculture; the description of the woods and of the cornfield is what Lanier had seen closely with his own eyes before he turned the raw matter into poetry. On a wider base, "The Symphony" is both an economic and a social protest; one may not agree with the idea that trade (materialism) inevitably debases or that nature etherealizes, but certainly there is no lack of valid subject matter. Yet it is as a religious poet that Lanier in his longer poems is at his best. All four are loosely constructed, and marred by rhetorical flourishes and illogical images. But the disordered though powerful "Sunrise" and the magnificent "Marshes of Glynn" express Lanier's mature religious belief: God is immanent, and He reveals himself to us through nature, in the ferns, the streams, the marsh, the trees, and the sun. When he complained that Poe did not know enough "to be a great poet," Lanier was not thinking of practical or scholarly knowledge, but of that intuitive comprehension by which a poet converts learning into wisdom (II, 6; VII, 94-96). This was what he attempted to do, and in "The Marshes of Glynn" he largely succeeded.

These faults cannot be found in a handful of his best lyrics. The early poems ("Night and Day," "Raven Days," "Life and Song," and one or two dialect poems) are simpler but not necessarily poorer than the later lyrics. He had not yet begun, in theory and in practice, to loosen the structure of English versification. As he developed, he found it hampering and nearly impossible to stay within a rigid framework: except for the Columbus sonnets in "Psalm of the West" and possibly "The Harlequin of Dreams," he wrote no sonnets that are comparable to those of Longfellow, Boker, and Hayne. He preferred to depend on musical cadence and a trained ear rather than on accent or rhythm; at times he may have carried this over into artifice, as in "Song of the Chattahoochee," but at his best ("Evening Song," "Marsh Song," and above all, "Ballad of Trees") he wrote some of the finest lyrics in American poetry.

It is a thin sheaf of authentic poetry that we can salvage from the occasional and the sentimental, but it remains an authentic one. Lanier never attained his goal of writing major poetry, but he produced a small number of poems that have never received the recognition they deserve. He is one of our most vital and most interesting minor poets.

LAFCADIO HEARN, "ONE OF OUR SOUTHERN WRITERS": A FOOTNOTE TO SOUTHERN LITERARY HISTORY

Lewis Leary

Columbia University

When in May, 1887, Charles W. Coleman contributed to *Harper's New Monthly Magazine* an essay on "The Recent Movement in Southern Letters," he included Lafcadio Hearn among "the score or more of ... writers" who had established "a worthy and characteristic Southern literature."[1] And well he might have, for during the past ten years Hearn had gained reputation in New Orleans and in Northern magazines as a recorder of the local scene and as a writer who could transform legends of any land to tales at once sensuous and elusive. One month later, he was to leave the American South in continuing search for the exotic and for a way of living compatible with his personal susceptibilities. He was to write better after 1887, with more restraint and controlled artistry. His sketches of island life in *Two Years in the French West Indies* three years later are unmatched for vividness and subtlety of impression, and the vignettes of Japanese life and lore which he produced in the decade preceding his death in 1904 bring continuing joy to readers who admire small things wrought with care. Because of these, Lafcadio Hearn has a secure and permanent place among writers of his time and kind, with Stephen Crane, Oscar Wilde, and Pierre Loti. His years in New Orleans were apprentice years when a young man moved into his thirties toward mastery of a medium, but during those ten years there was not another in the South who dedicated himself more assiduously and successfully to literature as an art.

1. LXXIV, 838. For biographical information throughout this essay I have drawn on Elizabeth Stevenson's *Lafcadio Hearn* (New York, 1961) and, for insight into some of Hearn's ideas, on Beongcheon Yu's *The Ape of the Gods* (Detroit, 1964). For the period of Hearn's life under consideration large debts are owed to Edward Larocque Tinker's *Lafcadio Hearn's American Years* (New York, 1924) and especially to Albert Mordell, who has identified and published in several indispensable volumes many of Hearn's contributions to the newspapers of New Orleans.

New Orleans was clearly a way-stop for Lafcadio Hearn. When he arrived there in November, 1877, after experience as a newspaperman in Cincinnati, where his reporting of slum and riverfront life brought local fame but his unconventional personal life brought disrepute, Hearn was admittedly in retreat. "Where shall I go? What shall I do?" he wrote soon after his arrival. "Sometimes I think of Europe, sometimes of the West Indies,—of Florida, France, or the wilderness of London."[2] Even after three years in Louisiana, he confessed, "I fancy that some day, I shall wander down to the levee, and creep on board, and sail away to God knows where."[3] But as a literary man of twenty-seven he was charmed with the old city: "The wealth of the world is here,—unworked gold in the ore, one might say; the paradise of the South is here, deserted and half in ruins. . . . I cannot say how fair and rich and beautiful this dead South is. It has fascinated me. I have resolved to live in it."[4]

Though his first months in New Orleans were starving months, Hearn soon made a satisfactory connection with a struggling four-page daily called the *Item*, which he livened with sketches in prose and with little drawings which pleasantly ridiculed local peculiarities. "I write as I please, go as I please, and quit work when I please," and he had time of his own to do as he pleased. He was full of literary schemes—for the publication of translations from Théophile Gautier which he had brought with him from Cincinnati; for collecting Creole songs and proverbs, which occupation brought him brief friendship with George Washington Cable, six years older than he, and already on the way toward literary fame; and for gathering Indian lore and legends in company with Adrian Rouquette, an eccentric Creole priest who had been educated in France, where in 1841 he had published a romantic poem about Louisiana called *Les Savanes*, which had received praise from Sainte-Beuve and caused Thomas Moore to acclaim its author as "the Lamartine of America." The company was good and the undertakings exhilarating, but literary work went slowly: "Life here is so lazy,—nights are so liquid with tropic moonlight,—days are so splendid with green and gold, . . . that I hardly know whether I am dreaming or awake."[5]

2. Elizabeth Bisland, *The Life and Letters of Lafcadio Hearn* (Boston and New York, 1906), I, 183.
3. *Ibid.*, I, 215.
4. *Letters from the Raven, Being the Correspondence of Lafcadio Hearn with Henry Walkin*, ed. Milton Bronner (London, 1908), pp. 42-43.
5. *Ibid.*, pp. 54-59.

The letters of Lafcadio Hearn, especially the letters written from New Orleans which describe the ups and downs, and ins and outs, of his ambitions and disappointments, his temper and temperament, are among the most lively of his writings. Like the letters of Edgar Allan Poe, who died the year before Hearn was born, and whom Hearn admired, it has been said, as spiritually an older brother in misfortune, they reveal more of the man and his moods, his aspirations and meannesses, than any chronicler has been able to set forth. No complete edition of his letters has been made, and at least a selected edition is certainly an urgent desideratum. They expose him as vain, crotchety, vituperative, and self-seeking, but often tender, and sometimes humble. After five years in New Orleans, and reading which his correspondence discloses as incredibly broad and seriously intensive, he confessed that he was "exceptionally ignorant": "Knowing that I have nothing resembling genius, and that any ordinary talent must be supplemented with some sort of curious study in order to place it above the mediocre life, I am striving to woo the Muse of the Odd, and hope to succeed in attracting some little attention."[6]

Attention was soon attracted, partly because of the subjects about which Hearn chose to write, and partly because of his extraordinary concern, expressed often in his letters, with words and their proper use. He spoke of the "elfish electricity" of words, of "mosaics of word Jewelry," of a poetical prose "fit to satisfy an old Greek ear,—like chants wrought in huge measures, . . . and just a little irregular, like Ocean-rhythm." The dark magic of Baudelaire, the patience of Flaubert, the delicate strokes of Gautier, who painted with words, and the skilled precision of Pierre Loti—these were his early enthusiasms. "It has long been my aim," he explained in 1883, "to create something in English fiction analagous to that warmth and colour and richness of imagery hitherto peculiar to Latin literature. Being of a meridional race myself, a Greek, I *feel* rather with the Latin race than with the Anglo-Saxon; and trust that with time and study I may be able to create something different from the stone-grey and somewhat chilly style of latter-day English or American romance."[7]

"I would give anything," he said, "to be a literary Columbus,"

6. *Life and Letters*, I, 290-291.
7. *Ibid.*, I, 275-276.

to visit strange lands, find new themes, awaken contemporaries to literature as passionate and vibrant as life should be. Unable now to travel, he sought among the streets and saloons, boardinghouses and bordellos of New Orleans, and the fishing villages on the Gulf, for the extraordinary, the sensuous, the common day-to-day happiness and heartbreak and passion which seldom found way into books. "Passion is the mighty electricity which vibrates through all human life and causes all grand vibrations"; writing should be voluptuous, and writers virile.[8] "I am seeking the Orient at home," he said, "among our Lascar and Chinese colonies, and the Prehistoric in the characteristics of strange European settlers."[9] He had no desire to be a realist of surfaces only, like William Dean Howells, whom he was later to identify as the favorite of mediocrities. He disliked the "atmosphere of Puritanism" in American writing, "in which no buds of fancy, no richly tinted flowers of art may live."[10]

As a literary commentator, Hearn is not often arresting or consistent. He had brief good things to say of Henry James, and he later admired Robert Louis Stevenson and Rudyard Kipling, but his estimates could be eccentric: Matthew Arnold was "one of the colossal humbugs of the century"; Longfellow wrote better nature poetry than Wordsworth; Joaquin Miller deserved a place among the greatest of American poets. What Hearn admired were "vapoury luminosities and golden glows, ... dream tints and transparent shadows," not the thing itself, but what it suggested which was finer or sweeter. He had no patience with Walt Whitman, who was "indecent and ugly, lascivious and gawky, lubricious and coarse."[11] Maupassant also was sometimes coarse, and Zola quite too frequently: "Strictly speaking, he has not written novels, he has only created a pseudo-literary museum." It is the unreality of art, its luminosity, explained Hearn, "that makes its charm." Like Poe, he would reach toward the supernal, to some ideal created in the searching mind of man: "In order to become better, nobler, wiser than we are, we must have a visible goal to strive for, an apparent model to copy, a beautiful in-

8. "The Sexual Idea in French Literature," *Item*, June 17, 1881, in *Editorials by Lafcadio Hearn*, ed. Charles W. Hutson (Boston, 1926), pp. 143-144.

9. *Life and Letters*, I, 291.

10. "Novels and Novelists," New Orleans *Times-Democrat*, Dec. 31, 1882, in Albert Mordell, *Discoveries: Essays on Lafcadio Hearn* (Tokyo, 1964), pp. 70-71.

11. Hearn's estimates of native writers are briefly set forth in Ray McKinley Lawless, *Lafcadio Hearn, Critic of American Letters* (Chicago, 1942), and Albert Mordell, "Hearn's Essays on American Literature," in *Discoveries*, pp. 60-77.

centive to urge to loftier exertion; and only he who is capable of seeing beyond the wretched boundaries of the baser senses, will ever seek consolation by striving to persuade his fellow-beings that they are as worms upon a dung-hill."[12]

So during these apprentice years Hearn steeped himself in the writings of European contemporaries, especially those who probed beyond convention toward controlled description of passionate joys or aspirations. Some of the translations from Gautier and Flaubert which he had made in Cincinnati were later to be published—"sins," he was to call them, "of my literary youth," and several hundred of the translations which appeared in the newspapers of New Orleans have now been identified or collected.[13] Pierre Loti, Jules Le Maître, Gerard de Nerval, Villiers de l'Isle-Adam, Maupassant, Zola, Daudet, Flaubert, and Gautier all attracted him, and many others, including Dostoevsky, Tolstoi, and Sienkiewicz. He polished and repolished, and he wished that other writers would join him in the task—"What a translation of Daudet could not Henry James give us?" It was difficult, demanding work, not to be carelessly attempted:

it is by no means sufficient to reproduce the general meaning of the sentence:—it is equally necessary to obtain a just equivalent for each word in regard to force, colour, and form;—and to preserve, so far as possible, the original construction of the phrase, the peculiarity of the rhetoric, the music of the style. And there is music in every master style,— a measured flow of words in every sentence; ... there are tints, sonorities, luminosities, resonances.... The sense, form, force, sonority, colour of every word must be studied; the shape of every phrase chiseled out, the beauty of every naked sentence polished like statuary marble.[14]

Thousands of Americans first read these foreign writers in the anonymous translations by Lafcadio Hearn. While during the 1880's America was discovering itself in the writings of Mark Twain and

12. *Essays in European and Oriental Literature*, ed. Albert Mordell (New York, 1923), pp. 4, 6, 14.

13. The Gautier collection was published at Hearn's expense as *One of Cleopatra's Nights, and Other Fantastic Romances* in 1882; the translations of Flaubert's *The Temptation of St. Anthony* was posthumously printed in 1910; a manuscript translation of Gautier's *Avatar*, which Hearn was reported to have destroyed because he could not find a publisher, was in 1959 in the hands of a private collector (see Jacob Blanck, *American Bibliography*, IV, 103). After leaving New Orleans, Hearn in 1890 did a hurried translation of Anatole France's *The Crime of Sylvester Bonnard* for Harper's; both it and *One of Cleopatra's Nights* remain today "standard" translations, the first in the Modern Library; the second in several paperback editions. Translations in New Orleans newspapers have been collected by Albert Mordell in *Saint Anthony and Other Stories* (New York, 1924), *Stories from Pierre Loti* (Tokyo, 1933), *Stories from Emile Zola* (Tokyo, 1935), and *Sketches and Tales from the French* (Tokyo, 1935).

14. *Times-Democrat*, Sept. 24, 1882, in Tinker, *Lafcadio Hearn's American Years*, p. 159.

Howells, Edward Eggleston and Cable and Parkman, Mary Murfree, James Whitcomb Riley, and many another who dwelt on the local scene, Hearn was more than any native contemporary extending literary horizons toward new themes and bold transatlantic notions of the proper substance of art. His contribution to the cultural expansion of his adopted country has sometimes been made to seem Hearn's whole and sufficient claim to being remembered, and praise has rightly been given New Orleans as the only city in the United States which at that time would have fostered so strange a talent. But New Orleans had more than that to offer, and translating was not in itself an end: "I see beauty here all around me,—a strange tropical, intoxicating beauty. I consider it my artistic duty to let myself be absorbed into this new life, and study its form and colour and passion."[15]

Wandering through the Vieux Carré, listening to street cries and street brawls, "the melancholy, quavering beauty and weirdness of Negro chants," absorbing sights and sounds and odors, listening to and reading of strange "traditions, superstitions, legends, fairy tales, goblin stories, impossible romances," blending them, he attempted a new form, based on brief impressions of scene fleetingly glimpsed or conversation overheard, and then painstakingly embellished— "moulded," he said, "and coloured by imagination alone."[16] He called these writings "Fantastics," and some thirty of them appeared through 1881, telling "of wonders and of marvels, of riches and rarities": in "Aphrodite and the King's Prisoners," of a captive kept in luxury, but alone with only an ebony statue of the Goddess of Love for company, until he kills himself at the foot of the statue in "Love which is brother to death"; in "El Vómito," which celebrates beauty and death, and "The Name on the Stone," in which a Ligeia-like maiden returns from the grave to inform her lover that "Love is stronger than death"; or in "The Fountain of Gold," a parable of eternal youth and love and happiness secured in death and dream.

Many of the Fantastics are slight indeed, like "The Idyl of the French Snuff-Box," from the enameled cover of which a nymph and faun come briefly but charmingly to life, or like "Spring Phantoms," which reminds man of visions of luscious ladies which may come to him as winter wanes. One borrows the semi-scientific manner made popular by Oliver Wendell Holmes as a doctor at a boarding-house

15. *Life and Letters*, I, 217.
16. "Some Fancies About Fancy," *Item*, March 28, 1881, in *Editorials*, p. 135.

table holds forth on "Hereditary Memories"—a theme obsessively intriguing to Hearn; another spoke in "A Dream of Kites," of children's windswept toys entangled in a web of telegraph wires, lost and tattered like the dreams of youth. Most of them are too fragile for quick retelling, and Hearn admitted them trivial. But he was right in refusing to be ashamed of them as unworthy of his talents. "I fancy the idea of the fantastics is artistic," he said. "They are my impressions of the strange life of New Orleans. They are dreams of a tropical city. There is one idea running through them all—love and death."[17]

"I live forever in dreams of other centuries and other faiths and other ethics," he said then, as he gathered from Brahmanic, Buddhistic, Talmudic, Arabic, Persian, Chinese, and Polynesian legend a collection of twenty-seven tales which James R. Osgood in Boston published in the spring of 1884 as *Stray Leaves from Strange Literatures.* Adapted from translations by other men, these fables, Hearn explained, are "reconstructions of what impressed me as the most fantastically beautiful in the exotic literature which I was able to obtain." Though he learnedly discussed sources, he made no claims to scholarship: he wished simply to share with others the delights which he had experienced among "some very strange and beautiful literatures."

The tales are brief, and often bold; they speak of passion, especially the passion of love, and of wisdom which may, but does not always, bring comfort or calm. Weirdness is their keynote: spectral lovers and enchantress wives, and love which leads to death. "The wise," he wrote in introduction to one tale, "will not attach themselves unto women; for women sport with the hearts of those who love them," and women die, even as love dies, so that memories are best, and sad, strange tales not shrouded in reality. He told of Polynesian lands "where garments are worn by none save the dead," of youth which might be eternal, and of dreams despoiled by phantoms, of intelligence greater than wisdom, and faith superior to truth.

Each tale is carefully chiseled, and meant to be enchanting. Each is frankly derivative, a retreat to ancient quietness. The language is honeyed with biblical phrasing, cloyed sometimes with alliterative rhythm, as Hearn strove to attain what Baudelaire had described as

17. *Life and Letters*, I, 220-221. Ten years after Hearn's death, Charles W. Hutson collected many of them in *Fantastics and Other Fancies* (Boston, 1914); reprinted in *The Writings of Lafcadio Hearn* (Boston and New York, 1922), II, 195-386.

"le miracle d'une prose poétic." They were exercises done by a young man who trained for something beyond virtuosity; "veritable poems," Charles W. Coleman thought them, "heavy with the perfume and glamour of the East, delicate, fragrant, graceful." Hearn was, however, to reach closer to an idiom of his own three years later in *Some Chinese Ghosts*, which Roberts Brothers published then in Boston. Having wandered, he said, through "vast and mysterious pleasure-grounds of Chinese fancy," he presented in this, his second volume, "the marvellous flowers there growing, ... as souvenirs of his curious voyage." He spoke again of spectral lovers, of nocturnal meetings, of passion sublimated to beauty, with no habitation in time or place, only in the questing spirit of man. Myth and legend, and the unlearned yearning of people, contained unchanging essences. He prefaced the book with an epigram from a Chinese poet: "If ye desire to witness prodigies and to behold marvels,/Be not concerned as to whether the mountains are distant or the rivers far away."

But there were marvels also in New Orleans and the bayou country beyond it. Hearn had at one time thought that his first published book would be a "tiny volume of sketches of our creole archipelago at the skirts of the Gulf." The local legends and songs which he had been collecting, and the impressions of the local scene, found place in the *Item* and the *Times-Democrat*, and in magazines of the North, in the *Century* or in *Harper's Weekly* or *Harper's Bazar*. In 1885 he published *La Cuisine Creole*, an assembly of culinary recipes "from leading chefs and noted Creole housewives who had made New Orleans famous," and *Gombo Zhèbes*, a dictionary of Creole proverbs. And he had begun a collection of "Ephemerae" or "Leaves from the Diary of an Impressionist," which included "Floridian Reveries" written on a journey to that peninsular coast in the summer of 1885. No publisher for this or for the Creole sketches was found during Hearn's lifetime,[18] but they contain his most impressive insights into the life and character of the tropical South, "its contrasts of agreeable color; its streets reëchoing with the tongues of many nations; its general look of somnolent contentment; its verdant antiquity; its venerable memorials and monuments; its eccentricities of architecture; its tropical gardens; its picturesque surprises; its warm atmosphere, drowsy perhaps with the perfume of

18. See, however, *Leaves from the Diary of an Impressionist*, ed. Ferris Greenslet (Boston and New York, 1911), in *Writings*, I, 1-99, and *Creole Sketches*, ed. Charles W. Hutson (Boston and New York, 1922), in *Writings*, I, 107-208.

orange flowers, and thrilled with the fantastic music of mocking-birds."[19]

Even more than George Washington Cable, who Hearn finally decided was handicapped by a Sunday-school compulsion to do something about things, he caught the lush languor of old New Orleans, its Mardi Gras, its Creole girls, its proud but purse-pinching lodging-house keepers, its tales of voodoo and ghostly apparitions, of women tantalizingly lovely, calculating, and bitter. He had a surer ear for words than eye for exact detail; he spoke more confidently of color and shadow than of particularities of place. His people are less often remembered as appearances than as voices, often Hearn's own voice, but often also in dialect which caught nuances of character. People in New Orleans rarely laugh, Hearn said; nor did he, for what he presents is not condescending but human, as when he presented the plaintive, exasperated voice of a Creole housewife explaining to another "Why Crabs Are Boiled Alive":

And for why you have not of crab? Because one must dem boil 'live? It is all vat is of most beast to tell so. How you make dem kill so you not dem boil? You can not cut dem de head off, for dat dey have not of head. You can not break to dem de back, for dat dey not be only all back. You not can dey bleed until they die, for dat dey not have blood. You can not stick to dem troo de brain, for dat dey be same like you—dey not have of brain.[20]

These Hearn did briefly best, renderings of people through what they said and how they sounded. But he did them seldom, preferring instead to turn his ear for tone and modulation to continuing re-creation of tales which came to him at second hand. His writings suggest that he knew few people well, and that what he observed of people was how they talked or what they thought, seldom how they looked or acted—except that he was curiously fascinated by eyes, by sparkling or furtive eyes, Venetian eyes challenging from behind a carnival mask. In telling a story or sketching a street scene, a seascape, or a sunrise, he seems at ease with words, evoking color and movement and sound; but people, unless overheard, eluded him. He was as bookish as he was sensually perceptive, and was finally most comfortable with the rhythm of words skilfully arranged to capture atmosphere or mood.

When Cable told him a sad story of storm and death which years before had visited an island on the Gulf coast, Hearn wove words

19. *Writings*, I, 108.
20. *Ibid.*, I, 133.

around it to produce a novelette called *Chita: A Memory of Last Island*, in part a magnificent tour de force, in part briefly evocative character portrayal, and in part pathos shaded toward sentimentality. In attempting a longer story, Hearn did not build well; he could decorate a plot better than he could resolve a situation, and so *Chita*, his single attempt at sustained narrative during his years in New Orleans, fails to please. However clear his intention to present man as part of, but caught relentlessly within, the power of nature, and to demonstrate that simple men who know and respect nature's force live more cleanly and satisfying lives than dwellers in cities to whom nature is hidden "by walls, and by weary avenues of trees with whitewashed trunks," the result is distorted more than Hearn could have meant it to be. As a child of nature, young Chita is never seen as clearly as the sea and sky whose color may be thought of as in itself a major theme.

For *Chita* is a book of blueness, and blueness is eternity. After mottled rage of storm or sudden glare at birth or death of day, the calmer color returns, inscrutable, insistent. Other colors are stroked boldly through the book: "the golden wealth of orange trees," "clouds brilliantly white and flocculent, like loose new cotton," "the quivering pinkness of waters curled by the breath of morning," the "vaporized sapphire" of cloudless summer days, and the redness of storm and death with which the action opens and closes—black redness like "heated iron when its vermillion dies." Forms are less distinct: "the rounded foliage of evergreen oaks," "beaches speckled with drift and decaying things," girls presented in outline only, "graceful as the palmettoeˢ that sway above them." Occasionally there is a memorable visual image, like that which fleetingly glimpses a passing gull "whirling its sickle wings" against a crimsoning sky. But sounds are everywhere: "the storm-roar of reptile voices chanting in chorus," "the monstrous and appalling chorus of frogs," "sinister, squeaking cries" of gulls, the perpetual rustle of the fiddler crab, and the "moan of the rising surf," the "voice of the sea," which is "never one voice, but a tumult of many voices . . . the muttering of multitudinous dead—the moaning of innumerable ghosts." And the sea, responding to the colors of the sky, implacably eats away at the shore, so that "Year by year that rustling strip of green grows narrower; the sand spreads and sinks, shuddering and wrinkling like a living brown skin; and at last standing copses of oaks, ever clinging with naked, dead feet to the sliding beach, lean more and more out of perpendicular. As the sands subside, the stumps seem to crawl, to writhe—like the reaching arms of cephalopods."[21]

Something of what *Chita* is about is suggested by the epigram from Emerson with which Hearn prefaces the book: "But Nature whistled all her winds,/Did as she pleased and went her way." It is the story of a child who is born to the world of nature by a storm in which her mother and, presumably, her father have lost their lives. They had been among lighthearted island vacationers who had not recognized signs of an approaching storm, for "Nature—incomprehensible Sphinx—before her mightiest bursts of rage, ever puts forth her divinest witchery, makes more manifest her awful beauty." All seemed so serene and blue that they failed to realize that there is also

something unutterable in this bright Gulf-air that compels awe—something vital, something holy, something pantheistic: and reverently the mind asks itself if what the eye beholds is not ... the Infinite Breath, the Divine Ghost, and the great Blue Soul of the Unknown. All, all is blue in the calm—save the land under your feet, which you almost forget, since it seems only a tiny green flake afloat in the liquid of eternity of day. Then slowly, caressingly, irresistibly, the witchery of the Infinite grows upon you; out of Time and Space you begin to dream with open eyes—to drift into delicious oblivion of facts—to forget the past, the present, the substantial—to comprehend nothing but the existence of the infinite Blue Ghost as something into which you would wish to melt utterly away forever.[22]

Hearn, perhaps inadvertently, is true to his imagery. After the storm had mounted wave after succeeding wave to attack the vacation island, its awful music in horrendous contrast to the waltz to which doomed revelers danced; after the waters had washed away all before it, the child Chita is found afloat "in the liquid of eternity" upon "a tiny green flake," which is a billiard table. The fisherman who rescued her knew and understood the sea, and when he had taught her to know it also, Chita's "soft, pale flesh became firm and brown, the meagre limbs rounded into robust symmetry...; for the strength of the sea had entered into her." How different the experience of her father, who also somehow miraculously had escaped death in the storm. Amid the "blindness and brutality of cities, where the divine light never purely comes," he practiced medicine, but could not save himself from yellow fever. When he arrives at the

21. *Ibid.*, IV, 153.
22. *Ibid.*, IV, 155.

gulfside settlement where Chita has lived, he recognizes her because she looks so like her mother, and then, after six pages of delirium, he dies.

The third section of *Chita*, called "The Shadow of the Tide," is crowded and incoherent. It attempts too much—Chita's development over ten years, her discovery of death in a gruesome woodland tomb, her conquering of fear of the sea; and then suddenly a shift in focus, from Chita to her father, his introduction to nature as he journeys to Viosca's Point, his illness, recognition of his daughter, and death. If in *Chita* Hearn was writing the narrative of which he had spoken earlier to friends, "constructed on totally novel principles," grounded in evolutionary philosophy as he had read it in Herbert Spencer and on the kind of benign fatalism he found attractive in Buddhism, such purpose does not come through—certainly not in this third section where he seems, almost frenetically, to be striving toward statement, about rough boatmen who break into beautiful song, about folk memories, and love discovered in death. Nor is the second section, "Out of the Sea's Strength," greatly better, though it is here, as Laroussel, a member of a rescue party which searches the bayou for remnants of the storm, questions the derelict child in Creole patois, that Chita is revealed, albeit briefly, as a person who is heard and known. Laroussel, who speaks and is real, then disappears, later dimly revealed as an enemy, then a friend, of Chita's father, was evidently intended to play a significant part in the development of the plot, though what exactly that part is Hearn never makes clear.

But the first section, "The Legend of L'Île Dernière," which has hardly a person in it, but which celebrates calm and storm and blueness, deserves place beside Mark Twain's "Old Times on the Mississippi" (which Hearn admired) and Thoreau's descriptions of Katahdin and Cape Cod. Hearn was later, he said, ashamed of *Chita* as overworked and overstylized, but he could not have been thinking of the first section, which is heightened surely, but which in tone and substance is almost exactly right. Word and mood and rhythm advance confidently side by side. Hearn's sea is a cradle endlessly rocking, but not by the hand of an elemental crone-mother. Mystery and beauty and menace there are one, not to be defined by eyes sharpened for daily use, or ears attuned to pleasing waltzes.

No Southern writer, except perhaps Sidney Lanier, had composed with more exultant fervor. Yet Hearn disliked the localizing of writers, as he might have disliked being remembered as shy, myopic, and irascible. Neither personal defect nor accident of place define an artist. Writing, he said, "which has no better claim to recognition than the fact that it is Southern, can never maintain its claim to recognition at all." Whatever its substance in locale or dialect, "the art itself must be founded upon catholic principles— upon those touches of nature which make the whole world kin." No work of true merit can be of "merely sectional interest."[23] Magic was needed, of a kind which might be searched out amid the mélange of wildness of the bayou country, or wherever simple people re- membered more than they had ever learned, where old songs and customs and superstitions defied corruption, and faith scoffed at learning. "We are nearer God in the South," wrote Lafcadio Hearn in 1887 as he was preparing to leave it, "just as we are nearer Death in that terrible and splendid heat of the Gulf Coast." By God, he ex- plained, "of course I mean only the World-Soul, the mighty and sweetest life of Nature, the great Blue Ghost which fills planets and hearts with beauty."[24]

Edmund Wilson in *Patriotic Gore* has dismissed Lafcadio Hearn as an impressionist and escapist, without interest in social move- ments—as if that were the gauge of any artist. Malcolm Cowley, in introduction to the only easily available collection of Hearn's writ- ing, speaks of him more leniently:

Unlike many authors of broader talents, he had the *métier*, the vocation for writing, the conscience which kept him working over each passage until it had the exact color of what he needed to say; and in most cases the colors have proved fast. Many books written by his famous con- temporaries are becoming difficult to read. One can't help seeing that Howells followed the conventions of his day, that Frank Norris was full of romantic bad taste; but Lafcadio Hearn at his best was in- dependent of fashion and was writing for our time as much as his own.[25]

Hearn had almost every minor literary virtue; he succeeded in minor genres, but he is real, as person and artist, and bold enough to stand, however unsteadily, alone. When the literary historian forgets him, something of literary heritage is lost, for he has added, said Paul Elmer More, "a new thrill to our intellectual experience,"[26] and people who care for writing as art will not pass him by, even when they are sure that he may finally disappoint them.

23. Mordell, *Discoveries*, pp. 66, 70.
24. *Letters from the Raven*, p. 86.
25. *The Selected Writings of Lafcadio Hearn*, ed. Harry Goodman (New York, 1949), pp. 1-2.
26. "Lafcadio Hearn: The Meeting of Three Ways," *Atlantic Monthly*, XCI, 205 (Feb., 1903).

KATE CHOPIN'S THE AWAKENING
IN THE PERSPECTIVE OF
HER LITERARY CAREER

George Arms

University of New Mexico

Republished in 1964 with an introduction by Kenneth Eble, *The Awakening* seems likely to take a permanent place among the American novels of distinction which appeared at the turn of the century. As Daniel S. Rankin's biography in 1932 showed, since the vigorous denunciation that accompanied the first publication in 1899, little had been written on Mrs. Chopin and less on her novel in the intervening decades. After Rankin's book both she and it received more attention: in 1936 Arthur Hobson Quinn called "Désirée's Baby" "one of the greatest short stories in the language" and praised the reality of the novel, though on the whole he decided against it; in 1951 Clarence Gohdes observed that Mrs. Chopin showed skill in character delineation, especially in *The Awakening*, which "deserves a worthy place in the history of sterner realism in nineteenth-century America"; but, three years earlier, in the *Literary History of the United States*, Carlos Baker had not mentioned the novel, though he treated her work with respect—"Even her failures are readable."[1]

In the 1950's the novel received its first extended treatment since Rankin's in a twenty-two page introduction by Cyrille Arnavon when he translated the work into French; but since this publication has had limited availability in this country, I think that it is fair to say that for most mid-century readers Kenneth Eble rediscovered the novel in his essay in 1956.[2] Since then, Edmund Wilson has

1. A. H. Quinn, *American Fiction* (New York, 1936), pp. 354-357; Gohdes, *The Literature of the American People*, ed. A. H. Quinn (New York, 1951), p. 654; Baker, *Literary History of the United States*, ed. Robert E. Spiller *et al.* (New York, 1948), II, 858-859.

2. Arnavon, *Edna* [i.e., *The Awakening*] (Paris, [1952]); Eble, "A Forgotten Novel," *Western Humanities Review*, I, 261-269 (Summer, 1956). Apparently Eble did not know Arnavon's essay; and I am indebted to William M. Gibson, of New York University, for calling it to my attention and for providing a copy. See also Robert Cantwell, "*The Awakening* by Kate Chopin," *Georgia Review*, X, 489-494 (Winter, 1956), and

written favorably of the work in *Patriotic Gore* (1962) —possibly with the result that a publisher reprinted it as Eble had urged in his earlier article. More recently in *The Ferment of Realism* (1965) Warner Berthoff has also shown an enthusiasm for *The Awakening* that equals that of Eble and Wilson.

Excellent as the commentary in general is, it leaves much to be said about the book and also about its background in the short stories, mostly earlier. Wilson has touched upon one of these stories, but only in the light of what he believes was the author's preoccupation with marital maladjustments and sexual freedom. Indeed, the four most recent commentators whom I have mentioned emphasize this subject; and the quotation from Wilson that appears on the cover of the paperback epitomizes their approach: "Quite uninhibited and beautifully written ... anticipates D. H. Lawrence, in its treatment of infidelity." Certainly I do not wish to controvert the importance of the subject, yet I think that Arnavon, Eble, and Wilson err in assuming a close sympathy and even identification of Mrs. Chopin and Edna Pontellier.

Arnavon does go beyond, especially in his use of continental literature as a frame of reference as well as in a variety of literary and psychological insights; and so does Eble, who in both his article and introduction (which are nearly the same) analyzes perceptively the characterization, structure, and the use of images and symbols. At one point he refers to "the warring within Edna's self" and compares it with Phaedra's struggle in the *Hippolytus* (p. xii).[3] Berthoff has also dealt with what seems to me this highly significant element. Noting "the conflict between two distinct ways of life" in the stories of New Orleans writers, he extends this contrast to *The Awakening*, in which "this conflict steadily underscores the main action, giving dramatic force to its psychological probings."[4] In my own remarks on the novel and its relation to other fiction of Mrs. Chopin I should like to treat more extensively this element of conflict, though not in the context of local color.

Briefly, the story of Edna Pontellier is that of a wife who becomes increasingly alienated from her husband. At the beginning of

Per E. Seyersted (who studied under Arnavon at Harvard in 1959 and will publish a biography toward the end of 1967), "Kate Chopin: An Important St. Louis Writer Reconsidered," *Bulletin of the Missouri Historical Society*, XIX, 89-114 (Jan., 1963).

3. "Introduction," *The Awakening* (New York, 1964). Page numbers in the text are those of this edition. I have not cited pages for quotations from short stories in Mrs. Chopin's own collections or that of Rankin.

4. *The Ferment of Realism* (New York, 1965), p. 88.

the tale she is vacationing in a summer resort frequented by Creoles on Grand Isle. There she falls in love with Robert Lebrun, a young bachelor, who upon becoming aware that a conventional flirtation will develop into a love affair leaves for Mexico. Upon her return to New Orleans in the fall, Edna still is in love with Robert, and, dissatisfied by his having left her, becomes involved with a man about town, Alcée Arobin. During her affair with him Robert returns; she offers herself to Robert, but he refuses her because she is married. The day following his refusal she goes to Grand Isle and swims out into the sea until she is drowned.

This summary does little to suggest the author's attitude toward her material and toward her principal character. Basically she writes as a non-intrusive author but principally presents her material with a sense of constant contrast, partly in the whole social situation, partly in Edna, but essentially as the author's way of looking at life. In the first of her two editorializing chapters she speaks of this contrast: "In short, Mrs. Pontellier was beginning to realize her position in the universe as a human being, and to recognize her relations as an individual to the world within and about her" (p. 33). Into the next chapter she extends this observation by remarking, "At a very early period she had apprehended instinctively the dual life—that outward existence which conforms, the inward life which questions" (p. 35). Yet Mrs. Chopin is unwilling to present Edna as simply struggling between two opposites, later remarking that her emotions "had never taken the form of struggles" (p. 121). On occasion the polarity reappears, as when the author writes that the husband could not see that his wife "was becoming herself and daily casting aside that fictitious self which we assume like a garment with which to appear before the world" (p. 148). In a much more adolescent fashion Edna speaks: "By all the codes which I am acquainted with, I am a devilishly wicked specimen of the sex. But some way I can't convince myself that I am" (p. 216).

On the whole, as she reveals herself, her aimlessness impresses us more than her sense of conflict. Early in the novel, recalling an incident from her childhood, Edna first interprets it as running away from the gloomy Presbyterianism of her father, but then goes on to say that her walk on that Sunday morning was "idly, aimlessly, unthinking and unguided" (p. 43). Thus Edna appears not so much as a woman who is aware of the opposition of two ideals but rather as one who drifts—who finally, even in death, is drifting when she again recalls having wandered on the blue-green meadow as a little girl. In the second editorial chapter, the author again considers the conflicts in Edna's life, but at this stage the contrasts have become a series of "multitudinous emotions." Edna is sensitive to many states of mind as the author describes her after the consummation of her affair with Arobin: irresponsibility, shock, her husband's and Robert's reproach, but not shame and not remorse, though regret that she has yielded from erotic longing rather than from love. Still, there is an "understanding" that hints of a polarity: "She felt as if a mist had been lifted from her eyes, enabling her to look upon and comprehend the significance of life, that monster made up of beauty and brutality" (p. 219).

At the time of Edna's suicide she thinks of many things, yet in the final paragraph the images that come to her are all those of her childhood. One is that of a cavalry officer whom she had romantically loved when he visited her father (pp. 44, 303). When she married, the author observes that "she felt she would take her place with a certain dignity in the world of reality, closing the portals forever behind her upon the realm of romance and dreams" (p. 47). And upon Robert's leaving for Mexico, "she recognized anew the symptoms of infatuation" of her earlier life, but the recognition "did not lessen the reality, the poignancy of the revelation by any suggestion or promise of instability" (p. 116). Thus one of the oppositions which the author develops throughout the novel is that of romance and reality, and she suggests that Edna remains a figure of romantic ideals in spite of her acting with a sexual freedom that the common reader would call realistic or even naturalistic. Part of Edna's romanticism derives from a sense of fate, as the comment late in the book suggests: "She answered her husband with friendly evasiveness, —not with any fixed design to mislead him, only because all sense of reality had gone out of her life; she had abandoned herself to Fate, and awaited the consequences with indifference" (p. 271). As so often in the novel, Mrs. Chopin made specific preparation by noting that marriages "masquerade as the decrees of Fate" (p. 46). So one can summarize that instead of identifying herself with Edna's actions, Mrs. Chopin tends to regard them as romantically motivated rather than as realistically considered. Yet, as if to say that there are other kinds of romanticism, the author introduces Adele Ratignolle, Edna's friend who is completely in love with her husband, in this fashion: "There are no words to describe her save the old ones that have served so often to picture the bygone heroine of romance and the fair lady of our dreams" (p. 19).

In all, the author presents these contrasts suggestively rather than systematically. Perhaps if she takes any stand at all it is to favor individualism against social obligation, for she writes of Edna, "Every step which she took toward relieving herself from obligations added to her strength and expansion as an individual" (p. 245). Yet even here she leaves the question open. What does the author mean when she writes that after her father and husband leave on trips, "Then Edna sat in the library after dinner and read Emerson until she grew sleepy" (p. 190)? Eble interprets this as a reaction against the father's Presbyterianism (p. ix), and such it may be; but to grow sleepy over a Transcendental individualist also hints that Edna's individualism lacks philosophical grounding.

This sleepiness from reading Emerson leads to the contrast, implicit in the title. In treating Edna's awakening, the author shows irony and even deviousness. We look upon Edna's awakening as archetypal in marking her passage from death to rebirth, but we may also look upon her awakening as not a rebirth but as another kind of death that is self-sought. Amusingly enough, the author, quite consciously I am sure, allows Edna to do an inordinate amount of sleeping throughout the novel, in spite of her underlying vitality. She first appears "with some appearance of fatigue" (p. 4, admittedly after she has been swimming); that night she is "fast asleep" (p. 11), and her weariness is noted many times, especially when she falls in love with Robert (pp. 73, 77), though at one time she only sleeps fitfully (p. 82). When she first openly seeks out Robert and takes him—again amusingly—to Sunday morning mass, she is so drowsy at the service that she has to leave, and sleeps the whole of the rest of the morning and afternoon at a nearby house, with Robert remarking at the end, "You have slept precisely one hundred years" (p. 96). Again, when she celebrates her decision to break with her husband at a dinner party, "the old ennui" overtakes her (p. 232). It is almost as if the author were saying: here is my heroine who at the critical points of her progress toward an awakening constantly falls asleep.

An even grimmer irony, of course, is in her awakening to an

erotic life not through Robert, whom she truly loves, but through Alcée, whom she uses merely as a convenience. Though Edna recognizes this, she hardly does so in the sense that the novel does. We are told that "Alcée Arobin's manner was so genuine that it often deceived even himself," but also that "Edna did not care or think whether it were genuine or not" (p. 201). We cannot help suspecting that Edna simplifies and melodramatizes her view of herself far more than the author does. After Robert's return, she exclaims to him, "It was you who awoke me last summer out of a life-long, stupid dream. Oh! you have made me so unhappy with your indifference. Oh! I have suffered, suffered!" (p. 283). Almost compulsively she is soon saying the same thing to the family doctor, who earlier had seen her as an "animal waking up in the sun" (p. 181) and now cautions her about the illusions of youth:

"Yes," she said. "The years that are gone seem like dreams—if one might go on sleeping and dreaming—but to wake up and find—oh! well! perhaps it is better to wake up after all, even to suffer, rather than to remain a dupe to illusions all one's life." (p. 292)

Finally, the underlying awareness of contrasting forces in the novel is exhibited in its use of children. Edna has two boys of four and five. With them she has little intimacy, and her husband accuses her of neglecting them, as does her mother-in-law—an accusation endorsed by the author, who early in the story announces, "In short, Mrs. Pontellier was not a mother-woman" (p. 19). Again we are somewhat perplexed as to whether or not the author approves of Edna's attitude toward her children. I suppose that those who look upon the novel as a defense of the New Woman would feel that Mrs. Chopin regards freedom from children as a necessary basis for complete freedom. But again I am doubtful, for Mrs. Chopin delights in the contraries which are present in Edna's response toward her boys.

Perhaps Edna most fully expresses her attitude in a conversation with Madame Ratignolle midway in the book:

"I would give up the unessential; I would give my money, I would give my life for my children; but I wouldn't give myself. I can't make it more clear; it's only something which I am beginning to comprehend, which is revealing itself to me." (p. 122)

This passage will be recalled for us at the time of Edna's death, but in the meantime we observe her constantly returning to her children as a kind of penance whenever she displays most markedly her love outside of marriage. When she suspects that Robert goes to

Mexico to avoid her, she shows an unusual intimacy with her children by telling them a bedtime story (p. 111). She had already coddled and caressed one of her sons immediately after her day spent with Robert (p. 100). After her second night with Alcée she visits her children in the country (p. 246)—one would think more as an act of penance than of affection. Just after Edna had fully admitted her love for Robert to a friend, she sent her children "a huge box of bonbons" (p. 213).

When Robert finally returns to New Orleans and Edna declares her love for him, she is called away from their reunion to attend the birth of another child of Adele Ratignolle. After the birth, which is not an easy one, Adele's parting injunction is: "Think of the children, Edna. Oh think of the children! Remember them!" (p. 289). From this scene she returns to discover that Robert has not waited for her, but instead has left a note, bidding her "Good-by—because I love you" (p. 294). The next day she goes to Grand Isle to drown herself, saying in the meanwhile again and again: "To-day it is Arobin; to-morrow it will be some one else. It makes no difference to me, it doesn't matter about Léonce Pontellier—but Raoul and Etienne!" (p. 299). Immediately afterward, she thinks back to her earlier conversation with Adele in which she had declared that she would give up everything for her children, including her life, but not "herself." This final opposition then leads directly to her death: "The children appeared before her like antagonists who had overcome her; who had overpowered and sought to drag her into the soul's slavery for the rest of her days. But she knew a way to elude them" (p. 300). Though she does not think of these things, the author tells us, when she walks toward the beach, her thoughts revert to the children and her husband as she tires in her swim toward death: "They were a part of her life. But they need not have thought that they could possess her, body and soul" (p. 302).

While the motivation from the children has been amply anticipated, its final realization produces something of a shift. Perhaps one might go so far as to say that the children, used in this way, somewhat flaw the novel. We recall that many of Mrs. Chopin's short stories first appeared in *Harper's Young People's Magazine,* the *Youth's Companion,* and also in *Vogue,* with the uneasy feeling that the author is still writing in a juvenile vein or from the conventional angle of a woman's magazine. Yet this difficulty might be answered by recognizing that the children stand for a stable society and the permanency of an unbroken home. Perhaps it would even be better to treat them as bringing another contrast into the story. Like those contrasts of purpose and aimlessness, of romance and realism, and of sleep and awakening, this one is not of absolute opposition but is complex and even blurred. As my argument has suggested, precisely this complexity may be what Mrs. Chopin is trying to achieve. She presents a series of events in which the truth is present, but with a philosophical pragmatism she is unwilling to extract a final truth. Rather, she sees truth as constantly re-forming itself and as so much a part of the context of what happens that it can never be final or for that matter abstractly stated.

When we turn to the approximately one hundred short stories and sketches by Mrs. Chopin, of which all but sixteen were published in periodicals or in books during her lifetime, it is hard to see a regular progression toward the complex sense of opposition that she realized in *The Awakening*. In *Bayou Folk* (1894), *A Night in Acadie* (1897), and the volume projected in 1898-1900, the development is not marked, even when one takes into account the dates of writing or first publication. As for the 1890 novel, *At Fault*, a contrast inheres in its two rival women characters, but it is melodramatically conceived and sentimentally resolved. This kind of opposition and resolution occurs often in the short stories, in which there is not much time for the complexity that we have seen in *The Awakening*. Still, in spite of the limits of form, Mrs. Chopin occasionally moves in the direction of her novel.

With the stories of *Bayou Folk*, I think that on the whole she goes least far, though Berthoff remarks that while her stories are less successful than her novel, the best are in this collection. In "Désirée's Baby" one has a contrast of racial opposition, and in its ending one sees something of Mark Twain's *Pudd'nhead Wilson*, which it preceded by a year; that is, both works raise the question of identity in a racial context. But though Mark Twain can be faulted on melodramatic elements, his novel makes a complex and pragmatic inquiry not present in Mrs. Chopin's story. Like many recent commentators, I wonder at the appearance of "Désirée's Baby" in so many anthologies, even while admitting its elegance as a well-made tale in the manner of Maupassant.

I would even suggest that "Beyond the Bayou," though a juvenile that first appeared in *Youth's Companion*, might better serve the author as representative of her work on a local-color level. This story relates how a former slave, because of a frightening experience in the Civil War, refuses to cross the bayou between her cabin and the plantation. But when a little boy whom she loves is injured, she breaks through the psychological barrier and carries him across the bayou to his home; and when she has done this once, she frees herself from her compulsive fear. Thus the author works out a problem in which there are elements of sentimentality, with the relationship of former slave and master or some variation of it that often appears in Mrs. Chopin's work. Yet the author has posed an opposition of hysteria and love that is realized in the situation itself rather than by an arbitrary solution. "Old Aunt Peggy" and "The Return of Alcibiade" also exemplify this blend of sentiment and pragmatism.

Much more directly presenting a contrast for the truth which is present in it are three stories: "Madame Célestin's Divorce," "A Visit to Avoyelles," and "A Lady of Bayou St. John." In the first of these a woman plans a divorce in spite of family and church opposition, but decides against it when her worthless husband returns after six months and promises to reform; in the second we have a comparison of a former lover's attitude toward a girl who has married into poverty and her actual situation—the lover sentimentalizes it, while the girl accepts the reality as her way of life; and in the third a soldier's wife who had agreed to run away to Paris with a lover, but who refuses his proposal of marriage when she is widowed, for now she has "memories to crowd and fill my life, if I live a hundred years!" In these stories Mrs. Chopin seems to be exploring conflict of attitudes not in conventional terms but with a humorous understanding of the obstinacy of emotions under pressure.

The second collection of short stories, *A Night in Acadie*, contains fewer stories than *Bayou Folk* that had originally appeared in juvenile magazines, one less story than had appeared in *Vogue*, three stories as against one in *The Century*, and three stories as against none in the *Atlantic*. These differences in magazine appearances suggest an increasing maturity in *A Night in Acadie*, and though many of its stories do not advance beyond sentimental episode, some come close to the accomplishment of *The Awakening*. My own choice of the best five are "A Night in Acadie," "Athénaïse," "Azélie," "A Sentimental Soul," and "A Respectable Woman." All deal more

openly with unconventional sexual experience than most of the
stories in the earlier collection. For example, in "Athénaïse," which
originally appeared in the *Atlantic,* a bride deserts her husband after
two months of marriage. Both agree that they have made a mistake
in marrying, though after the first desertion when the husband goes
to her home to get her, she returns with him. A couple of weeks later
she disappears again, this time going to New Orleans, where she
meets a newspaperman with whom she perhaps falls in love. But
suddenly aware that she is going to have a baby from her marriage,
she returns to her husband and for the first time responds to his
embrace with passion. As for the newspaperman, he "had gathered
that she was self-willed, impulsive, innocent, ignorant, unsatisfied,
dissatisfied." In love with her himself, he takes his defeat gracefully
when she eagerly returns to her husband. Still, "By heaven, it hurts,
it hurts!"

The newspaperman also appears in "A Respectable Woman,"
which was first published in *Vogue.* When Gouvernail visits the
Barodas on their plantation, Mrs. Baroda begins to like him in
spite of a preconceived distaste, falls in love with him, and then leaves
during his visit to escape the temptation of an affair. About a year
later, however, she asks her husband to invite Gouvernail to visit
again, with the open hint to the reader that this time she will yield
to her impulse. As the author observes, "Besides being a respectable
woman she was a very sensible one; and she knew there are some
battles in life which a human being must fight alone." In both these
stories as in the other three, one thus finds an experience explored
without final judgment and with the sense that the truth may be
found only transiently rather than emerging absolutely from it. Interestingly too, one discovers that the oppositions present in *The
Awakening* are present in these stories, though without the probing
manifest in the novel.

But frequently we have a sentimental slickness, as exemplified in
"At Chênière Caminada," which takes place in the Grand Isle area,
introduces the Lebrun family, and has as its protagonist Tonie, the
son of Madame Antonine, in whose house Edna slept when she first
realized fully her love for Robert. Tonie has fallen in love with one
of the summer visitors, who is tolerantly amused by the rough fisherman's affections and gives him a necklace in a "a spirit of coquetry."
He realizes that they can never marry, but loves the girl throughout

the following winter even when he does not see her. It is a morbid, sickening sort of love, and when he hears she has died of a cold that presumably developed into pneumonia, he is revived—"He did not know why it was so; he could not understand. But from that day he felt that he began to live again, to be once more a part of the moving world about him." Up to this point we have a story in Mrs. Chopin's realistic mode. But when Tonie finally explains that he has recovered because in heaven Claire "will know who has loved her best," I think that the author asks the reader to share his view. Perhaps she does not, or perhaps she consciously avoids disappointing the conventional expectations of her readers.

In 1898 Mrs. Chopin sent the publishers of *A Night in Acadie* a new collection of short stories, *A Vocation and a Voice*, which they accepted, but then it was transferred to Herbert S. Stone & Company in November, 1898, and returned to her in February, 1900. Rankin speculates that her new publishers, who by late 1898 had presumably accepted *The Awakening*, rejected *A Vocation and a Voice* because of the stir created by the novel.[5] Of the twenty-one titles that he lists in the proposed collection he prints six in his group of ten in the second part of his biography. Of these six, three belong to Mrs. Chopin's finest, in my opinion. Perhaps I should include the story "The Dream of an Hour," since Wilson finds a great deal of interest in it, but his conern with it is more biographical than literary. There is irony in this story of a woman, who upon learning of the supposed death of her husband, murmurs in the privacy of her room, "Free, free, free!" and then dies of a heart attack when she finds her husband is still alive. The irony, however, strikes me as too neat if not too cheap, and though I recognize its importance in suggesting the author's attitude toward husbands, I can hardly regard it as more than one of her better *Vogue* stories. Those that seem to me most successful in the Rankin group much more subtly explore situations. "Lilacs" (written in 1894 and published in 1896) is properly described by Rankin as having as its burden "the moral collision of two natures." But when he adds that it also conveys "a shock rending the hearts of others,"[6] I think that he melodramatizes a conflict that is presented essentially for its perceptions within a realistic frame of reference. In this story an opera singer returns for a visit to the convent of her childhood, once a year when lilacs bloom, and

5. *Kate Chopin and Her Creole Stories* (Philadelphia, 1932), p. 195.
6. *Ibid.*, pp. 166-167.

brings a handsome present for the chapel along with great bunches of lilacs. The Mother Superior looks upon her action as a self-indulgence that also gives her a too special place in the convent life. Accordingly, on a last visit she is not allowed to enter, and our final view is that of a lay sister sweeping away the lilac blossoms which the singer had let fall upon the portico. Everything is presented; no interpretation is forced upon the reader, who is not shocked but simply understands. In "Two Portraits" (written in 1895) the author presents sketches of a "wanton" and a "nun." Both begin with precisely the same paragraph: "Alberta having looked not very long into life, had not looked very far.... They were mysterious eyes and love looked out of them." The brief biography of the wanton ends with the suggestion that she will murder one of her lovers, and that of the nun that she may become a saint. Though the author touches slightly on naturalistic elements of heredity or environment, we are primarily given these two lives as a suggestion of the constant paradox of life itself. Finally in "The Vagabonds" (written in 1895) we have one of the few stories Mrs. Chopin told in first person. The narrator, a woman, meets a vagabond she knows, perhaps a distant cousin. He begs unsuccessfully from her, and she responds to him with a kind of disdainful sympathy. "I called him names; but all the same I could not help thinking that it must be good to prowl sometimes; to get close to the black night and lose oneself in its silence and mystery." Then she continues her walk: "I was glad the vagabond did not want money. But for the life of me I don't know what he wanted, or why he wanted to see me." In the author's titling her story with a plural, we recognize in this confrontation of two such different people a common bond that neither character fully understands.

Since all three of these stories belong to the mid-nineties, no development can be argued from them. However, they give further assurance of Mrs. Chopin's real strength and accomplishment. Some of the stories of the projected third volume are just as weak as those of the other two, but in all three books she occasionally examines the opposites of her situation with skill and insight. Even if she often falls into commercial sentimentalism, she refuses to be satisfied with this; she refuses to yield to the temptation of becoming a final interpreter out of her conviction that a realist may reveal most successfully that truth exists in a constant state of tension.

Mrs. Chopin did not review many books, but when she did she clearly exhibits her basic realism. For Garland's *Crumbling Idols* she expressed an essential sympathy—"he is one of us"—in spite of her dislike of his brashness. But she dislikes something else: "And, notwithstanding Mr. Garland's opinion to the contrary, social problems, social environments, local color and the rest of it are not of themselves motives to insure the survival of a writer who employs them."[7] With Zola's *Lourdes* she makes a more explicit comment. Though having a faith in the sincerity of his work, "I am yet not at all times ready to admit its truth, which is only equivalent to saying that our points of view differ, that truth rests upon a shifting basis and is apt to be kaleidoscopic." What she objects to is "the disagreeable fact that his design is to instruct us."[8] Mainly she condemns Hardy's *Jude the Obscure* for its didacticism: "The characters are so plainly constructed with the intention of illustrating the purposes of the author, that they do not for a moment convey any impression of reality."[9] She herself follows the traditional method of the realist when she mockingly defends her novel *The Awakening*:

> Having a group of people at my disposal, I thought it might be entertaining (to myself) to throw them together and see what would happen. I never dreamed of Mrs. Pontellier making such a mess of things and working out her own damnation as she did. If I had had the slightest intimation of such a thing I would have excluded her from the company. But when I found out what she was up to, the play was half over and it was then too late.[10]

In a somewhat distracted meditation, "A Reflection," written in the same year, she exclaims: "What matter if souls and bodies are falling beneath the feet of the ever-pressing multitude! it moves with the majestic rhythm of the spheres. Its discordant clashes sweep upward in one harmonious tone that blends with the music of other worlds—to complete God's orchestra." Here, I think, she contemplates an easy reconciliation of opposites which in her most accomplished work she does not attempt, even though she attributes this to those "with a vital and responsive energy." Perhaps one may find a clue to the weakness of her sentimental stories in this feeling that the discordant clashes ought to blend into an uplifting unity. She concludes her meditation, however, with resigned acceptance:

7. *Ibid.*, pp. 144, 143.
8. *Ibid.*, p. 145.
9. *Ibid.*, p. 152.
10. *Ibid.*, p. 173.

Oh! I could weep at being left by the wayside; left with the grass and the clouds and a few dumb animals. True, I feel at home in the society of these symbols of life's immutability. In the procession I should feel the crushing feet, the clashing discords, the ruthless hands and stifling breath. I could not hear the rhythm of the march.

Salve! ye dumb hearts. Let us be still and wait by the roadside.

In such literary neutrality, in spite of her apparent envy of those who achieve more—but still "do not need to apprehend the significance of things"[11]—Mrs. Chopin is most successful. As she observes the procession of life, she sees in it a constantly forming truth but never a truth that becomes an absolute or conventional one.

A green and yellow parrot opens *The Awakening* by repeating over and over: "*Allez vous-en! Allez vous-en! Sapristi!* That's all right!" (p. 1). Perhaps to the image of the bird with the broken wing first referred to by a friend and then seen by Edna at her drowning (pp. 217, 301), the parrot forms the ultimate contrast. Cynically and impiously he presents the human situation, but with
a profounder sense of its inconsistencies
Mrs. Chopin might conclude with
him, "That's all right."

11. *Ibid.*, pp. 190-191.

O. HENRY AS A REGIONAL ARTIST

E. Hudson Long

Baylor University

O. Henry, who was christened William Sidney Porter, was born in Greensboro, North Carolina, in 1862, where his boyhood was spent during the Reconstruction period of the South. Barely twenty years of age, he went to Texas, and lived for two years on a ranch at a time when the cattle industry was thriving. From the ranch he moved to Austin, where he remained from 1884 until 1896, with short interludes in Houston and San Antonio. Fleeing, unfortunately, from charges of embezzlement, which he had not intended, Porter paused briefly in New Orleans on his way to Honduras. Upon his return in 1897 he was brought to trial and in 1898 entered the federal penitentiary at Columbus, Ohio. After being released, he found his way to New York, and lived there from 1902 until his death in 1910. His life is as romantic as any story he ever wrote, and rarely has any other American writer of the short story possessed such varied experiences to draw from.

O. Henry's stories remain vividly alive because he drew his material directly from life, and he viewed the scene with a freshness and interest that make it ever new. He treated his characters with sympathy and understanding, and his occasional touches of irony are never devoid of tolerance. His keen interest in setting and atmosphere make them pervasive in his stories, integrating plot and characters.

In New York, as a Southerner who had lived in the Southwest and Central America, O. Henry was acutely aware of regional differences, which with him never became sectional. Writing for magazines and newspaper supplements, he was by instinct a local colorist, who placed his romances against realistic backgrounds, as he turned out a story a week. Naturally his fiction was bright, rapid, and mechanical, much like the life he was depicting. Employing the latest slang and every-day expressions, he presented his unusual characters with sentiment and humor, at times with a dash of slapstick, often to the detriment of his art.

As a clerk in his uncle's drug store in Greensboro, where he worked for several years, young Porter had heard the old-timers exchanging yarns about the ante-bellum South, the Confederacy, and Reconstruction. As they played dominoes or checkers, these Southern character types refought the Civil War and discussed politics in a manner that was to influence his later fiction. From them came such portraits as that of old Doc Millikin of "Two Renegades," "the red-hottest Southerner that ever smelled mint. He made Stonewall Jackson and R. E. Lee look like Abolitionists" (p. 538).[1] Another was Col. Aquila Telfair of "The Rose of Dixie," whose watchword for his magazine was "Of, For, and By the South" (p. 683). And there was Major Pendleton Talbot in "The Duplicity of Hargraves," whose dearest subject was "the traditions and history of his beloved Southland" (p. 871).

In "The Emancipation of Billy," O. Henry pictured the drug store of a small Southern town, no doubt drawing on his own memories from Greensboro days. In the same story one sees Governor Pemberton's "old, old square-porticoed mansion, with the wry window-shutters and the paint peeling off in discolored flakes" (p. 469), while the click of the old gentleman's gold-headed cane sounded on the "rugged brick sidewalk" as, wearing his "plug hat," he passed through the gate of a "rickety paling-fence."

Many years later, following a visit to Nashville, Tennessee, where he stayed at the Maxwell House, praising its fine food and service, O. Henry wrote one of his best Southern stories, "A Municipal Report." Showing the peaceful town drowsing under a slow, heavy drizzle, he captures its essence. The old Negro hack driver, loyal and devoted, is a relic of bygone days, while Azalea Adair is a tenderly protected lady of the old regime. By contrast, Major Caswell, degraded and dishonest, represents the type of "professional Southerner" that O. Henry abhorred.

The tale, written to refute a statement by Frank Norris that the only real "story" cities were New York, New Orleans, and San Francisco, proves that such a conventional place as Nashville could equal any other in human interest. Making artistic use of the prosaic quotations from a Rand and McNally atlas, much in the manner of a Greek chorus, O. Henry contrasts the uneventful, material city against his romantic plot. The accurate depiction of background and

1. The page numbers after each quotation from O. Henry refer to *The Complete Works of O. Henry* (2 vols.; Garden City, N. Y., 1953).

characters and the reality of narration blend the obvious and mysterious into a convincing, dramatic situation.

There is a profound touch when the old Negro, who had demanded an exorbitant fare, discovers that his passenger is a Southerner:

> "Boss," he said, "fifty cents is right; but I *needs* two dollars, suh; I'm *obleeged* to have two dollars. I ain't *demandin'* it now, suh; after I knows whar you's from; I'm jus sayin' that I *has* to have two dollars to-night and business is mighty po."
>
> Peace and confidence settled upon his heavy features. He had been luckier than he had hoped. Instead of having picked up a greenhorn, ignorant of rates, he had come upon an inheritance.
>
> "You confounded old rascal," I said, reaching down to my pocket, "You ought to be turned over to the police."
>
> For the first time I saw him smile. He knew; *he knew;* HE KNEW. (p. 1558)

For two years Will Porter lived in Texas on the Dull Ranch, 250,000 acres extending from La Salle County into the adjoining ones of Frio and McMullen. The ranch was managed by the famous Texas Ranger, Captain Lee Hall, now retired, who was joined by several members of his old command. Here the young North Carolinian came to know the chaparral, the drouth, and the norther. He became well acquainted with cowboys, sheepherders, and Mexican *vaqueros*, while from Captain Lee Hall he derived much about rangers and outlaws.

During this period of war between the ranchmen and cattle thieves Will Porter saw something of the real desperadoes, learning enough about outlaws and rangers to put them convincingly into such stories as "An Afternoon Miracle," "The Reformation of Calliope," and "A Departmental Case."

Sheepherders appear in "The Hiding of Black Bill," "The Missing Chord," and "The Pimienta Pancakes," for young Porter had suffered the routine of sheepherding, escaping the monotony before, as he expressed it, "the wool entered my soul" (p. 700) . Porter could have had no better mentors than the cowboys on the Dull Ranch to teach him about the plains and the chapparal. J. Frank Dobie has stated: "Nobody has written a better description of a prickly pear flat than O. Henry in his story of "The Caballero's Way."[2] The real cowboy who liked to sing and play his guitar, before the motion pictures debased the type, appears in "The Last of the Troubadours,"

2. *Guide to Life and Literature of the Southwest* (rev. ed., Dallas, 1952), p. 16.

a story Dobie designates as "a classic," saying, "I nominate it as the best range story in American fiction."[3] The houses of the cattle owners and the sheep men are described with vividness and accuracy against their natural backgrounds. O. Henry has pictured the home of a successful rancher of South Texas in "The Higher Abdication." The plastered adobe walls, the wooden ell, the gallery that was twenty feet wide and ran completely around the house, and the "live-oaks and water-elms" with their "massive pendants of the melancholy gray moss" become an integral part of the narrative. So well did he recognize this essential flavor that the chief historian of the Southwest has declared, "His stories may be classed as among the best of the region and of their kind."[4] And O. Henry caught the essence of the Texas towns he lived in: Austin, Houston, and San Antonio. In "An Afternoon Miracle" he wrote:

Consider that at that time San Antone was the hub of the wheel of fortune, and the names of its spokes were Cattle, Wool, Faro, Running Horses, and Ozone. In those times cattlemen played at crack-loo on the side-walks with double-eagles, and gentlemen backed their conception of the fortuitous card with stacks limited in height only by the interference of gravity. (p. 168)

"Bexar Scrip No. 2692" owed its inception to the old Land Office building in Austin, both for background and plot. The old building with its furnishings, "consecrated by the touch of hands that Texas will never cease to honor" (p. 1051), takes its place among those settings that become vital parts of O. Henry's narratives. "Georgia's Ruling" was frankly based on the methods of Land Commissioner Richard Hall, and "Witches' Loaves," though given another setting, was an outgrowth of Land Office experience.

In "The Enchanted Kiss" Tansey stumbled into that section of San Antonio which still makes it unique among American cities:

Here was the City's quarter once given over to the Spaniard. Here were still his forbidding abodes of concrete and adobe, standing cold and indomitable against the century. From the murky fissure, the eye saw, flung against the sky, the tangled filigree of his Moorish balconies. Through stone archways breaths of dead, vault-chilled air coughed upon him; his feet struck jingling iron rings in staples stone-buried for half a cycle. (p. 480)

During his years in Texas O. Henry came to know the region intimately, and with accuracy and artistry he pictured Easter and

3. *Ibid.*, p. 94.
4. Walter Prescott Webb, *The Great Plains* (New York, 1931), p. 464.

Christmas holidays. He put into numerous stories detailed accounts of the pleasures then afforded by the growing towns, as his characters danced at "germans," went serenading, gave amateur theatricals, played dominoes or checkers, and attended summer opera. Baseball was popular, and in the larger places there were hotels, restaurants, and sometimes the equivalent of night clubs. All found their way into his Texas stories.[5]

The exact duration of Porter's sojourn in New Orleans is not known, but in a brief period he absorbed enough of its atmosphere to give an authentic flavor to his stories. "Whistling Dick's Christmas Stocking," his first story published under the name of O. Henry, had its setting in Louisiana, while another of his better efforts, "The Renaissance at Charleroi," pictures New Orleans and a nearby aristocratic plantation. In "Blind Man's Holiday" he captured the spirit of the old French quarter:

The Rue Chartres in New Orleans is a street of ghosts. It lies in the quarter where the Frenchman, in his prime, set up his translated pride and glory; where, also the arrogant don had swaggered, and dreamed of gold and grants and ladies' gloves. Every flagstone has its grooves worn by footsteps going royally to the wooing and the fighting. Every house has a princely heartbreak; each doorway its untold tale of gallant promise and slow decay. (p. 1224)

"Cherchez la Femme" conveys the reader to a small, dark "Creole-haunted cafe," where at the polished tables one "may sit and drink the best coffee in New Orleans, and concoctions of absinthe equal to Sazerac's best" (p. 444). Near Congo Square, Captain Malone, sipping his cognac, told the story of "Phoebe," with its surprise ending in Poydras Market.

His first book, *Cabbages and Kings* (1904), treating also the shoes, ships, and sealing-wax of Lewis Carroll's walrus song, consists of tales about fugitives and fortune seekers in Central America. The book is peopled with fantastic creations—beachcombers, revolutionists, soldiers of fortune, American and English exiles, local politicians, and foreign consuls. Here in a land of flowers and perpetual afternoon Porter saw the steamers loaded with bananas, the smuggling of arms to the revolutionaries, and the adventurers who sought concessions from the rulers of these small republics of thatched huts, adobe shacks, and grass houses. If many of the tales recounted in

5. Cf. E. Hudson Long, "Social Customs in O. Henry's Texas Stories," *A Good Tale and A Bonnie Tune*, Publications of the Texas Folklore Society No. XXXII (Dallas, 1964), pp. 148-167.

Cabbages and Kings seem theatrical, life in Honduras was sometimes strange and turbulent. Porter met many of the characters he later transferred to the pages of his first book. He did no writing in Honduras, but later drew vividly upon his recollections. Trujillo became Coralio: "The town lay at the sea's edge on a strip of alluvial coast. It was set like a little pearl in an emerald band. Behind it, and seeming almost to topple, imminent, above it, rose the sea-following range of the Cordilleras" (p. 554).

Even his prison experience furnished material. On night rounds as druggist in the penitentiary at Columbus, Ohio, Porter picked up stories from confidence men and safe-crackers. There he found the original of Jimmy Valentine of "A Retrieved Reformation," who could open any safe. There, too, he listened to the yarns that inspired him to create Jeff Peters and Andy Tucker of *The Gentle Grafter* (1908), those kindly rogues who fleeced only people who could afford the loss. From Al Jennings, the train robber then serving time, he derived the incidents to be retold as "Holding-up a Train."

It was New York City, however, that inspired his finest work. In "The Duel" he wrote:

Far below and around lay the city like a ragged purple dream. . . . And out of the violet and purple depths ascended like the city's soul sounds and odors and thrills that make up the civic body. There arose the breath of gaiety unrestrained, of love, of hate, of all the passions that man can know. There below him lay all things, good or bad, that can be brought from the four corners of the earth to instruct, please, thrill, enrich, despoil, elevate, cast down, nurture, or kill. Thus the flavor of it came to him and went into his blood. (p. 1626)

His interest, moreover, extended to all walks of life. With his preface to the original edition of *The Four Million* (1906), O. Henry took issue with Ward McAllister's arbitrary restriction on New York society: "Not very long ago some one invented the assertion that there were only 'Four Hundred' people in New York City who were really worth noticing. But a wiser man has arisen—the census taker —and his larger estimate of human interest has been preferred in marking out the field of these little stories of the 'Four Million.' "

O. Henry's first biographer declared, "If ever in American literature the place and the man met, they met when O. Henry strolled for the first time along the streets of New York."[6] O. Henry became a social historian of his decade, and his vignettes form a period piece.

6. C. Alphonso Smith, *O. Henry Biography* (New York, 1916), p. 173.

Two later biographers who knew him in the city have attested: "Were all other records lost, from the forty-odd tales against the definite New York background, a future historian might rebuild a grotesque and alluring city that would somehow be the city of that decade from 1900 to 1910...."[7] And Van Wyck Brooks felt that he caught its spirit: "O. Henry sought for its particular essence and flavor. His feeling of the mystery of the city and the will with which he probed it dignified some of the stories he wrote about New York."[8]

More recently, J. Donald Adams has said, "On generation after generation, the Big Town, as they like to call it, has cast its spell. Many writers have tried to capture that magic, and of them all, none so successfully as O. Henry."[9] Adams then adds, "It is the warmth and the wisdom with which he viewed it then, and would view it now, that makes these tales of his New York a rewarding experience for the reader."[10]

A born storyteller, O. Henry found drama on every street. A bit of overheard conversation or a glimpse through a window could suggest a tale. If Mouquin's has since become Henri's, and though the old brownstone Waldorf-Astoria has changed to a modern structure with twin towers, the essence remains the same. Through his fiction one still hears the rattle of the elevated trains from the now-departed Third Avenue "El."

O. Henry's decade brought automobiles, airplanes, electricity, and motion pictures into the new century; and in 1900 Mayor Van Wyck spaded up the first earth for the first of the New York subways, which figure, also, in some of the stories. Yet the old gas lights, vaudeville shows, and hansom cabs remained a part of the daily lives of the people. In his story "From the Cabby's Seat" O. Henry explored the cab driver's "concentrated view of life" (p. 68). In "Sisters of the Golden Circle" the "Rubberneck Auto was about to start" with the "merry top-riders" in place, as the "megaphone man raised his instrument of torture" (p. 81). There was the old-fashioned Blue Light Drug Store of "The Love-Philtre of Ikey Schoenstein," located "between the Bowery and First Avenue, where the distance between the two streets is the shortest" (p. 49). Here Ikey, the night

7. Robert H. Davis and Arthur B. Maurice, *The Caliph of Bagdad* (New York, 1931), p. 174.
8. *The Confident Years, 1885-1915* (New York, 1952), p. 276.
9. *O. Henry's New York* (Greenwich, Conn., 1962), p. vii.
10. *Ibid.*, p. xi.

clerk, still rolled pills as of long ago to be put into "round paste-board pill-boxes" (p. 50).

Coney Island attracted his attention, and with "Tobin's Palm" we see the chutes, tintype men, moving pictures, Punch and Judy shows, and fortune tellers. There is the smell of popcorn to greet the arrivals from the ferry boat with its musicians on deck and waiters serving beer inside. To Dennis Carnahan of the Bricklayers' Union in "The Greater Coney," " 'Twas a fine sight. The Babylonian towers and the Hindoo roof gardens was blazin' with thousands of electric lights, and the streets was thick with people" (p. 912). So much did Coney Island figure as amusement for Masie, one of the "3,000 girls in the Biggest Store"—"She was eighteen and a saleslady in the gents' gloves"—that she mistook the description of a wedding journey to Europe and the Orient for a trip to Coney Island.

The Greenwich Village section appealed strongly to O. Henry, and in the old winding streets he found hints for plots. Here lived Hettie of "The Third Ingredient," while the "crumbling red mansions" suggested the setting for "The Furnished Room," with the worn carpet, tainted air, and shadowy hall which become an active force in the story, as O. Henry pictures in detail the reminders of its departed guests (pp. 100-101). "Between Rounds" reveals Mrs. Murphy's boarding house, where enjoying a spring night, the "boarders were seated on the high stoop upon round, flat mats like German pancakes" (p. 15), such as used to be served at Luchow's. A bare, dreary yard and blank wall between the houses on Grove Street gave him the idea for "The Last Leaf."

On Fifteenth Street a short distance east of Fourth Avenue was the Hotel America, frequented by Latin Americans, who, if they were not planning revolutions, made mysterious appearances that suggested the arch-conspirators for such a story of South American intrigue as "The Gold That Glittered."

During his most prolific period, 55 Irving Place was O. Henry's home. Here through the large window that covers the front of the first-floor room of this old, four-story brownstone house he looked upon the street. The saloon of "The Lost Blend," a neighborly establishment in an orderly neighborhood, was on the corner of Eighteenth Street and Irving Place, opposite O. Henry's dwelling at number 55. Six blocks north Irving Place stops against the iron fence of Gramercy Park, open only to the elite with keys to this private sanctuary, then bordered by aristocratic mansions. Adept at making localities an integral part of his stories, he made Gramercy Park figure prominently in "The Discounters of Money."

Within walking distance of his home were Union Square and Madison Square; the former with Broadway skirting one corner was presided over by the statue of Washington, called by O. Henry "George the Veracious" (p. 1493). In Madison Square, he mingled with the drifters who were its night tenants, giving them hand-outs and eliciting the tales of those unfortunates, cast aside by the city's currents. Lounging on a bench with the park dwellers, he gazed at the statue of Diana over the clock tower rising above the wooded square, listening and learning. Soapy in "The Cop and the Anthem," one of the "regular denizens of Madison Square," annually sought refuge for the winter by getting himself arrested and sent for three months to Blackwell's Island. "The Fifth Wheel" presents the indigents of the Bed Line in the "delta of Fifth Avenue and Broadway" looking across at the Flatiron Building, famous for its odd triangular shape, "with its impious cloud-piercing architecture looming mistily above them on the opposite delta . . ." (p. 1508).

Shop girls, cab drivers, waiters, policemen, laundry workers found their way into his plots. If his New Yorkers were sometimes sunken in their daily existence, they were never futile. O. Henry, moreover, was no mere photographer; through the alembic of his imagination the drab lives of his subjects were colored with romance and adventure. He was able to convey to his readers the same interest in the tawdry streets and their dwellers that he felt. He knew the shop girl's story of "insufficient wages, further reduced by 'fines' that go to swell the store's profits; of time lost through illness; and then of lost positions"—stories, "such as the city yawns at every day" (pp. 66-67).

He depicted, too, the living conditions of the respectable poor. The description of Dulcie's room in "An Unfinished Story" reveals the character of the girl who earned six dollars a week in a department store, and whose meager existence denied her all "those joys that belong to woman by virtue of all the unwritten, sacred, natural, inactive ordinances of the equity of heaven" (p. 74). "The Skylight Room" reveals a scant seven-by-eight floor space, furnished with only an iron cot, chair, washstand, and a shelf substituting for a dresser. The only light against the four bare walls came from the skylight above; but to its occupant the blue sky by day and the stars at night brought hope and courage.

By instinct O. Henry was attuned to the reform movements of Theodore Roosevelt, and he wrote for the McClure syndicate, which was engaged in exposing social abuses and municipal corruption. Theodore Roosevelt stated, "It was O. Henry who started me on my campaign for the office girls."[11]

O. Henry explored the grime, dirt, and squalor of the slums, inhabited by the helpless poor. "The Guilty Party" shows the damning effect of such surroundings on the children condemned to live there, and "Brickdust Row" is an indictment against the owners of slum property. On the lower East Side "the push carts and trash heaps" and the "tangled-haired, bare-footed, unwashed children" of Delancey Street became part of his narrative.

Observing the byways of the city at first hand, he wrote of the underworld with true knowledge of the Bowery toughs, the dance-hall prostitutes, and gangsters from Hell's Kitchen, where a subdistrict called the Stovepipe "runs along Eleventh and Twelfth avenues on the river, and bends a hard and sooty elbow around little, lost homeless De Witt Clinton Park" (p. 1415). Here was the hangout of such lawless elements as the gangster Kid Brady of "Vanity and Some Sables." Watching the inhabitants of the Sixth Avenue district, aptly termed "Satan's Circus," O. Henry made their appearance, conversation, and mannerisms part of his panorama. At any hour of the day or night he walked along the river fronts or down the Bowery, where he met the "sports" who talked glibly of the race track and boxing ring.

He saw the leaders of the underworld who controlled the gunmen and lesser criminals, and the politicians like Billy McMahan, district leader of "The Social Triangle," upon whom "the Tiger purred and his hand held manna to scatter" (p. 1420). He viewed the counterpart of Cork McManus, hiding outside the law until Tim Corrigan, a shady politician, returned from Europe to make the "fix" for him in "Past One at Rooney's." Rooney's illegally run night spot, where, contrary to accepted rules, women were permitted to smoke, was announced by "incandescent lights against a signboard over a second-story window." Inside "a human pianola with drugged eyes hammered the keys with automatic and furious unprecision," and waiters

11. *Mentor*, XI, d (Feb., 1923).

occasionally sang "coon" songs, composed by "natives of the cotton fields and rice swamps of West Twenty-eighth Street" (p. 1606).

Restaurants of all types, ranging from the cheap all-night variety to the elaborate dining rooms of the luxury hotels, became his favorite haunts as he sat, night after night, an interested spectator, drawing directly upon reality for his characters and settings. In "The Brief Debut of Tildy" the atmosphere of "Bogle's Chop House and Family Restaurant" with its two rows of tables, tasteless condiments, and "steaming, chattering, cabbage-scented" air permeates the whole narrative. On Third Avenue, Scheffel Hall, made distinct by its smoky rafters, rows of steins, portrait of Goethe, and verses on the walls, became Old Munich of "The Halberdier of the Little Rheinschloss." At the rathskeller of Koster and Bial on Sixth Avenue, O. Henry listened to the singing waiters and conversed with the prostitutes who made it their place of rendezvous. He knew, too, the cheap little cafés off Fourteenth Street, but with equal facility he wrote in "Transients in Arcadia" of a Broadway hotel, where "in the cool twilight of its lofty dining-room . . . watchful, pneumatically moving waiters hover near supplying every want before it is expressed" (p. 1330).

O. Henry did not, however, confine his art to picturing the less fortunate. On occasion he wrote of expensive clubs, brownstone mansions, and the owners of motor cars. In the glow of the Great White Way he imagined the varied adventures that transformed the city into his "Little Old Bagdad-on-the-Subway." He visited the roof gardens, then popular with café society; and he wandered into the wealthy sections, inhabited by the millionaires he liked to call the Caliphs. In his stories appear actresses, chorus girls, and men-about-town of the Richard Harding Davis type.

"An Unfinished Story" shows the lure of the dazzling lights of Broadway making Manhattan into "a night-blooming cereus . . . beginning to unfold its dead-white, heavy-odored petals." On Broadway in "The Pride of the Cities," "the electrics are shining and the pavements are alive with two hurrying streams of elegantly clothed men and beautiful women attired in the costliest costumes . . . ." With such tales as "Lost on Dress Parade," "While the Auto Waits," and "Transients in Arcadia" he reversed the Harun-al-Rashid plot by having humble characters wander incognito among the expensive playgrounds of the rich.

While writing "The Complete Life of John Hopkins" he expressed the excitement and suspense of New York: "In the Big City large and sudden things happen. . . . Fate tosses you about like cork crumbs in wine opened by an un-feed waiter. The City is a sprightly youngster, and you are red paint upon its toy, and you get licked off" (p. 1258). O. Henry was far more than a factual reporter, evoking the magic of the great modern city, which he saw in terms of the Arabian Nights. As he once put it: "If you have the right kind of eye—the kind that can disregard high hats, cutaway coats, and trolley cars—you can see all the characters in the 'Arabian Nights' parading up and down Broadway at mid-day."[12]

Though a journalist by trade, O. Henry was an artist who followed the school of regional writing. What Harte did for the miners of California, Page for the Virginia aristocracy, Cable for the Creoles of New Orleans, and Craddock for the Tennessee mountaineers, O. Henry did for New York, and to a lesser extent for Texas. Indeed, he successfully depicted every locality in which he ever lived.

12. George MacAdam, "O. Henry's Only Autobiographia," *O. Henry Papers* (Garden City, N. Y., 1924), p. 21.

EDWIN ARLINGTON ROBINSON
IN PERSPECTIVE

Floyd Stovall

University of Virginia

The history of Robinson the poet is one of early neglect, increasing critical recognition during his middle years, a brief period of fame before his death, and afterwards a rapid decline in popularity accompanied by a more gradual decline in critical esteem. To understand this history, though it follows with variations a pattern all too common in the annals of literature, one should read the poems in the light of the author's known temperament and the circumstances of his life. In addition, one must take account of the revolutionary changes in moral and aesthetic values that occurred during his lifetime and after his death.

Born four years after the close of the Civil War, he grew to manhood during the decades when materialism was rampant, even in his native state of Maine, and when new ways and ideas, which appealed to his young intelligence, clashed head-on with old ways and ideas to which by temperament he was attached. Since wealth was almost the sole criterion of success, those who could not rise above poverty were considered failures. Theological dogmas crumbled under the impact of biological and physical science; Transcendentalism, trying to absorb both neo-Hegelian and Spencerian principles, was diluted to a watery humanism; on the literary scene the realism of Howells and Garland stood at one extreme of the scale of taste and the decadent romanticism of Edgar Saltus at the other, while, cutting across this scale, popular variants ranged from the sentimental piety of E. P. Roe to the sardonic humor of Ambrose Bierce. The production of good poetry, even in literary Maine, was at a low ebb. By the time Robinson entered Gardiner High School, Longfellow and Emerson were dead; Whitman, though living, was not read; and Emily Dickinson was yet unpublished. There was a plentiful supply of popular verse, ranging in style from the polished elegance of Thomas Bailey Aldrich to the nostalgic banality of James Whitcomb Riley.

In Britain, Tennyson and Browning had been taken over by the literary clubs, and Kipling, both in Britain and in America, pleased the man in the street. The bright young men were following other gods, including the English Pre-Raphaelites, the French symbolists, and the imitators of Villon and other fifteenth-century improvers of Provençal verse. The revival by Austin Dobson and others of the early French forms, the ballade, the rondeau, the villanelle, quickly spread to America, even to Gardiner, where Robinson's friend, Dr. A. T. Schumann, became so addicted to their fabrication that he is said to have neglected his medical practice. Not a very good poet, Dr. Schumann nevertheless had technical skill, and he became Robinson's critic and champion. His title to literary fame, such as it is, rests on the fact that he encouraged the young poet and presently introduced him to others of the literary elite in Gardiner. Robinson seems to have written many poems in the old French forms, though only five ever got published, and one of these was omitted from the *Collected Poems*. It was a way to develop verbal skill, like the musician's finger exercises.

Thus we find Robinson busy with verse writing before he was out of high school, and a dedicated poet before the end of his two years at Harvard in 1893. Thereafter, except for a few fruitless attempts at prose stories and plays, he never wavered in his devotion to the muse. He insisted to his family and friends that he was unfit for anything except writing verse.

After Harvard he returned to Gardiner, where he faced the grim struggle between self-assurance and the knowledge that in the eyes of his neighbors and the world at large he was a failure. He worked at such jobs as came to him, or were required by the circumstances of his family, and he read a great deal in conscious preparation for a literary career. His letters to Arthur Gledhill and Harry de Forest Smith, old high school friends, preserve the record of his self-education and of his persistent determination to prove himself a poet in spite of all discouragements. He composed deliberately, painfully, and with studied, meticulous art, but the editors of the literary monthlies found his poems unacceptable; their taste accorded with the genteel manner of Bayard Taylor and E. C. Stedman, or the stale romanticism of Madison Cawein and Father Tabb. The publishers of books were equally unresponsive. His first volume, *The Torrent and the Night Before*, was privately printed and issued with a paper binding in 1896. The author sent these first fruits to friends, professors at Harvard, and established critics, and received a number of encouraging responses. The next year, with the help of a subsidy provided by Gardiner friends, he brought out a more substantial edition, *The Children of the Night*, but his publisher's undistinguished imprint contributed nothing to the small success of the book. It was not widely circulated, but such critics as noticed it at all usually spoke well of the poems, though some of them objected to what they conceived to be the poet's pessimism. Then and always thereafter he denied that he was a pessimist, though he admitted that life is hard. He wrote his friend Smith on May 17, 1897: "This world is a grind and the sooner we make up our minds to the fact the better it will be for us. That, to my mind, is the real optimism."

"Captain Craig," the first of his long narrative poems, was begun in 1898 and published with some shorter poems in 1902 in a volume with the same title. It is a philosophical poem based in part on the character and conversation of a New York acquaintance, an elderly man once prominent in England but now indigent and somewhat decayed. The sometimes tedious "wisdom" of the poem, though put into the mouth of the "Captain," is essentially Robinson's own brand of optimism maintained against the indifference of an unfriendly world. The shorter poems of the volume, notably "Isaac and Archibald" and "Aunt Imogen," strike a somewhat different note, equally Robinsonian, in which the optimism seems more spontaneous and less contrived to bolster a philosophy. In this edition at last Robinson's poems had the advantage of appearing under the imprint of a reputable publisher.

Before *Captain Craig* was accepted for publication, Robinson learned that the family fortune was gone; he would have to earn his living. He had already tried working in the administrative offices of Harvard without happiness or notable success; he called the ordeal his "six months in hell." He tried journalism with even less success. Friends came to his rescue when he could not pay his rent. Nevertheless, in February, 1902, while the manuscript of *Captain Craig* was still making its rounds, he wrote to Mrs. Laura Richards that his experience with publishers only confirmed him in the determination to write in his own way. "A dozen lines of real matter," he declared, "is worth more to me than a dozen volumes of 'creditable verse.'" But when it became evident that *Captain Craig* would not sell, and that magazine editors would not buy his short poems, he was forced to conclude that he could not live by poetry alone. He turned, one might almost say in desperation, to writing prose. Thinking the theater offered the best chance of quick rewards, he planned a trilogy; but nothing came of this, or, for a while, of other plans for writing for the stage. For two or three years he lived, as Hagedorn says, "from hand to mouth" in New York, chiefly on loans from his friends.

Late in 1903, to escape this humiliation, he took a job at two dollars a day checking workmen and trucks in and out of the subway, then under construction. For eight or nine months he was able to live on his small earnings, but the work was depressing, and he could not write. To make life endurable, he drank heavily. In June, 1905, fortune looked more kindly on him. President Theodore Roosevelt, who had read *Children of the Night* and liked it, found a place for Robinson in the New York Customs House with nominal duties and and a salary of $2000 a year. Roosevelt also, a little later, published an article in the *Outlook* in which he praised Robinson's poetry. Magazine editors, perhaps influenced by Roosevelt's notice, began to recognize his talent and actually accepted a dozen of his poems. These were included among the thirty-one poems in *The Town Down the River*, published in 1910. But Robinson gave up his job when Roosevelt left the White House in March, 1909, and in an effort to compensate for the loss of income turned again, this time more seriously, to the writing of plays, completing two, *Van Zorn* and *The Porcupine*. Both were rejected by the theaters but afterwards published.

The Town Down the River received some favorable attention from the critics and that revived Robinson's confidence in his poetic powers, but it did not provide the income needed. He rewrote *Van Zorn* as a novel, but it was wanted as little as the play had been. He worked at other plays and other novels, but in the spring of 1913 he decided to give up prose and return to poetry altogether. He wrote John Hays Gardiner in March, 1913: "When I come down out of myself and try to write for the crowd, I perpetrate the damndest rubbish that you ever heard of, and I seem to have no guiding hand to let me know what I am doing." Within a few months he was back at work in his proper field, preparing another collection of short poems and poems of medium length. This, *The Man Against the Sky*, was published in February, 1916, and was praised by a number of reviewers, including Amy Lowell. Robinson's reputation as a major American poet seemed assured. It was his failure as a prose writer, coupled with his arrangement, beginning in 1911, for summer residence at the MacDowell Colony at Peterborough, that had led to his first success as a poet.

Success was not an unmixed blessing for it encouraged him to write too rapidly and too much. From Peterborough he wrote to Hagedorn on June 1, 1916: "I came here a week ago, and by way of getting 'oiled up' I wrote a more or less dramatic poem of 250 lines in three days." This was "Genevieve and Alexandra," not one of his best poems. Ten days later he again wrote Hagedorn: "I'm writing at a most immoral rate, but I don't yet know what I am writing, or who is going to read it." This must have been *Merlin*, published the next year, for other letters reveal that he had written 2200 lines of that poem by the end of July and that he had finished it by the middle of August. On June 3, 1917, he told Lewis Isaacs that he had written 500 lines of *Lancelot*. Before the end of the summer he had finished the first draft of that poem in 3400 lines, later reduced to 2700. Such speed was, by Robinson's standards, indeed immoral! He confessed in a letter to L. N. Chase, also on June 3, 1917, that when he was writing his first book he "thought nothing" of working for a week over a single line, and that he had "tinkered" one sonnet, "The Clerks," for a month, but that he had recently written a sonnet, "Another Dark Lady," in twenty minutes. On August 25, 1918, he wrote Mrs. Ledoux that though he could "throw together" a small book by the end of the year, he hoped he would have sense enough not to do it. He recalled his "old dictum regarding one book of poetry in five years" but admitted he would probably not stick to it.

So it went, with some variations, for the next fifteen years. The critics were cool toward *Merlin*, but received *Lancelot* in 1920 more favorably. In a minor literary competition it won a $500 prize. The first collected edition of the poems appeared in October, 1921, and won for Robinson the Pulitzer prize for poetry. In spite of the labor of proofreading the collected edition, he began and finished the first draft of *Roman Bartholow* that summer—a poem of 3500 lines. Between *Lancelot* and *Roman Bartholow* he had completed two more collections, *The Three Taverns* (1920) and *Avon's Harvest* (1921), and after *Roman Bartholow* was published in the spring of 1923, he set to work on still another collection, which was published in 1925 as *Dionysus in Doubt* and won for him his second Pulitzer prize. By this time Robinson was hard at work on *Tristram*, which he had been thinking about for years. On its publication in 1927 he was awarded his third Pulitzer prize, and, even more important for his popular success, the book was adopted by the Literary Guild as its book of the month. After *Tristram* Robinson wrote Mrs. Ledoux that his "well was pumped entirely dry" and must have time to fill up again. He had not long to wait, for *Cavender's House* was done by July, 1928, and before his death in 1935 he had produced five other book-length poems and another collection.

Even before *Tristram*, critics had recognized that the promise of *The Man Against the Sky* was fulfilled. In two small books, Lloyd Morris (1923) and Ben Ray Redman (1926) hailed him as America's greatest living poet, and in 1926 also the young Edmund Wilson named him "one of the poets of our time most likely to survive as an American classic." In another book-length study published in the same year with *Tristram*, Mark Van Doren praised the poem as a complete "tragic picture" of human passion in conflict with destiny; and three years later, in the first full-scale study of Robinson's poetry, Charles Cestre predicted that *Tristram* would attain "an exalted rank among the few works that unite dramatic force with depth of observation." But the poem rapidly lost credit with other critics, who almost invariably, since 1930, have rated it below *Merlin* and *Lancelot*. The new note in criticism was struck by Louise Bogan in a review of *The Glory of the Nightingales* that appeared in *Poetry* for January, 1931. "To the present writer," she wrote, "Mr. Robinson's Arthurian poems and the non-legendary narratives of his later period mark a distinct lapse in power: a lessening grasp not only on technical, but on psychological essentials." In a review of *Talifer* in the *New Republic*, October 25, 1933, Allen Tate also lumped the Arthurian poems with the other long narratives, asserting that all the long poems "lose outline and blur into one another. They really constitute a single complete poem that the poet has not succeeded in writing, a poem of which these indistinct narratives are partial formulations." Morton D. Zabel was somewhat more judicious. Reviewing the *Collected Poems* for the *Nation*, August 28, 1937, he admitted Robinson's faults of style, characterization, and plot, but pointed to the compensating virtues of "enduring strength, sobriety, perspective, sustained thought, verbal intensity," and the successful combination of "passion with judgment, sympathy with prudence." He perceived a relation between the style and "dramatic properties" of Robinson's narrative poems and the novels of James, Meredith, and Conrad. Others have noted such a relation, particularly with the novels of Meredith.

Since Robinson's death there have been, besides Herman Hagedorn's biography (1938), a number of book-length studies of his poetry, including those of Yvor Winters (1946), Emery Neff (1948), Ellsworth Barnard (1952), and Edwin Fussell (1954). In 1965 Chard Powers Smith published *Where the Light Falls*, which is interesting as biography rather than as criticism, since the author is more concerned with identifying the characters of Robinson's poems with his family and friends than in objective interpretation. The only one of these authors who undertakes to evaluate the poems individually and as a whole is Yvor Winters, who makes a higher estimate of Robinson's worth as a poet than any other critic with a comparable reputation. In his opinion Robinson is "essentially a counter-romantic," and his style is "distinguished by classical restraint," though his language is sometimes deficient in richness. In the rank of poets writing in English since Milton and Dryden, he puts Robinson at or near the top. It must be remembered, however, that Winters has a poor opinion of most nineteenth-century poetry, either British or American. He considers the Arthurian poems the best of the long narratives, and of these he finds *Lancelot* the best and *Tristram* the worst.

Like most other critics, Winters judges Robinson to be at his best in the short poems and the poems of medium length; unlike many, he prefers the poems of the middle period, 1916 to 1925, to the early ones. He names eleven short poems which he thinks can be equaled in the work of only four or five English and American poets of the past century and a half. Of these, two were published in the collection of 1897, one in 1910, four in 1916, one in 1920, two in 1921, and one in 1925. He selects as the four best short poems "Hillcrest" and "Eros Turannos" from the 1916 collection, "The Wandering Jew" from 1920, and "Many Are Called," a sonnet, from 1921. As the two best poems of medium length he names "Rembrandt to Rembrandt," which he ranks first, and "The Three Taverns," which he calls "one of the greatest poems of its kind in English." Some of the poems which have been most popular with critics as well as other readers he ignores or depreciates. "Richard Cory," he says, builds to a "very cheap surprise ending"; "Flammonde" is "reminiscent of the worst sentimentalism of the nineties"; "The Man Against the Sky" is philosophically unimpressive, stylistically weak, and structurally self-defeating; "Ben Jonson Entertains a Man from Stratford" is "no more than a secondary poem at best." By contrast Emery Neff says that "The Man Against the Sky" "towers above any other poem written upon American soil"; and Ellsworth Barnard, though not given to value judgments, affords high praise to "Richard Cory" and names "Flammonde" and "Ben Jonson" among Robinson's greatest triumphs.

The relative decline in Robinson's popularity since 1930 is revealed by the anthologies. In 1930 Louis Untermeyer allowed 28 pages each to Robinson and Frost, 12 to Eliot, 9 to Pound, and 11 to Stevens. In the 1962 edition of the same work he gave Robinson 23 pages, Frost 28, Eliot 27, Pound 15, and Stevens 14. Although the later edition contains eleven Robinson poems not in the earlier one, his total space, relatively, is considerably reduced. The anthology edited by Sanders and Nelson shows a comparable change. In 1930 they gave Robinson 38 pages, Frost 17, and Pound 8, and did not include any poems by Eliot or Stevens. In 1962 their revised edition allotted Robinson 33 pages, Frost 42, Eliot 33, Pound 22, and Stevens 23. Both these anthologies are addressed primarily to college students and their professors and may be assumed to represent a conservative point of view. However, another anthology, in 1966, also prepared by college professors for class use, allots Robinson only 10 pages while Frost is given 25, Eliot (the poetry alone) 32, Pound 22, and Stevens 16. As a rule, the anthologies which appeal more to the non-academic reader give less prominence to Robinson. In *A Little Treasury of American Poetry* (1952 edition) Oscar Williams allows Robinson 23 pages, Frost 22, Eliot 35, Pound 34, and Stevens 33. In his *Pocket Anthology* (1955) he gives Robinson only 8 pages, whereas he allots Frost 25, Pound 19, and Stevens 33. Eliot is omitted as not American, but he is replaced by Auden with 27 pages. The Williams anthologies are not limited to the recent period. In an anthology called *Discovering Modern Poetry* (1961), the stated purpose of which is "to make readers and lovers of poetry, especially modern poetry," the editors, Elizabeth Drew and George Connor, select from thirteen American poets, including Emily Dickinson, Frost, Stevens, and Eliot among the older poets, but Robinson is not mentioned, even to explain why he is omitted.

In the histories of American literature the story is much the same. Here, too, Robinson's poetry receives more attention when considered as part of the whole of American poetry than when it is included with modern poetry exclusively. Critical histories intended for the college student, like the anthologies, are more generous with Robinson than those addressed to the more general reader. In the *Literary History of the United States* (1948), Robinson is given 14 pages, Frost 8, Eliot 7, Pound 5, and Stevens 2. In *The Literature of the American People* (1951), Robinson is allotted 3 pages, Frost 4, Eliot 7, Pound 3, and Stevens less than 2. By contrast with these academic works, Louise Bogan, in *Achievement in American Poetry: 1900-1950*, disposes of Robinson in three pages, mentioning of his many volumes only *Children of the Night*, whereas she devotes ten pages each to Eliot and Pound. Frederick J. Hoffman, although he barely mentions Robinson and Frost in *The Twenties* (1949), requires 20 pages for Pound and 13 pages for Eliot's *The Waste Land* alone. In *The Modern Poets* (1960), M. L. Rosenthal can spare only 4 pages each for Robinson and Frost, yet allots 32 pages to Eliot, 26 to Pound, and 11 to Stevens. Roy Pearce finds 14 pages adequate for Robinson and 12 for Frost in his *Continuity of American Poetry* (1961), but needs 22 for Eliot, 18 for Pound, and 45 for Stevens. He is unique among critics in the importance given to Stevens.

It is evident that, allowing for a few exceptions, we can arrange Robinson's critics since 1930 into two groups. The critics in one group, chiefly literary historians and others with a strong sense of the continuity of culture, still think very well of Robinson's poetry, though perhaps not as well as formerly. They recognize in it the individualism and much of the idealism of the nineteenth century, but they discern also something of the disillusionment, the pessimism, and the obsessive concern with psychological problems that we have come to expect in literature of the twentieth. These critics, conceiving cultural growth as evolutionary, see Robinson as a transitional figure, linking two cultural periods and belonging equally to both. Critics in the other group, conceiving cultural growth as revolutionary, are convinced that there is a radical difference between this century and the last. They question the traditional American faith in social democracy and in the integrity of the self.

They reject or deplore the romantic sentiment and verbal music of nineteenth-century verse, but embrace the cool hardness of the imagists and encourage an intellectual poetry that combines the contemporary frustration of thought and feeling with the stylistic complexities of the English metaphysicals and the French symbolists. These anti-romantic critics are inclined to think Robinson a belated spokesman for the nineteenth century who was never at home in the twentieth. Winters is the exception, but he calls Robinson anti-romantic. This division among critics may not last. Each age, we know, finds newness somewhere in the past, as our own found it in the seventeenth century; it would not be surprising, therefore, if a later generation, seeking a newness to sharpen its sense of identity, should look back to the nineteenth century with tolerance if not with nostalgia.

Meanwhile, readers not fully acquainted with Robinson's work are tempted to accept one or the other of these critical attitudes, assume that his case is settled, and not read his poetry. The temptation is the more inviting because there is so much verse to be read before any sound judgment of its worth can be made. Those who are interested in exploring the whole of Robinson's verse, with its variety and changing patterns from youth to age, may find the following statistical table both interesting and helpful. Somewhat arbitrarily I have designated as short all poems of 100 lines or less and as poems of medium length all those which have between 100 and 520 lines. All other poems, ranging from 1000 to 4300 lines, are considered long. As a matter of convenience I count all sonnets as separate poems, although two or three may have a common title, and I count the 1897 sequence of twenty-three octaves as a single poem of medium length. I divide the forty years of Robinson's poetic career into three periods, the first of which, it will be noted, is as long as the second and third combined. The number of lines of the long poems is only approximate. To calculate the percentage of irregularities in the blank verse I have used liberal samples of continuous lines drawn from poems in all three periods.

The most striking fact revealed by these statistics—one I have already commented on—is Robinson's enormous productivity during the last twenty years of his life. During the first two decades of his active career he wrote, published, and collected an average of 300 lines per year, whereas during the next ten years his average was over

1600 lines, and during his last ten years his average was 2200. Only 13 per cent of his total output was published during his first twenty years. His poems also tended to become longer as the years passed, though there is less difference between the last two periods than between either of them and the first. All of his long poems and two-thirds of his poems of medium length are in blank verse. This amounts to more than 85 per cent of his total number of lines. His use of blank verse increased from 52 per cent in the first period to 75 per cent in the second and 95 per cent in the third. Irregularities of rhythm and meter in the blank verse increased progressively through the three periods. The one important exception I have

TABLE SHOWING THE DISTRIBUTION OF ROBINSON'S POEMS CLASSIFIED ACCORDING TO LENGTH, METRICAL PATTERN, STANZA ARRANGEMENT, AND THE PERCENT- AGE OF IRREGULAR LINES IN THE BLANK VERSE

	FIRST PERIOD (1895-1914)		SECOND PERIOD (1915-1924)		THIRD PERIOD (1925-1934)		TOTALS	
LENGTH	poems	lines	poems	lines	poems	lines	poems	lines
Short	100	2269	58	1969	23	428	181	4666
Medium	7	1684	12	3047	10	3258	29	7989
Long	1	1800	5	11400	7	18500	13	31700
Totals	108	5753	75	16416	40	22186	223	44355
BASIC METRICAL PATTERN								
Sonnet	47	658	23	322	19	266	89	1246
Trimeter	3	107	1	32	0	0	4	139
Tetrameter	36	1414	23	1323	2	206	61	2943
Rhymed Pentameter	10	202	9	364	3	144	22	710
Hexameter	1	32	0	0	0	0	1	32
Octameter or Heptameter	4	128	5	305	0	0	9	433
Ode-like	2	194	1	280	1	370	4	844
Blank Verse	5	3018	13	13790	15	21200	33	38008
Totals	108	5753	75	16416	40	22186	223	44355
STANZA LENGTH (excluding ode-like poems and poems not divided into stanzas)								
Four Lines	20	792	14	620	2	232	36	1644
Eight Lines	17	916	16	620	1	72	34	1608
All Others	11	453	4	172	1	24	16	649
PERCENTAGE OF IRREGULAR LINES IN THE BLANK VERSE POEMS								
More than Ten Syllables	7%		23%		30%		27%	
Irregular Rhythm	10%		31%		45%		39%	
Feminine Endings	4%		18%		25%		22%	
Run-on Lines	25%		34%		34%		32%	

noted is in "Ben Jonson Entertains a Man from Stratford," published in 1916, which has a freer and more fluid rhythm than *Merlin*, published the next year, or "The Three Taverns" and "John Brown," both published four years later. This may be in part the consequence of the poet's adapting his verse form to the informal and somewhat humorous tone of "Ben Jonson." It must be admitted, however, that Robinson achieves a comparable informality and lightness with fewer irregularities in the early story of "Isaac and Archibald."

All of the short poems are in rhyming verse, and all but one that have more than eight lines are either sonnets or poems arranged in stanzas. Among the short poems his favorite form was the sonnet. He published 95 sonnets altogether, of which 89 were collected in the volume of sonnets published in 1928 and later incorporated in the *Collected Poems*. One, "An Evangelist's Wife," published in 1920, follows the Shakespearean form; the rest have the octave and sestet division of the Italian sonnet. The three rhymes of the sestet appear in fifteen different arrangements, but the favorite sequence was *cde cde*, which was used thirty times, including three of the uncollected sonnets. The best of them, with few exceptions, are those of the 1897 collection and those of the 1925 collection. They are best chiefly because they are more intense in thought and language and are more varied in rhythm yet at the same time simple, clear, and single in effect. Why the poet lost his sonnet power and then regained it after a quarter of a century would be difficult to discover.

Next to the sonnet Robinson's favorite form for poems in rhyme was the tetrameter verse in stanzas of four or eight lines. Of all his rhymed poems, both short and of medium length, not counting the sonnets, 68 per cent were in tetrameter in the first period, but only 58 per cent in the second, and 28 per cent in the third. The predominant rhythm of these poems is iambic, but a considerable number of them through 1910 are either trochaic or trochaic and dactylic combined. In the early poems the iambic rhythms are more frequently varied with the introduction of anapests than in the later ones. After 1916 there is no poem that is predominantly trochaic. This movement toward greater regularity in later rhymed poems is just the opposite of the development of his blank verse. Only once after he outgrew his interest in early French forms did he allow himself the privilege of attempting a difficult or unusual pattern. His 1920 poem "Late Summer" is composed in unrhymed tetrameter verse with a complicated rhythm in imitation of the classical alcaics. The poem has some effective lines, but as a whole it seems less suited to the theme—that of lost faith and love, a common one in Robinson —than a simpler rhythm would have been. Several poems in his early and middle years have the vigorous rhythms, predominantly trochaic octameter, which were popular about the turn of the century and which vaguely suggest Kipling's verse. Four poems, including "The Man Against the Sky," have an ode-like irregularity of line and stanza. One of those has no rhyme, and in the others the rhymes have no perceptible pattern. Occasionally a line is introduced that rhymes with no other.

Robinson would probably have agreed with Emerson that a good poem is not made by meters, but by a meter-making argument—a thought so passionate that it has a life and architecture of its own. This passion of thought is conveyed more by individual words, in which nouns and verbs predominate, than by rhetorical elaboration, and when Robinson uses figures of speech and other intangible elements of style they are integral with his thought. I have not attempted to represent these elements statistically, but they cannot be ignored. He was not fond of simile, probably because it contributed to diffuseness. His metaphors, however, are both frequent and skilfully used, whether in their primary form or in their derivative forms of metonymy and synecdoche, which bridge the gap between metaphor and symbol. So far as I can tell, the frequency of such figures of speech is about the same in the early, middle, and late periods. In the 1897 volume, for example, "Cliff Klingenhagen" is composed in the simplest language without any figures of speech, whereas "The Garden" is composed in figurative language almost altogether; similarly, in the 1925 volume, "The Sheaves" has little imagery, and what there is is so nearly integral with the thought that it is scarcely noticed, whereas "New England" is a complex of metaphor and personification. All these sonnets have been admired by competent critics, but they do not agree on which style is the better. I confess that my own taste inclines toward the simpler style, although I heartily agree with those who are moved by the metaphorical language of such poems as "Luke Havergal," "Vickery's Mountain," and "The Man Against the Sky."

Natural phenomena are the source of most of Robinson's symbols as well as his metaphors—sunlight, shadow, stars, the mountains, the sea. His favorite symbol, as has often been noted, is light, often spelled with a capital as *the* Light. It is the symbol of transcendental and ultimate truth, the ground of faith, which is revealed rather by intuition than by supernatural agency, and is seen, if seen at all, only in glimpses. Its presence throughout his poetry from 1897 to 1935 is proof of an Emersonian strain of idealism in his thinking, hardly maintained in an uncongenial world, but persistent and undimmed by circumstance. Among his many other symbols, the following are memorable: the town down the river, Merlin's beard, Vivian's green dress, Guinevere's golden hair, the rain that accompanies the tragic failures of Lancelot and Tristram, the white birds that fly about the coast of Brittany, the cold waves that wash the rocky coast of Cornwall, the dark rock like an Egyptian door in *Matthias*, the eyes of Amaranth in which one sees himself as he really is, and in *King Jasper* the chimneys, the unseen hands moving to destroy them, and Zoë's knife, which like Amaranth's eyes brings self-knowledge to those who feel it. In *King Jasper*, and to a lesser degree in *Merlin* and *Lancelot*, the symbolism is so all-pervasive as to give them the character of allegories. Many of the short poems might be called parables, such as "Richard Cory," "Flammonde," and "Two Gardens in Linndale." "Sainte-Nitouche," a poem of medium length, has much of the character of an allegory or extended parable.

Perhaps Robinson's most effective figure of speech, if it may be called that, is irony. I say "if" because irony in Robinson's verse is not merely a rhetorical device, but, more important, an attitude toward his characters and toward life—very nearly a philosophy. Some of the best examples of irony as a figure of speech are to be found in "Ben Jonson Entertains a Man from Stratford," of which I shall mention only Shakespeare's comment on his story of the housemaid that kills the spider that eats the fly: "That's Nature, the kind mother of us all." Another example in a more tragic vein is Guinevere's remark to Lancelot when he tells her he is taking her back to Camelot after rescuing her from King Arthur's penal fire: "What more, in faith, have I to ask/Of earth or heaven than that!" It may be that Robinson's mood grew sharper as he grew older. In any case, the bitterest twist of his rhetorical irony is found in a Christmas sonnet of 1925 in which a man, as a sign of repentance for past ill deeds, gave "A dime for Jesus who had died for men."

Even in these instances, the irony is as much in the character of the speaker or the one spoken of as in the language itself. Sometimes the irony is less in the character involved than in the general situation, or else it is in some relationship of character to situation. From the earlier volumes one thinks of "Richard Cory," who seemed to have all that heart could desire, yet felt the lack of something that drove him to suicide; or of the wife in "Partnership," who suffered half a lifetime of hardship so that her husband might achieve his ambition, and then died at the moment of his success. From later volumes there is the story of Tasker Norcross, who had neither taste nor talent, and knew it, but was never reconciled to his condition; or there is Mr. Flood, who once had many friends, but has no comforter in his old age but his jug; or there is the unloved wife of Ben Trovato, who puts on the furs of the woman he loved so that in his blindness he could take her in his arms and die happy. In the long poems we have first the sleazy Socrates, Captain Craig, for whose funeral the Tilbury band played, with trombones, "the Dead March in Saul"; then Merlin, the king-maker, who was last seen on his way to a lowly tavern accompanied by the dead king's fool; after that, Fernando Nash, the would-be rival of Bach, who ends his days beating the drum in a Salvation Army band; and, after these, others—at least one in every long poem: Guinevere, Queen of the Christian world, who, shorn of her golden hair, finds refuge among the nuns of Almesbury, or Gabrielle, who learned to love her husband only after she had lost him and has left no refuge but the dark water of the river, or Natalie, who chose security with Matthias over love with the less durable Timberlake but finds no security until she follows Garth through the dark Egyptian door.

But along with these who fell there were others who rose. We are told that Matthias, though driven to the threshold of the Egyptian door, will not enter there but rise to make a new and more useful life, partly because Garth and Natalie and Timberlake have died. And Roman Bartholow, who is saved from despondency by the wise counsel of a friend and because he is saved cannot respond to his wife's newly awakened love, finds that a new life opens up for him after her death. Here we have something like irony in reverse—the apparently dead live anew, the supposed failure succeeds at last, and the sufferer, through wisdom, achieves an overbalance of happiness. This theme of good out of evil was a favorite one with the poet and is developed in numerous short poems. Among the early poems one remembers Cliff Klingenhagen, who wins happiness by a willing acceptance of life's bitter moments, and Reuben Bright, the butcher who turns out to be a tender sentimentalist, and Aunt Imogen, the spinster, who is reconciled to seeking happiness in the love of her sister's children, and Clavering, the ne'er-do-well, now dead, who clung to phantoms but also to friends. From later poems we may recall the mother who found "The Gift of God" in her love for an unworthy son, and the man who in his lifetime was scorned as "The Rat" but is recognized after his death to have been no less humane than those who scorned him.

Whether Robinson is judged by these creations of the imagination or by his poems commenting directly on social problems and historical persons and events, he may appear, like Thomas Hardy, to view human life as a texture of ironies. He praises George Crabbe for his hard realism, contrasting him with the "little sonnet-men" of his own time who "consecrate the flicker, not the flame," and fashion songs without souls. He sees poets and kings as but "the clerks of Time." The kingdoms of history and legend have all been destroyed by the gnawing rats of time and human imperfection. Napoleon in his island prison discovers that rats prevail because a king has no cats. Yet, for Robinson, popular democracy is not the remedy, for democracy has its rats likewise, two of which are materialism and a false equality. The true Demos may speak for Robinson in warning that "the few shall save/The many, or the many are to fall." But the materialistic Demos of "Demos and Dionysus" is a false god. In that poem Dionysus, who also speaks for the poet, warns Demos that he will make machines of men who in the end will destroy him. The few who can save the many must have the vision to see truth and the courage to uphold it. Those who, like Nicodemus, recognize the truth but fear to support it openly are little better than slaves. The true saviors of mankind are men like Lincoln, an Olympian, who met rancor and ridicule with cryptic mirth or with patient silence and in the end achieved a greatness that shamed his critics.

It is an inescapable effect of our human need that we should strive to wrench form out of chaos and long for permanence in a world of change. In Robinson's view an optimist is one who believes that with intelligent effort these ends may be achieved in time, and a pessimist is one who feels sure that such a belief is a delusion. He called himself an optimist. Those who thought him a pessimist either misread his poems or defined the terms more narrowly than Robinson. He has also been called an idealist in the tradition of Emerson, and with reason; yet he acknowledged the existence in the world of something very like Schopenhauer's irrational will that makes use of the human intellect to achieve its ends but is not necessarily guided by it. All that he certainly knows is that the world we live in is one of perpetual change; but he believes that through faith, symbolized by the Light, he can see beyond knowledge, and that what he sees justifies the hope that somehow and at an indeterminate date this change will produce a better world. Merlin has viewed the light afar, and he has made Arthur a king, but he cannot sustain him against the law of change, which is a kind of fate. The light itself is the herald of change. As Lancelot realizes at last as he rides through the darkness away from Almesbury and his last sight of Guinevere, "Where the Light falls, death falls." Galahad has seen the Light, and the Light may have revealed to him, as he believed it would, all that man might become, but he dies because he cannot return to a world still unready for what the Light revealed. Sir Bedivere said that another age "will have another Merlin,/Another Camelot, and another King." Between Robinson's King Arthur and his King Jasper there was room for other Camelots and other kings, but apparently none for another Merlin. The kingdom that Jasper built was more advanced and may have been better than the one built by Merlin and Arthur, but it was not more lasting.

Robinson was no Merlin to foresee clearly what kind of world the destroyers of Jasper's kingdom would build, but from the glimpses he gives us in the poem of its coming I assume that he meant some form of pseudo-democracy that is in fact a tyranny such as Dionysus had warned Demos he might produce. The poem leaves no doubt that it will be a change for the worse. We are not left without comfort, however, for Zoë survives, and she is the symbol of man's undying faith and the ground of his hope that somehow, sooner or later, he will create, or help to create, a better world for men to live in. How many failures, and how much suffering, must precede or accompany this change for the better, he leaves us to conjecture. This was the nature of his pessimism and the extent of his optimism.

But philosophy, whether optimistic or not, will not sustain a poet's fame. Neither will long poems, which are inaccessible to young readers because they are not included in anthologies and books of selections. My own pleasure in the long poems, which I read along with all the rest in the *Collected Poems* thirty years ago, remains undiminished, but they are little read by the present generation and in the future will be mostly unread. For this reason future historians are likely to record the opinion that Robinson's early poems, which are nearly all short, are better than his later ones, which are nearly all long. Even so, he will surely retain a prominent place among the modern poets who were his contemporaries, perhaps not the first place as I thought at the time of his death, but a secure one. If in the future we should be so fortunate as to produce greater poets, poets in comparison to whom he must lose stature, Robinson would be the last to complain.

IDEAS AND ACTION
IN JACK LONDON'S FICTION
Franklin Walker

Mills College

In the United States some dozen books by Jack London remain in print or have been reissued in paper covers, the principal survivors among the fifty volumes that he produced during his short, strenuous writing career which spanned two decades at the beginning of the century. As the editions of his books ran into fairly sizable numbers, it is not difficult to find copies of almost all of them in the second-hand market. In England, The Bodley Head is currently publishing a series of London's works edited by Arthur Calder-Marshall, and in non-English-speaking countries he continues to be extensively translated, as the UNESCO figures in *The Index Translationum* testify. Thus he is much more alive than are most of his "popular" contemporaries. There is no persuasive sign, however, of serious attention to Jack London among professional and academic circles. Such critics showed little enthusiasm for his work when he was alive; sixty years later they show even less, although occasionally a Maxwell Geismar or Kenneth Lynn gives him detailed consideration without suggesting a revival. He plays a modest part in American social history but has earned no place of importance in surveys of American literature. He has yet to be the subject of a scholarly biography.

Paradoxically, as a folk hero, correctly or incorrectly understood, he remains very much alive. Americans who have never heard of his principal competitors know the name "Jack London" and have a strong, though somewhat stereotyped conception of his personality and his work. He is the poor boy who made good, the radical who successfully challenged The Establishment, the hyperthyroid extrovert who lived dangerously and adventurously for all of his forty years. In Oakland, an area beside the waterfront from which he sailed to the South Seas in his ketch, *The Snark*, has been named Jack London Square and been blessed by the city fathers, including Joseph Knowland, Senior. It has become the heart of the city's very successful restaurant and imported goods section. In front of the city hall, on the spot where Jack was arrested for breaking a municipal ordinance by mounting a soap box to preach militant socialism in a place prohibited to public speakers, there grows a beautiful live oak dedicated to London by one of Oakland's mayors. Near Glen Ellen, the Jack London State Park, made up of a large section of his "Beauty Ranch," including his grave and the mournful ruins of his huge stone mansion which burned down just before it was completed, is one of the most visited of California's historical monuments. In California London is better known to residents and visiting tourists than Bret Harte, Mark Twain, Joaquin Miller, and Frank Norris all put together.

Among his books which still have vitality, *The Sea-Wolf* remains a favorite. Part of its appeal undoubtedly lies in the melange of social Darwinism and Nietzschean lauding of the superman that is to be found in the words and behavior of Wolf Larsen, the ruthless skipper who shanghaied the bookish protagonist and took him on a voyage off Siberia to capture seals. But Larsen is more than a reflection of ideas taken from books; he is the incarnation of London's persistent idea that the strong men should run the earth. He fails, not because his ideas are faulty but because his brain goes to pieces. *The Sea-Wolf* is a fine adventure story, except for its childish love plot, and gains much of its appeal from London's use of his own experiences on a sealer when he was seventeen. *Martin Eden*, another favorite, which has actually earned something of an audience in colleges, wins its way because it is Jack London's own story of how he pulled himself up from poverty by learning to write salable fiction. In addition to containing a sermon in favor of Herbert Spencer, it gives a vivid picture of a young fellow fighting against the social and economic order of his day; Martin Eden is a sort of early twentieth-century angry young man who forces the stolid burghers to recognize him and then commits suicide in contempt.

A number of other books which are drawn from London's experiences continue to have considerable appeal. *John Barleycorn*, purportedly written in support of prohibition, attempts to portray its protagonist as a victor over alcohol when every third line forecasts his ultimate defeat. *The Road* is a significant social document based on young London's adventures in stealing rides on freight and passenger trains, panhandling for funds to see America, and suffering in a county penitentiary after being jailed for vagrancy. *The People of the Abyss* tells of the squalor of London's East End as Jack saw it after living in disguise in one of the slums.

The writings of London which have shown the greatest vitality are, however, his books about the Far North. Products of a winter in the Klondike during the great rush, experienced when London had not yet started on his writing career, they constitute not only the earliest but the best of London's contribution to letters. They are great adventure stories partly because they catch the spirit of the last (and the most insane) mass rush towards a new frontier, partly because they embody London's perceptive view of the difference between the wilds and civilization. They appeal because they embody every man's desire to get away from daily routine, to gamble on a quick success, and to cope with nature in its more rugged aspects. Whether London's hero is a man, or a man disguised as a dog, he is full of vigor, there is a sparkle in his eyes, and he escapes the dull features of a humdrum existence. So it is that there continues to be a steady world audience for *The Son of the Wolf, The Call of the Wild, White Fang,* short stories such as "Love of Life" and "To Build a Fire," and even *Burning Daylight* and *Smoke Bellew,* in spite of their weak endings. London's Yukon fiction reveals him at his best.

It is significant that *The Call of the Wild* and the other Klondike books are read chiefly for their plots and characters and the settings in which the action takes place, not for their intellectual concepts. It is true that in them there is some rather vague concern with atavism, and an even more constant lauding of Anglo-Saxon proficiency and worth, with Anglo-Saxon success revealed as a natural concomitant of the operation of the survival of the fittest. Yet these ideas are presented without any detailed argument in their support; they are only mildly academic. In the opinion of this writer, London is never less successful than when he is putting theories obtained from his reading into fiction. It is true that he was tremendously impressed by his reading, and thus a novel like *Martin Eden* owes part of its appeal to the reflection in it, often in an appropriately confused state, of many of the economic and social issues of the period in which it was written. London was no more confused, however, than most men around him, with whom thoroughness and consistency were no more common than they are today. He has, it is to be admitted, some of the appeal of writers like Mark Twain and Melville who approach discursive books and current theories without the sometimes dulling effects of an academic orientation. London could mix with enthusiasm (and without a qualm) the manifest destiny of Kipling, the belief in free will and eventual cosmic justice of Browning, the materialism of Ernest Haeckel, the social Darwinism of Herbert Spencer, the economic determinism of Marx, and the rugged individualism of Nietzsche. When his books are colored in only a peripheral way by theory, as in *The Call of the Wild*, he is effective; when they are dominated by theory, as in *The Iron Heel*, he is lost. It is worthwhile to consider in detail two of his novels which can be truly called "idea" novels, *The Iron Heel* and *The Valley of the Moon*, and a third, in which academic concepts are less dogmatic and pervasive, *The Scarlet Plague*.

With the exception of one or two short stories like "The Mexican" and a handful of essays, *The Iron Heel* is the only work by London to reflect in any detail his enthusiasm for socialism and particularly Marxism. During the year before its composition he had lectured widely throughout the United States in support of the Intercollegiate Socialist Society, of which he was the first president; often sounding more revolutionary than his supporters, he had come to feel, in the face of the proletarian revolts in the Russia of 1905, that violence rather than the ballot was the true path for the socialist in America. His picture of the social and economic struggle in *The Iron Heel*, written in 1906 and published shortly after the staggering shock of the panic of 1907, emphasized the weakness of socialist reform achieved through parliamentary procedures and pictured the rise of totalitarianism imposed by big business which by 1918 would crush the working class under "the iron heel of a despotism as relentless and terrible as any despotism that has blackened the pages of the history of man."[1] Though the novel forecasts an eventual victory for the proletariat in three hundred years, it does so only through footnotes; its action ends in a most fearful blood bath when the proletarian revolutionists, who have been driven underground, set up a short-lived commune in Chicago. Though *The Iron Heel* impressed such widely different rebels as Eugene Debs, Anatole France, and Leon Trotsky, and though it has received considerable credit for anticipating fascism, its significance as an exposition of Marxist ide-

---

1. Jack London, *The Iron Heel* (New York, 1908), p. 152.

ology is not today taken very seriously. According to Deming Brown in his *Soviet Attitudes toward American Writing*, more than thirty years ago the Russian critics decided that the novel showed a very faulty conception of Marxism and it is today read in Russia principally as a picture of contemporary American society![2] The Russians, who have published more works by London than by any other American writer, are fascinated by his books about the Far North rather than by his revolutionary writings, which they consider "naive and confused."[3] They have decided that London's ideology is representative of the faulty thinking of the petty bourgeoisie.

Though Trotsky found *The Iron Heel* both stimulating and prophetic, he pointed out its greatest weakness: "The author is intentionally sparing in his use of artistic means."[4] Even among utopian novels, a genre not noted for skilful writing, it stands out as ineptly done. The first half of the book is given over to the presentation of Ernest Everhard, the revolutionary hero, arguing with everyone in sight in order to advance his theories linking the eventual success of the proletariat with the evolutionary process discovered by Darwin. Ernest alternates between lecturing his wife, the awed daughter of a University of California physics professor, and browbeating industrialists at dinner parties and discussion clubs. He is clearly Jack London making his ideas emphatically known, winning every argument, never letting up on his opponents. When they lose their heads, he becomes even more calm, confounding them with his logic. "It was always his way to turn the point back upon an opponent, and he did it now, with a beaming brotherliness of face and utterance."[5] Everhard, who runs into no worthy competitors in debate, puts forward all sorts of ideas from W. J. Ghent or Herbert Spencer or Karl Marx with all the assurance of an Old Testament prophet. The tone of these chapters is well illustrated by a letter which London wrote to F. I. Bamford, the president of the Oakland Ruskin Club, to which London proposed to read two chapters from the manuscript of his novel in progress. "These are new in content and are devoted to the perishing middle class, and I think it would go splendidly. Incidentally, I handle surplus value in them, and the inevitable breakdown of capi-

---

2. Deming Brown, *Soviet Attitudes toward American Writing* (Princeton, 1962), pp. 223-226.

3. *Ibid.*, p. 228.

4. Leon Trotsky to Joan London, quoted in Joan London, *Jack London and His Times* (New York, 1939), p. 313.

5. *The Iron Heel*, p. 11.

talism under the structure of profits it has reared."[6] The two chapters read like the arguments of a high school sophomore who has just begun to explore the theories he expounds.

When action does come, it is expressed mainly through summary. Before they are driven underground, the socialists of the United States and Germany stop a world war by calling a general strike—all done in six pages; later, it takes Jack only one page to dispose of the middle class. Only in his description of the horrors of the putting-down of the Chicago commune does he become graphic and moving. Earlier much of the plot is derivative and tenuous; for instance, a great deal is made of the neglect by mill owners of a worker named Jackson who has lost his arm in an accident in handling the mill machinery. Ernest Everhard's sweetheart, who leaves the manuscript which tells the story of *The Iron Heel*, is won over to her future husband's point of view by following his suggestion that she investigate the circumstances of the accident and the abortive law suit brought by the injured worker. The whole episode, spun out by London to considerable length, is taken from a typical muckraker article by Jocelyn Lewis.[7] Miss Lewis's workman is named Jackson, he ends up peddling rattan chairs (as he does in *The Iron Heel*), and the author, interviewing lawyers and industrialists' wives, gets exactly the same answers as does London's heroine. The article itself is unimpressive—one is never certain whether it is fiction or fact—and the fault in London's use of it lay not in his borrowing the material (he prided himself on the process of what he called "turning journalism into literature," and he listed the article in a footnote in *The Iron Heel*) but in his attempt to blow up a not untypical case of industrial mismanagement before the days of a satisfactory workmen's compensation law into an overwhelmingly serious episode indicating the complete venality of American financiers.

The essentially artificial, forced nature of the narrative is well illustrated by the revelations which followed a contretemps which developed between Frank Harris and Jack London over London's use in *The Iron Heel*, with only minor alterations and no acknowledgement, of a thousand-word item which Harris had published in England in 1901. Harris, amused at what he considered the pompous

6. Jack London to F. I. Bamford, Oct. 10, 1906, quoted in Georgia Loring Bamford, *The Mystery of Jack London* (Oakland, Calif., 1931), p. 214.

7. Jocelyn Lewis, "Was It Worth While?", *Outlook*, Aug. 18, 1906, pp. 902-904. See footnote in *The Iron Heel*, p. 70.

behavior of a group of English clerics, headed by the Bishop of London, who had indulged in the usual platitudes at a meeting called to promote public morality, wrote a satirical squib for the *Candid Friend* titled "The Bishop of London and Public Morality." "It occurred to me that it would be amusing to picture what would be the effect on the meeting if the Bishop of London had suddenly become a Christian."[8] The Bishop's speech, as Harris wrote it, revealed most unorthodox behavior.

"I was in my brougham, driving along Picadilly.... Now and then I looked through the carriage windows, and suddenly my eyes seemed to be opened, and I saw things as they really are. At first I covered my eyes with my hands to shut out the awful sight, and then, in the darkness, the questions came to me: What is to be done?... What would the Master do?... and I saw my duty sun-clear, as Saul saw his on the way to Damascus.

"I stopped the carriage, got out, and, after a few minutes' conversation, persuaded two of the public women to get into the brougham with me. If Jesus was right, these two unfortunates were my sisters, and the only hope of their purification was in my affection and tenderness.... I took the two women of the street to Fulham Palace, and they are going to stay with me. I hope to fill every room in my palace with such sisters as these."[9]

The bishop continued for a few more sentences and then sat down in the midst of great excitement.

In writing *The Iron Heel*, London, who never suspected that the squib was a spoof but felt that it was a telling social document, incorporated it into his text, changing the English cleric to "Bishop Morehouse of San Francisco," altering Fulham Palace into a palatial home in Menlo Park, but keeping the "brougham" and most of the rest of the words. In London's version Bishop Morehouse had to be hushed and led from the platform, the capitalistic newspapers joined in a conspiracy to ignore his speech, and the speaker was persuaded to take a vacation. When he returned holding the same revolutionary ideas, and carried them further by selling all his goods for charity and going to live with the poor, he was locked up in the insane asylum, obviously a victim, and a touching one, of the "Iron Heel." When Frank Harris discovered the passage and printed it in *Vanity Fair* in parallel columns with his own squib, titling his exposé "How

8. Frank Harris, "How Mr. Jack London Writes a Novel," *Vanity Fair* (London), April 14, 1909, p. 454.
9. The *Candid Friend* article by Harris (May 25, 1901) was reproduced verbatim in Harris, "How Mr. Jack London Writes a Novel," p. 454. For London's version, see *The Iron Heel*, pp. 112-113.

Mr. Jack London Writes a Novel," the public received it as merely one more charge of plagiarism. (It certainly was a good case of the smoked pan calling the kettle black.) London, in reply, asserted that Harris's squib had been reprinted in America in a socialist journal as a bona fide speech given by the Bishop of London, and that he had filed away the clipping as an excellent bit of evidence which could some day be used to give verisimilitude to his fiction.[10] London admitted being a sucker but denied he was a thief. Harris continued to act very small about the whole matter, asking such questions as "Are we to take it that Mr. Jack London's novels are a *réchauffé* of newspaper stories?"[11]

The principal significance of the incident, other than its reflecting the personalities of the two writers, is that London revealed that, as a social critic, he was quite unable to distinguish between an account of a real event and a broad satire. The speech of London's bishop does not strike one as ridiculous in the sense Frank Harris intended it to be because it is quite in keeping with most of the speeches in *The Iron Heel*. The bishop's speech is no more ridiculous than most of the arguments delivered by Ernest Everhard. A tone of unreality is pervasive throughout the book.

This cannot be said of *The Valley of the Moon*, written half a dozen years after *The Iron Heel* came out when London's enthusiasm for Marxist socialism had fallen off considerably. Now, instead of returning from a lecture tour devoted to the coming revolution, he was busy developing his ranch near Glen Ellen. The theme of *The Valley of the Moon* is the return to the land. Its hero and heroine, more nearly members of the proletariat than any other characters London created, flee from their working-class environment because "poor people can't be happy in the city where they have labor troubles all the time."[12] Billy Roberts and Saxon Brown, a teamster and a laundry worker who live in the very section of Oakland where London had spent his poverty-stricken boyhood, are appropriately inarticulate and youthfully happy in their courtship; their meeting at a bricklayers' picnic in Weasel Park is accompanied by one of the best workmen's brawls in American fiction. They are very real people in the early days of their marriage, with Saxon thrilling at being able

10. Jack London to *Vanity Fair*, July 1, 1909, in *Letters from Jack London*, ed. King Hendricks and Irving Shepard (New York, 1965), pp. 280-281.
11. Frank Harris in *Vanity Fair*, Oct. 27, 1909.
12. Jack London, *The Valley of the Moon* (New York, 1913), p. 332.

to take daily baths for the first time in her life and Billy stubbornly excited about his first safety razor. Billy gives up prizefighting, by which he has been making money on the side, only to have his teamster work come to a halt when his union goes out on strike. Bad times, the prevalence of scab labor, and police persecution of the strikers prove too much for Billy. He takes to drinking, becomes involved in brawls, and even grows hard-hearted towards his young wife after she suffers a miscarriage induced by a labor riot which takes place in their front yard. After spending a term in jail for beating up a boarder whom Saxon has taken into the house to help pay expenses, Billy emerges sober and ready to accept his wife's suggestion that they get out of Oakland and look for a new life elsewhere.

Though Saxon's brother is a socialist and feebly attempts to persuade them that they should wait for the coming utopia, the Robertses show no more interest in revolutionary theories than did the author at this stage in his life. As he wrote his agent, "For once in my life I have a story that will not be offensive to bourgeois morality and bourgeois business ethics,"[13] adding that in spite of these circumstances, he absolutely and passionately believed in his new thesis —"back to the land." Two thirds of the way through his novel he sent his uprooted couple on what he described as "a magnificent, heroic odyssey." The trouble is that the odyssey rang hollow, whereas the description of troubles in the city was very effective. For some reason or other, in spite of the fact that he himself had shaken the dust of Oakland from his feet, London had not been able to make his retreat to the hills look like a success. True, he had a great deal of land, most of which was heavily mortgaged, a blooded Shire stallion for which he had paid $25,000 after it had won first prize at the state fair, and plans to build a baronial mansion to be named "Wolf House." He was erecting the first concrete silo in California, starting to terrace his slopes like the Italians, scheming to grow Angora sheep to keep his hillsides cropped, and already planting the first of thousands of eucalyptus trees which were intended to bring him a fortune. In the meantime it took every cent he could earn from his writing to make his return to the land economically feasible. No wonder that the reader of *The Valley of the Moon* is not wholly convinced that London has found the solution for every man's troubles, much less for those of Billy and Saxon Roberts.

13. Jack London to Paul R. Reynolds, June 24, 1911, MS in the Huntington Library,

It was London's plan that his young couple should wander up and down California to observe farming methods and to find the ideal plot on which to settle. As they trudged along, their observations reflected the second theme of the novel, the plight of the displaced pioneer. Both Billy and Saxon were children of pioneers who had crossed the plains and fought Indians; moreover, they were of good Anglo-Saxon stock (Saxon's name was given to her by her family to remind her of her superior racial heritage). During their search, the Robertses frequently complain: "We crossed the plains and opened up this country, and now we're losing even the chance to work for a living in it."[14] This resulted from the fact that foreign immigrants like the hard-working, thrifty Portuguese were not only willing to labor long hours but were putting into practice many of the effective methods of making every inch of soil produce that they had learned in their native lands. The Robertses did not blame them for this activity; they blamed the Anglo-Saxon pioneers for failing to work the soil to its greatest potential yield.

The rather pretentious presentation of farming methods in this section of the novel, together with Billy's and Saxon's activities when they finally, after three years of wandering, settle on the ideal spot—in the Valley of the Moon next to London's "Beauty Ranch"—are doubtless responsible for Charmian London's sweeping assertion after Jack's death that this novel ought to be used as a text in an agricultural college. An examination of his protagonist's discoveries, however, indicates that practically every detail is taken from a series of articles by Forest Crissey which appeared in the *Saturday Evening Post* in 1911.[15] These tell not only about the ingenious Portuguese in San Leandro but the hard-working Dalmations in the Pajaro Valley and the persistent Chinese in the Sacramento delta, all of whom appear in the novel. Even "the San Jose woman" who shows the Robertses how successfully a retired librarian can live off the land is taken from another magazine article. And in treating the Sacramento delta country, where Jack had sailed his boat for weeks at a time, and in his account of conditions in northern California, where he made a four-horse driving trip at the very time he was working on

14. *The Valley of the Moon*, p. 205.
15. See the file of source materials for *The Valley of the Moon* in the Huntington Library. Among articles by Forrest Crissey see particularly "Neglected Opportunities," *Saturday Evening Post*, Sept. 2, 1911; "John Chinaman as a Crop-Coaxer," *ibid.*, Sept. 16, 1911; "Lessons from our Alien Farmers," *ibid.*, Oct. 7, 1911; and "Lessons from our Alien Farmers," *ibid.*, Nov. 18, 1911.

the novel, he failed to use his own observations but fell back on ephemeral, unscientific articles from popular magazines to form the bases for his comments on California agriculture.

Not all of the Robertses' hegira is devoted to investigating farming methods; they spend most of a year at Carmel, thus giving London an opportunity to describe with very thin disguises the members of the active literary colony there which then centered upon George Sterling, his closest friend. He does not introduce himself in fictional guise as one of the Carmelites, but he does elsewhere slip himself into the book three times—once as the nameless twelve-year-old boy who takes Saxon fishing in his small rowboat and cheers her up when she is most despondent, and twice as Jack Hastings, traveling with his wife Clara (Charmian), first aboard *The Roamer* and then driving his four horses gaily through the redwood forests. It is not surprising that the optimistic urchin is far more attractive than the successful novelist in these portraits—the difference reflects the difference in tone of the two parts of the book.

When the Robertses acquire their dream ranch, starting with a modest five acres, they hardly carry on in the typical "small-scale farming" manner which London described to his publisher.[16] It is true they raise chickens and put in some berries and other produce which they plan to peddle to nearby hotels. Billy at once begins buying and breeding draught horses for the Oakland market; it is not long before he and Saxon, who is now allowed to do no work except launder her "flimsies," which Billy so admires, are proud owners of riding horses. The work on the farm is done by hired labor, a motherly housekeeper and two paroled Chinese convicts from San Quentin, who work for very little and even lend their employers money when they are pressed. It is not long, however, before the twentieth-century frontiersmen have solved their financial problems by discovering a deposit of pottery clay on their ranch (now expanded to one hundred and forty acres) and realize that, by damming up the stream which runs through their property, they can hold up the citizens of Glen Ellen for a good price for drinking water. These are but trivial matters, however, in the light of Saxon's discovery that she is pregnant. After she whispers the news out in the woods to an embarrassed but happy Billy, the novel ends on an appropriate tone. "Saxon felt

16. Jack London to Roland Phillips, of the *Cosmopolitan Magazine*, May 30, 1911, published in *Letters from Jack London*, pp. 347-348.

Billy's finger laid warningly on her lips. Guided by his hand, she turned her head back, and together they gazed far up the side of the knoll where a doe and a spotted fawn looked down upon them from a tiny open space between the trees."[17]

The immediate action of London's short novel *The Scarlet Plague* is pleasantly uncomplicated. An eighty-seven-year-old man called "Granser" by his three grandsons is accompanying the boys while they herd goats and catch and roast crabs on the beach—near where the Cliff House had once stood in San Francisco. Although the youngsters tease the old man in a somewhat cruel fashion, they are eager to hear his story of the scarlet plague and its aftermath in spite of the fact that he uses many big words that they cannot understand. He explains patiently that it is sixty years since a newly developed germ wiped out all of mankind except for a few score who were strangely immune to it. The disaster had come swiftly in 2013; Granser, who is now the sole survivor of those fearful days, tells his story vividly, in spite of the fact that the sixty years in which he had seen primordial life sweep back and recapture the land had somewhat disoriented his thoughts.

In the fateful time when the plague struck, he had been an English professor in the University of California at Berkeley. While men died and civilized life lost its routine impetus, he and four hundred others isolated themselves in the Chemistry Building. There they were safe from the fearful rioting which went on all around them but not safe from the germ, which worked its ravages among them until there were only forty-seven survivors. This group set out trekking south away from the cities; within a week Professor James Howard Smith was the only remaining survivor. Determined to escape from the stench of rotting corpses, he made his way up to Yosemite, where he lived alone for three years. Returning to a much changed San Francisco Bay Region, where most material signs of civilization had already disappeared, he found a few other survivors like himself.

These people had certainly not won survival on any basis of virtue or physical strength—they had simply been immune to the deadly germ. The first one the narrator met was a brutal chauffeur who had mated with the young widow of one of the most powerful tycoons in the world; he beat her constantly and mercilessly. Later the

17. *The Valley of the Moon*, p. 530.

protagonist joined a group of eighteen survivors who lived near Glen Ellen and came to be known as the Santa Rosa tribe. Two of the group were feeble-minded adults from a nearby asylum. The professor had difficulty in finding a wife but eventually did so and fathered children, even becoming the progenitor of several grandchildren.

Under the changing conditions, he saw man's senses become more acute, his physique more supple, but his mind less concerned with abstractions. Long before the time that he ate crabs with his grandsons on the beach, he had seen them lose the ability to read as well as the interest in doing so, and now they could count no higher than ten. Along with the formerly domestic animals, they grew wild and cruel. Through natural selection the many breeds of dogs were replaced by packs of wolves; the cats, always loners, became wild-cats; the horses grew smaller and learned to fight for forage. The bears multiplied.

Though Granser had developed many doubts as to the virtues of civilization, he patiently did what he could to contribute to its return in the distant future. With the greatest of care he tried to show the boys what a hundred, a thousand, a million might represent. He warned them against being deceived by the growing number of medicine men. He urged them to pass on to their children and grandchildren the all-important truths that steam could be harnessed for man's good, that the lightning had in it a form of energy of great value, that the alphabet was worth preserving even if they for the moment found picture writing more satisfactory. In a cave on Telegraph Hill he had cached as many basic books which might help future generations as he could—and these included the classics. He knew that another day would come.

All things pass. Only remain cosmic force and matter, ever in flux, ever acting and reacting and realizing the eternal types—the priest, the soldier, and the king. Out of the mouths of babes comes the wisdom of all the ages. Some will fight, some will rule, some will pray; and all the rest will toil and suffer sore while on their bleeding carcasses is reared again, and yet again, without end, the amazing beauty and surpassing wonder of the civilized state.[18]

The Scarlet Plague presents ideas, but it presents them quietly and without distortion. Above all, it pleads no special case. The book ends in almost an idyllic mood; wild horses stand by the surf,

18. Jack London, *The Scarlet Plague* (New York, 1915), pp. 178-179.

silhouetted against the sunset. Close at hand the sea lions are bellowing their ancient chant. "And old man and boy, skin-clad and barbaric, turned and went along the right of way into the forest in the wake of the goats."[19] In spite of the current proliferation of survival novels, *The Scarlet Plague* remains fresh and vivid. In its brooding sense of the kinship of man and nature, it is a minor companion to *The Call of the Wild* and *White Fang*. It merits a wider reading public.

9. *Ibid.*, p. 181.

VACHEL LINDSAY: AN APPRAISAL

John T. Flanagan

University of Illinois

There can be no question that the reputation of Vachel Lindsay has declined sharply since the days when he won fame as a bardic poet and recited "The Congo" to thousands of tense listeners. When Norman Foerster published the first edition of his popular anthology *American Poetry and Prose* in 1925, he naturally included Lindsay and selected six poems to represent one of the freshest American talents since Poe. A quarter of a century later, F. O. Matthiessen in *The Oxford Book of American Verse* allotted Lindsay twenty-one pages and chose to include six poems. But in 1965 the situation was quite different. In their anthology entitled *American Poetry*, Gay Wilson Allen, Walter B. Rideout, and James K. Robinson resurrected Frederick Tuckerman, gave space to H.D., and allocated forty pages to many obscure and untested poets such as Robert Creeley and Wendell Berry, but failed to include a single poem by Vachel Lindsay. The nadir of Lindsay's fame has certainly been reached when a collection of American verse running in excess of twelve hundred pages completely omits his work.

This abrupt shift in critical esteem of a poet who once enjoyed international recognition can hardly be unexpected. In an age of abrasive sound, of deliberate harshness and shock, Lindsay's often musical lines seem to find small appeal. In an age of intellectual poetry when thought seems to transcend form or is even consciously muddy in the hope that it will impress readers as profound, Lindsay's ideas seem vague and naïve. In an age of dissidence and revolt, when nonconformity in both action and thought becomes freakish, Lindsay's romanticism is jejune. In an age of ringing asseveration of civil rights and human dignities, Lindsay's patriotism seems parochial, a pallid imitation of Whitman's grander sympathies which is clearly out of joint with the times. Even Lindsay's symbolism, his frequent use of the butterfly and the spider, of the rose and the lotus, appears obvious and commonplace at a time when symbols are extremely complex and personal.

Contemporary poets have their causes and are sometimes annoyingly insistent in pleading them. It is not only the hirsute folksingers who argue in verse for Marxist proletarianism or desegregationism. But Lindsay also had causes for which he crusaded—temperance, a mild agrarianism, municipal beautification, the replacement of the Mammon-soul of avarice in public life with the spirit of beauty. The trouble is that in comparison these goals seem naïve and elusive. Today's partisans of a militant church will hardly be much impressed by the dream of a world religion in which Springfield, Illinois, would become the site of a great cathedral open to all and adorned by statues of Gautama Buddha, St. Francis of Assisi, and Johnny Appleseed. The Village Improvement Parade, symbols and lines from which decorate the end pages of Lindsay's *Collected Poems*, seems as ineffectual and pointless now as the miscellany of sketches and proclamations which once filled his "annual" periodical, the *Village Magazine*. Lindsay was unquestionably sincere, but many of his esoteric visions carried little conviction to his readers. As he once wrote in his journal, "I scarcely think one thought a year, and visions come in cataracts."

Indeed a chief factor accounting for Lindsay's decline in popularity is the illusionary character of much of his thinking. He had a rich and colorful imagination but virtually no sense of logic. Stephen Graham, the English writer who accompanied Lindsay on a hiking trip through the Rockies, observed that his companion "loves oratory more than reason, and impulse more than thought." Edgar Lee Masters, his first important biographer and an acquaintance of the poet, expressed it differently; according to him, Lindsay's religion made him "myopic to reality." It should be remembered that the poet's mother, a dominant personality and an orthodox Campbellite, often thought of her son as a great Christian cartoonist. Egyptian hieroglyphics, first garnered from a close study of Rawlinson's history of Egypt, adorn his drawings, and the Orient was never far from his fancy. His sister Olive had married a medical missionary and had lived for some time in China; by sending him pictures of the Kamakura Buddha and other sculptures she provided another channel of images for the poet. Lindsay's interest in the graphic arts, his reading in art periodicals, his vicarious experience of exotic countries—all inflamed his imagination without giving substance or firmness to his own work. As Masters pointed out, Lindsay with all his interest in drawing was never able to sketch the human face.

Any appraisal of Lindsay must of necessity take into account his deep nationalism. He was proud of being an American and once wrote in "Doctor Mohawk": "The soul of the U.S.A.: that is my life-quest." It pleased him to think of an Indian strain somewhere in his remote lineage and to remember that his mother could possibly claim some Spanish blood. Even greater than his profound Americanism was his pride in his Southern ancestry. "No drop of my blood from north/Of Mason and Dixon's line," he wrote in his tribute to Alexander Campbell. His "Litany of the Heroes" introduces Lincoln and in the final stanza equates Woodrow Wilson and Socrates as martyrs to a cause, the one figuratively and the other literally drinking a cup of hemlock. A late poem, entitled "The Virginians Are Coming Again," utilizing the title as a refrain, pours scorn on the Babbitts of the world he knew with their avarice and their rackets and cites Washington, Jefferson, and Lee as exemplars of a different code. The statue of Old Andrew Jackson striding his charger and bearing a sword "so long he dragged it on the ground" became a symbol to the poet of native power and glory.

Lincoln of course received his sincerest accolade and in Springfield, Illinois, Lincoln's town, Lindsay was born and died. The poet visualized the tall gaunt figure, still wearing his shawl and his top hat, pacing restlessly near the old court house, unable to sleep because the world was sick. For Lincoln the poet retained a lasting devotion. But Lindsay found American heroes elsewhere and often in strange locations. He imagined himself on a mining camp street in California listening to Edwin Booth as the actor enunciated a "whispering silvery line" which he was resolved to speak aright. He praised Governor Altgeld of Illinois, savior of the Chicago anarchists, as "the eagle that is forgotten." He could celebrate John L. Sullivan, the strong boy of Boston, who "fought seventy-five red rounds with Jake Kilrain." William Jennings Bryan, of course, won his admiration, and in the poem with the quadruplicate title he praised the "gigantic troubadour" who "scourged the elephant plutocrats/With barbed wire from the Platte." Bryan's defeat for the presidency Lindsay saw as a plot engineered by Mark Hanna in which Western democracy collapsed before the onslaught of Wall Street and State Street.

And always Johnny Appleseed fixed his attention, the gentle

Swedenborgian horticulturist who came down the Ohio River with a cargo of tracts and apple seeds determined to distribute both along the frontier. Johnny Appleseed was the man who "ran with the rabbit and slept with the stream" and who as a knotted and gnarled septuagenarian still planted trees in the clearings of Ohio and Indiana. Once Lindsay even imagined his saintly pomologist as praying on Going-to-the-Sun Mountain in Glacier Park surrounded by a flood of dark rich apples.

For a time Lindsay was the victim of his own success. Harriet Monroe printed his early poems in *Poetry: A Magazine of Verse*; and H. L. Mencken some of his later ones in the *American Mercury*. But he won his fame on the recital platform, in a thousand churches, schools, auditoriums, lecture halls—declaiming, shouting, whispering as his lines ebbed and flowed, providing his own acoustical accompaniment, his own clarion and tympani. Inevitably the spell faded and the fountain dried up. Lindsay could and did write better verse than "The Congo" but audiences demanded "The Congo" just as concert-goers demanded the C sharp minor "Prelude" from Rachmaninov. In a letter to his friend Lawrence Conrad he referred to the poems on General Booth and the Congo with positive disgust. "I have *had* to recite those two poems and those only, since 1913, till I have nearly cracked up the back." Lindsay lost his touch even when he tried to write in the same vein. Later poems like "The Trial of the Dead Cleopatra" reveal both the poet's orientalism and his lush fancy but lack the magic of "The Chinese Nightingale." In the late 1920's, as many letters confirm, Lindsay grew physically tired and emotionally frustrated. Also, according to the latest biographical dicta, he was a victim of epilepsy. It is small wonder that he eventually chose the path trod earlier by Hart Crane and later by Ernest Hemingway, becoming one of the three great American literary suicides of the twentieth century.

Early in his life, perhaps when he was peddling "The Cup of Paint" and "We Who Are Playing" along New York's Broadway, selling his poetic leaflets for two cents, Lindsay resolved to write brassy, stentorian verse, verse suitable for oral delivery and immediately challenging to his audiences. He even devised a label for it, the "higher vaudeville." Generations of listeners became familiar with these fortissimo poems, rich in alliteration, heavy of accent, full of spondaic feet and emphatic caesuras. Transposed to the printed page, they carried elaborate stage directions. "John Brown" he envisaged as a classical antiphony, with a leader and a chorus alternating, the leader providing the substance of the poem, the chorus or audience interrupting with leading questions: *What did you see in Palestine?"* "Daniel" was intended to combine touches of "Dixie" and "Alexander's Ragtime Band." "The Santa-Fé Trail" was to be sung or read at times with great speed, preferably in a rolling bass, the interpreter was advised to utter the resonant place names of the second section like a union depot train-caller, but to enunciate the synonyms for auto horns with a "snapping explosiveness" and finally to end with "a languorous whisper." Carl Van Doren pointed out years ago many of the ingredients of Lindsay's poetic style: the revival hymn, the sailor's chantey, the military march, the Negro cakewalk, even fragments of patriotic songs. The result of this mélange, as seen conspicuously in "The Congo," "General William Booth Enters into Heaven," and "The Santa-Fé Trail," became Lindsay's trademark and one of the most distinctive achievements in the whole range of American poetry. Even in the booming verses so familiar to audiences there are memorable phrases or lines, but chiefly they linger in the memory because of their stridency.

What readers and critics of Lindsay's work often overlook today is the poet's gentler side, his attention to little things, his softness, his tender romanticism, which led Masters to term "The Beggar's Valentine" one of the "most moving love poems in the language." The subject matter of these briefer poems is in itself revealing. Lindsay could write about mice, turtles, snails, crickets, toads, grasshoppers, crows, butterflies, and meadowlarks. The dandelion as well as the rose and the lotus appealed to him, and memories of long hours of toil in the wheat fields under a blazing sun could not erase the pleasure in being in the open air, as a reading of "Kansas" will confirm. Some of the larger mammals also attracted his attention, the buffalo of the prairies and the golden whales of California, although inevitably these creatures became symbolic. He remembered the experience of watching hands on a Western ranch attempting to discipline a young horse, and he later transmuted this experience into "The Broncho That Would Not Be Broken." These poems are brief, whimsical, sometimes wryly humorous, though in general humor was not Lindsay's forte. There is probably no better example of the poet's delicate touch than "What the Rattlesnake Said":

The moon's a little prairie-dog,
He shivers through the night.
He sits upon his hill and cries
For fear that *I* will bite.

Here the sly anthropomorphism, the simple language, the use of the familiar ballad stanza in an unpretentious lyric—all suggest Lindsay's deftness.

As a love poet Lindsay was generally less successful. He seemed unable to get away from triteness and conventional hyperbole. Early poems to unknown inamoratas are hardly memorable. "With a Rose, to Brunhilde" was addressed to Olivia Roberts, a Springfield neighbor and writer who attracted him briefly. Sara Teasdale, to whom he dedicated his *Collected Poems*, was his Gloriana, but although he exaggerated her physical qualities (her "burning golden eyes" and her "snowy throat"), his romantic admiration for her never achieved impressive form. Briefly he thought that a girl he had met while he was teaching at Gulf Park Junior College in Mississippi, Elizabeth Wills, was his Dulcinea, but although he compared her to a bird's wing which "spreads above my sky," his devotion was not transformed into imperishable verse and his offer of marriage was spurned. After his marriage in 1925 to Elizabeth Conner he published a number of love poems, collected in *The Candle in the Cabin* and suffused with a romantic color, but this "weaving together of script and singing," as the subtitle has it, is not particularly successful. Most of the poems reflect the Glacier Park scenes which the couple viewed on their honeymoon, and even the landscape descriptions are curiously subdued and flat.

The subjects which moved Lindsay most deeply were places and people intimately associated with his own early life, or subjects with which he could achieve a family and almost a racial intimacy. "The Proud Farmer," a quietly impressive tribute to his maternal grandfather E. S. Frazee which in tone and workmanship reminds one of Masters's tribute to his own grandmother, "Lucinda Matlock," is genuine and devoted. The Hoosier preacher-farmer who read by night and built his world by day left an indelible mark on both his daughter and his grandson and became the subject of one of Lindsay's best elegies. "Dr. Mohawk," the account of a half-mythical figure who is both the poet's putative aboriginal ancestor and his physician father, suggests the son's fear of and respect for his parent and Dr. Lindsay's understandable bewilderment at the occasional behavior of his gifted son. "Billboards and Galleons," inscribed to Stephen Graham, is a fantasy inspired by his days at Biloxi and contains the reference to Don Ivan, his Spanish ancestor, whom Lindsay conceived as a friend of Columbus and a guest of Queen Isabella.

Lindsay's natal town of Springfield, even though he spent many years away from it, always cast a spell on him. His hope for the future of the community was unrealistic but genuine. "A city is not builded in a day," he declared and added that a great city need not be large; neither Athens nor Florence achieved immensity. What was needed most was "many Lincoln-hearted men." He certainly envisaged the Village Improvement Parade as taking place in Springfield and hoped that farm boys, builders, craftsmen, marchers of all kinds carrying banners inscribed with slogans would bring about a municipal revolution. But even though the slogans might win approval ("Bad public taste is mob law—good public taste is democracy"), the parade in Springfield or anywhere else never got started. To his chagrin Springfield remained the city of his discontent.

Of a different nature were the tributes paid to public figures, the well-known encomiums to Jackson, Lincoln, Altgeld, Bryan, Alexander Campbell, Governor Bob Taylor of Tennessee, sincere if not always highly perceptive, terse characterizations which seized upon familiar details and phrased them memorably. Lindsay attempted no career judgment but sought rather a brief illumination, a vision of light or a brilliant profile, and often achieved more than pages of expository prose could do.

Some of his most striking effects occur in poems less familiar than "The Congo" or "The Santa-Fé Trail" although he employed identical methods. "Simon Legree—A Negro Sermon," the first part of the Booker T. Washington trilogy, is a fanciful account of a meeting between the ignominious overseer and the Devil in Hell where each tries to outdo the other in viciousness. Legree's puffed-out cheeks which were a fish-belly white in color probably owe something to Mark Twain's description of Huck's father but are not necessarily less vivid because of the similarity, and the picture we are given of the overseer gambling, eating, and drinking with the Devil on his wide green throne is one of Lindsay's magnificent achievements.

Equally vivid is "The Ghost of the Buffaloes" with its extraordinary picture of the animals stampeding madly,

> Stamping flint feet, flashing moon eyes,
> Pompous and owlish, shaggy and wise.

One remembers, too, the parade of fabulous animals invoked in "Bryan, Bryan, Bryan, Bryan," the bungaroo and giassicus, the rakaboor and hellangone, all mixed up with prairie dog and horned toad and longhorn. In a very different key is the poem "I Know All This When Gipsy Fiddles Cry" in which his own experiences on the open road, begging and tramping in a way that Whitman never did, breed a sympathy in him for those wanderers who for centuries have been itinerant without losing their identity or their interest.

The critics have not always been kind to Lindsay, although he has had his defenders. Conrad Aiken, writing in *Scepticisms* in 1919, was willing to credit the poet with originality but objected to the orotund style, the echolalia, the banalities. He also found fault with Lindsay for being overly topical, thus denying him the very virtue celebrated by others of making use of the American scene in a frank and unhackneyed manner. Aiken gave Lindsay small chance for survival unless he abandoned the traits which inhere basically in the higher vaudeville. Llewellyn Jones was less harsh, but he also preferred the quieter poems. Yet he felt that some of Lindsay's tributes might well be grouped together into a kind of American hagiography. T. K. Whipple in *Spokesmen* asserted categorically that Lindsay was the author of *six* poems, the chosen six including of course all the famous bravura pieces plus "The Chinese Nightingale." Writing in 1928, only three years before the poet's death, Whipple could say, "His achievement has not yet been commensurate with his possibilities." Stephen Graham in a kind of obituary letter alluded to Lindsay's bitter disillusionment in love and to his deliberating grief at the time his mother died; he also termed Lindsay the greatest American poet of his age. Willard Thorp wrote in the *Literary History of the United States* that the twenty or so of Lindsay's poems which the poet's audiences clamored to hear over and over again "are as exciting as when they were first declaimed." William Rose Benét was convinced that Lindsay's best work would be read with admiration by posterity at the very time that he as the editor of an important literary periodical was constrained to refuse the poet's latest productions.

Ludwig Lewisohn, William Marion Reedy, and Carl Van Doren all thought highly of Lindsay's gifts although none was willing to deny obvious imperfections. In *Many Minds* Van Doren pointed out Lindsay's limited range but praised him for his free use of the American language, for his willingness to introduce a new idiom into poetic practice. Edgar Lee Masters cited nine poems as being among the poet's best, added another twenty as being significant, and concluded that collectively these poems constituted "the most considerable body of imaginative lyricism that any American has produced." To offset this enthusiasm one might allude to Allen Tate's cautious assertion that Lindsay's early poems had an original rhythm but that his use of language was undistinguished and his poetic subjects on the whole rather dull. Horace Gregory and Marya Zaturenska in their *History of American Poetry* quote liberally and approvingly from Lindsay, although they discourage anyone from reading through the *Collected Poems* and feel that some of the verse would not have been allowed to stand if Lindsay himself had been a more reliable self-critic. It is interesting that they found "I Heard Immanuel Singing"—a poem which Lindsay himself treasured—a valuable and interesting American spiritual.

In one of the last poems of the late Theodore Roethke, entitled "Supper with Lindsay," the author imagined Lindsay stepping into his chamber carrying the moon under his arm and deluging the furniture with a flood of creamy light. The two poets ate a meal of homely food together—corn bread, cold roast beef, and ice cream—until the lunar glow began to fade. With that change Lindsay decided that the feast was over and rose to depart, asking as he did so to be remembered to William Carlos Williams and Robert Frost. Of the three names Lindsay's in his time was the best known, as celebrated as a platform performer and declaimer as the Russian poet Andrei Voznesensky is today. Lindsay's verse has earned him a permanent place in American literature, and future anthologists who deny him that place will reflect only their own myopic vision.

WILLIAMS'S PATERSON
AND THE MEASURE OF ART
Bernard I. Duffey

Duke University

Although William Carlos Williams is still insisted upon as a poet of things only, a poet of the noun, it seems more evident that the course of his poetry reflects a varying imbalance between the world and the poet's own mind. In many cases the weight swings in favor of the world. Imagist tenets have their way, and mind is subordinated to what it beholds. But "Objectivism" for Williams was a declaration of the poem's self-sufficiency[1] as well as its rooting in things, and sometimes, as in "The Yachts," there is a kind of stand-off in which mind at first effaces itself to serve as a sensing medium only but later reasserts creative independence at the expense of distorting, of making the world over in its own momentary image and so producing a vision blurred between the two. Some poems are plainly didactic. Throughout, the pervading drama is that of idea, as theme or form, counterpointed against things. And nowhere is it more plain than in the longer poems, especially the first four books of *Paterson*.

A most elusive entity there is the reality of the central noun image itself. Town, mankind, poet, doctor, or the city's masses, the name's references shift again and again. The roar of the falls drowns out clear hearing just as their flood and spray forbid plain sight. Or the rush of the stream carries everything past and away before one can really see. Frederick Eckman has suggested the dominance of a verb rather than a noun effect in Williams, of motion and change rather than presence, and however this may be with the individual shorter poems, it exercises a strong power in *Paterson*.

Each of the first four books has a recurrent image of veiling or vanishing as its most obvious unifying force. In the first it is the

1. Cf. the comment in his essay "Marianne Moore" in *Selected Essays* (New York, 1954), p. 125. "But what I wish to point [sic] is that there need be no stilled and archaic heaven, no ducking under religiosities to have poetry and to have it stand in its place beyond 'nature.' Poems have a separate existence uncompelled by nature or the supernatural. There is a 'special' place which poems, as all works of art, must occupy, but it is quite definitely the same as that where bricks or colored threads are handled."

stream of history containing the manifold events, the things of the poem. In the second there is the poet's walk through the park which brings more events and, especially, the evangelist whose sermon gushes forth a message of divine riches never realized outside the sadly ironic flow of its own sentiments. In the third book the Babel of the library is silenced only by the holocaust that seemingly burns up library and town alike, and, in the fourth, personal disintegration is matched by atomic and economic breakdown and apparent death in the sea except for a lone swimmer who makes an ambiguous way to shore and his future: but, "the future's no answer," declares the poet, "I must/find my meaning—or succumb."[2]

If there is no answer in the future, there is only a hazy reality in past or present. Williams's "things" in *Paterson* are very sparse in themselves, insubstantial and inherently unsuggestive of much except surface characteristics. In this they resemble objects in his shorter poems. Locust trees, snow lying on the ground, workmen or idlers, lakes, spring shoots, an old woman eating plums, fountains, multitudinous birds, flowers, and plants, and images of the poet himself pop up and down in a verse where the charm of everything lies in the moment rather than in dominating presence or dwelt-upon actuality. To look at one of the shorter poems by itself is, most often, like looking at a sketch whose detail, relations, and import are only tentatively suggested, and to read through a group of the shorter poems is to experience a *perpetuum mobile* (in the phrase Williams used as a title) not very unlike reading *Paterson* itself.

Despite his occasional parallels to Joyce, the town of Paterson is not a Dublin for the American. A falls, a bridge, a park, industry (generalized), occasional buildings or streets, these are most of what we get of the city in an effect vastly different from the Dublin of *Ulysses* and different even more from the Dublin, or the rivers, of *Finnegans Wake* where things and ideas are without question bound to each other in words alone. Williams is an impressionist, simplifying language, using it to catch onto a few flamboyant shapes and colors for whatever immediate arrest of attention compels him. But he is also an impressionist with a message, and as a result his poem

2. *Paterson* (New York, [1963]), p. 173. In future references to Williams's work the following abbreviations will be used: *P, Paterson; CEP, Collected Early Poems* (New York, [1951]); *CLP, Collected Later Poems* (revised edition; New York, [1963]); *PB, Pictures from Breughel* (New York, [1962]); *SE, Selected Essays* (New York, 1954); *SL, Selected Letters* (New York, [1957]); *W, I Wanted to Write a Poem* (New York, 1958).

grows into an argument. It posits ideas, supplies examples, and draws conclusions.

It would not be outrageously paradoxical to suggest of *Paterson* I-IV that it presents few things but in ideas, that it is the forms themselves of meaningless flux, unreal stasis, and the poet's despair of language which are really the generative force for his images. In Book One, Part I, for example, the people associated with Paterson are set forth as automatons, and as automatons they are made to act, "Who because they/neither know their sources nor the sills of their /disappointments walk outside their bodies aimlessly/for the most part" (*P*, 14). The second part of Book One then contemplates history as a possible source of meaning but rejects it because such learning rejects experience: "Divorce is/the sign of knowledge in our time/divorce! divorce!" (*P*, 28), and there follow some dozen images of divorce. In the third part, argument is raised a degree into allegory, but earth as the "father of all speech" is seen only dimly under the flood of false speech and false learning which enshrouds him.

The poem is not so much lyric or epic as it is a book of parables showing mind and will fallen from a sovereign place in the kingdom of experience. Sister M. Bernetta Quinn has seen *Paterson* as the expression of idealistic mind denied its office. "In the Word alone is life," she notes, referring to logos as reason or thought, "and the contemporary Paterson feels that Word to be inaccessible." Williams's imagination cannot really trust things here despite its affirmations to itself because it cannot find itself reflected in them. It can only behold their existence outside itself. The result is unhappiness apprehended as a sense of poetic failure: one suggested by the "lame or limping iambics" (*P*, 53) cited from John Addington Symonds at the end of Book One; by the ironic self-injunction toward the end of Book Two, "Go home. Write. Compose./Ha!/Be reconciled, poet, with your world, it is/the only truth!/Ha!/—the language is worn out" (*P*, 103); by the distant comfort, "in a hundred years, perhaps—/the syllables," (*P*, 171) at the end of Book Three; or by the nostalgic cry of Book Four,

> Oh that the rocks of the Areopagus had
> kept their sounds, the voices of the law!
> Or that the great theater of Dionysius
> could be aroused by some modern magic
> to release

> what is bound in it, stones!
> that music might be wakened from them to
> melt our ears.
>
> (*P*, 235)

Paterson, in these passages and many like them, takes a place in that long line of laments for failed imagination heralded by Coleridge's "Dejection, an Ode" or, in America, by Poe's "Israfel."

The subject of *Paterson* I-IV is not things, though these are its occasions. It is rather the dejection of the idealistic imagination, conning one more time its own inability to raise the show of things to the desires of the mind. I am suggesting, thus, my agreement with those views of the poem which have seen its unity as one essentially of parallel themes developed by examples, though the same argument may also suggest that it is too long, that its whole substance is brought into view well before its conclusion. Certainly the parallelisms forward this recognition. As history can redeem nothing in Book One, neither can religion in Book Two, the library or the fire in Book Three, or the world of science or economics in Book Four. None of these is of use within the world of Paterson itself, or to the poet's search for his language, and their failure becomes increasingly predictable as the poem unfolds.

Paterson I-IV presents no alternative to failure. Elsewhere, in verses like "The Botticellian Trees" or "Burning the Christmas Greens," the subject had undergone a change natural to its circumstances, and one in which the poet found progress and form. Coherence lay in natural change itself. In his poem titled "Lear" Williams wrote about such trust in the nature of things:

> When the world takes over for us
> and the storm in the trees
> replaces our brittle consciences
> (like ships female to all seas)
> when the few last yellow leaves
> stand out like flags on tossed ships
> at anchor—our minds are rested.
>
> (*CLP*, 237)

To set *Paterson* I-IV off against these more integral uses of what Mrs. Linda Wagner calls the "transitional metaphor," against poems whose meaning is a reflection of natural process in its human aspect, suggests an important but shifting operation of the pathetic fallacy. "The Botticellian Trees" welcomes the trees' change from winter bareness to summer opulence as a metamorphosis of abstract language into full reality and of male into female. In such a poem the world does take over for the poet and for us and, in doing so, forms the poem. *Paterson* I-IV, in turn, operates on a middle but not very happy ground created by the discovery and multiplication of elements decisively foreign or hostile to the mind's desires, an alien or blank process inaccessible to understanding or fellow feeling, capped by the totally unassimilable image of the sea "which is *not* us."

Williams occasionally reaches something like an opposite condition, suggested perhaps in "Choral: The Pink Church," where the poet's mind attempts to accept its own idealistic loyalties as normative. The poetic cost of this third phase is great, however. To celebrate abstract loyalties in a verse designed to cope with concrete and personal experience is to risk a variety of failures, and "The Pink Church," along with *Paterson* I-IV, achieves its share. One is confusion of meaning as the abstract and concrete awarenesses jostle against each other:

> Sing!
> transparent to the light
> through which the light
> shines, through the stone,
> until
> the stone light glows,
> pink jade
> —that is the light and is a stone
> and is a church—if the image
> hold . . .
>
> (*CLP*, 159-160)

I think it doubtful that the image does hold in this case, and that such failure of fusion parallels the incoherence of *Paterson* I-IV, an inability to raise the pathetic fallacy; here to put light and stone together and by them suggest something out of nature properly discernible as a church. Another risk, when the poem leaves nature out, is stridency and sloganizing. Or, when the poem at its close bears down on poetic and political positions without exactly depending on them, there is the risk of a smudged invocation of party lines— dimming them to an even remoter degree of abstraction than their original one:

> Joy! Joy!
> —out of Elysium!
> —chanted loud as a chorus from
> the Agonistes—

> Milton, the unrhymer,
> singing among
> the rest ...
> like a Communist
> (*CLP*, 162)

Perhaps "The Pink Church" strives for what Theodore Roethke once admired under the name of "sophisticated looniness," but it also strives for rather heavy spiritual affirmation, and the two aims clash. There is no container for them, no single medium within which they can work together.

Such, at any rate, is the suggestion of *Paterson* V (1958) and the poems collected in *Pictures from Breughel* (1962) as they turn away from nature and abstract ideas to draw a large share of their themes and images from music, painting, and other literature. Glauco Cambon has suggested that *Paterson* I-IV had washed itself clean of aestheticism in the dirty Passaic, but the later poems affirm a new-found dependence, a newly discovered parent imagination in art. Such a change in content is paralleled by Williams's growing concern with "measure," most immediately the rhythm of his own verse as experimentation carried him toward a degree of regular form in the "variable foot." But metrical concern is only one expression of the larger idea defined in capital letters and italics at the beginning of *Paterson* V.

> "What has happened to Paris
> since that time?
> and to myself"?
>
> A WORLD OF ART
> THAT THROUGH THE YEARS HAS
> *SURVIVED*!
> (*P*, 243-244)

And, as Book Five progresses, it seems clear not only that a world of art has survived, but that it has come to heal the nature-mind divorce of Books I-IV. The composite Paterson vanishes out of the poem except for a single reference, and the word otherwise is used only to mean the poet himself. In place of its earlier associations comes another kind of catalogue. There is Toulouse-Lautrec, to whom the poem is dedicated, who made his own kind of wittily re-deeming measure. He is followed by Lorca, the Unicorn tapestry of the Cloisters (which becomes a new central image), Philippe Sou-pault, Audubon, Jackson Pollock, Ben Shahn, Ezra Pound, Mezz

Mezzrow, the dance (a second extended image), Gertrude Stein, Paul Klee, Arabic art, Dürer, Leonardo, Bosch, Picasso, Juan Gris, Beethoven, and Breughel himself. Most of these become examples of the artist's power to make the world his home whether it be in Toulouse-Lautrec's brothels or Jackson Pollock's world of pure paint.

This particular use of art to the poet is suggested in the excerpt he includes in *Paterson* V from an interview with Mike Wallace. As he uses art to reshape his own world, he eases himself away from the starkness of encounter prevailing in the earlier work and discovers the possibility of a poetry sufficient to itself as it is sufficient to its creator.

Q. Mr. Williams, can you tell me, simply, what poetry is?

A. Well ... I would say that poetry is language charged with emotion. It's words, rhythmically organized. ... A poem is a complete little universe. It exists separately. Any poem that has worth expresses the whole life of the poet. It gives a view of what the poet is. (*P*, 261)

One can only guess how aware Williams may have been of his combined use and alteration of Pound's formula, "language charged with meaning" to "language charged with emotion." But the formula in itself suggests his awareness of shifting from the pragmatic and mimetic intent of the earlier parts of the poem to an expressive one, of abandoning the outright reconciling of people with stones for the different and more congenial function of creativity, declared and exhibited as such. The change does not remake *Paterson*, but it eases the overwhelming burden of Books I-IV, the stark, unaided effort at harmonizing mind and the jumble of circumstance.

To recognize art as an act only of imagining and forming within mind itself is to liberate creativity from impossible tasks. This Kant-like doctrine is at the center of Williams's new awareness. As the transcendental aesthetic was for Kant a freedom obtainable without affecting the real limits of pure or practical reason, so Williams's imagination, on the evidence of art, is a freedom of mind attainable within a world still defined by idea and experience. Art does not become a means of special knowledge. It does become the area within which mind can exercise itself in the limits and attainments of its own measuring nature. Williams made this explicit in a letter of 1955 to John C. Thirlwall.

But in the arts, the art of the poem, lie resources, which when we become aware of their existence make it possible for us to liberate ourselves, or so I believe and think. ...

The first thing you learn when you begin to learn anything about this earth is that you are eternally barred save for the report of your senses from knowing anything about it. Measure serves for us as the key; we can measure between objects; therefore we know they exist. Poetry began with measure, it began with the dance, whose divisions we have all but forgotten. . . . (*SL*, 330-332, *passim*)

Pictures from Breughel, from the title poems on, is largely an exploration out and into this sense of poetry, the plainest token of which is its frequent return to art objects as touchstones of accomplished thought or feeling. With great frequency, it achieves through them the junctures whose failure was the burden of the first four books of *Paterson*. "How shall we get said what must be said?" Williams asks in "The Desert Music" (*PB*, 108-109). The question is familiar in its repetition, but there is now an answer.

> Only the poem.
>
> Only the counted poem, to an exact measure:
> to imitate, not to copy nature, not
> to copy nature
>
> NOT, prostrate, to copy nature
>
>   but a dance! to dance
> two and two with him—
>
>   sequestered there asleep,
>   right end up!
>
>   (*PB*, 108-109)

Whether the sleeping Mexican of "The Desert Music" is like the sleeping Paterson, or, being "right end up," different, Williams's lines here find an Aristotelian formula of parallel measure between nature and art that declares creation to be possible.

The metrical experimentation that had marked all his work continues on into this poetry of the last two volumes, and the poems themselves continue to function as associative wholes, though they gain a new framework for association. But "Measure," here, goes beyond metrics to relate poetry to a perennial creative enterprise, and personal association is given an impersonal backing. Williams's sparrow still cries out lustily, but his crying is "a trait/more related to music/than otherwise" (*PB*, 129), and his "image/is familiar as that of the aristocratic/unicorn" (*PB*, 130). A woman fussing with her hair is a "classic picture" (*PB*, 142), and the hitherto intractable sea calls to mind "the *Iliad*/and Helen's public fault/that bred it" (*PB*, 158). Through measure, our experience of it combined with a constant imagining of it, even the sea may be taken into account, for art and life both.

> There is no power
> so great as love
> which is a sea,
>
> which is a garden—
> as enduring
> as the verses
>
> of that blind old man,
> destined
> to live forever
> (*PB*, 166)

These lines are an associative sequence almost exactly like the first of my quotations from "The Pink Church," but their allusion to Homer puts an image of achieved and admirable order-in-chaos between the pattern of nature and the pattern of feeling instead of leading from nature through personal feeling to a largely wishful postulation of order. Personal acts of discovery need not bear the form of the poem, or its truth, by themselves. Homer has written of the power of love and of the sea, and his verses, which are like a garden, can be invoked by the poet as the defining part of an environment.

Williams had discovered a kind of allusion useful to his poetry as Pound's and Eliot's had been to theirs. Before about 1950 two Americans had lain heavily in his awareness. With Walt Whitman he acknowledged somewhat grudgingly a sense of shared dilemma, and he had taken Poe's radical loneliness as prototypical of American poetry. But the later work indicates a change. Poetry is still to be of his own time and place, but these, unlike Whitman's vision of himself especially, are included in a contemporary world of art. In the idea of art things and thoughts (still existing to themselves) can be seen integrally, under an aspect of contemplation rather than estrangement. Williams's sense of art is more like Poe's, though it is much more richly furnished. In it the idealistic imagination can live freely as it cannot do in the realm of pure fact.

Art works poetically for Williams like a recasting of nature, or the finding of a second nature, of something to "take over for us" in the failure of mind's power to reclaim its alienation. It is thus more an aspect of poetic relation than any advance into new language or new values as such. Paterson shrinks from his somewhat pretentious vagueness into the one form that had always really been his, that of the poet's perception seeking peace with itself. What the exercise of the pathetic fallacy or of moral idealism had failed to sustain, the power of a comparing, measuring imagination might accomplish. Imagination comes to see the need and use of a harmony to be achieved in imagination itself. This is, for example, the idea of later love poems like "The Ivy Crown" and "Asphodel, That Greeny Flower." Their whole substance is imagination conceived as the fabric of love.

> Medieval pageantry
>   is human and we enjoy
>   the rumor of it
>
> as in our world we enjoy
>   the reading of Chaucer,
>   likewise
>
> a priest's raiment
>   (or that of a savage chieftain).
>   It is all
>
> a celebration of the light.
>   All the pomp and ceremony
>   of weddings,
>
> "Sweet Thames, run softly
>   till I end
>   my song,"—
> Are of an equal sort.
>   (*PB,* 181)

And whatever of sharp encounter may be lacking in this later poetry is to be compensated for by something at last discovered and adhered to.

> Light, the imagination
>   and love
>   in one age,
>
> by natural law,
>   which we worship,
>   maintain
>
> all of a piece
>   their dominance
>   (*PB,* 180)

Here the figure of light means something like sensation or experience, imagination the measuring or comparing activity of art, and love the fruit of the two. Under this total aspect, experience can be conceived freely and in an achieved relation.

Is such an idea too sentimental, the retreat of an old and ailing man into cliché? On some occasions it can sound that way. The figure of the dance, as Hugh Kenner noted in his review of *Paterson, Book V*, seems all too available, but the idea of dance had been one of Williams's earliest as well as one of his later ideas of art. He had made the claim as early as *Kora in Hell*, and repeated it throughout the pages of that volume of 1920. Speaking against the simile, urging the need for sensing particulars as such, he yet maintained a need for imagined relation, for measure.

All is confusion, yet it comes from a hidden desire for the dance.
But one does not attempt by the ingenuity of the joiner to blend the tones of the oboe with the violin. On the contrary, the perfection of the two instruments is emphasized by the joiner; no means is neglected to give to each the full color of its perfections. It is only the music of the instruments which is joined, and that not by the woodworker but by the composer, by virtue of the imagination.
On this level of the imagination all things and ages meet in fellowship. Thus only can they, peculiar and perfect, find their release. This is the beneficent power of the imagination. (*SE*, 15)

And *Kora* was "the one book I have enjoyed referring to more than any of the others," Williams said. "It reveals myself to me" (*W*, 26).

In the place of simile, too bindingly explicit an analogy, Williams this early postulated the freer measuring activity of art figured here as dance or the shifting relation of discrete things. His idea was certainly not very different in theory or practice from Pound's "superimposition" of images. But the measure of art, the patterning of complementary or contrasting images, contained a principle of poetic self-sufficiency which over the years of his writing Williams had mixed with the pathetic fallacy or with even more outright thematic principles like those of "The Pink Church." In such cases, the poem inhered partly in the measure of art, or the free shaping of images, and partly in the assertion of ideas. *Kora in Hell*, perhaps, revealed more of the poet to himself as it, more than any other text, allowed for a free dance of mind in relation to its objects.

Dance reappeared briefly in Williams's next volume, *Sour Grapes* (1921), in "Overture to a Dance of Locomotives."

> Gliding windows. Colored cooks sweating
> in a small kitchen. Taillights—
>
> In time: twofour!
> In time: twoeight!

—rivers are tunneled: trestles
cross oozy swampland: wheels repeating
the same gesture remain relatively
stationary: rails forever parallel
return on themselves infinitely.
                                        The dance is sure

                    (*CEP*, 195)

Here again the figure asserted is freedom to organize the descriptive detail of the train in motion according to a free selection and patterning of detail, images juxtaposed like those of a cinematic montage. In *Spring and All* (1923), Neil Myers has argued, the theme itself of the volume is to be found in its shattering of the "natural" image in favor of new and cubistic designs. Certainly the awakening force of spring in "On the Road to the Contagious Hospital," the poem opening the sequence, is measured off not only against the equally asseverant forces of disease implied in the title but also against the "pink confused with white" of a pot of flowers in the poem which follows. The same measure continues into poem three where "the artist figure of/the farmer" stands in early spring "composing" his fields against their natural inclination to wilderness.

Paterson I-IV, unlike these works, had been shaped in what might be called the mixed mode of Williams's composition. Its assertive logical core was an explicitly developed essay on the poet's difficulties with a world of experience to which none of the analogies for poetry available to him seemed very congruent, and it also contained an abundance of imagery. But though some of this latter seemed patterned according to its own inherent suggestiveness, more lay under control by the theme. *Paterson* V changed the theme to assert the measure of art as an aesthetic idea stemming from the "WORLD OF ART/THAT THROUGH THE YEARS HAS SURVIVED." The sensuous and aesthetic was saved from its own dissolution by being made explicitly into a world of its own reference sufficient to itself as a mode of order. Art survives where nothing else has. The measure of art became the highest organization of human experience, the genetrix of beauty, and of comprehension, freedom, and love.

Williams's measure of art was a sufficient relation of things, discerned despite their failure to speak a logical or pragmatic relationship in themselves. It was a marriage ritual of otherwise separate or fleeting impressions. Imagining the sea as a garden by virtue of its likeness to Homer's poetry would be truer to art than rejecting the sea flatly as chaos, because such measuring was the idea of art. The poet, Williams had told Mike Wallace, makes his own world, and he now declared the principle by which such a world could be made.

Williams's late poetry could achieve few if any unconditional victories over experience, but that effort had been the weakness of "The Pink Church" as despair of it had plagued the first four books of *Paterson*. What was needed more, in any case, was the forming of objects for the mind so that the mind need not instantly be defeated by them and so of avoiding the fool's mate of despair. The measure of art was the practice of an aesthetic freedom among the given particulars of nature. And now, beyond that, it became the aesthetic principle itself validated by the world of art within which the poet had grown.

DASHIELL HAMMETT
THEMES AND TECHNIQUES
Walter Blair

University of Chicago

I

The influence of subliterary works (sentimental fiction and poetry, popular humor, melodrama, and the like) on literary works, or the ways literary works shape subliterature often are fascinating. Without Gothic fiction Poe and Hawthorne would have been impossible; without Scott and Dickens nineteenth-century American humor, with all its vulgarity, could not have been written. An instance is the career of Dashiell Hammett (1894-1961), writer of detective fiction. Two uncertainties furnish difficulties but add interest to a consideration of him: (1) the possibility that Hammett's writings, despite their genre, are good enough to classify not as subliterature but as literature, and (2) the impossibility of one's being sure about the precise direction of the influence—about who influenced whom. Regardless, affiliations between the detective story fictionist and some of his more reputable contemporaries, particularly Ernest Hemingway, have great interest, and in his best novel, Hammett brilliantly, and I think uniquely, adapted current techniques to his genre.

Hammett's lasting popularity and repute suggest that his work may be of more than ephemeral value. Having crowded practically all his writing into a decade, he published practically nothing after January, 1934. But between that date and his death twenty-seven years later, his novels and collected short stories sold four million copies in paperback editions; three of his novels (*Red Harvest,* 1929; *The Dain Curse,* 1929; and *The Maltese Falcon,* 1930) were collected in an *Omnibus* in 1935; and *The Complete Novels* (the three above plus *The Glass Key,* 1931, and *The Thin Man,* 1934) appeared in 1942. A few months after Hammett's death, a million copies in paperback of his various works were issued; in October,

1965, *The Novels of Dashiell Hammett* was reset and printed from new plates; in June, 1966, his *The Big Knockover: Selected Stories and Short Novels* appeared;[1] and, the following month, three of his novels (*Glass Key, Falcon, Thin Man*) were reissued in paperback editions.[2]

The nature of the critical acclaim that accompanied such successes raises the strong possibility that something more than sensational appeals was responsible. Granted, a share of these sales may well have been stimulated by portrayals of Hammett's characters in popular movies, in radio and television series, even in comic strips. But surely a good share was stimulated by Hammett's remarkable— perhaps unique—reputation.

Indicative of the nature of this is the fact that *The Maltese Falcon* went through at least fifteen printings as part of a prestigious collection, the Modern Library. Indicative, too, is the esteem in which the author was held by enthusiastic readers who belonged to a rather unusual group. Detective stories for about five decades (since World War I) were read, liked, and discussed by many professional men, political leaders, pundits, and professors. As a result, a genre of subliterature was assessed and in some instances praised by highly influential—as well as perceptive and articulate—readers. The admiration of these readers for Hammett's writings has been consistently strong and widespread. In addition, leading reviewers of mystery novels and informed historians of the genre such as Howard Haycraft and Ellery Queen, and famous practitioners such as Raymond Chandler and Erle Stanley Gardner habitually and casually—as if there were no possible question about the matter—referred to him as the greatest writer in his field, perhaps even "a genius."[3] Finally, respected literary men not as a rule much interested in mystery fiction manifested warm admiration for Hammett— Somerset Maugham, Peter Quennell, and Robert Graves of England;

1. Previously nine books of his short stories had been collected in paperback editions by Ellery Queen.

2. Raymond Chandler, another adept and highly praised (and a more prolific) author of detective novels, died in 1959. Since that year, he has been commemorated in a scholarly biography and a collection of his letters and articles. In 1966 nine of his books in paperback, two novels in hardcover printings, and an *Omnibus* (published in 1965) were in print.

3. "*The Maltese Falcon* may or may not be a work of genius, but . . . . Once a detective story can be as good as this, only the pedants will deny that it *could* even be better."—Howard Haycraft. "I think that of all the early pulp writers who contributed to the new format of the detective story, the word 'genius' was more applicable to Hammett than to any of the rest."—Erle Stanley Gardner.

André Malraux and André Gide of France; and a trio of American Nobel prize winners—Sinclair Lewis, William Faulkner, and Ernest Hemingway. Quennell in 1934 correctly remarked that Hammett was almost alone among mystery writers "in being praised by writers as a serious writer and by good novelists as a master of their business."

II

Available details about Hammett's life before he began to write indicate that it provided unusual and exploitable experiences but scant training for a writing career. Born in 1894 in St. Mary's County on the eastern shore of Maryland, he attended a technical school, Baltimore Polytechnic Institute, and was a dropout from its non-literary program at thirteen. During the next several years he had a number of quite unliterary jobs—messenger, newsboy, freight clerk, timekeeper, stevedore, yardman, and machine operator. After that for eight years he was an operative for the Pinkerton Detective Agency, his chief literary exercises presumably being the writing of reports on his cases.[4] He then served during World War I as a sergeant in the ambulance corps. After emerging from the war with damaged lungs and after a period of hospitalization and a brief return to detective work, he began to make use of remembrances of his sleuthing in articles and stories.

His writings were first published early in the 1920's, some in *Pearson's Magazine*, some, unpredictably, in H. L. Mencken's *Smart Set*, most of them in a pulp mystery magazine, *Black Mask*. At first the writings attracted little attention, in part it may be because one Carroll John Daly had briefly preceded Hammett in writing what would in time be dubbed hard-boiled detective stories,[5] in part because the importance of originating this genre was not recognized or at least discussed at the time, in part because before long other writers (Gardner, for instance) began to publish similar stories. Then an editor, Joseph T. Shaw, decided that since Hammett was "the leader in the thought that finally brought the magazine its distinctive form," he should be featured and the featuring, coupled with Hammett's outstanding talent, gave his stories pre-eminence. And when

4. Two cases on which he worked were those of Nicky Arnstein and Fatty Arbuckle.
5. Daly's pioneer creation was Private Operative Race Williams, worldly wise, hard-boiled, and laconic. "The papers," said Race, poetically, "are always either roasting me for shooting down some minor criminals or praising me for gunning out the big shots. But when you're hunting the top guy, you have to kick aside—or shoot aside—the gunman he hires. You can't make hamburgers without grinding up a little meat."

between 1929 and 1934, Hammett's five novels were published by Alfred A. Knopf and individually and collectively were enthusiastically praised far and wide, justifiably or no, he came to be known as the founder of the school.

The short stories as well as the more famous novels in time were appreciated for their innovations. For, drawing upon memories of his Pinkerton career, Hammett pictured crime and the work of a private operative (so everybody said) in a much more "real" fashion than they had been pictured before; and since the first-person narrator in many stories was a detective and since in all the stories the dialogue was largely that of dicks and criminals he used an economical vernacular style which seemed unusually lifelike.

Especially when compared with that of earlier mystery stories, Hammett's subject matter was revolutionary. From the time of their most venerable ancestor, Poe's C. Auguste Dupin, leading fictional detectives had been gentlemen and they had been erudite. In 1927, in a review of a book about one of the most exquisite and purportedly learned of such sleuths, Hammett himself scoffs at the type and at the ignorance of its portrayers about crime:

> This Philo Vance is in the Sherlock Holmes tradition.... He is a bore when he discusses art and philosophy, but when he switches to criminal psychology he is delightful. There is a theory that anyone who talks enough on any subject must, if only by chance, finally say something not altogether incorrect. Vance disproves this theory: he manages always, and usually ridiculously, to be wrong. His exposition of the technique employed by a gentleman shooting another gentleman who sits six feet in front of him deserves a place in a *How to be a detective by mail* course.[6]

Raymond Chandler praised Hammett for doing away with the unrealities here attacked:

> Hammett gave murder back to the kind of people that commit it for reasons, not just to provide a corpse; and with the means at hand, not with hand-wrought duelling pistols, curare, and tropical fish. He put them down on paper as they are, and made them talk and think in the language they customarily used for these purposes.

The linking of matter that is "real" ("put them down on paper *as they are*") with a style that is "real" occurs in much of the praise of the detective story writer. Chandler further remarks that at its best the style "is the American language."

6. Review of *The Benson Murder Case, Saturday Review of Literature*, Jan. 15, 1927. Hammett also is critical of the author's manner of writing: "The book is written in the little-did-he-realize style."

Anyone familiar with discussions of developments in presumably more serious American fiction during the 1920's will recognize oft-repeated concerns—with the increased "reality" of the matter and with the "Americanization" of the style. Edmund Wilson saw both in Ernest Hemingway's earliest fiction and mentioned them in a *Dial* review of it in October, 1924. "Too proud an artist to simplify in the interest of conventional pretenses," went one sentence, "he [Hemingway] is showing you what life is like." Elsewhere:

... Miss Stein, Mr. Anderson, and Mr. Hemingway may now be said to form a school by themselves. The characteristic of this school is a naïveté of language, often passing into the colloquialism of the character dealt with. ... It is a distinctively American development in prose—as opposed to more or less successful American achievements in the traditional style of English prose. ...

After *Red Harvest* appeared in 1929, critics of Hammett frequently compared him to Hemingway. "It is doubtful," wrote Herbert Asbury in a review of that first novel, "if even Hemingway has ever written more effective dialogue. ... The author displays a style of amazing clarity and compactness, devoid of literary frills and furbelows, and his characters speak the crisp, hard-boiled language of the underworld ... truly, without a single false or jarring note." Gide asserted that the author's dialogues "can be compared [among American writers] only with the best in Hemingway." Peter Quennell held that the last of the novels, *The Thin Man* of 1934, provides interior evidence that Hammett admired Hemingway, since it "contains portraits, snatches of dialogue written in a terse colloquial vein —and lurid glimpses of New York drinking society, that Hemingway himself could not have improved upon."

Quennell was not alone in believing that Hemingway influenced Hammett, but a few critics wondered whether Hammett might not have influenced Hemingway. Gide said that some of Hammett's dialogues could "give pointers to Hemingway or even Faulkner." However, since both authors began to write and to publish obscurely almost simultaneously, the likelihood appears to be that neither shaped the earlier writings of the other. And by the time each had mastered his craft, the possibility of either shaping the work of the other was very small. Resemblances arose more probably because of similarities in temperament, in experiences, and in background.[7]

7. Joseph Haas in a review of *The Big Knockover* in the Chicago *Daily News,* June 18, 1966, writes: "It seems probable that neither man was familiar with the works of

Not only were the two alike in picturing a world that met the post-World War I demand for "more reality" and in using a style that was "more laconic" and "more colloquial"; they were alike in other important ways. Wounded by the war and unhappy in the postwar world, both were battered by disillusionment and cynicism, and both created worlds and characters justifying their attitude. Their protagonists are forced to cope with such worlds and their inhabitants. "Hemingway's favorite characters," André Maurois has noticed, "are men who deal with death and accept its risk": the same remark of course could be made about Hammett's favorite characters. Moreover, as Joseph Haas recently remarked, "Their similarities don't end there, either. Their heroes were much alike, and we find it easy to put Sam Spade in Jake Barnes' place, or to imagine that Robert Jordan and the Continental Op[erator] could have become good friends. They all lived by that simple, sentimental code of loyalty, courage and cynicism in a world of betrayal." Many discussions of Hemingway's morality indicate that his code was a rather more complex one than Haas suggests; and so, I venture to say, was Hammett's. Interestingly, both men were accused from time to time of having no standards—probably because they both were contemptuous of many pre-World War I standards and because they both admiringly portrayed heroes who were. Oscar Handlin has said of Hammett's heroes: "Their virtues were distinctly personal—courage, dignity, and patience; and to them the hero clung for their own sake, not because the client for whom he fought had any worth. Honor to Sam Spade was conformity to a code of rules which he himself invented, a means of demonstrating his own worth against the world." The same, or something very like it, could be said of the codes of Hemingway's heroes.

Both men's lives were shaped by similar personal codes. That Hemingway's life was has been clearly demonstrated. Hammett's code compelled him at the age of forty-eight to enlist in the United States army for service in World War II and to carry out a dull assignment in the Aleutians not only with meticulous care but with gusto. Lillian Hellmann tells of another instance in 1951:

He had made up honor early in his life and stuck with his rules, fierce in his protection of them. In 1951 he went to jail because he and two other trustees of the bail bond fund of the Civil Rights Congress refused

the other, in those [early] years. What is likely is that their like approaches to prose were the products of two similar minds affected by comparable influences."

to reveal the names of the contributors to the fund. The truth was that Hammett had never been in the office of the Committee and did not know the name of a single contributor. The night before he was to appear in court, I said, "Why don't you say that you don't know the names?" "No," he said, "I can't say that. . . . I guess it has something to do with keeping my word . . . but . . . if it were my life, I would give it for what I think democracy is and I don't let cops or judges tell me what I think democracy is."

He served a term of six months in a federal prison.

The codes of both Hemingway and Hammett related not only to their lives but also to their writing. "The great thing," remarked the former in 1932, "is to last and get your work done and see and learn and understand; and write when there is something that you know." In a late uncompleted story, "Tulip,"[8] a character obviously voicing Hammett's opinions states a similar belief that an author must write only about matters that have real significance for him. The speaker, a professional fictionist, has never written a word about some of his experiences: "Why? All I can say is that they're not for me. Maybe not yet, maybe not ever. I used to try now and then . . . but they never came out meaning very much to me."

Both authors believed strongly that harsh self-discipline was an essential to good writing. Hemingway did not go to Stockholm to receive the Nobel prize in 1954 because he refused to interrupt his writing of a novel that was going well. His manuscripts attest to the fact that, word by word, he wrote with infinite care. Lillian Hellmann testifies that, when writing a novel (*The Thin Man*), Hammett similarly let the task of composition possess him: "Life changed: the drinking stopped, the parties were over. The locking-in time had come and nothing was allowed to disturb it until the book was finished. I had never seen anybody work that way: the care for every word, the pride in the neatness of the typed page itself, the refusal for ten days or two weeks to go out even for a walk for fear something would be lost."

III

During the last few decades probably no other aspect of the technique of fiction has loomed as large in the concerns of critics and the conscious creative procedures of authors as the fictional point of view. Fictionists as different—and as influential—as Mark Twain and a bit later Henry James independently noticed the tremendous

8. First published in *The Big Knockover* in 1966.

significance the choice of this had in shaping their fiction. James, and after James many leading critics, have discussed exhaustively the authors' or the narrators' insights into characters' thoughts and feelings, and the authors' or the narrators' biases and attitudes, as the narratives reveal them. Often the discussions have been very illuminating.

In about twenty-five short stories and in the first two of Hammett's novels, *Red Harvest* and *The Dain Curse,* the first-person narrator and the solver of the puzzle is an operative employed by the Continental Detective Agency. Unlike the exquisites of chiefly ratiocinative mystery stories this man (whose name is never revealed) is short, plump, and middle-aged, thus in his very ordinary appearance contrasting with a Dupin or a Sherlock Holmes. In an early story, "The Gutting of Couffignal," he explains that for him his enthusiasm about his job is a strong motive:

"... I like being a detective, like the work. And liking work makes you want to do it as well as you can. Otherwise there'd be no sense to it. ... I don't know anything else, don't enjoy anything else, don't want to know or enjoy anything else. You can't weigh that against any sum of money. Money is good stuff. I haven't anything against it. But in the past eighteen years I've been getting my fun out of chasing crooks and solving riddles. ... I can't imagine a pleasanter future than twenty-some years more of it."

As Leonard Marsh has noticed, the Op's methods were accordingly different:

The conventional tale focused on the investigator's mental prowess; the later variety stressed the detective's physical engagement with the criminal. ... in [Hammett's] stories he saw crime not as a completed history to be attacked with the mind, but as a dynamic activity to be conducted with force as well as cunning. ... the Op adapts venerable investigative concepts to modern police methods. He painstakingly collects facts. He goes to the street, not to the study or the laboratory, fortified by familiarity with criminal behavior, by his wit, courage, endurance, luck. ... He obtains information by surveillance and by questioning anyone remotely associated with crime. Finally, he often seeks help from other private operatives, from hotel and police detectives, from hired informants, from taxi drivers and railroad employees.
   These techniques would be worthless, however, without the Op's ability to deduce the relevance of information and to exploit errors or weaknesses while in direct contact with his adversaries. ...

Since action plays so large a part in the process, and since the detective's ratiocination is detailed at intervals and briefly, the narrator can (like a Twain, a Conrad, or a Hemingway) tell much of his story very concretely. Erle Stanley Gardner notices that the Continental Op stories in *Black Mask* "were told in terms of action . . . told objectively, and there was about them that peculiar attitude of aloofness and detachment which is so characteristic of the Hammett style." The same might be said of the novels in which the Continental Op appeared. And the operative's frequent concentration on the action and withholding of statements about his own reactions added mystery and suspense. Gide noticed this in *Red Harvest*, which he called "a remarkable achievement, the last word in atrocity, cynicism, and horror": "Dashiell Hammett's dialogues, in which every character is trying to deceive all the others and in which the truth slowly becomes visible through the haze of deception, can be compared only with the best in Hemingway."[9]

Even the first-person narrator's feelings and thoughts are often withheld. An outstanding instance is in Chapter xxvi of *Red Harvest*, wherein, after a drugged sleep on Dinah Brand's living room Chesterfield, the Op awakens to find himself in the dining room, his right hand holding an icepick, the sharp blade of which is buried in Dinah's left breast. "She was lying on her back, dead," he goes on. Then he tells of his actions—his examining the body, the room, the adjacent rooms, and of his departing—all without a word detailing his emotional reactions or his thoughts about the woman's death.

The Continental Op disappears after *The Dain Curse*, and the next two novels, *The Maltese Falcon* and *The Glass Key*, are told in the third person. I shall return to the *Falcon*, but here want to notice that in both books the author abjures insight into any of the characters' thoughts or feelings. What Walter R. Brooks says about *The Glass Key* is true of both: "Mr. Hammett does not show you [the characters'] thoughts, only their actions. . . ." Because not one but practically all the characters are either tight-lipped stoics or superb liars, the reader's attempts to discover what makes characters tick, what they are trying to do and how, are baffled, and the mystery is greatly augmented.

In *The Thin Man*, Hammett returns to the first-person narrator, here a former detective, Nick Charles, who is persuaded to make use of his detecting skills again. Nick is very different from the Continental Op: he is attractive, sophisticated and witty. He resembles the

9. Elsewhere, soon after reading one of Hammett's novels, Gide was critical of Conrad's *Chance* because "Its finical slowness seems even more tiresome after the lively gait of Dashiell Hammett."

earlier narrator in being cynical and worldly and in being unrevealing about his emotional and intellectual responses to most people and events. In the final novel as in the first, the author therefore utilizes a fictional point of view that is well adapted to the genre which he is writing—one productive of mystery and suspense.

IV

The Maltese Falcon is generally conceded to be Hammett's best detective novel, and at least some reasons for its pre-eminence may be discovered. The fable ranges over a wide area including Russia (vaguely), Constantinople, Hongkong, Marmora (wherever that is), and San Francisco. The order in which its details are revealed is admirably managed for the puzzlement of the reader. In many of the conversations, the author shows his flair for reproducing colloquial speech. As I have said, suspense is increased because so many characters are untruthful and enigmatic.

Most important, Hammett employs a procedure which is particularly deceptive when combined with an objective dramatic narrative method. I have in mind the association of deceptive images and descriptive details with the characters. Writers of mystery novels long have employed this in representing some of their characters, e.g., in the classic representation of a humble butler who turns out to be a ruthless killer. But Hammett, in his picturing of all his leading enigmatic and deceitful characters, gives them outward aspects incongruous with their actual natures.

Joel Cairo, for instance, perfumes himself with chypre, wears many jewels, dresses carefully in fawn spats, a black derby, and yellow chamois gloves. He sucks violet pastilles. He walks with "short, mincing, bobbing steps." His hands are "soft and well cared for." He is meticulously polite. On the occasion of his first appearance, coughing apologetically and smiling nervously, this gorgeous creature pulls a pistol on the tough detective Sam Spade. And throughout the rest of the book he constantly reveals a toughness that his sissified appearance belies.

Another character whose name is "Wilmer" is constantly described as "the youth in the cap," "the kid," "the schoolboy," and "the boy." At close hand he is seen to have small features, white beardless cheeks, hazel eyes with curling lashes. This baby-faced youngster, it develops, is a sadistic gunman.

Again, there is Casper Gutman (translate "Goodman"), whose appearance—if recognized signs of character generally believed in by readers are to be trusted[10]—has the looks of a jolly, harmless, lovable fellow. For he is "a fat man . . . flabbily fat with bulbous pink cheeks and lips and chin and neck, with a great soft egg of a belly . . . and pendant cones for arms and legs." He "beams" at his visitor; he laughs heartily, his belly shaking like that of a Santa Claus, smiles benevolently, chuckles. His talk has an old-fashioned vocabulary and rhythm: "We begin well, sir. . . . Well, sir, here's to plain speaking and plain understanding. . . . You're the man for me, sir, a man cut along my own lines. . . . Well, sir, if I told you—by Gad, if I told you half!—you'd call me a liar." This jolly fat man, with his antique way of talking, is the master-mind behind the attempt to secure the falcon—a cruel, unrelenting searcher.

Then there is Brigid O'Shaughnessy, if not the heroine the chief feminine character of the narrative, who enters detective Spade's office as the book starts. Everything she does indicates that here is a shy unworldly young thing. She speaks softly through trembling lips, puts a hand to her mouth when startled, walks with "tentative steps," sits nervously on the edge of her chair, and at frequent intervals achieves the old-fashioned and all but forgotten feat of blushing. At one point, after she has "flushed slightly . . . a becoming shyness [not having] left her eyes," Spade accuses her of not being exactly the sort of person she pretends to be: "Schoolgirl manner . . . stammering and blushing and all that." Blushingly, she grants that the charge has justification. And indeed it does, for in the collection of scoundrels pictured here, the stammering, blushing Brigid is probably the most treacherous and vicious, having deceived, stolen, and murdered her way around a good part of the world.

The first paragraph in the book describes the detective with the ominous name of Spade:

Samuel Spade's jaw was long and bony, his chin a jutting v under the more flexible v of his mouth. His nostrils curved back to make another, smaller, v. His yellow-grey eyes were horizontal. The v *motif* was picked up again by thickish brows rising outward from twin creases above a

10. Whether science has approved or not, the lay public always has associated certain physical features with inward characteristics. As Kingsley Amis has noted, the typical siren pictured by Ian Fleming in his James Bond novels ordinarily has a wide mouth— "a supposed pointer to a sensual nature: Aristotle goes on about it." Readers of romantic fiction will recall the stock sisters, the blond, blue-eyed one who is innocent, sweet and shy, and the dark-haired, brown-eyed one who is gay, a bit more acid, and more worldly wise.

hooked nose, and his pale brown hair grew down—from high flat temples —in a point on his forehead. He looked rather pleasantly like a blond satan.

The satanic aspects of the detective, thus introduced, recur at many intervals in the book, the feature most recurrently stressed being the yellow-grey eyes which in time, like those of Chillingworth in *The Scarlet Letter*, can hardly be mentioned without the additional statement that they are burning or blazing. Through his reading of much of the book the reader is kept in the dark as to what makes Spade tick. But as the story concludes, Spade's actions make clear that he is the only character who has integrity, who obeys a code. The outcome of Spade's investigation is the discovery not only of Brigid's distant past but also of her more recent past during which she killed Spade's partner. Despite the fact that he has fallen in love with Brigid, he determines to turn her over to the police. He tells why:

"When a man's partner is killed he's supposed to do something about it. It doesn't make any difference what you thought of him. . . . Then it happens we were in the detective business. Well, when one of your organization gets killed it's bad business to let the killer get away with it. . . . Third, I'm a detective and expecting me to run criminals down and let them go free is like asking a dog to catch a rabbit and let it go. . . . Fourth, no matter what I wanted to do now it would be absolutely impossible for me to let you go without having myself dragged to the gallows . . . ."

His concluding reason is that he refuses to let himself be "played for a sucker," and Brigid from the start has depended upon her personal relationship to bring her release.[11] The code undoubtedly is an unusual and highly individual one—a mixture of what is admirable and what is not—which here clearly undergoes a stern test. And the technical procedures followed by the author, particularly the handling of the point of view and the attribution of deceptive physical qualities of the characters, testify that a technician of unusual skill has used this skill in telling his story.

11. In a much earlier short story, "The Gutting of Couffignal," for very similar reasons the Continental Op had similarly refused to let a woman interfere with his performance of duty. Philip's ultimate refusal of Dorothy in Hemingway's *The Fifth Column* offers what seems to me to be an interesting parallel.

THE BRIDGE OF
THORNTON WILDER

Alexander Cowie

Wesleyan University

Thornton Wilder enjoys life: this is the testimony of all who know him personally. He seems to have remained unscathed by potentially traumatic phenomena to which the first half of the twentieth century has exposed him: two world wars, one depression, the advent of Freud, the invention of the hydrogen bomb, the escalation of race conflict, the birth of existentialism, the disclosures of space explorations, etc. He seems an imperturbably cheerful person. Life, he says —and his books say—is eminently worth living. It may present troubling questions; but Wilder is a man who can entertain doubts without being destroyed by them. He does not resolve the doubts; he lives with them—equably. He seems to have his own version of Keats's "negative capability." He is not tormented or rendered schizophrenic by being unable to decide which of two opposing theories is the "correct" one. He manages to subsist in between them. If he does not achieve certainty, he has established for himself a kind of balance or equilibrium which serves him well both as a lay philosopher and as an artist.

In his own life, too, Wilder has been a sort of in-between person. He was born on April 17, 1897, at Madison, Wisconsin, but he did not stay put in the Middle West. As a youngster he was whisked off to China, where his father was Consul General and where he spent two intervals, one of a few months and one of two years. His early schooling was in China; in California (a school in Berkeley: Wilder was to spend many years first and last in academic communities); and, for the first two years of college, at Oberlin. After a period of military service in World War I he completed his work for the A.B. degree at Yale University; his Master's degree was from Princeton (1935). Meantime he had studied archaeology at the American Academy at Rome, taught French at Lawrenceville, and had begun his career as a writer. From 1930 to 1935 he was on the faculty of the

University of Chicago. Later he taught at Harvard. During World War II he served as intelligence officer with the Air Force in northern Africa and in Italy. In recent years he has lived in his own house (he has remained unmarried) in Hamden, Connecticut.

In some ways the career of Wilder has been an anomaly. It seems a bit odd that a writer of his apparent stature, a writer who has been before the public forty years, should have received so little formal criticism. Granted that he is apparently not destined to be ranked ultimately as one of the giants of our literature—the peer, say, of Faulkner or Mark Twain or Melville—he has at least been a serious, highly talented professional writer devoted to his art: the author of best sellers, the recipient of three Pulitzer prizes, the author of a play (*Our Town*) that has been performed probably more frequently than any other recent American play, and a box-office success with movie versions of his works. Yet until recently there was only one book-length study of him published in this country (now there are three) besides one medium-length German monograph. There has been a moderate number of articles about him, but often these have amounted to little more than personalia. In a number of books on American literary history of the twentieth century his name is not mentioned. Moreover, the tone of those writers who do discuss his works is often curiously reluctant or embarrassed. No one has fully explained this anomaly. His latest biographer, Malcolm Goldstein, hazards the thought that Wilder has been the victim of chronology: he came to his artistic maturity under the influence of the New Humanists (Paul Elmer More, Irving Babbitt, and others) at the very time, in the late teens and the early twenties, when naturalism was beginning to steal the show, later to be followed by the existential era—schools of literature with which Wilder has had little affinity. To critics bred in the naturalist-existentialist atmosphere Wilder seemed to show very little of life as it is actually lived. His books were too tame, too pretty, too little involved with "the fury and the mire of human veins." Perhaps there are other reasons for the anomaly that may appear if one surveys his production.

Wilder's first book, *The Cabala* (1926), created little critical stir, but it revealed characteristic elements that in later books would earn the author more flattering attention. It is a youthful book, a comedy flecked with farce and fantasy as well as invested with darker tones that do not comport well with comedy. Set in almost contemporary Rome, it deals with a group of decaying aristocrats whom the reader is asked to think of as reincarnations of ancient gods. There is an interview with dying John Keats near the beginning, and near the end the young American narrator (and protagonist) conjures up Virgil in quest of his advice. The body of the novel is concerned particularly with the problems of three of the elegant, learned, sophisticated members of the somewhat mysterious Cabala, which is beginning to lose some of its long-held political and social sovereignty in the Eternal City. In each case the aid of the narrator, Samuele, is sought. When Marcantonio, scion of a distinguished line, seems about to destroy himself in a sexual marathon with a series of girls of less than patrician provenance (and thus, his mother fears, deal a mortal blow to family pride), the mother prevails on Samuele to try to cope with the lad's condition. But the effect of the narrowly Puritanical Samuele's well-meant "lecture" only accentuates the young man's perversity (he takes to incest with his sister), and the result is tragedy. A second sufferer is a neurotic princess Alix d'Espoli, who conceives a vain passion for Samuele's American friend Blair, a young man who seems as little available for love and sex as Samuele himself. Blair seeks safety in a flight from Rome, and Samuele can do nothing to help the princess. The third person to solicit aid is Mlle Astrée Luce de Morfontaine, a sensitive older woman who is pathetically obsessed with the idea that the way to secure Church authority is to have the Divine Right of Kings established as part of Church dogma: will Samuele try to get Cardinal Vaini to help? The Cardinal, however, a veteran cleric who has drifted into skepticism anyway, politely declines the gambit. At the end Samuele gets a hint from Virgil that since Rome is on the way out, the hero had best go home and concern himself with building a new city in the new world. It is an assignment pretty heavy, one thinks, for the frail shoulders of the attractive, graceful, innocent scholar-dilettante Samuele, who has little aptitude for the practical, no apparent capacity for love, and only a surface knowledge of the messier problems of mankind. Frequently the author-narrator adopts a tone of self-mockery which cues the reader not to take his role too seriously. After all Samuele is but a youngster, and he seems best qualified to render the external scene: the streets and alleys of Rome, the mansions and acres of the aristocrats, the play of fountains on the terrace, the contours of the distant hills seen from a parapet in the lingering twilight. This he does with charm and skill. He loves the country: "It was Virgil's country and there was a wind that seemed to rise from the fields and descend upon us in a long Virgilian sigh, for the land that has inspired sentiment in the poet ultimately receives its sentiment from him."[1] Even if the phrasing (influenced, thinks Edmund Wilson, by Proust) is occasionally a bit precious, it is also phrasing that is to the last degree disciplined in accordance with Wilder's ideals at that stage in his career. If not the philosopher, Wilder is at least the artist in this, his first book.

The Bridge of San Luis Rey (1927), Wilder's next novel, was a brilliant popular success, and it has retained its place in the affections of many people. It is again a book of no great philosophical weight. Its action is spectacular and in a sense tragic, but it creates no unbearable emotions in the reader. The deaths of five people who went down when the bridge gave way are rendered tolerable by their remoteness in time (1712) and place (Peru). One remembers them sadly but without acute distress: the old Marchesa whose daughter has cut herself off in cold disdain from a mother she could not endure; the little servant Pepita whom the Abbess sends to aid the old woman; Esteban, the lonely young public scribe, stricken by the death of a twin orphan brother to whom he had been profoundly, perhaps homosexually, devoted; Uncle Pio, who had made a great actress out of the wilful, sensual Camila Perichole; and young Don Jaime, Camila's illegitimate son. What does it all mean— the summary snuffing out of the lives of these five? The reader never knows; this book is open-ended. Brother Juniper, who witnessed the fall of the bridge, thought he could prove that the event did not represent an accident but the will of God; these lives, he believed, could be shown to be "perfect wholes." This presumptuousness in explaining God's ways earned Brother Juniper the stigma of heretic and the doom of being burned at the stake. Wilder himself does not resolve the problem: his first chapter is entitled "Perhaps an Accident"; his last, "Perhaps an Intention." Apparently he believed man's condition to be governed by a mixture of partly un-

1. Thornton Wilder, *The Cabala* (New York, 1926), p. 7. There is no uniform edition of Wilder's writings. A useful bibliography is J. M. Edelstein's *A Bibliographical Checklist of the Writings of Thornton Wilder* (New Haven, 1959). Biography and criticism may be found in Rex Burbank, *Thornton Wilder* (New York, 1961); Helmut Papajewski, *Thornton Wilder* (Frankfurt am Main, 1961); Malcolm Goldstein, *The Art of Thornton Wilder* (Lincoln, Neb., 1965).

knowable factors. He once wrote, in phrasing reminiscent of Melville, "It is the magic unity of purpose and chance, of destiny and accident, that I have tried to describe in my books."[2] That "magic unity" is never elucidated. Throughout most of his writings, whether through an awareness of the limitations of his own intelligence or a natural propensity to leave things in suspension—on a bridge— Wilder refrains from dogmatizing regarding religion. A kind of stoic acquiescence in the inevitable—what must be—seemed to help him to harmonize such intuitions as he had regarding the mystery of life. And this without any descent into despair or pessimism. He knew (and demonstrated in *The Bridge*) the pain of immediate circumstance, but, as he was to suggest in *The Woman of Andros*, he deprecated prolonged emphasis on grief and suffering. Ultimately, he seems to say, the sadness that inheres in the human condition will be easily borne. At the end of *Our Town* the dead speak gently and equably to each other; and throughout "The Long Christmas Dinner," during which no less than eight persons silently move into the realms of the hereafter, the audience participates in the drama without suffering acute pain. Lucia in the latter play suggests one clue to the tone of Wilder when she says: "But sad things aren't the same as depressing things."[3] And so with the ending of *The Bridge of San Luis Rey*: it is sad but not depressing. Not even the assurance of life after death seems to be requisite; at the end of the book, indeed, Wilder appears to deny it. The sole indubitable comfort he offers is the high premium he appears to place on human love as an end in and of itself. This emerges in the thoughts assigned to the kindly Abbess at the very end of the book.

Even now [she thought] almost no one remembers Esteban and Pepita, but myself. Camila alone remembers her uncle Pio and her son; the woman Donna Clara her mother. But soon we shall die and all memory of those five will have left the earth, and we ourselves shall be loved for a while and then forgotten. But the love will have been enough; all those impulses of love return to the love that made them. Even memory is not necessary for love. There is a land of the living and a land of the dead and the bridge is love, the only survival, the only meaning.[4]

2. Walther Tritsch, "Thornton Wilder in Berlin," *Living Age*, CCCXLI, 4380, 44-47 (Sept., 1931). This is a translation of a report that first appeared in *Die Literarische Welt* for June 12, 1931. See Edelstein, *op. cit.*, p. 43.

3. Thornton Wilder, *The Long Christmas Dinner & Other Plays in One Act* (New York and New Haven, 1931), p. 10.

4. Thornton Wilder, *The Bridge of San Luis Rey* (New York, 1928), pp. 234-235.

Skipping for the moment the plays Wilder published in the 1920's, one comes to his next novel, *The Woman of Andros* (1935). Although based on a comedy, Terence's *Andria*, Wilder's novel is, characteristically, neither comedy nor tragedy. Often its tone is pastoral. Its setting is in pre-Christian Greece: the obscure beautiful Aegean island of Brynos. Here the courtesan Chrysis, a disciple of the teachings of Socrates, holds symposia during which there are readings and discussions in part designed to serve as therapy for many young men who come to her with their problems, their anxiety about a life they can neither understand nor master. One of her visitors is Pamphilus, a youth of aristocratic lineage, for whom she has a passion but who falls in love with Glycerium, her sister. When Pamphilus announces to his family that he proposes to marry this charming suffering peasant girl (by now pregnant), his parents are shocked by this threat to their dignity and affront to society. Ultimately the patrician father begins to relent. In the end both Glycerium and her baby die. This is the simple external action of the book, but it is featured much less than the meanings with which Wilder aims to invest his story, chiefly meanings related to Greek humanism, through the agency of Chrysis the prostitute. She emphasizes love for one's fellow-men; the wisdom of trying to realize and savor life moment by moment (a theme which Wilder also stressed in *Our Town*); and the acceptance of this world in its every guise, whether apparently beneficent or baneful and whether or not there is an after-life:

"I want to say to someone ... that I have known the worst that the world can do to me, and that nevertheless I praise the world and all living. All that is, is well. Remember ... me as one who loved all things and accepted from the gods all things, the bright and the dark."[5]

She also insists that one must not pay too much attention to suffering as such:

"Why cannot someone tell him [Pamphilus] that it is not necessary to suffer so about living.... Let him rest some day, O ye Olympians, from pitying those who suffer. Let him learn to look the other way. This is something new in the world, this concern for the unfit and the broken.... That is some god's business."[6]

The pagan acceptance of what must be is a characteristic Wilder response, but he chooses to fix his novel in time partly by two allu-

5. Thornton Wilder, *The Woman of Andros* (New York, 1930), p. 107.
6. *Ibid.*, pp. 77-78.

sions to the Christian religion. Christ's birth is adumbrated at the beginning, and at the end Glycerium's role is seen to symbolize that of Mary: "And in the East the stars shone tranquilly down upon the land that was soon to be called Holy and that even then was preparing its precious burden."[7] This, the last sentence in the novel, provides an example of Wilder's mastery of a stylistic mode which has been denigrated by some critics as "sentimental" or "precious" but applauded by others as "classical" in its clarity, poise, and grace.

Wilder's public response to adverse criticism has been the wise one: absolute silence. There have been two major periods of attack on his work, one of them occurring in the early 1930's. At that time, when the United States was in the midst of the Great Depression, it was natural to evaluate a play or a novel partly on the basis of its economic and/or sociological stance. By this time even Wilder's friends found it a bit curious that a man of such talents as he, the author of three books, should have paid so little attention to his own country. Why, outspoken critics asked, did he expend his talents on remote places, flimsy fables about fake gods, the corrupt idle rich, neurasthenic young men lolling around when they might have been better employed digging potatoes? Why so much toying with fine and fancy images: viola d'amore, ivory, terra cotta, spices, silks, alabaster figurines, paintings on fans, etc.? Critics seemed now to be retroactively angry that a Pulitzer prize had been given to a writer who apparently regarded himself as too elegant to address himself to the reek and racket of contemporary America. The most notable outburst was that of Michael Gold, who found in Wilder's books only "a pastel, pastiche, dilettante religion . . . a day-dream of homosexual figures in graceful gowns moving archaically among lilies. . . ." He called for a treatment of "the blood, horror, and hope of the world's new empire." "Where," he asked, "are the modern streets of New York, Chicago and New Orleans in these little novels? Where are the cotton mills . . . the child slaves of the beet fields . . . the stockbroker suicides, the labor racketeers . . . ?"[8] A number of Wilder's friends rushed to his defense, but he himself made no answer to the charges.

Or did he? Was his next novel, *Heaven's My Destination* (1935), a tacit attempt at confession and restitution? Geographically it seemed

7. *Ibid.*, p. 162.
8. Michael Gold, "Wilder: Prophet of the Genteel Christ," *New Republic*, LXIV, 267 (Oct. 22, 1930).

to be, in the amount of American soil it embraces in some twelve states of the Union. There were changes in personnel and in subject matter too. Here are many characters obviously not top-drawer society, not Ariadne-like Greek girls mourning their dejected state, not scented young men of debatable masculinity. Here are village bums; here is a whorehouse; here are roadside adventures in Kansas, Michigan, Oklahoma; here is some discussion of commerce and finance; here are American businessmen in convention; here is a traveling salesman; here is a good deal of American dialogue that rings true in accent and syntax; and here are many other notations of contemporary American life.

The central character, George Marvin Brush, is an incurably idealistic young man chock-full of benevolent impulses and a strong will to reform society, which he thinks rotten in its basic structure. He is a pacifist, a believer in racial equality, and a perfectionist. Armed with texts from the Sermon on the Mount and other scriptural counsel, imbued with the ideas of Gandhi, he sets out to crusade for his conception of the true life. His constant campaigning against tobacco and alcohol creates only minor irritation among people on whom he foists himself, but his theories of voluntary poverty and non-violence finally evoke anger, even rage, against him. A little like a latter-day Thoreau, who ridiculed the rationale of insurance, Brush has decided that the theory of banks is wrong; and when he comes to take his savings out, he refuses to accept the interest accrued: he says it doesn't really belong to him. "To save up money," he tells the president of the bank, "is a sign that you're afraid, and one fear makes another fear . . . . No one who has money in banks can really be happy."[9] Imprisonment for crime and capital punishment are also wrong, he tells a judge:

"It's a crime to kill, and the government does that, and it's a crime to lock somebody up in a room for years on end, and the government does that by the thousands. The government commits thousands of crimes in a year. And every crime makes more crimes. The only way out of this mess of crimes is to try this other way."[10]

The other way is to freely give the potential criminal what he wants —yes, even if he is raping your sister: this good act (of forbearance) will "make an impression" on the man. Indeed Brush had got arrested for giving a robber forty dollars that did not belong to him—

9. Thornton Wilder, *Heaven's My Destination* (New York, 1935), pp. 22-23.
10. *Ibid.*, pp. 242-243.

though he was going to pay it back. If he were in a war, he said, he would refuse to kill a man who was trying to kill him. This seems a bit extreme to the judge: "Suppose," says the judge, "that man in the shell-hole shot you. What becomes of your lesson to him then?" "Well, Judge," replied Brush, "*ahimsa* would have been in my mind. That's Gandhi's word for it, Your Honor. And if somebody has *ahimsa* in his mind, I believe it has a chance of jumping from mind to mind."[11] Brush is allowed by Wilder to present his arraignment of society with considerable skill and persuasiveness. Even Mrs. Efrim, whose money he lifted without permission (in her presence) to give to the robber, is half won over. Brush himself is a handsome, strong, essentially likable person with a marvelous tenor voice which enchants listeners. His very presence sometimes has a healing effect on people—they feel as if they had somehow been blessed—a little like the effect that Rabbit Angstrom has on people in John Updike's *Rabbit, Run*. Of course the trouble is that besides having the odor of divinity about him he is a man lacking in ordinary good sense—a specimen of the holy fool. He pesters people and tries to prevail by sheer logic, making little or no allowance for the fallibility and weakness of ordinary human nature. Says Lottie plaintively near the end of the book: "Nobody's strong enough to live up to the rules."[12] Inevitably people finally think that he is really crazy. The stout oak of rooted purpose and enduring wisdom which sustained Thoreau and Gandhi is but feebly parodied by this tumbleweed of the prairie. Brush's behavior becomes farcical. Sooner or later he violates, under extenuating circumstances perhaps, a great many of his own principles: he gets drunk, he slugs a man, he smokes a pipe, and (no one knows how) he gets a girl with child. He later spends months trying to find the girl in order to make up for his sin by marrying her. Of course the girl, a simple farmer's daughter, does not want to marry him, but she finally gives in to his magnetic ways—with dire results, chiefly because Brush is really incapable of love. Brush has his moments of discouragement, and he is intelligent enough to diagnose part of his trouble: "I made the mistake all my life of thinking that you could get better and better until you were perfect." Like Holden Caulfield in *The Catcher in the Rye*, he has been quixotically tilting against "phony" elements in society. And like Holden he eventually

11. *Ibid.*, p. 241.
12. *Ibid.*, p. 290.

has a severe breakdown, suffering utter physical and psychological prostration; but he recovers and resumes his former ways.

What is Wilder's attitude toward his monstrous creation? He has avowed that his portrait of Brush is heavily autobiographical. One wonders. In any case critics remonstrated with the author for his ambivalence—again his remaining on the bridge—regarding Brush's behavior. One gets the impression that Wilder is glad of the chance to ventilate social theories, to force society to examine the assumptions on which it lives—no doubt taking some sly pleasure in the process, for, as Judge Carberry says, "Most people don't like ideas."[13] Yet Wilder stays far short of committing himself to Brush's idealistic program; indeed he undercuts his protagonist to the point of making him absurd. Moreover, he seems to have no love for his own literary progeny. He permits one of the other characters, Burkin, to destroy much of what has been built up, by showing what a half-baked person Brush essentially is—even to the point of letting Brush know that the woman-evangelist originally responsible for his conversion had been under the influence of drugs at the time. If Wilder began by modeling his hero on himself as a Calvinistically bred, pinched, censorious Puritan young man, he escalated him into a full-blown blunder-boy such as Wilder has surely never been. By a process of canceling out values, then, Wilder almost completely destroys the philosophical validity of the protagonist's position. Possibly the reader is expected to take some comfort in the thought of the indestructibility of a moral idea and in the presence of disinterested human love symbolized by a silver spoon sent to the ailing Brush by a Catholic priest who had never met him. But Wilder did not destroy the story interest of *Heaven's My Destination*: it remains a critically ambiguous but very readable book. Although Brush is humorless, the jams he gets into are often productive of real comedy and some farce. A trifling example may suffice; it highlights the character of Brush. In a jail-yard Brush walks up to a fellow-violator of the law who is lying on a bench. Emitting bonhomie at every pore, Brush shakes hands and says in his best, brisk American manner:

"My name is George M. Brush. I come from Michigan and I sell text-books for Caulkins and Company."
"Any birth marks?"
"What?"

13. *Ibid.*, p. 247.

The man lay down again. "My name is Zoroaster Eels. I lie on benches for a living."[14]

One fears that the lesson was lost on George M. Brush.

In *The Ides of March* (1948) Wilder returned after a non-novel-writing interval of more than a decade to an old love of his, the Eternal City, his project this time one of more weight than that of the delicate *Cabala*. This book attains the character of a novel by reason mainly of three matters for action: (1) the conflict of Caesar and Mark Antony vis-à-vis Cleopatra; (2) the celebration of the mysteries of the Good Goddess, a festival intended to be participated in by women of high birth and irreproachable reputation; and (3) the downfall of Caesar. The social and political atmosphere of Rome is richly supplied by much movement of distinguished people; the presence of Catullus and Cicero reminds the reader that the era was one in which poetry and oratory existed in close liaison with statecraft. Cunning intrigue spices the action, part of it instigated by the pathetic but cruel Clodia in quest of revenge on all men for her having been violated by her uncle when she was twelve. She is the Lesbia of Catullus, whom she takes delight in torturing. The conditions and events which made Caesar's death inevitable are fully presented, but the actual day of the assassination receives only a one-page account written many years later by Suetonius. The structure of the book is original. Instead of relating events in chronological order as the more or less omniscient author, Wilder chose to bring his material to the reader in the form of ingeniously juxtaposed documents of one sort or another: letters, journals, commonplace books, proclamations, graffiti, etc., which are in a few cases historical but for the most part of Wilder's devising.

Many memorable portraits emerge from Wilder's packed pages, but of course Caesar's multi-faceted portrait remains central. The diversity of traits commonly attributed to him is here: he is at various times practical, pragmatic, decisive, ruthless, sardonic, credulous, disillusioned. Like Wilder, he is far from monolithic in his thinking. His strong sense of responsibility and his capacity to make needed decisions in the interest of the welfare of Rome and her people are stressed. Although often scornful of the ignorant, self-seeking mob, he is capable of compassion for the afflicted. He affects not to be interested in philosophical speculation; yet it is clear that the subject

14. *Ibid.*, p. 214.

does interest him. His own response to the universe—especially the question of the relative influence of volition and destiny on man's fate—is mixed. He thinks at times that there is a possibility of "a mind in and behind the universe which influences our minds and shapes our actions."[15] And he intermittently acknowledges the hypothesis "that my life and my services to Rome seem to have been shaped by a power beyond myself" or by "the *daimon* within me."[16] In a depressed moment he asserts to his friend Turrinus that "Life has no meaning save that which we may confer upon it."[17] In sum he can never resolve his teleological doubts, and he often gives the impression of thinking it foolish to spend time worrying over the past and over a possible after-life: the daily agenda is enough to absorb one's energies. At any rate he carries on vigorously even though it becomes more and more apparent that his downfall is inevitable. His was a harassed life, often a sad and lonely one as well: "The condition of leadership adds new degrees of solitariness to the basic solitude of mankind."[18] In some ways Wilder's Caesar is a tragic figure, but the book does not create the impression of being "*a* tragedy"; Caesar does not quite qualify as an Aristotelian tragic hero. It is finally a reflective book. Wilder's own involvement in his theme is theoretically forbidden by reason of the adoption of a technique based on objectivity, but it is natural to think that he could sympathize with Caesar's speculations on the meaning of the universe—speculations which were troubling but fell short of creating anguish or panic. Ambivalent like Caesar, he seems to believe that life must be lived out with equanimity, with courage, if possible with relish.

The Ides of March is the last long fiction Wilder has written up to the present time,* and it would seem that his interest at present is more in the drama: he is writing cycles of plays. His interest in playwriting goes far back in his career: as early as 1928 he had published *The Angel That Troubled the Waters and Other Plays.* What has been responsible for his great and enduring success in the theater can be pretty well seen in two plays: *Our Town* (1938) and *The Skin of Our Teeth* (1942.)

Prone as he was to remain ambivalent about philosophical

---

15. Thornton Wilder, *The Ides of March* (New York, 1949), p. 38.
16. *Ibid.*, pp. 39, 40.
17. *Ibid.*, p. 232.
18. *Ibid.*, p. 105.
*Wilder's novel *The Eighth Day* (1967) appeared after Mr. Cowie had read the proofs of his essay.—Ed.

the audience gratefully accepts his words as a kind of benedict.
For this is a play that, although sad, reconciles one to the eterↄ
life-and-death cycle. All that happens is presided over shrewdly, hu
morously, tenderly by the Stage Manager, who is sure that "*something*
is eternal. And it ain't houses and it ain't names, and it ain't earth,
and it ain't even the stars .... everybody knows in their bones that
something is eternal, and that something has to do with human
beings."²² The author does not spell out doctrinally what humanity
may hope for. Indeed he envisions a future time so remote that even
Christianity will exist only in records. But he gives assent to a process
not fully defined when he has Mrs. Gibbs say to Emily: "When you've
been here longer you'll see that our life here is to forget all that
life on earth], and think only of what's ahead, and be ready for
vhat's ahead."²³ Pretty cold comfort, one might say, for conventional
ↄelievers. Yet the testimony is that almost no viewers of the play
ↄre distressed by the absence of specific orthodox consolation and
ↄromise—and that all are comforted somehow by viewing life
ↄd death under the aspect of eternity. Like the author of "Thana-
ↄpsis," Wilder can treat candidly of death without frightening his
ↄdience. The reason, of course, is that the play tends to be allegori-
ↄl. Even the very real details used to describe George and Emily at
ↄe soda fountain are seen through an almost invisible screen. As
ↄten, Wilder is on the bridge between two strategies—that of the
ↄncrete and that of the universal. Always he discreetly limits one's
ↄgree of involvement, one's degree of responsibility, one's anxieties,
ↄe's overt hopes. With T. S. Eliot he sometimes almost seems to be
ↄoning: "Teach us to care and not to care." Yet finally he places
ↄ emphasis slightly on the positive side: the wisdom of trying to
ↄize to the full one's participation in the never-ending pageant of
ↄnkind from the cradle to the grave.

ↄ *The Skin of Our Teeth* alternately scares and entertains people
ↄe than it comforts them. Yet there is optimism here also, for
ↄ play underlines the indestructibility of the human will to sur-
ↄ. The characters are again double: both real people with home
ↄesses and figures in an allegory of man. The Antrobus family
ↄt times a suburban New Jersey family and at times stand-ins for
ↄkind through the ages. Part of the time we see them as Adam and

Ibid., p. 52.
Ibid., p. 58.

matters, especially the question of autonomy versus det
Wilder was pretty constant in one belief, namely, that wh
may or may not mean the important thing is to live, to s
be aware. This is not easy. The theme of *Our Town*, he I
pointed out, is "the difficulty of . . . 'realizing life whil
it.' "[19] The first act, called Daily Life, gives an ordinary
lives of the ordinary inhabitants of Grover's Corners, :
small town in New Hampshire. Through the very arti
Manager, who speaks from a bare stage, we come to kn
as if in a series of genre pictures: its physical features, :
its municipal organization, its population—the milkr
paper boy, the banker, the town drunk, the undertaker—
activities of the people in their business and their pr
pecially in the latter case the lives of the Webb and C
The second act, called Love and Marriage, brings to
Gibbs and Emily Webb in a delightful courtship—hom
touching. The act ends as the couple move into the
their wedding. Act Three, set in the cemetery, revea
dead, among whom Emily presently arrives, taking h
her mother-in-law, Mrs. Gibbs: she has died in child
with the privilege of speaking and of looking on at
living, the dead have been discussing life down th
life awful—and wonderful?" says Mrs. Soames.[20] I
assent of the Stage Manager but against the advic
Emily decides to go back to earth for a day, choosii
relive, her twelfth birthday. She is glad soon to re
for although she still loves the things she had onc
she now knows that earthly life goes too fast: "W
to look at one another . . . . Oh, earth, you're too
body to realize you . . . human beings are . . . [j
Turning to Mrs. Gibbs, she says: "They doi
they?"[21] And Mrs. Gibbs replies: "No, dear. They
As the play nears its end, the Stage Manager
announce that the Albany train has just gone
everybody's asleep" in Grover's Corners. And i
audience directly, he says: "You get a good re

v
l
a
p
a
t
a
ca
th
of
co
de
on
in
his
rea
ma

mo
the
viv
add
are
man

22
23

19. *Writers at Work*, ed. Malcolm Cowley (New York, 1
20. *Three Plays by Thornton Wilder* (New York, 196
Bantam Books, Inc., paperback containing *Our Town*, TI
The Matchmaker, is provided with a Preface by Wilder.
21. *Ibid.*, pp. 62, 63, 64.

Eve and Cain. The maid Sabina is a symbol of aeons-old sensual desire. Time is unmistakably the present, and it is scooped up by centuries. Today Mr. Antrobus is eating ham and eggs; only yesterday he was inventing the wheel. The scenery and props, such as they are, have to be tossed about pretty smartly to keep up with the jumps in time. The threats to mankind from which he emerges by the skin of his teeth include natural disasters: the flood, fire, the descent of glaciers. In addition there are troubles—war is one—for which mankind is partly responsible. God made the world, the author implies, but left mankind to run it—even to the point of saving himself from the flood. There would seem to be (says Malcolm Goldstein) a degree of psychological determinism in the play. In Henry (also Cain) is embodied the urge to violence, hatred, and self-destruction; yet after wandering, he is also under a compulsion to come home again just to see the old place. Toward the end George Antrobus, like George Brush, has a phase of discouragement: he has lost "the desire to begin again, to start building." But he regains it—he has to, mankind has to, and will—and the play closes with the maid expecting Mr. Antrobus back from the office any moment now. She says at the end: "Mr. and Mrs. Antrobus' heads are full of plans and they are as confident as the first day they began." Wilder is said to have written this play partly "to encourage the troubled public in 1942." Maybe it did. Anyone trying to follow the action in its whirlwind and kaleidoscopic chaos would certainly have to get his mind off the war. *The Skin of Our Teeth* won a Pulitzer prize. It also evoked a storm of criticism occasioned by the disclosure that Wilder had made substantial and for a time unacknowledged use of Joyce's *Finnegans Wake* as a source. Finally it appeared that most people were less disturbed by Wilder's borrowing from *Finnegans Wake* than astonished at his having been able to understand the book well enough to make use of it. Though not so popular as *Our Town*, *The Skin of Our Teeth* has frequently been revived, and in June, 1966, was being played at the Tyrone Guthrie Theater in Minneapolis.

Thornton Wilder is one of the most difficult American writers to evaluate and interpret under a few rubrics. He tends to fall between categories. This is apparent when one considers him in terms of (1) his choice of material, (2) his philosophical outlook, and (3) his technique.

First for his materials. It is obvious that he exhibits great diversity in both his novels and his plays with respect to scene and dramatis personae. No such homogeneity characterizes him as exists, for example, in John O'Hara, in whom one discerns a large degree of sameness as year after year he adds another unit to his sociological, sexual saga of his beloved Gibbsville. Or in Faulkner, who tends one domain. Or in Marquand, whose cup of tea is Boston and environs. Wilder has no favored plot of ground: no Yoknapatawpha, no Poictesme, no Wessex, or Gibbsville, or Combray, or Winesburg. He gets around. He has a certain attraction to classical soil, setting two novels in Rome and one on a Greek island—not to mention shorter pieces. *The Bridge of San Luis Rey* took him to Peru. The clamor for him to pay attention to his native land resulted (indirectly) in stories and plays set in a variety of verifiable American regions: New Jersey, New England, the Middle West. Inevitably his characters constitute a variegated personnel, ranging from Roman aristocrat to Manhattan busboy; from devoted, learned eighteenth-century South American priest to quasi-illiterate twentieth-century Kansas farm girl; from shy, naïve soda-sipping New Hampshire high-school girl to Cleopatra. The characters tend to be lightly delineated, in crayon rather than oils, but they are representative of many strata —social, professional, cultural, economic—in many milieux. Diversity also characterizes Wilder's narrative and dramatic actions. He does not confine himself to one or all of the traditional matters for novel or play, namely, making money, making war, and making love. Instead it is a matter of interpreting a complex, sophisticated in-group (*The Cabala*); the philosophical causes and human effects of a major catastrophe (*The Bridge of San Luis Rey*); the psychology of characters trying to cope with the problem of suffering (*The Woman of Andros*); the adventures of an idealist embattled against the proponents of a rotten society (*Heaven's My Destination*); the average daily behavior of small-town people who realize too late the value of life (*Our Town*); the deeply implanted instinct of mankind to survive and rebuild after no matter what or how many disasters (*The Skin of Our Teeth*). The nearest to "standard" material appears in *The Match-Maker*, in which a wealthy sixty-year-old man decides to get married—with hilariously farcical consequences.

In the second place, philosophically Wilder—to judge by his writings—is neither an affirmer nor a nay-sayer. He arrives at no camp of dogma but remains on a bridge of reflection. In him one finds no basis for a strong Christian faith or for bleak existential despair, still less nihilism. He seems to imply that one must take the long view. Nor is he an adherent of the cult of the absurd. About the "government" of the universe he makes no final statement. Like his Caesar, he just doesn't know; like Caesar he seems to have a pagan poise, ready to accept what the gods decree. Even about whether there is an after-life he appears to have no settled convictions. Yet in *Our Town* we see characters in a cemetery, between life and death, apparently taking off on some strange spiritual voyage or evolutionary sequence which may argue an off-beat version of immortality.

For a writer who proffers so little overt religious or philosophical assurance, Wilder has been remarkably acceptable to average readers. At the very least they know that he has no paralyzing fears and that, unlike some of his juniors, he has no self-pity. Perhaps they sense, too, that he has intuitions, only in part given expression, which proceed beyond the area of demonstrable proof. They like his emphasis, in *The Bridge of San Luis Rey* and *The Woman of Andros*, on the necessity and the good effects of the love of human beings for one another. There is vague comfort also in the Stage Manager's insistence that there is *"something"* eternal about man. At times, too, he seems to believe in the existence of some good principle operating among men which, if indefinable and unprovable, is perhaps indestructible. No sentiment of goodness or love is ever lost—as with Gandhi's *ahimsa*, it may "jump from mind to mind." Wilder, then, is often ambivalent philosophically, but he is not tormented and torn to pieces: he is not schizophrenic, and he is not "lost." In fact he comes close to harmonizing such opposing views as he harbors. If life exists in halves, he seems to say, try to join the halves—make a unity as well as you can. Such counsel comports with a kind of over-all classical balance and repose that characterizes Wilder in general.

Thirdly, Wilder's technique evinces the same tendency to move freely between alternative modes. He uses the concrete well but he veers toward abstraction. He is capable of clear, straightforward characterization of individuals: Samuele in *The Cabala* is an example of this; and there are patches of very effective small realism in most of his books. Yet in general he is not attracted to the slice-of-life school of the late-nineteenth-century realists or the endless factual Dreiser-like documentation of the naturalists of the twentieth century. Wilder clearly does not think that 20-20 vision is an asset to the artist. He is less interested in transcription than in representation. The "busy little world of door-bell and telephone," he once said, was a bore to him. The single fact, he thought, has little significance unless its relationship to a general law is felt. Accordingly, he used abstraction, sought the universal. For this reason he resorts much to emblems, symbols, allegory, myth—the instruments of universality. For this reason many of his characters, though tagged with small tokens of "reality," are not quite real in the usual sense of the word—not the girl-next-door type of person—but, rather, pallid figures slightly misted over and blurred. They are finally figures in a parable or pageant, who have their exits and their entrances at the will of a master of ceremonies or puppeteer. Ultimately they are absorbed into the universal.

In this quest for universality through abstraction Wilder used his three handmaids: distance, time, and recurrence or repetition. Distance enabled him to see mankind as a group, as community, even, in *The Skin of Our Teeth*, as race. Depth in time also helped him to understand the dimensions of mankind. Individuals as such are often allowed only scant rights as separate identities—only a tenuous momentary validity in the colossal reaches of time that extend back behind their immediate movements in the fast-ebbing present and forward into endless future ages. Birth, procreation, death; something built, something lost, something aspired toward: the patterns of man repeat themselves endlessly. In this enormous perspective the importance of the individual's agenda shrinks. Death is not clinical but symbolic. One soon finds it hard to remember the five persons on the bridge at San Luis Rey who were dashed to their deaths in a rocky gorge or boiling torrent; for the reader they are dropped into eternity, their legacy a philosophical problem. Brother Juniper died the agonizing death of one burned at the stake; but in his account of the burning Wilder all but annuls reality: "he [Brother Juniper] called twice upon St. Francis and leaning upon a flame he smiled and died."[24] The eight people in "The Long Christmas Dinner" who one by one pass off the stage, silently, without protest, without religious consolation, are being absorbed, as noiselessly as Ahab, into universality. "I am interested," said Wilder, "in those things that repeat and repeat and repeat in the lives of the millions."[25] Even

24. *The Bridge of San Luis Rey*, p. 220.
25. Quoted in Goldstein, *The Art of Thornton Wilder*, p. 152.

the characters in *Our Town*, which provides so many winning details of New England village and domestic behavior, are being translated into the universal language of eternity, fractions being converted into an integer whose size no one can conceive of. George and Emily relinquish their tiny identities to become emblems of innocent young love anywhere, any time. And even Emily's death (which we never see) only ranges her in an uncountable sisterhood, among the billions of mankind "dreaming through the twilight that doth not rise nor set." George Brush has a million kinfolk, in history past and to come, who pit their strength if not always their common sense against apparent evils in our lives. The Antrobus family in *The Skin of Our Teeth* carries the process even further: Mr. and Mrs. Antrobus, symbols of the survival quotient of mankind, have been married five thousand years—surely a record for steady employment in the theater. Son Henry (for Henry read Cain) had been around wandering almost equally long, before Wilder drafted him for a tiny exposure in twentieth-century New Jersey. He will soon be at large again. He will finally belong nowhere—and everywhere. So what becomes of the importance of the town of Excelsior, New Jersey, in 1942?

Thus Wilder, vendor of abstractions. What is the effect of this technique on his works in the large? It is mixed. For some readers and audiences it is disquieting to see characters in whom they have staked an interest dissolving into symbols. For people who like cash on the narrative line, Wilder's proffered long-term investments are somehow unsatisfactory. He himself recognized this problem when he wrote that although *Our Town* is "an attempt to find a value above all price for the smallest events in our daily life," he "made the claim as preposterous as possible" for he has "set the village against the largest dimensions of time and place."[26] He notes that "buried [back] in the text . . . is a constant repetition of the words 'hundreds,' 'thousands,' 'millions.' It's as though the audience . . . is looking at that town at ever greater distances through a telescope."[27] Yet most audiences and readers appear to bear with him in his quest for generalized truth. On a bare stage or amid exploding scenery, on a remote myth-enshrouded island, on a bridge that has its existence more in allegory than in veritable space, Wilder has cast humanity itself in age-old roles destined to be re-enacted ceaselessly as the future replaces the present.

26. *Three Plays by Thornton Wilder*, Preface, p. xi.
27. *Writers at Work*, p. 113.

For the rest, Wilder's technique in detail is often superb. Making no pretensions to Olympian stature as a writer, he is yet one of the most finished craftsmen in American fiction and drama of the past generation, one of the most devoted disciples of art. In this respect his books *are* homogeneous. His thinking may be open-ended but his art is fixed and finished. His most serious limitations are a certain thinness in invention (most of his works have been primed by sources) and some ineptitude in handling larger structures. His architectonics are sometimes shaky as in *The Bridge* and *The Cabala*. He himself said he had a "passion for compression," and he admitted that this was an offset to his "inability to sustain a long flight."[28] He approaches perfection in many small units, within which he makes the most of his skill in image, in line and mass, in tone, in cadence and resonance. His dialogue tends to be superior, whether of the formal sort suited to allegorical sequences or the modified colloquial speech of average citizens in a village square. All is controlled, all is finished. Every paragraph executes its author's will; no sentence or phrase escapes him without knowing its assignment. Within his own realm—a principality, perhaps, rather than a kingdom—he rules with unquestioned authority.

Thornton Wilder has had a successful career. Yet as a writer he has a curious relationship with his public. Some of his books have been best-sellers, and he has been greatly admired, but readers do not seem to feel that they know *him* or that he belongs to them. He is gregarious as a man, one hears, but somehow he seems to forbid intimacy: a distance exists between author and reader. He does not confide his hopes and fears, his private life, to the reader; his books are not (what is the mode at present) "confessional." He does not woo or exhort or frighten the reader. He has no program to gun for, no point of view to sell. He is less the debater than the moderator. This is no doubt partly because he is not too sure of conclusions himself.

Thornton Wilder is a spectator, an observer of life. In a sense he is himself a man on a bridge. A bridge enables you to see much but commits you to nothing. Beneath you, at uncertain depths, are the arteries of communication and transport: railroad, river, or motor highway. Freight of all kinds is moving, some of it marked

28. Thornton Wilder, *The Angel That Troubled the Waters and Other Plays* (New York, 1928), Foreword, p. xiii.

fragile. Yonder, perhaps, is the teeming city. Far away are the hills, purpled with distance and the invitation to reflection. Overhead is the sky, a route, not well marked, to eternity. So you may linger, bemused, immobilized for the time being—yourself for the moment frozen into a fragment of parable or pageant. The bridge is open at either end, but you are under no immediate compulsion to choose a way. You are in balance. For a while your thoughts may be in suspension between alternative ways of doing. Wilder is often an in-between sort of person, unable or unwilling to commit himself to one mode. He is between comedy and sadness; between realism and parable; between a dimly apprehended mystical faith and cool skepticism; between the conviction that man can order his own existence and the acceptance of a distant cosmic determinism; between the will to reform and the awareness that man must not strive fanatically for perfection—a bridge must not be too rigid, must allow for expansion and contraction; between the pulsing present and a nobody-knows-how-old past. Thornton Wilder is there, listening to the old earth sigh and beginning to order his own thoughts.

Readers sometimes wish Wilder would get off the bridge, be an actor in life rather than observer and recorder of it. They wish he would be more involved personally. They wish he would get more excited, make more downright decisions, really lose himself, and go all out for *something*. He is too exasperatingly cool, has too steady a pulse, never runs a fever. At times he seems a man wearing gloves, surgically safe from life's infection. Why doesn't he ever portray passion or pain, his own or his characters', at close range? Why is he so prim and prissy about sex? And does he really have love for his characters? Does Wilder love George Brush in the way Salinger loves Holden Caulfield? And why doesn't he deliberately run more risks? Why doesn't he take off on some titanic Melvillean voyage in quest of the deeper wisdom, or with Walt Whitman on a "passage to India," risking self, ship, and all? Why does he never get out of sight of shore?

How foolish to ask. How unreasonable of his readers. Aren't they in effect asking him to jeopardize the very qualities which subtend his greatest asset, the principal benefit he may confer on the reader, namely, his balance, his classical repose and poise, his fine sense for order and harmony, his long-range vision of things? If he shows passion, ecstasy, agony, tragedy only obliquely, doesn't he serve his readers by helping to put *their* troubles, big and small, their sorrows and griefs, even their fun (all the dark and the light of life) into a perspective that may help them to experience life with fullness and equanimity as well as help to prepare them for a time when they too will be gathered into the artifice of eternity? If he doesn't seem to be capable of the love of individuals, he at least has a broad-gauge human tenderness, and he does love mankind in general. He is in a way a comforter and a healer. Yet as a humanist he is less concerned finally with worrying about or preparing for the next world than he is in celebrating things of this world. He is acquainted with suffering and doubt, but (like Chrysis in *The Woman of Andros*) he counts upon man's ability to transcend suffering and to live with his doubts. He insists not only upon the dignity of man but also upon his capacity for the enjoyment of life. He thinks of man as a fun-having animal; and he knows the uses of humor. To him this world is not necessarily the best of all possible worlds, but he thinks of it as mainly a good place.

THE INFLUENCE OF SPACE
ON THE AMERICAN IMAGINATION*

Gay Wilson Allen

New York University

I

Although the key symbol of *Leaves of Grass* is botanical, the grass "sprouting alike in broad zones and narrow zones,"[1] the aesthetic dimension most often employed by Whitman in his poems is space—usually geographical, but sometimes interstellar or cosmic. "Salut au Monde!" states explicitly the poet's psychology and exhibits the structure of most of his longer poems, especially the earlier ones. "What widens within you Walt Whitman?" the poet's practical self asks, and his daemon replies:

> Within me latitude widens, longitude lengthens,
> Asia, Africa, Europe, are to the east—America is provided for in the west,
> Banding the bulge of the earth winds the hot equator,
> Curiously north and south turn the axis-ends,
> Within me is the longest day, the sun wheels in slanting rings, it does not set for months,
> Stretch'd in due time within me the midnight sun just rises above the horizon and sinks again,
> Within me zones, seas, cataracts, forests, volcanoes, groups, Malaysia, Polynesia, and the great West Indian islands.

In reply to the ensuing questions, "What do you hear . . . [and] see Walt Whitman?" the poet's fantasy widens and stretches, like the sprouting grass in all latitudes.

> I see a great round wonder rolling through space,
> I see diminute farms, hamlets, ruins, graveyards, jails, factories, palaces, hovels, huts of barbarians, tents of nomads upon the surface,
> I see the shaded part on one side where the sleepers are sleeping, and the sunlit part on the other side,

* This paper was written for a Conference on American Studies held at the Newberry Library on May 6, 1961, with the title "Whitman and the Influence of Space on American Literature." A summary of the discussion was published in the *Newberry Library Bulletin*, Vol. V, No. 9, pp. 299-314, but the essay itself is published here for the first time.

1. "Song of Myself," sec. 6.

I see the curious rapid change of the light and shade,
I see distant lands, as real and near to the inhabitants of them as my
    land is to me.

Of course here the subject is the "great round wonder rolling
through space," but the "I" of Whitman's poems often takes as its
point of observation some imaginary position high in the sky in order
to give the widest possible angle of vision. No doubt many readers
have noticed that Whitman's imagination was especially strong in
space imagery, which cumulatively produces a sense of moving past
many objects. And movement also involves time, but the resulting
aesthetic effect is *space empathy*, for what is experiential space but
objects observed in successive positions and patterns, near or far to
the stationary observer, or seen one by one as the observer moves
past them? From his imaginative awareness of space, time, and
movement Whitman derived his mystic "wisdom" in "Song of the
Open Road" (section 6) or "truth" in "Song of Myself" (sections
20 and 30) :

To me the converging objects of the universe perpetually flow,
All are written to me, and I must get what the writing means.
       .   .   .   .
All truths wait in all things, . . .

In Whitman's fantasy transcending of time and space, the "I" of
his poems expands to cosmic dimensions, so that

My ties and ballasts leave me, my elbows rest in sea-gaps,
1 skirt sierras, my palms cover continents,
I am afoot with my vision.[2]

In his 1855 Preface Whitman related his poetic doctrine of space
and size to his nationalistic program: "Here [in the United States] are
the roughs and beards and space and ruggedness and nonchalance
that the soul loves." But, "The largeness of nature or the nation were
monstrous without a corresponding largeness and generosity of the
spirit of the citizen." Thus spatial qualities were both symbolic and
the means of expanding the American mind and character.

Not only must the American poet "tally" the dimensions of nature, but he must also himself grow with the expanding nation:

The blue breadth over the inland sea of Virginia and Maryland and
the sea off Massachusetts and Maine and over Manhattan bay and over
Champlain and Erie and over Ontario and Huron and Michigan and
Superior, and over the Texan and Mexican and Floridian and Cuban

2. "Song of Myself," sec. 33.

seas and over the seas off California and Oregon, is not tallied by the blue breadth of the waters below more than the breadth of above and below is tallied by him [the American poet]. When the long Atlantic coast stretches longer and the Pacific coast stretches longer he easily stretches with them north or south. He spans between them also from east to west and reflects what is between them. On him rise solid growths that offset the growths of pine and cedar and hemlock and liveoak . . . &c., &c.

The poet's spatial metamorphosis is interesting to observe: "On *him* rise solid growths . . . ." He *becomes* the broad continent, and the content of his poems is the space-filling objects of the land embraced. Whitman's cumulative images—his so-called "catalogues"— are his poetic means of creating space-empathy, of enlarging the reader's vision by making him see and feel the size and abundance of the nature whose spirit he is to match in his own soul and character and imagination. Thus Whitman's conception and use of space is basic to the theory and practice of his art.

II

Anyone who knows Whitman at all knows that he aspired above all else to be *the American poet* of his 1855 Preface, and today he is widely accepted as the poet who best represents the American spirit. Certainly in foreign countries he is reputed to be "the poet of democracy." Personally, I value Whitman more as a poet than as the epitome of anything, but there does seem to be almost universal agreement that, for good or bad, he is intrinsically American. Assuming this to be so, is there anything characteristically American in his absorbing interest in space?

Perhaps an approach to the answer is suggested by an experience I had in Japan while trying to lecture on Whitman.[3] The Japanese complained that they found his poems much more difficult to understand than Emily Dickinson's. When I asked them why, they could only say that Whitman's poems were too long; they got lost in his long lines and mass of images. Further questions revealed that his poems conveyed no space-empathy to them. Evidently the difficulty was not entirely linguistic because the cryptic subtleties of Emily Dickinson gave them less difficulty. Her terse, compact poems were something like their own *haikus*. Of course we have two problems here, length of poem and imagery of space, but I have tried to in-

3. Conference on American Studies sponsored by the U. S. State Department, Nagano, Japan, August, 1955.

dicate above that Whitman achieved his space-empathy partly by cumulative imagery and quite literally a spacious structure, as in "Song of Myself" and the other long poems.

The space which has aesthetic meaning for the Japanese is confined, manipulated, controlled, whether in a poem or a miniature tree. It is formal, decorative, artificial (contrived). It has none of the dynamic connotations of freedom, power, growth that it has for Americans. The giants of their folklore are merely ogres, not national heroes like our Paul Bunyan, John Henry, or Mike Fink.

For the Japanese, Taine's[4] theory of the shaping influence of race, environment, and epoch works very well, for it is easy to see parallels between their aesthetic sense and their compact island life, their dense population, and the stony face of nature in their mountainous, volcanic geography. Some of their mountains are tall, but livable space is scarce, and every inch of soil must be cultivated to the limits of human ingenuity. Substitute "syllable" for "inch" and this is almost a description of their *haiku,* a seventeen-syllable poem so packed with symbolism and allusion that it is practically untranslatable and hence almost unintelligible to a Western mind.

And perhaps Taine's theory works equally well for Spain. Lorca declared in his lecture on "The Duende": ". . . in Spain, all [symbols] bear little grass-blades of death, allusions and voices perceptible to the spiritually alert, that call to our memory with the corpse-cold air of our own passing. It is no accident that all Spanish art is bound to our soil, so full of thistles and definitive stone; the lamentations of Pleberio or the dances of the master Josef Maria de Valdivielso are not isolated instances . . . ."[5]

But Japan and Spain are nations whose culture has slowly evolved through centuries of human and natural history, whereas as a nation, our culture is still less than two centuries old. For us Taine's theory is hardly applicable (and is not at present in high repute anyway). As I have tried to indicate, there was no blind determinism for Whitman in his theory of the relation of nature and art; rather it was American determination to match, consciously and wilfully, the size, abundance, and free growth of nature. Yet in a way never en-

4. Hippolyte Adolphe Taine, Introduction to *History of English Literature,* translated by H. van Laun (Edinburgh, 1873).
5. "The Duende: Theories and Divertissement," translated and edited by Ben Belitt, in *Poet in New York,* by Federico Garcia Lorca (New York, 1955), pp. 160-161.

visioned by Taine, American history illuminates the emphasis on space in Whitman's theory and practice of art.

Crèvecœur, whose observations mainly antedate the American Revolution, declared in his *Letters from an American Farmer* (1782):

An European, when he first arrives, seems limited in his intentions, as well as in his views; but he very suddenly alters his scale; two hundred miles formerly appeared a very great distance, it is now but a trifle; he no sooner breathes our air than he forms schemes, and embarks in designs he never would have thought of in his own country. There the plenitude of society confines many useful ideas, and often extinguishes the most laudable schemes which here ripen into maturity. Thus Europeans become Americans.[6]

Francis Lieber, another European who spent many years in this country, first as visitor and later as immigrant, elaborated and explicated in his *Letters to a Gentleman of Germany* (1834) the influence of space on the American mind:

What distances and cheapness! ... distances are not considered in this country as in Europe; if they were, we should not have crept much beyond the Alleghany mountains by this time. And what is the reason that a thousand miles in the United States are not as much as a thousand miles in Europe? There are several reasons for it, in my opinion. First, the early settlers had to think of many thousands of miles off, whenever they thought of their beloved home. Thus, a far different unit by which to estimate other distances was laid down in their minds. It is clear that a person settling a hundred miles from them could not appear far away to those who had their original home some thousand miles off.... This feeling, together with the vast unsettled continent before them, induced people to push on and settle at great distances, especially as the life of the early colonists was such as to develop a daring spirit of enterprise, which gradually has settled down into a fixed trait of American character....[7]

Lieber also thought "the comparatively small number of mountain chains" to be "another reason why distances appear shorter to us." But equally important, he added, was another contemporary historical event: the growth of American oceanic commerce. The "clipper" ships had made possible the American "passage to India," to borrow Whitman's phrase. And we might remember that Herman Melville, like many another young man of the northeast coastal towns of the United States, was soon to sail in a whaling vessel for adven-

6. Hector St. John De Crèvecœur, *Letters from an American Farmer* (New York, 1940), p. 58.
7. Francis Lieber, "Ten Years in America Are Like a Century Elsewhere," in *Letters to a Gentleman in Germany*, reprinted by Henry Steele Commager, ed., *America in Perspective* (New York, 1948), p. 34.

ture in the Pacific Ocean. In its own way, *Moby-Dick* is no less space-conscious than *Leaves of Grass*; and like *Leaves of Grass*, too, its very structure is spacious.

But nautical history alone could not, as Lieber pointed out, account for the American attitude toward distance, for if this were so "the English, whose possessions in all quarters of the globe would make them consider distance as still less than the Americans, were their own country not itself so very confined. Every mile has there its full value."[8] So we come back to geography and American experience.

Both Crèvecœur and Lieber wrote before the most space-conscious—if not space-obsessed—period in the history of the United States, that of Westward expansion, which was precisely the movement that led Whitman to envision the American poet as *stretching* with every increase in the coastline or boundary.

Although westward migration was inevitable once Europeans had established a foothold on the North American continent,[9] "Manifest Destiny" was not announced until 1845, and Bernard DeVoto has called 1846 "the year of decision."[10] With the settlement of the Oregon dispute the United States became in actual fact a continental nation. The effect on the American imagination can hardly be exaggerated. Even a New Englander like Thoreau, who feared that expansion was merely another means of spreading slavery, could not help being exhilarated by the thought of the West: "Eastward I go only by force; but westward I go free . . . the forest which I see in the western horizon stretches uninterruptedly toward the setting sun . . . . I should not lay so much stress on this fact if I did not believe something like this is the prevailing tendency of my countrymen. I must walk toward Oregon, and not toward Europe."[11]

However, like Emerson and the other Transcendentalists, Thoreau was more interested in subjective than objective space. In *A Week* he declared, in his best paradoxical manner:

In what enclosures does the astronomer loiter! His skies are shoal, and imagination, like a thirsty traveler, pants to be through their desert.

8. Lieber, p. 35.
9. Henry Adams emphasized this point in his *History of the United States during the First Administration of James Madison* (1889-1891), especially in Vol. II, chap. iv.
10. Bernard DeVoto, *The Year of Decision: 1846* (Boston, 1943).
11. Henry Thoreau, "Walking," written in his *Journal* for 1850-1851, first published in the *Atlantic Monthly*, June, 1862, quoted from *The Works of Thoreau*, ed. Henry S. Canby (Boston, 1937), p. 668.

The roving mind impatiently bursts the fetters of astronomical orbits, like cobwebs in a corner of its universe, and launches itself to where distance fails to follow, and law, such as science has discovered, grows weak and weary. The mind knows a distance and a space of which all those sums combined do not make a unit of measure—the interval between that which *appears* and that which *is*. I know that there are many stars, I know that they are far enough off, bright enough, steady enough in their orbits—but what are they all worth? They are more waste land in the West—star territory—to be made slave States, perchance, if we colonize them. I have interest but for six feet of star, and that interest is transient. . . .[12]

But Thoreau, like Whitman, could fancifully transcend space. At Walden, "I lay down the book and go to my well for water, and lo! there I meet the servant of the Bramin, priest of Brahma and Vishnu and India, who still sits in his temple on the Ganges reading the Vedas. . . . The pure Walden water is mingled with the sacred water of the Ganges."[13] However, this man who "traveled much in Concord," was not interested in visiting distant lands. One should, instead, explore his own "streams and oceans; explore your own higher latitudes . . . . Nay, be a Columbus to whole new continents and worlds within you, opening new channels, not of trade, but of thought."[14] But his delight in space-imagery reflected his period and his American mind.

After the Civil War the West lost something of its mystery as it became in reality an integral part of the nation, but Americans were no less space-conscious. Now they were busy devouring space with the construction of railroads. The locomotive was added to the Pantheon of American deities. It was a train that carried the remains of the martyred Lincoln, in reality and in Whitman's poem,

> Over the breast of the spring, the land, amid cities,
> Amid lanes and through old woods, where lately the violets peep'd
> from the ground, spotting the gray debris,
> Amid the grass in the fields each side of the lanes, passing the endless
> grass,
> Passing the yellow-spear'd wheat, every grain from its shroud in the
> dark-brown fields uprisen,
> Passing the apple-tree blows of white and pink in the orchards,
> Carrying a corpse to where it shall rest in the grave,
> Night and day journeys a coffin.

And Whitman's space imagery symbolized not only the historical journey from the national Capitol to Springfield, but also the con-

12. *Works of Thoreau*, p. 238.
13. *Ibid.*, p. 442.
14. *Ibid.*, p. 457.

solidation of space, the cementing of the continent into one nation which took place under Lincoln's administration.

The whole nation participated vicariously in another celebration on May 10, 1869, when the Union Pacific and the Central Pacific tracks were joined in Utah. It is not surprising that Currier and Ives sold more copies of their locomotive and railroad prints than any other.[15] In 1876 Whitman wrote a poem "To a Locomotive in Winter" in which he called this machine the "pulse" of the continent,

> Launch'd o'er the prairies wide, across the lakes,
> To the free skies unpent and glad and strong.

Even Emily Dickinson's nursery-rhyme train, "docile and omnipotent," lapped up the miles, licked the valleys up, pared the quarries to fit its sides, and stepped prodigiously around mountains. But by the end of the century her playful animal had turned into Frank Norris's monster, an octopus stretching its horrible tentacles into every valley of the Garden of Eden, choking the life out of the New World Adam. And in the fantasy world of Stephen Crane's poems space had become the unattainable horizon, the blue distance mocking man's naïve dreams, a world in which heavy clouds muffled the valleys and the peaks looked toward God alone.

Stephen Crane's space was outside the Whitmanian tradition, even though William Dean Howells thought his poems derived from Emily Dickinson and Whitman. Whether it could be said to have been outside the main American tradition is another matter, for his solipsism was a forerunner of the barren spaces of the generation of wastelanders. But that movement was not confined to our own country and was led by an expatriate, and need not be considered here.

The one twentieth-century poet who deliberately took up Whitman's space-symbolism was Hart Crane in *The Bridge*. In his Proem Crane prayed that the mythical bridge, which he envisioned spatially (from adoring the actual Brooklyn Bridge), "vaulting the sea, [and] the prairies' dreaming sod," would "lend a myth to God." And just as his worship *stretched* the bridge out over the continent (at least as far as the prairies), so did he also symbolize the soul of the nation as a person of supernatural dimensions, namely, Pocahontas, the "body under the wide rain" known by the hoboes riding the rods:

15. See Morton Cronin, "Currier & Ives: A Content Analysis," *American Quarterly*, IV, 317-330 (Winter, 1952).

Yet they touch something like a key perhaps.
From pole to pole across the hills, the states
—They know a body under the wide rain;
Youngsters with eyes like fjords, old reprobates
With racetrack jargon,—dotting immensity
They lurk across her, knowing her yonder breast
Snow-silvered, sumac-stained or smoky blue—
Is past the valley-sleepers, south or west.
—As I have trod the rumorous midnights, too,

And past the circuit of the lamp's thin flame
(O Nights that brought me to her body bare!)
Have dreamed beyond the print that bound her name.
Trains sounding the long blizzards out—I heard
Wail into distances I knew were hers.
Papooses crying on the wind's long mane
Screamed redskin dynasties that fled the brain,
—Dead echoes! But I knew her body there,
Time like a serpent down her shoulder, dark,
And space, an eaglet's wing, laid on her hair.[16]

Crane's imaginative feat is grotesque and more paradoxical than Whitman's literal space imagery, but it accomplishes the same empathy. In this poem we find also Whitman's space-devouring train, or more accurately, the hoboes and the Pullman riders who use the train to transport them across the continent.

The Mississippi River in this section of *The Bridge* is a symbol of time and American history rather than specifically space, but in its "slow . . . sliding" down the valley it is a space- as well as a time-binder, until it loses its identity in the Gulf of Mexico. Nothing could be more Whitmanesque than this motif of merging, which also poses a space paradox: by extending itself to meet a greater mass (Whitman's ocean or "measureless float") the finite object loses its dimensions and hence its identity. But the metaphysics of the separate self and the "en-masse" need not concern us here.

An American writer whose space imagery seems almost an exaggerated caricature of all that has been said in this essay about American space-consciousness was Thomas Wolfe. He even thought of himself as a sort of Paul Bunyan, whose hungers were Gargantuan, who was always peering into "a thousand faces," or striding "a million streets"—he seemed to know no number less than a thousand and more often it was a million. In the famous scene in *Of Time and the River* in which the drunken hero is crossing Virginia at night by train

16. *The Collected Poems of Hart Crane*, ed. Waldo Frank (New York, 1933), pp. 15-16.

geographical space is described in a manner strongly reminiscent of Whitman's 1855 Preface:

> Then the moon blazed down upon the vast desolation of the American coasts, and on all the glut and hiss of tides, on all the surge and foaming slide of waters on long beaches. . . . it came in with the sea, it flowed with the rivers, and it was still and living on clear spaces in the forest where no men watched. . . . The moonlight slept above dark herds moving with slow grazings in the night, it covered lonely little villages; but most of all it fell upon the unbroken undulations of the wilderness, and it blazed on windows, and moved across the face of sleeping men.
>
> Sleep lay upon the wilderness, it lay across the faces of the nations, it lay like silence on the hearts of sleeping men; and low upon lowlands, and high upon hills. . . .[17]

The effect of this space-imagery is also Whitmanesque (cf. "The Sleepers"), the embracing of all space—and life occupying it—in a kind of pantheistic merging. But at the end of the book space has a surrealist character never encountered in Whitman:

> He moved on ceaselessly across a naked and accursed landscape and beneath a naked and accursed sky, an exile in the centre of a planetary vacancy that, like his guilt and shame, had neither place among things living nor among things dead, in which there was neither vengeance of lightning, nor mercy of burial, in which there was neither shade nor shelter, curve nor bend, nor hill, nor tree, nor hollow, in which—earth, air, sky, and limitless horizon—there was only one vast naked eye, inscrutable and accusing, from which there was no escape, and which bathed his naked soul in its fathomless depths of shame.[18]

"Limitless horizon" no longer has Whitman's connotations of plenitude, potential power, and freedom: only barrenness and alienation. Once again this is waste-land imagery, but not all American writers since 1920 have accepted it. Since I can mention only a few exceptions, I will begin with Archibald MacLeish. He is not so often compared to Whitman as Sandburg is, but in the following passage from "American Letter" he shows what it means to occupy American space:

> It is a strange thing to be an American.
> It is strange to live on the high world in the stare
> Of the naked sun and the stars as our bones live.
> Men in the old lands housed by their rivers.
> They built their towns in the vales in the earth's shelter.
> We first inhabit the world. We dwell
> On the half earth, on the open curve of a continent.
> Sea is divided from sea by the day-fall. The dawn
> Rides the low east with us many hours;

---

17. *Of Time and the River* (New York, 1935), pp. 72-73.
18. *Ibid.*, p. 885.

First are the capes, then are the shorelands, now
The blue Appalachians faint at the day rise;
The willows shudder with light on the long Ohio:
The Lakes scatter the low sun: the prairies
Slide out of dark: in the eddy of clean air
The smoke goes up from the high plains of Wyoming:
The steep Sierras arise: the struck foam
Flames at the wind's heel on the far Pacific.
Already the noon leans to the eastern cliff:
The elms darken the door and the dust-heavy lilacs.[19]

Perhaps no American poet has exploited the topography of a limited locality more relentlessly than William Carlos Williams in his *Paterson* books, but his details of space give only psychological symbols, not space-empathy to any marked extent. Robinson Jeffers does, and he deserves to be discussed here,[20] but I must draw this discussion to a close, and will end with brief attention to Wallace Stevens. He is comparable to Whitman in the sheer delight he takes in space, whether in "Thirteen Ways of Looking at a Blackbird," or "Sea Surface Full of Clouds," or "Chocorua to its Neighbor":

To speak quietly at such a distance, to speak
And to be heard is to be large in space,
That, like your own, is large, hence, to be part
Of sky, of sea, large earth, large air . . . .

Stevens seems more indifferent than Whitman about where he takes his slice of space (though Walt liked to measure the cosmos), but to S. F. Morse, "We have made too much of certain aspects of Stevens . . . and too little of the native element. I do not mean any sort of Factitious Americanism; but I do mean a quality of mind, a sense of the world, and the character of the poet."[21] Central in Stevens's theory of poetry is the marriage of imagination and reality. Though the reality he most cherished was less spacious than Whitman's, he has himself intimated a comparison in his lines on Whitman in "Like Decorations in a Nigger Cemetery":

In the far South the sun of autumn is passing
Like Walt Whitman walking along a ruddy shore.
He is singing and chanting the things that are part of him,
The worlds there were and will be, death and day.
Nothing is final, he chants. No man shall see the end.
His beard is of fire and his staff is a leaping flame.[22]

19. *Collected Poems* (Boston, 1952), p. 64.
20. William White compares the use of space by Whitman and Jeffers in "Robinson Jeffers's Space," *Personalist*, LXIV, 175-179 (Spring, 1963).
21. S. F. Morse, "The Native Element," *Kenyon Review*, XX, 446 (Summer, 1958).
22. *The Collected Poems of Wallace Stevens* (New York, 1957), p. 150.

III

In the discussion above I have mentioned several folklore and comic characters, and since the American fascination with space (including distance, size, and exaggerated dimensions of all kinds) is nowhere more evident than in American humor, I should at least mention some examples of this revealing aspect of the American imagination. Here I pretend to no originality, because the subject has been expertly covered by Walter Blair,[23] Constance Rourke,[24] and others. Miss Rourke's chapter on "The Gamecock of the Wilderness" in her *American Humor* provides abundant examples. We learn that the "tall tale" began as early as the American Revolution. In his irreverent history of the Puritans in Connecticut the Reverend Samuel Peters described the Connecticut River as so swift it would float a crowbar, and he also began the fabulous un-natural history of America. He told about the "humility" bird, "which spoke its own name, had an eye as piercing as that of a falcon, and could never be shot as it skimmed the ground, for it always saw the spark in the flintlock before the powder was kindled and darted out of range."

Though the Reverend Mr. Peters plainly anticipated the rise of backwoods (later called "Western") humor, it was not until the time of the War of 1812 that the backwoodsman emerged as a mythical national hero, a creature part human, part beast, part god, and obsessed with size, scale, and power. As Miss Rourke says:

He was not only half horse, half alligator, he was also the sea-horse of the mountain, a flying whale, a bear with a sore head. He had sprung from the Potomac of the world. He was a steamboat, or an earthquake that shook an enemy to pieces, and he could wade the Mississippi. "I'm a regular tornado, tough as hickory and long-winded as a nor'wester. I can strike a blow like a falling tree, and every lick makes a gap in the crowd that lets in an acre of sunshine."[25]

Probably every tribal hero (and in many ways frontier life in the United States was tribal) has unusual physical dimensions and/or strength. Beowulf had the strength of eight men and could crush his opponent with a bear hug. But though he used a magic sword and conquered a fabulous monster, he was not truly a giant when compared to such cosmic heroes as Paul Bunyan, Mike Fink, and Davy

23. Walter Blair published *Two Phases of American Humor* in 1931 and has published at least half a dozen books on the subject since then, such as *Tall Tale America: A Legendary History of Our Humorous Heroes* (1944).

24. Constance Rourke, *American Humor: A Study of the National Character* (New York, 1931); Anchor Book, n.d.

25. *American Humor* (Anchor Book ed.), p. 39.

Crockett—at least after they had grown supersized in legend. The cosmic dimensions are particularly interesting. Crockett's characteristic boast was that he could "eat a painter" (panther), "hold a buffalo out to drink, and put a rifle-ball through the moon."[26] Even as a baby he slept on a rock bed and drank buffalo milk.

Of course these were the myths of Jacksonian America, but the "size of Texas" folklore still flourishes. And I need not emphasize the psychology of abundance in the formation of the myth of giantism. Although a few Americans have begun to fear that our natural resources are not inexhaustible, the effect of diminishing wealth on the national conduct is scarcely apparent yet.

Along with the confidence in abundance has also existed a somewhat concealed obsession with fecundity. Oscar Cargill remarked in his *Intellectual America* that "The fear of being thought scatological has kept critics and scholars from assigning Whitman his true place in our literary history—the natural voice of breeding and prolific America, the Priapus of the new continent." Cargill also pointed out that "human proliferation for economic purposes began in America with the founding of the colonies"; hence "there is in American letters in the nineteenth century what might almost be termed the 'Cult of Fecundity.'"[27] This was certainly true of Whitman, but not for economic reasons. With him fecundity was only another evidence of the unlimited fertility and power of Nature.

But are not these myths and "tall tales" survivals of our primitive past? No doubt, but they were also stimulating and useful to the imagination of men and women trying to conquer a continent and build a nation conforming to their dreams. Preference for bigness, crude strength, and the natural as opposed to the artful or artificial, etc., are still obvious manifestations of the American imagination. Where else has the "natural man" been so dear to the novelist, or so flattered and wooed by the politician? Hemingway's hero still has something of the strength, endurance, and violence of Davy Crockett; and Hemingway contended that all American literature began with Mark Twain,[28] the master of the "tall tale." In Faulkner, too, we still find the American love of exaggeration—in humor, violent action, an almost superhuman endurance, and the

26. *Ibid.*, p. 54.
27. Oscar Cargill, *Intellectual America: Ideas on the March* (New York, 1941), p. 541.
28. *Green Hills of Africa* (New York, 1935), chap. 1.

fantastic metaphor—not to say the fantastic plot! In no other country has the "Gothic" tale (in which exaggerated space is particularly conspicuous) had so long and distinguished a history, stretching from Charles Brockden Brown at the beginning of the nineteenth century, to Poe and Hawthorne forty years later, to Faulkner and Robert Penn Warren today—and nearly the whole "Southern school" for the past half century. Leslie Fiedler would trace this Gothicism back to faulty sexual adjustments in our cultural (and physical) life,[29] but it certainly derives in part at least from American geography and history, in which space has been both a physical and a psychological influence.

29. Leslie A. Fiedler, *Love and Death in the American Novel* (New York, 1960).

JAY BROADUS HUBBELL
VITA

Compiled by Ray M. Atchison

Samford University

Born May 8, 1885, in Smyth County, Virginia, the son of the Reverend
David Shelton Hubbell and Ruth (Eller) Hubbell
Married Lucinda Smith in Dallas, Texas, June 1, 1918. Children: Jay B.
Hubbell, Jr., and David Smith Hubbell, M.D.
Student, Windsor Academy, Windsor, Virginia, 1901-1902
Student, Richmond College (now University of Richmond), 1902-1905;
B.A., 1905
Instructor in Latin and Greek, Bethel College, Russellville, Kentucky,
1905-1906
Graduate student in English, Harvard University, 1906-1908; M.A., 1908
Instructor in English, University of North Carolina, 1908-1909
University Scholar, Columbia University, 1909-1910
Head of English Department, Columbus, Georgia, High School, Spring,
1911
Associate Professor of English, Wake Forest College, 1911-1914
Graduate student, Columbia University, 1914-1915, 1919; Ph.D., 1922
Field Artillery Central Officers Training Camp, Camp Zachary Taylor,
Kentucky, 1918; First Lieutenant, Officers Reserve Corps, 1918-1923
Assistant Professor of English, Southern Methodist University, 1915-1916;
Associate Professor, 1916-1918, 1919-1921; E. A. Lilly Professor of
English and Chairman of the Department, 1921-1927. In 1915 or-
ganized the Extension Division (which later became Dallas College)
and taught the first courses offered in English; organized the Cor-
respondence Division in July, 1921; founded the S.M.U. Poetry
Club ("The Makers") in April, 1922
Editor, *Southwest Review* (formerly *Texas Review*), 1924-1927
Professor of English, Duke University, 1927-1946; Professor of American
Literature, 1946-1954; Emeritus, 1954–. Director of Graduate Studies
in English, 1943-1948. Organized the Graduate English Club in
1928
Chairman, Board of Editors, *American Literature: A Journal of Literary
History, Criticism, and Bibliography* (the semi-official organ of the

American Literature Section of the Modern Language Association), 1928-1954; Founding Editor, 1954—

Summer Session Appointments

University of Colorado, 1923, 1933
University of Texas, 1924
Columbia University, 1929, 1930, 1932, 1938
University of California at Los Angeles, 1949

Visiting Professorships

Visiting Professor of American Literature and Expert to the Secretary of the United States Army, University of Vienna, Austria, Spring semesters of 1949 and 1950

Fulbright Professor of American Literature and Civilization, University of Athens, Greece, Spring, 1953

Visiting Professor of English, University of Virginia, 1954-1955

Visiting Professor of English, Clemson University, Spring, 1956

Smith-Mundt Professor of American Literature, Hebrew University, Jerusalem, Israel, 1956-1957 (At the outbreak of the Suez War, on orders from the U. S. State Department, Dr. and Mrs. Hubbell were evacuated, along with other refugees on an American warship on October 31, 1956.)

Visiting Professor of English, Columbia University, 1957-1958

Visiting Professor of English, Texas Technological College, Spring, 1960

Visiting Professor of English, University of Kentucky, Spring, 1961

Professional Activities and Honors

THE MODERN LANGUAGE ASSOCIATION OF AMERICA: Chairman, American Literature Section, 1924-1927, 1939; Program Committee, 1937-1941; Committee on Research Activities, 1944-1947; Executive Council, 1946-1949 and 1951 (ex officio); Vice-President, 1951; Committee on Resolutions, 1950, 1954

THE SOUTH ATLANTIC MODERN LANGUAGE ASSOCIATION: Organized the first English section for the meeting at Davidson College in 1929

OTHER ORGANIZATIONS: At present a member of Phi Beta Kappa, Modern Language Association (since 1917), South Atlantic Modern Language Association (since 1929), North Carolina Folklore Society (charter member, 1913), Andiron Club of New York City, English Graduate Union of Columbia University, Duke University Faculty

Club, Erasmus Club of Duke University (President, 1928-1929 and 1948-1949)

Before retirement from Duke University a member of American Association of University Professors, Southern Historical Association, Society of American Historians, Virginia Historical Society, Poetry Society of Texas, and Poetry Society of America

Honors and Awards

At Windsor Academy in 1902 awarded the Prince Medal and a scholarship to Richmond College (now University of Richmond) which was awarded again each year until graduation in 1905

At the University of Richmond in senior year won the Tanner Greek Medal, the Crump Prize in Mathematics, and the Philologian Society's Medal for Improvement in Debating

Faculty Editor of the Wake Forest College annual *(The Howler)* in 1914

American Life in Literature (2 vols., 1936) was reprinted in 4 vols. by Harper & Brothers for the United States Armed Forces Institute, 1944, 1945, 1947 (This anthology was selected on the recommendation of one hundred university and college teachers of American literature.)

John Hay Whitney Lecturer for the Richmond Area University Center (now the University Center in Virginia), November, 1955

Delivered the Inaugural Frederic William Boatwright Fine Arts Lecture, "Contemporary Southern Literature," University of Richmond, November 5, 1955

Awarded the Mayflower Cup by the North Carolina Literary and Historical Society for *The South in American Literature* as the best non-fiction book written by a resident of North Carolina, November, 1955

Delivered the Eugenia Dorothy Blount Lamar Lectures at Mercer University in November, 1959. Published by the University of Georgia Press as *Southern Life in Fiction* (1960)

Awarded the first Jay B. Hubbell Medal by the American Literature Section of the Modern Language Association for distinguished service to scholarship in the field of American literature, December, 1964

Honorary Consultant in American Cultural History to the Library of Congress, 1964-1966

Honorary Degrees: Litt.D., awarded by Southern Methodist University, 1951; University of Richmond, 1956; Clemson University, 1961

Books Dedicated to Jay B. Hubbell

George E. DeMille, *Literary Criticism in America: A Preliminary Survey* (1931). Dedicated to William S. Knickerbocker, Jay B. Hubbell, and Matthew W. Rosa

Roy P. Basler, *The Lincoln Legend: A Study in Changing Conceptions* (1935)

Lewis Leary, *Articles on American Literature, 1900-1950* (1954)

Ralph Purcell, *Government and Art: A Study of American Experience* (1956)

Clarence Gohdes, *Bibliographical Guide to the Study of the Literature of the U. S. A.* (1959, 1963)

Edd Winfield Parks, *Henry Timrod* (Twayne's United States Authors Series, 1964)

Authorship

A List of the "Publications of Jay B. Hubbell" appears
in his *South and Southwest: Literary Essays
and Reminiscences* (1965), pp. 365-369.

Index